P9-CAL-429

LIVING LANGUAGE®

ITALIAN
DICTIONARY

ITALIAN–ENGLISH
ENGLISH–ITALIAN

REVISED & UPDATED

THE LIVING LANGUAGE® SERIES

Living Language® Basic Complete Courses Revised & Updated

Spanish*   *Japanese**
French*   *Russian*
German*   *Italian**
Portuguese
Inglés/English for Spanish Speakers*

Living Language® Intermediate Skill Builder Courses

Spanish Verbs   *French Verbs*
German Verbs   *Italian Verbs*

Living Language® Advanced Courses, Revised & Updated

Advanced Spanish   *Advanced French*

Living Language® Ultimate™
(formerly **All the Way™**)

Spanish*   *Advanced Spanish**
French*   *Advanced French*
German*   *Advanced German*
Italian*   *Advanced Italian*
Russian*   *Advanced Russian*
Japanese*   *Advanced Japanese*
Inglés/English for Spanish Speakers
Advanced Inglés/English for Spanish Speakers
Mandarin Chinese
Portuguese

Living Language® Essential Language Guides

Essential Spanish for Healthcare
Essential Spanish for Social Services
Essential Spanish for Law Enforcement
Essential Language Guide for Hotel & Restaurant Employees

Living Language® English for New Americans

Everyday Life
Health & Safety
Work & School

Living Language® All-Audio™
Spanish* *French** *Italian** *German**

Living Language® American English Pronunciation Program

Fodor's Languages for Travelers
Spanish* *French** *Italian** *German**

Living Language® Parent/Child Activity Kits

Learn French Together
Learn Italian Together
Learn Spanish Together
Learn French Together: For the Car
Learn Italian Together: For the Car
Learn Spanish Together: For the Car

Living Language® Business Companion

Chinese
German
Spanish

*Available on Cassette and Compact Disc

If you're traveling, we recommend
Fodor's guides

Available in bookstores everywhere

Visit our Web site at: **www.livinglanguage.com** for more informaiton

Living Language® publications are available at special discounts for bulk purchases for sales promotions or premiums, as well as for fund-raising or educational use. Special editions can be created in large quantities for special needs. For more information, write to Special Sales Manager, Living Language, 280 Park Avenue, New York, NY 10017.

ITALIAN DICTIONARY

ITALIAN–ENGLISH
ENGLISH–ITALIAN

REVISED & UPDATED

REVISED BY RENATA ROSSO

AND LORRAINE GATTO

Original edition by Genevieve A. Martin and Mario Ciatti

◆

Based on the dictionary developed by

Ralph Weiman,

Former Chief of Language Section,

U.S. War Department

LIVING LANGUAGE®
A Random House Company

This work was previously published under the title *Living Language™ Common Usage Dictionary—Italian* by Genevieve A. Martin and Mario Ciatti, based on the dictionary developed by Ralph Weiman.

Published by Living Language®, A Random House Company, New York, New York.

Random House, Inc. New York, Toronto, London, Sydney, Auckland

www.livinglanguage.com

LIVING LANGUAGE and colophon are registered trademarks of Random House, Inc.

Printed in the United States of America

ISBN 1-4000-2017-4

10 9 8 7 6 5 4 3 2 1

CONTENTS

INTRODUCTION

The *Living Language® Italian Dictionary* lists more than 15,000 of the most frequently used Italian words, gives their most important meanings, and illustrates their use. This revised edition contains updated phrases and expressions, as well as many new entries related to business, technology, and the media.

1. More than one thousand of the most essential words are capitalized to make them easy to find.

2. Numerous meanings are illustrated with everyday phrases, sentences, and idiomatic expressions. If there is no close English equivalent for an Italian word, or if the English equivalent has several different meanings, the context of the illustrative sentences helps to clarify the meanings.

3. Because of these useful phrases, the *Living Language® Italian Dictionary* also serves as a phrasebook and a conversation guide. The dictionary is helpful both to beginners who are building their vocabulary and to advanced students who want to perfect their command of colloquial Italian.

4. The Italian expressions have been translated to their English equivalents. Literal translations have been added to help the beginner. The user is thus furnished with

numerous examples of how even idiomatic and colloquial Italian expressions can best be translated into
English. This feature makes the dictionary useful for
translation work.

EXPLANATORY NOTES

All nouns that end with an -*o* are masculine, and all nouns
that end with -*a* are feminine, unless otherwise indicated by
m. for masculine and *f.* for feminine. The abbreviations *m.*
and *f.* are also used to indicate the gender of nouns that end
in -*e*.

Adjectives, abbreviated *adj.* where necessary, are given in
their masculine singular forms.

Singular is abbreviated as *sing.*, plural as *pl.*, adverb as *adv.*,
object as *obj.*

In the phrases and sentences that illustrate the meanings of
the words, some subject pronouns are omitted because the
form of the verb indicates who the speaker is (I, you, he,
etc.). For example, *Parlo italiano* is translated as "I speak
Italian," even though the Italian sentence doesn't include the
subject pronoun *io* (I).

Italian-English

A

A, AD (used in front of words beginning with vowels) *to, at.* Also:

agli (plural; contraction of *a* plus *gli*).

ai (plural; contraction of *a* plus *i*).

al (contraction of *a* plus *il*).

alla (contraction of *a* plus *la*).

alle (plural; contraction of *a* plus *le*).

allo (contraction of *a* plus *lo*; used in front of words beginning with *z*, *s* followed by a consonant, and *gn*).

alle tre *at three o'clock.*

andare a piedi *to go on foot.*

cucinare all' italiana *to cook the Italian way.*

A domani. *See you tomorrow. (Until tomorrow.)*

Andiamo al cinema! *Let's go to the movies!*

È andato allo stadio. *He went to the stadium.*

È la prima strada a destra. *It's the first street on the right.*

Hai dato la mancia ai portabagagli? *Did you tip the porters?*

Io vado a Roma. *I'm going to Rome.*

Mi preparo ad andar via. *I'm getting ready to leave (go away).*

Questi libri appartengono agli studenti. *These books belong to the students.*

Siamo andati alla fiera. *We went to the fair.*

Ti condurrò alle corse. *I'll take you to the races.*

abbachio *lamb.*

abbaglianti *headlights.*

abbagliare *to dazzle.*

abbaglio *mistake.*

abbaiare *to bark.*

abbandonare *to abandon.*

abbandono *abandonment, desertion.*

abbassare *to lower; to reduce.*

abbasso *down, downstairs.*

abbastanza *enough, rather.*

abbattere *to throw down; to demolish; to pull down; to fell; to bring down.*

Un aereo è stato abbattuto. *An airplane has been shot down.*

Hanno abbattuto gli alberi del giardino. *They felled the trees in the garden.*

La minima cosa lo abbatte. *The least thing depresses him.*

abbattersi *to get disheartened; to get depressed.*

Non bisogna abbattersi così facilmente. *One should not get discouraged so easily.*

abbattuto *dejected, downhearted.*

L'ho trovato molto abbattuto. *I found him very downhearted.*

abbazia *abbey.*

abbellimento *improvement, embellishment.*

abbellire *to improve; to beautify.*

abbigliamento *clothes, apparel.*

industria dell'abbigliamento *garment industry.*

abbisognare *to be in need of; to need.*

abboccamento *interview, talk.*

abbonamento *subscription.*

Lui ha un biglietto d'abbonamento ferroviario. *He has a season train ticket.*

Ho un abbonamento a questa rivista. *I have a subscription to this magazine.*

abbondante *abundant, plentiful.*

un raccolto abbondante *a plentiful crop.*

abbondanza *abundance, plenty.*

abbondare *to abound; to be plentiful.*

La selvaggina abbonda in questo paese. *Game is plentiful in this country.*

abbordare *to board (a ship); to accost (a person).*

Mi ha abbordato scortesemente. *He accosted me rudely.*

abbottonare *to button.*

Abbottonati la giacca. *Button up your jacket.*

abbozzo *sketch.*

abbracciare *to embrace.*

abbreviare *to make shorter; to abbreviate.*

abbreviazione, f. *abbreviation.*

Qualche abbreviazione italiana (Some Italian abbreviations):

mons. (monsignore) *Mgr.*

N.B. (nota bene) *N.B.*

P.T. (Poste e Telegrafi) *post and telegraph office.*

Sig. (signore) *Mr.*

Sig.a (signora) *Mrs.*

Sig.na (signorina) *Miss.*

abbronzare *to bronze; to tan.*

abbronzarsi *to get a suntan.*

abbrustolito *toasted.*

abbuiare *to darken, to obscure.*

abdicare *to abdicate.*

    abdicare al trono *to abdicate the throne.*

abete, m. *fir tree.*

abietto *base, abject.*

abile *able, skillful.*

abilità *ability, capability.*

abisso *abyss.*

abitabile *habitable.*

ABITANTE, m. *inhabitant.*

abitare *to live; to dwell.*

abitazione, f. *habitation, house.*

ABITO *suit, dress.*

    abito da sera *evening gown.*

abituale, m. & f. adj. *habitual, usual.*

abituarsi *to get used to.*

ABITUATO *accustomed; used to.*

abitudine, f. *habit, custom.*

abolire *to abolish.*

abolizione, f. *abolition.*

abominevole, *abominable.*

aborrire *to abhor.*

abortire *to miscarry; to have an abortion.*

aborto m. *miscarriage; abortion.*

abrasione, f. *abrasion.*

abusare *to take advantage of; to misuse.*

    Lui abusa della mia pazienza. *He is trying my patience.*

    Lui abusa di tabacco. *He smokes too much.*

abuso *abuse.*

accademia *academy.*

    Accademia di Belle Arti. *Academy of Fine Arts.*

accademicamente *academically.*

accademico n. *academician;* adj. *academic.*

ACCADERE *to happen.*

    Che cos'è accaduto? *What happened?*

    È accaduta una disgrazia. *An accident happened.*

    Non accade mai. *It never happens.*

    accadde che *it happened that.*

accaduto m. *event, happening.*

accaldarsi *to become excited (nervous); to get hot; to become angry.*

accampamento *camp, camping.*

accampare *to camp; to encamp (military).*

    I soldati si sono accampati ai piedi della collina. *The soldiers have encamped at the foot of the hill.*

accanimento *obstinacy, persistence.*

ACCANTO *beside, near, by.*

    Il ristorante si trova accanto al museo. *The restaurant is near the museum.*

    Le bambine camminano una accanto all'altra. *The little girls are walking side by side.*

    Siedi accanto a me. *Sit by me.*

accappatoio *bathrobe.*

accarezzare *to caress; to pet; to fondle; to cherish.*

    accarezzare un'idea *to cherish an idea.*

    Il ragazzo accarezza il suo cane. *The boy is petting his dog.*

accartocciare *to wrap up.*

accatastare *to heap up.*

accattare *to beg; to borrow.*

accattone, m. *beggar.*

accecare *to blind.*

accedere *to accede; to enter.*

accelerare *to accelerate; to hasten.*

    Dobbiamo accelerare il passo. *We must hasten (quicken our steps).*

accelerato *accelerated.*

acceleratore, m. *accelerator.*

    Premi l'acceleratore. *Step on the gas. (Press the accelerator.)*

ACCENDERE *to light; to kindle; to turn on.*

    Accende la luce. *He turns the light on.*

    Accendi il fuoco nel caminetto. *Light a fire in the fireplace.*

    Ho acceso la candela. *I lit the candle.*

accendersi *to light up; to ignite; to get excited.*

accendino *lighter.*

accennare *to hint; to point out.*

accenno *hint, nod.*

accentare *to accent.*

accentato *accented.*

L'ultima sillaba è accentata. *The stress is on the last syllable.*

accento *accent, stress.*

Lui ha un leggero accento. *He has a slight accent.*

accentuare *to emphasize; to accent.*

accerchiamento *encircling; surrounding.*

accerchiare *to surround; to encircle.*

accertare *to ascertain; to verify.*

accertarsi *to make certain.*

Me ne voglio accertare. *I want to make sure of it.*

acceso *alight, aflame.*

La folla è accesa d'ira. *The crowd is in a fit of rage.*

La luce nel corridoio è accesa. *The light is on in the hall.*

accessibile *accessible.*

ACCESSO *access, admission, attack, fit.*

Lui ha avuto un accesso di rabbia. *He had a fit of rage.*

accessorio *accessory.*

accettabile, m. & f. adj. *acceptable.*

ACCETTARE *to accept.*

Accetti le mie scuse. *Accept my apology.*

Ho accettato il suo invito. *I accepted his invitation.*

Le condizioni furono accettate da tutti. *Everyone agreed to the conditions.*

Non posso accettare questo regalo. *I can't accept this gift.*

ACCEZIONE *accepted meaning (of words); acceptation.*

La moderna accezione di alcune parole differisce grandemente da quella antica. *The modern meaning of some words greatly differs from the ancient one.*

accialo *steel.*

accidentale *accidental.*

ACCIDENTE, m. *accident.*

Accidenti! *My goodness! Damn!*

accigliato *gloomy, frowning.*

acciochè *in order that.*

acciottolato *pavement; cobblestone.*

acciuffare *to catch; to grasp.*

acciuga *anchovy.*

acciamare *to acclaim.*

acciamazione, f. *acclamation.*

acclimatarsi *to become acclimated.*

ACCLUDERE *to enclose.*

Accludo una fotografia di mio figlio. *I am enclosing a snapshot of my son.*

Non si dimentichi di accludere la fattura. *Don't forget to enclose the invoice.*

accluso *enclosed.*

accoccolarsi *to squat; to crouch.*

accoglienza *reception, welcome.*

Mi han fatto una bella accoglienza. *They welcomed me warmly.*

accogliere *to receive; to welcome.*

Lui fu accolto male. *He was not welcome. (He was poorly received.)*

accollarsi *to take upon oneself; to assume.*

Mi sono accollato questa responsabilità. *I assumed this responsibility.*

accollato *burdened; uptight.*

accolta *meeting, gathering.*

accoltellare *to stab.*

accomiatarsi *to say good-bye, to take one's leave; to dismiss.*

accomodabile, m. & f. adj. *adjustable.*

ACCOMODARE *to mend; to repair; to suit; to settle; to fix.*

Bisogna far accomodare questa lampada. *This lamp must be repaired.*

accomodarsi *to sit down; to make oneself comfortable.*

Prego, si accomodi. *Please, have a seat.*

accompagnamento *accompaniment (musical).*

ACCOMPAGNARE *to accompany.*

Il pianista lo ha accompagnato magnificamente. *The pianist accompanied him magnificently.*

Mi ha accompagnato a casa. *He saw me home.*

accompagnatore, m. *accompanist (musical); escort.*

accomunare *to join; to write.*

acconciare *to adorn.*

accondiscendere *to acquiesce.*

acconsentire *to consent; to agree.*

Chi tace acconsente. *Silence is consent.*

accontentare *to content; to please.*

accontentarsi *to be content.*

Mi accontento facilmente. *I'm easy to please.*

ACCONTO *account.*

Lui mi ha dato una somma in acconto. *He gave me some money as a deposit.*

accoppiare *to couple.*

accoppiarsi *to unite; to (become a) couple.*

Sono bene accoppiati. *They make a fine couple.*

accorare *to grieve; to worry.*

accorciare *to shorten.*

accorciarsi *to become shorter.*

D'inverno le giornate si accorciano. *In winter the days become shorter.*

accordabile *allowable.*

ACCORDARE *to grant; to accord; to tune.*

Devo fare accordare il pianoforte. *I must have the piano tuned.*

Ti posso accordare solo dieci minuti di tempo. *I can give you only ten minutes' time.*

accordarsi *to come to an agreement.*

Dopo lunga discussione si sono finalmente accordati. *After lengthy discussion they finally came to an agreement.*

ACCORDO *agreement, accord, harmony.*

D'accordo! *Agreed!*

Gianna e Maria sono venute ad un accordo. *Jean and Mary reached an agreement.*

In casa nostra regna un perfetto accordo. *There is complete harmony in our home.*

Siamo perfettamente d'accordo. *We are in complete agreement.*

Si è stabilito un accordo fra i due. *An agreement was reached between the two.*

accorgersi *to take notice; to become aware of; to realize.*

Mi sono accorto d'aver lasciato l'ombrello in treno. *I've noticed I'd left my umbrella in the train.*

accorrere *to run up; to run.*

accortezza *shrewdness, sagacity.*

accorto *careful, clever.*

accostare *to approach; to put beside.*

accreditare *to credit.*

La somma gli fu accreditata. *The sum was credited to him.*

accreditato *reliable, accredited.*

accrescere *to increase.*

accrescimento *increase, growth.*

ACCUDIRE *to attend; to take care of.*

Devo accudire alle mie faccende. *I must attend to my duties.*

ACCUMULARE *to accumulate; to amass.*

Lui ha accumulato una gran fortuna. *He amassed a fortune.*

accuratamente *accurately, carefully.*

accuratezza *accuracy, care.*

accurato *accurate, careful.*

accusa *charge, accusation.*

ACCUSARE *to accuse; to charge.*

Lui fu accusato ingiustamente. *He was unjustly accused.*

accusato, n. & adj. *accused, defendant (legal).*

L'accusato fu rimesso in libertà. *The defendant was freed.*

accusatore, m. *accuser.*

acerbamente *bitterly, sharply.*

acerbo *unripe.*

acero *maple.*

acetato *acetate.*

aceto *vinegar.*

acetone *acetone.*

acidità *sourness, acidity.*

acido *acid, sour.*

ACQUA *water.*

acqua salata *salt water.*

acqua dolce *fresh water.*

acqua minerale *mineral water.*

acqua ossigenata *peroxide.*

un bicchiere d'acqua *a glass of water.*

acquaforte, f. *etching.*

acquaio *sink.*

acquarello *watercolor.*

acquario *aquarium.*

acquavite, f. *brandy.*

acquazzone, m. *shower (of rain).*

acquedotto *acqueduct.*

acquietare *to quiet; to appease.*

acquirente, m. *buyer.*

acquistare *to buy; to acquire.*

acquisto *purchase.*

> Vado a fare degli acquisti in città.
> *I'm going shopping in town.*

acre *acrid.*

acrobata, m. *acrobat.*

acustica *acoustics.*

acustico *acoustic.*

acutamente *acutely, shrewdly.*

acuto *acute, sharp, keen, harsh.*

ad *see A.*

adagiare *to lay; to place.*

adagio *slowly.*

adattare *to adapt.*

adattarsi *to suit; to conform; to submit.*

ADATTO *qualified for; suitable; right.*

> Non sono adatto per questo impiego.
> *I am not qualified for this position.*
> Quest' abito non è adatto per me.
> *This suit is not right for me.*

addestrare *to train.*

ADDÍ *This day of.*

> Addí 18 guigno 1999. *The 18th of
> June 1999.*

ADDIO *good-bye, farewell.*

addirittura *really, quite, completely,
even.*

additare *to point at; to point out.*

additivo *additive.*

addizionale *additional.*

ADDIZIONARE *to add; to sum up.*

addizione, f. *addition.*

> A scuola i bambini imparano a fare
> l'addizione. *In school children
> learn to add.*

addobbare *to decorate; to furnish.*

addoicire *to sweeten; to soften.*

addoicirsi *to become sweet.*

ADDOLORARE *to grieve.*

addoiorato *sorry, grieved.*

addome, m. *abdomen.*

addomesticare *to tame.*

addormentare *to put to sleep.*

ADDORMENTARSI *to fall asleep.*

> Mi sono addormentato sul divano. *I
> fell asleep on the divan.*

addossare *to lay on; to throw on.*

> Mi hanno addossato la colpa di
> questo incidente. *They blamed me
> for this incident.*

addossarsi *to take upon oneself; to
saddle oneself with.*

> Mi sono addossato tutte le
> responsabilità. *I assumed all the
> responsibility.*

addosso *upon; on; on one's back.*

> Mettiti addosso un vestito e vieni.
> *Put some clothes on and come.*
> Gli furono tutti addosso. *They all fell
> on him.*

addotto *alleged.*

addurre *to allege.*

> addure delle scuse. *to allege some
> excuses.*

adeguatamente *adequately.*

> Furono adeguatamente compensati.
> *They were adequately repaid.*

ADEGUATO *adequate.*

adempiere *to accomplish.*

adempimento *accomplishment.*

aderire *to adhere to.*

adesione, f. *adherence, assent.*

adesivo *adhesive.*

ADESSO *now.*

> Volete uscire adesso? *Would you like
> to go out now?*

adiacente *adjacent, adjoining.*

adirarsi *to get angry.*

adirato *angry.*

adocchiare *to eye.*

ADOLESCENTE n. & adj. *adolescent.*

ADOPERARE *to use; to make use of.*

> adoperare il cerevello. *to use the
> brain.*
> adoperare lo strumento adatto. *to use
> the proper tool.*

adorare *to adore.*

adorazione, f. *adoration.*

adornamento *ornament.*

adornare *to adorn.*

adorno *adorned.*

ADOTTARE *to adopt; to pass.*

> È stato adottato un nuovo sistema. *A
> new system was adopted.*
> Hanno adottato un bambino. *They
> adopted a child.*
> Le nuove leggi furono adottate. *The
> new laws were passed.*

adottivo *adopted.*

adozione, f. *adoption.*

adulare *to flatter.*

adulatore, m. *flatterer.*

adulazione, f. *adulation, flattery.*

adulterio *adultery.*

adultero *adulterer.*

ADULTO *adult.*

adunanza *meeting.*

adunare *to assemble.*

AEREO, adj. *of the air; airy;* n. *aircraft, airplane.*
   aeronautica militare *air force.*
   linea aerea *airline.*
   posta aerea *airmail.*

aeroplano *airplane.*

aeroporto *airport.*

afa *sultriness; sultry weather.*

affabile *affable, kind.*

affaccendato *busy.*

AFFACCIARSI *to present oneself; to appear.*
   affacciarsi alla finestra *to lean out the window.*

affamare *to starve.*

affamato *starving, hungry.*

affannare *to pant; to make uneasy.*

affannarsi *to be anxious.*

affanno *difficulty of breathing (panting); uneasiness.*
   È una salita che procura l'affanno. *This rise in altitude causes shortness of breath.*

AFFARE, m. *business, affair.*
   Gli affari sono affari. *Business is business.*
   Non sono affari tuoi. *It's none of your business.*
   Si tratta d'un affare spiacevole. *It's an unpleasant affair.*

affascinante *charming, fascinating, attractive.*

affascinare *to charm; to enchant; to bewitch.*

affascinato *fascinated; charmed.*

affaticare *to tire; to fatigue.*

affaticato *fatigued, weary.*

AFFATTO *quite, entirely.*
   È affatto impossibile. *It's quite impossible.*
   niente affatto *not at all.*

affermare *to affirm; to state; to say.*

affermativamente *affirmatively.*

affermativo, adj. *affirmative.*

affermazione, f. *affirmation, statement.*

afferrare *to seize; to catch.*

affettare *to cut into slices; to affect.*

AFFETTO *affection.*

AFFETTUOSAMENTE *affectionately.*

affettuoso *affectionate.*

affezionarsi *to become attached to, to be fond of.*

affezionato *affectionate, fond.*

affidamento *assurance, confidence, trust.*
   non dare affidamento *not to be dependable.*
   non fare affidamento su di *not to rely on.*

affidare *to commit; to entrust.*
   affidare alla memoria *to commit to memory.*
   Mi affido a te. *I trust you. (I entrust myself to you.)*

affilare *to sharpen.*

affiliare *to affiliate.*

affinare *to refine.*

affinchè *in order that.*

affissione *bill posting.*
   Divieto di affissione. *Post no bills.*

affisso *bill, poster, placard.*

affittare *to let; to lease.*
   stanza da affittare *room to let.*

affitto *rent, lease.*

affiggente *distressing.*

affiggere *to distress; to sadden.*

afflitto *afflicted.*

affogare *to suffocate; to drown.*

affollato *crowded.*

affondare *to sink.*

affrancare *to stamp.*
   Questa lettera non è affrancata. *This letter is not stamped.*

affrancatura *postage.*

AFFRETTARE *to hasten; to hurry.*
   affrettare il passo *to quicken the pace.*

affrettato *hurried, hasty.*

affrontare *to meet; to face.*

agente, m. *agent.*

AGENZIA *agency, branch.*
   agenzia di viaggi *travel agency.*
   agenzia pubblicitaria *advertising agency.*

agevolare *to facilitate; to help.*

agevolazione, f. *concession, facilitation.*

agganciare *to hook; to hang up.*

aggettivo *adjective.*

aggiornare *to adjourn; to postpone; to update.*

aggiungere *to add.*

aggiunta *addition.*

agglustare *to arrange; to fix.*

aggrapparsi *to cling to.*

aggravare *to aggravate.*
> La situazione si è aggravata. *The situation grew more serious.*

aggredire *to assault, to attack.*

aggressivo *aggressive.*

aggressore *aggressor.*

agguato *ambush, trap.*

agiatezza *comfort, wealth.*

agiato *wealthy.*

agile *agile.*

agio *leisure, ease, comfort.*
> Mettersi a proprio agio *to make oneself at home; to make oneself comfortable.*

AGIRE *to act; to behave.*
> Questo non è modo d'agire. *This is no way to behave.*

AGITARE *to shake; to wave.*

agitarsi *to get excited; to toss.*
> Mi agito inutilmente. *I'm needlessly anxious.*

agitato *excited, agitated.*
> mare agitato *rough sea.*

agitazione, f. *anxiety, restlessness.*

aglio *garlic.*

agnello *lamb.*

ago *needle.*

agonia *agony, torment.*

agonizzare *to agonize.*

agosto *August.*

agricolo *agricultural.*

agricoltore, m. *farmer.*

agricoltura *farming, agriculture.*

agro *sour, bitter.*

agrodolce *bittersweet.*

agrumi *citrus fruits.*

aluola *flower bed.*

alutante, m. *assistant, helper, mate.*

AIUTARE *to help.*

aluto *aid, assistance.*
> Aiuto! *Help!*

ala *wing.*

alba *dawn.*

albeggiare *to dawn.*

alberare *to plant trees.*
> alberare una nave *to mast a vessel.*

alberatura *masting.*

albergare *to lodge; to harbor.*

albergatore, m. *hotel keeper.*

ALBERGO *hotel, inn.*
> scendere ad un albergo *to stay at a hotel.*

albero *tree, mast (of a ship).*

albicocca *apricot.*

albóre *brightness.*
> primi albori *dawn.*

albume *albumen, egg white.*

alcolico *alcoholic.*

alcova *alcove, recess.*

alcuno *some, none* (with negative sentences); *any* (with interrogative).
> alcuni giornali *some newspapers.*
> Sono venuti alcuni amici. *Some friends came.*
> Non ne ho alcuno. *I don't have any. I have none.*

alfabeto *alphabet.*

alfine *at last.*

alga, pl. **alghie** *seaweed.*

alienare *to alienate.*

alienazione *alienation, estrangement.*

alimentare, adj. *alimentary;* v. *to feed.*
> generi alimentari *foodstuffs, groceries.*

alimentarsi *to feed on; to nourish oneself.*

ALIMENTO *food.*

allacciare *to lace; to link.*
> allacciare le cinture *to fasten one's belt.*
> allacciare le scarpe *to tie one's shoes.*

allagamento *inundation, flood.*

ALLARGARE *to widen; to enlarge; to broaden.*

allarmante *alarming.*

allarmare *to alarm.*

ALLARME, m. *warning, alarm.*
> segnale d'allarme *warning signal.*

alleanza *alliance.*
> fare alleanza con *to ally oneself to.*

ALLEGGERIRE *to lighten; to relieve.*
> alleggerire la sofferenza *to relieve the suffering.*

allegramente *cheerfully, gaily.*

allegrezza *cheerfulness, joyfulness.*
ALLEGRÌA *cheerfulness.*
allegro *cheerful.*
allenamento *training.*
allenare *to train.*
   Si è allenato per l'incontro. *He trained himself for the match.*
allenatore, m. *trainer.*
allentare *to relax; to loosen.*
   allentare la stretta *to relax the hold.*
allergico *allergic.*
allestire *to prepare.*
allevamento *breeding, rearing, farm.*
allevare *to breed; to bring up; to raise.*
   allevare un bambino *to raise a child.*
allevatore, m. *breeder.*
alleviare *to alleviate; to mitigate.*
   alleviare i dolori. *to relieve pain.*
allievo, m. **allieva**, f. *pupil.*
allodola *lark, skylark.*
ALLOGGIARE *to lodge.*
   alloggiare in un albergo *To lodge at a hotel.*
alloggio *lodging.*
   prendere alloggio *to put up at.*
   vitto e alloggio *room and board.*
ALLONTANARE *to remove.*
   allontanarsi da *to go away from.*
   allontanarsi dall'argomento *to digress; to stray from the subject.*
ALLORA *then.*
   d'allora in poi *from that time on.*
   fin d'allora *since then.*
allorchè *when, whenever.*
alluce, m. *big toe.*
alludere *to allude (to); to hint.*
   Non alludevo a lui. *I wasn't referring to him.*
alluminio *aluminum.*
ALLUNGARE *to lengthen; to extend.*
   allungare il passo *to quicken one's pace.*
   allungare il vino coll'acqua *to dilute wine with water.*
   allungare la mano *to extend one's hand.*
   allungare un vestito *to lengthen a dress.*
allungato *lengthened, diluted.*
allusione, f. *allusion, hint.*
   fare allusione a *to hint at.*
alluvione, f. *flood deposit.*

alquanto *somewhat; a good deal.*
altamente *highly.*
   altamente qualificato. *highly qualified.*
altare, m. *altar.*
ALTERARE *to alter; to change.*
   alterarsi *to get angry.*
alterazione, f. *change, alteration.*
alterigia *pride; arrogance; conceit.*
ALTEZZA *height; width (of material).*
altitudine, f. *altitude.*
ALTO *high; lofty; loud (voices).*
   ad alta voce *in a loud voice.*
   dall'alto della montagna *from the mountaintop.*
   in alto *on high.*
altoparlante, m. *loudspeaker.*
altopiano *plateau.*
altresì *also, too.*
ALTRETTANTO *as much as; so much; equally.*
   altrettanto lontano *as far as; equally far.*
   Altrettanto a lei. *The same to you.*
   Grazie e altrettanto. *Thank you and the same to you.*
   Ne ho altrettanti. *I have as many.*
ALTRIMENTI *differently; otherwise; or else.*
ALTRO *other.*
   dell'altro *some more.*
   l'un l'altro *each other.*
   l'uno o l'altro *one or the other.*
   né l'uno, né l'altro *neither one.*
   qualcos'altro *something else.*
   quest'altra settimana *next week.*
   senz'altro *immediately; at once.*
   tutt'altro *not at all; anything but.*
   un altro *another.*
ALTROVE *elsewhere.*
ALTRUI *another's; of others.*
   la casa altrui *other people's homes.*
altruismo *altruism.*
altura *high ground.*
alunno, m. *alunna*, f. *pupil.*
alveare, m. *beehive.*
ALZARE *to raise; to lift.*
alzarsi *to get up; to rise.*
   alzarsi in piedi *to stand up.*
alzata *lifting up; raising.*
   l'alzata del sole *the rising of the sun.*
alzato *up.*

È alzato? *Is he up?*

amabile *lovable, amiable.*

   vino amabile *sweet wine.*

amaca *hammock.*

amante, m. & f. *lover, admirer.*

amaramente *bitterly.*

AMARE *to love.*

amareggiare *to embitter; to grieve.*

amareggiarsi *to fret; to grieve.*

amarezza *bitterness.*

AMARO *bitter, harsh.*

   amaro digestivo *bitters.*

ambasciata *embassy, message.*

   fare un' ambasciata *to bring a message.*

ambasciatore, m. *ambassador;* **ambasciatrice,** f. *ambassadress.*

ambedue *both.*

ambidestro *ambidextrous.*

ambire *to desire ardently.*

ambito *sphere.*

   entro l'ambito della legge *within the limits of the law.*

ambizione, f. *ambition.*

ambizioso *ambitious.*

ambulante *itinerant.*

ambulanza *ambulance.*

ambulatorio *doctor's office.*

ameno *agreeable, pleasant, amusing.*

americano *American.*

amichevole *friendly.*

amichevolmente *in a friendly manner.*

amicizia *friendship.*

AMICO, m. **AMICA,** f. *friend.*

amido *starch.*

ammaestrare *to train.*

AMMALARSI *to become ill.*

AMMALATO *ill.*

ammassare *to amass.*

ammasso *heap, mass.*

ammazzare *to kill.*

ammazzarsi *to kill oneself; to commit suicide.*

   ammazzarsi di lavoro *to kill oneself with work.*

ammesso *admitted.*

AMMETTERE *to acknowledge; to admit.*

   Ammetto il mio errore. *I admit my mistake.*

AMMINISTRARE *to manage; to administer.*

amministrare la giustizia *to administer justice.*

amministrare un'azienda *to manage a business.*

amministrativo *administrative.*

amministratore, m. *administrator.*

   amministratore delegato *CEO. chief executive officer.*

amministrazione, f. *administration.*

   consiglio d'amministrazione *board of directors.*

AMMIRARE *to admire.*

ammiratore, m. **ammiratrice,** f. *admirer.*

ammirazione, f. *admiration.*

ammissibile *admissible, permitted.*

AMMISSIONE, f. *admission.*

   esame d'ammissione *entrance examination.*

   tassa d'ammissione *entrance fee.*

ammobiliare *to furnish (a home).*

ammodo, adj., *nice, well-bred, respectable;* adv. *properly.*

ammogliare *to marry.*

ammogliarsi *to get married.*

ammogliato *married (man).*

ammonire m. *to warn.*

ammontare, m. *sum;* v. *to reach (a figure); to amount.*

   A quanto ammonta la somma? *What is the sum? How large is the sum?*

ammorbidire *to soften.*

ammorbidirsi *to become soft.*

amo *fishing hook.*

AMORE, m. *love, affection.*

   amor proprio *self-esteem.*

   fortunato in amore *lucky in love.*

   per amor del cielo *for heaven's sake.*

   per amore or per forza *by hook or by crook.*

   È un amore *It's a darling. It's adorable.*

amoreggiare *to flirt.*

amoroso *loving.*

amplamente *amply, sufficiently.*

   ampiamente ricompensato *amply rewarded.*

amplo *ample, wide.*

ampolla *cruet.*

amputare *to amputate.*

anagrafe, f. *register of births, deaths, and marriages.*

analcolico *nonalcoholic.*
analfabeta adj. & n. *illiterate.*
analfabetismo *illiteracy.*
analisi, f. *analysis.*
   analisi del sangue *blood test.*
   in ultima analisi *after all.*
analizzare *to analyze.*
analogia *analogy.*
anarchia *anarchy.*
anatomia *anatomy.*
anatra *duck.*
ANCHE *also, too.*
   anche se *even though; even if.*
   quand'anche *even if.*
   Anche questo finirà. *This too shall
     end.*
àncora *anchor.*
   gettar l'àncora *to cast anchor.*
   levar l'àncora *to weigh anchor.*
ANCORA *yet, still.*
   Ancora qui? *Still here?*
   Non sono ancora andato. *I haven't
     gone yet.*
ancorare *to anchor.*
ANDARE *to go.*
   a lungo andare *in the long run.*
   andare a cavallo *to go horseback
     riding.*
   andare a piedi *to go on foot.*
   andare di fretta *to be in a hurry.*
   andare in auto *to go by car.*
   Come va? *How are you?*
   Come va questa faccenda? *How is
     this matter?*
   Come vanno gli affari? *How is
     business?*
   Come vanno le tue cose? *How is
     everything with you?*
   Il mio orologio va avanti. *My watch
     is fast.*
   Il tuo orologio va indietro. *Your
     watch is slow.*
   Quest' orologio va male. *This watch
     is not working right.*
ANDATA *departure, going.*
   biglietto d'andata *one-way ticket.*
   biglietto d'andata e ritorno *round-
     trip ticket.*
   viaggio d'andata *outward journey.*
andatura *gait.*
androne, m. *lobby, entrance hall.*
ANELLO *ring (jewelry); link (chain).*

anello nuziale *wedding ring.*
   l'anello più debole della catena *the
     weakest link in the chain.*
anfibio, adj. *amphibious;* n. *amphibian.*
anfiteatro *amphitheater.*
angelico *angelic.*
angelo *angel.*
ANGOLO *angle, corner.*
   l'angolo della strada *street corner.*
angoscia *anguish.*
anguilla *eel.*
angusto *narrow.*
   una camera angusta *a narrow room.*
anima *soul, spirit.*
   con tutta l'anima *with all one's heart.*
   senz' anima *without spirit.*
   Non e'è anima viva . . . *There's not a
     soul . . .*
animale, m. *animal.*
   animale feroce *wild animal.*
animare *to animate.*
animarsi *to become animated; to get
   excited; to take courage.*
animo *mind, heart.*
   avere in animo di . . . *to intend to . . .*
   farsi animo *to take heart.*
   mettersi l'animo in pace *to set one's
     mind at rest.*
   mettersi in animo di *to make up
     one's mind to.*
   Animo! *Come on! Take heart!*
   stato d'animo *mood.*
   animo gentile *kindhearted.*
annebbiamento *dimming, clouding,
   obscuring.*
annebbiare *to fog; to dim.*
annebbiarsi *to become foggy; to grow
   dim.*
   Mi si sta annebbiando la vista. *My
     eyesight is growing dim.*
   Si è annebbiato il tempo. *The
     weather has become foggy.*
annegare *to drown.*
annerire *to blacken; to darken.*
annesso *annexed, attached.*
   annessi e connessi *appendages.*
annettere *to annex; to include.*
anniestare *to annihilate.*
ANNIVERSARIO *anniversary.*
   anniversario della nascita *birthday.*
   anniversario di matrimonio *wedding
     anniversary.*

ANNO *year.*
> anni fa *years ago.*
> anno di nascita *year of birth.*
> capodanno *New Year's Day.*
> di anno in anno *from year to year.*
> essere avanti negli anni *to be on in years.*
> il primo dell'anno *New Year's Day.*
> per anni e anni *for years and years.*
> tanto all'anno *so much a year.*
> Buon Anno! *Happy New Year!*

annodare *to knot.*

ANNOIARE *to annoy; to weary.*
> annoiare la gente *to bore people.*

annoiato *bored, weary.*

annotare *to note; to annotate.*

annotazione, f. *note, annotation.*

annottare *to grow dark.*

annoverare *to count; to number.*
> Ti annovero fra i mei amici. *I number you among my friends.*

ANNUALE *yearly, annual.*

annualmente *annually.*

annullamento *annulment.*

annnullare *to annul; to cancel.*

annunciare *to announce.*

annunciatore, m. **annunciatrice,** f. *announcer.*

annuncio *announcement, advertisement.*

annuo *annual, yearly.*

annusare *to sniff; to smell.*

annuvolato *cloudy.*

anonimo *anonymous.*
> società anonima *joint stock company.*

anormale *abnormal.*

anormalità *abnormality.*

ansante *panting; out of breath.*

ansare *to pant.*

ansia *anxiety.*

ansiosamente *anxiously.*

ansioso *anxious, desirous.*
> Sono ansioso di vederti. *I'm anxious to see you.*

anteguerra *prewar period.*

antenato *ancestor.*

antenna *antenna (animal & radio).*

anteriore *previous, fore.*
> le ruote anteriori dell'automobile *the front wheels of the car.*

antiaereo *antiaircraft.*

antibiotico *antibiotic.*

antichità *antiquity, antique.*

ANTICIPO *anticipation, deposit, advance.*
> arrivare in anticipo *to arrive ahead of time.*
> Ho ricevuto un anticipo sullo stipendio. *I got an advance on my salary.*

ANTICO *ancient, old, antique.*
> gli antichi *people of old, the ancients.*

anticoncezionale *contraceptive.*

antimeridiano *morning.*

ANTIPASTO *hors d'oeuvre.*

antipatìa *dislike.*

antipatico *disagreeable, unpleasant.*

antiquariato *antique trade.*

antiquario *antique dealer.*

ANZI *on the contrary; rather.*

anzianità *seniority, age.*

ANZIANO *aged, old, senior.*

ANZICHÈ *rather than.*
> Preferisco pernottare all'albergo anzichè viaggiare di notte. *I'd rather stay the night at the hotel than travel through the night.*

anzidetto *aforementioned; above mentioned.*

ANZITUTTO *first of all; above all.*
> La salute anzitutto. *Health above all.*

ape, f. *bee.*

aperitivo *aperitif.*

APERTAMENTE *openly, frankly.*
> Mi ha detto apertamente quello che pensava di me. *He told me frankly what he thought of me.*

APERTO *open.*

apertura *opening.*
> apertura mentale *open-mindedness.*

apolide, n. *stateless person;* adj. *stateless.*

apostrofo *apostrophe.*

appagare *to satisfy; to please.*
> appagarsi di poco *to be pleased with little.*

appannare *to dim; to obscure.*

apparecchiare *to prepare.*
> apparecchiare la tavola *to set the table.*

apparecchio *apparatus, machine.*

APPARENTE *apparent.*

apparentemente *seemingly.*

APPARENZA *appearance.*
> Non si può giudicare dall'apparenza. *You can't judge from appearances.*

APPARIRE *to appear; to seem.*
> apparire improvvisamente *to appear suddenly.*
> apparire stanco *to seem tired.*

apparizione, f. *apparition.*

APPARTAMENTO *flat, apartment.*
> Affittasi appartamento. *Apartment for rent.*

appartarsi *to withdraw.*

appartenente *belonging to.*

APPARTENERE *to belong to; to be a member of.*
> Questo libro mi appartiene. *This book is mine (belongs to me).*

appassionare *to interest; to impassion.*
> La lettura di questo libro mi appassiona. *This book interests me.*

appassionato *passionate; fond of; partial.*
> giudizio appassionato *a biased judgment.*
> appassionato della musica *fond of music.*

appassire *to wither; to fade.*

appassito *faded, withered.*

appello *call, appeal.*

APPENA *hardly; scarcely; barely; as soon as.*
> Erano appena usciti. *They had just left.*
> Riesco appena a camminare. *I can hardly walk.*
> Siamo appena in tre. *We are only three (people).*
> Verrò appena posso. *I'll come as soon as I can.*

APPENDERE *to hang up.*

APPETITO *appetite, hunger.*
> avere appetito *to be hungry.*
> Buon appetito! *Enjoy your meal!*

appezzamento *lot, plot.*

appianare *to settle; to soothe; to level.*

applaudire *to applaud; to cheer.*

applauso *applause.*

applicabile *applicable.*

APPLICARE *to apply; to enforce.*
> applicare una legge *to enforce a law.*
> applicarsi *to apply oneself; to devote oneself.*

applicazione, f. *application.*

appoggiare *to lean; to lay; to rest; to back; to support.*
> appoggiare al muro *to rest against the wall.*

appoggiato *leaning.*

appoggiatolo *support, stair rail.*

appoggio *support, protection.*

apporre *to affix.*

apportare *bring, fetch.*

APPOSTA *on purpose; just for.*
> È stato fatto apposta. *It was done on purpose.*
> L'ho conservato apposta per te. *I saved it just for you.*
> L'ho fatto apposta per indispettirlo. *I did it just to spite him.*

APPRENDERE *to learn; to hear.*
> apprendere facilmente *to learn easily.*
> apprendere una notizia *to hear a piece of news.*

apprendista, m. *apprentice.*

apprensione, f. *apprehension, fear.*
> essere in apprensione *to be apprehensive.*

APPRESSO *near by; close to; then; after.*
> Che cosa viene appresso? *What comes next?*
> la casa appresso alla mia *the house next to mine.*

APPREZZARE *to appreciate.*
> Ho apprezzato molto la sua cortesia. *I appreciated his courtesy very much.*

apprezzato *esteemed.*

approdare *to land; to get ashore.*

approdo *landing, landing place.*

APPROFITTARE *to profit (by); to take advantage of.*
> approfittare dell'occasione *to take the opportunity.*
> approfittare troppo *to abuse.*

appropriarsi *to appropriate.*

appropriato *appropriate, proper.*
> usare i termini appropriati *to use the proper words.*

appropriazione, f. *appropriation.*

appropriazione indebita
embezzlement.
APPROSSIMATIVAMENTE
approximately.
approssimativo *approximate.*
APPROVARE *to approve.*
approvare una legge *to pass a law.*
approvazione, f. *approval.*
APPUNTAMENTO *appointment.*
Ho un'appuntamento alle tre. *I've an
appointment at three.*
APPUNTARE *to sharpen; to pin; to
note.*
appunto *note, remark.*
APPUNTO, PER L'APPUNTO
precisely; just so; just.
Per l'appunto! *Exactly!*
Stavo appunto per partire. *I was just
about to leave.*
apribottiglie *bottle opener.*
aprile *April.*
pesce d'aprile *April fool's joke.*
APRIRE *to open.*
Apri la porta. *Open the door.*
La porta si è aperta. *The door
opened.*
Non posso aprine questo documento.
I can't open this (computer) file.
apriscatole *can opener.*
aquila *eagle.*
aquilone *kite.*
arabo *Arab.*
arachide *peanut.*
aragosta *lobster.*
aranceto *orange grove.*
arancia *orange.*
spremuta d'arancia *freshly squeezed
orange juice.*
succo d'arancia *orange juice.*
aranciata *orangeade.*
arancione *orange* (color).
arare *to plow.*
arazzo *piece of tapestry.*
arazzi *tapestry.*
arbitro *arbiter, arbitrator, umpire.*
fare da arbitro *to referee.*
arcata *arcade.*
archeologia *archaeology.*
architetto *architect.*
architettura *architecture.*
archiviare *to file.*
arcivescovo *archbishop.*

arco *bow, arch.*
strumento ad arco *stringed
instrument.*
arcobaleno *rainbow.*
arcuato *curved, bent.*
ardente *burning, ardent.*
amore ardente *ardent love.*
fiamma ardente *burning flame.*
ARDERE *to burn; to be on fire.*
Ardo dal desiderio . . . *I'm very
desirous . . .*
ardimento *boldness, daring,
impudence.*
ARDIRE *to dare; to have the courage
to; to have the impudence.*
arditamente *boldly.*
arditezza *boldness.*
ardito *bold, fearless.*
arduo *arduous, difficult.*
area *area.*
area fabbricabile *building ground.*
arena *arena, sand.*
arenile *sandy shore.*
argentare *to silver.*
argentato *silvered, silverplated.*
argenteria *silver plate.*
ARGENTO *silver.*
argine *dam, embankment, bank;
obstacle.*
ARGOMENTO *subject, topic.*
argomento in discussione *subject
under discussion.*
entrare in argomento *to broach the
subject.*
trattare l'argomento *to treat a subject.*
ARIA *air.*
all'aria aperta *in the open air.*
aver l'aria di *to look like.*
buttar per aria *to fling; to upset.*
darsi delle arie *to put on airs.*
in aria *in the air.*
per via aerea *by airmail.*
aridamente *aridly, drily.*
aridità *aridity, aridness, dryness.*
arido *arid, dry.*
terreno arido *barren land.*
aristocratico *aristocratic.*
aristocrazia *aristocracy.*
aritmetica *arithmetic.*
ariecchino *harlequin.*
ARMA *weapons.*
arma da fuoco *firearm.*

arma tagliente *sharp weapon.*

deporre le armi *to lay down arms;* (fig.) *to give up.*

armadio *wardrobe closet.*

armamenti *arms.*

riduzione degli armamenti *arms reduction.*

armare *to arm.*

armarsi *to arm oneself.*

armato *armed.*

armato di coraggio *armed with courage.*

cemento armato *reinforced cement.*

armistizio *armistice.*

armonia *harmony.*

armoniosamente *harmoniously.*

armonioso *harmonious.*

armonizzare *to harmonize, to match.*

AROMA, m. *aroma, fragrance.*

arrabbiarsi *to get angry.*

arrabbiarsi per niente *to get angry over nothing.*

arrabbiato *enraged.*

arredamento *furnishing; interior design.*

arredare *to furnish.*

arrendersi *to surrender; to surrender oneself.*

arrendersi all'evidenza *to yield to the facts.*

arrestare *to arrest; to stop.*

arrestarsi a metà frase *to stop in the middle of a sentence.*

Fu arrestato e condannato. *He was arrested and condemned.*

arretrato *behindhand; in arrears.*

paese arretrato *underdeveloped country.*

essere arretrato *to be behind.*

Ho molto lavoro arretrato. *I am behind in my work.*

arricchire *to enrich; to make rich.*

arricchirsi *to become rich.*

arricchito *newly rich; profiteer.*

arricciare *to curl.*

arricciare i capelli *to curl hair.*

arricciarsi il naso *to frown.*

arricciato *curled.*

ARRIVARE *to arrive.*

arrivare a destinazione *to reach one's destination.*

arrivare in tempo *to arrive on time.*

arrivare in ritardo *to arrive late.*

arrivare sano e salvo *to arrive safely.*

ARRIVO *arrival.*

all'arrivo *on arrival.*

gli ultimi arrivi *the latest supplies.*

l'ora d'arrivo *the hour of arrival.*

Non ci arrivi? *Don't you understand?*

arrogante *arrogant.*

arroganza *arrogance.*

arrossire *to blush; to turn red.*

arrostire *to roast.*

ARROSTO *roast.*

arrotolare *to roll up.*

arruffare *to disorder; to ruffle.*

arrugginire *to rust; to make rusty.*

arrugginirsi *to become rusty.*

arrugginito *rusty.*

arsenale *arsenal.*

ARTE, f. *art, skill; cunning.*

fare con arte *to do skillfully.*

belle arti *fine arts.*

arteria *artery.*

articolo *article.*

articolo di fondo *editorial.*

artificiale *artificial.*

artigianato *craftsmanship.*

artigiano *craftsman.*

artista *artist,* m. & f.

artistico *artistic.*

arto *limb.*

ascendere *to ascend; to amount to.*

Gli utili ascendono a tre milioni. *The profits reaches three million.*

ASCENSORE, m. *elevator.*

ascesa *ascent.*

ascia *axe.*

asciugacapelli *hair dryer.*

asciugamano *towel.*

ASCIUGARE *to dry; to dry up; to wipe.*

asciugare all'aria *to dry in the air.*

asciutto *dry.*

ASCOLTARE *to listen; to hear.*

ascoltare la radio *to listen to the radio.*

Ascoltami bene. *Listen to me carefully.*

ascoltatore, m. **ascoltatrice,** f. *listener.*

ascolto *listening.*

dare ascolto a *to heed; to listen to.*

stare in ascolto *to be listening.*

indice d'ascolto *audience.*

asfalto *asphalt.*

asfissia *asphyxia.*

ASILO *asylum, shelter, refuge.*

asilo infantile *kindergarten; nursery school.*

chiedere asilo *to seek shelter.*

asino *ass; donkey;* **asina** *female donkey.*

asparago, pl. **asparagi** *asparagus.*

ASPETTARE *to wait for.*

aspettare con ansia *to look forward to.*

non mi aspettavo di *I didn't expect.*

Lo aspetto da un momento all'altro. *I expect him any minute.*

Ti aspetterò alla stazione. *I'll wait for you at the station.*

Vi aspetto alle tre. *I expect you at three.*

ASPETTO *look, aspect.*

al primo aspetto *at first sight; at first.*

aver l'aspetto di un signore *to look like a gentleman.*

sotto tutti gli aspetti *from every point of view.*

un aspetto serio *a serious mien.*

aspirapolvere, m. *vacuum cleaner.*

aspirare *to breathe in; to inhale.*

aspirare a *to aspire to.*

aspro *harsh, sharp.*

con voce aspra *in a harsh voice.*

vino aspro *sharp wine.*

assaggiare *to taste; to try; to test.*

assai *very much; enough.*

assalire *to assail; to assault; to attack.*

assalto *assault; attack.*

assassinare *to assassinate.*

assassino *assassin.*

asse, m. *board, plank, axis.*

assegnamento *reliance; allotment.*

Non fare assegnamento su di me. *Don't count on me.*

assegnare *to assign; to allot.*

Gli fu assegnato il primo premio. *He was given first prize.*

Questo posto mi è stato assegnato. *This place was assigned to me.*

ASSEGNO *check, allowance.*

contro assegno *C.O.D.*

pagare con un' assegno *to pay by check.*

Ho ricevuto il mio assegno mensile. *I received my monthly allowance.*

assemblea *assembly.*

assennato *wise, judicious.*

assenso *assent.*

assentarsi *to absent oneself.*

Si assentò qualche minuto dal lavoro. *He left work for a few minutes.*

ASSENTE *absent.*

assente da casa *away from home.*

assente dal lavoro *away from work.*

assente dalla scuola *absent from school.*

ASSENZA *absence, lack.*

fare troppe assenze dalla scuola *to be absent from school too often.*

ASSERIRE *to assert; to declare; to affirm.*

asserire il contrario *to say the opposite.*

asserzione, f. *assertion, declaration.*

assetato *thirsty.*

ASSICURARE *to assure; to secure; to insure.*

Ho assicurato la mia casa contro gli incendi. *I insured my home against fire.*

Mi ha assicurato che sarebbe venuto. *He assured me he would come.*

ASSICURARSI *to make sure; to insure oneself.*

Mi sono assicurato per cinquemila dollari *I took out a five thousand dollar policy.*

Mi voglio assicurare che la porta sia chiusa. *I want to make sure the door is closed.*

assicurazione, f. *insurance.*

polizza d'assicurazione *insurance policy.*

assistente, n. & adj. *assistant.*

assistenza *assistance, aid, help.*

assistenza pubblica *welfare.*

ASSISTERE *to assist; to aid; to nurse; to be present.*

I forti assistono i deboli. *The strong help the weak.*

Molti assisterono alla cerimonia. *Many were present at the ceremony.*

L'infermiera assiste l'ammalato. *The nurse is assisting the patient.*

asso *ace.*

associare *to associate; to take into partnership.*

associazione, f. *association.*

assoggettare *to subject; to subdue.*

ASSOLUTAMENTE *absolutely, completely.*

ASSOLUTO *absolute, complete.*
> autorità assoluta *complete authority.*

assolvere *to absolve; to forgive.*

ASSOMIGLIARE *to look like; to be like; to resemble; to compare.*
> Si assomigliano come due gocce d'acqua. *They are as alike as two drops of water.*

assopirsi *to get drowsy.*

assorbente *absorbing.*
> carta assorbente *blotting paper.*
> assorbente igienico *sanitary napkin.*

assorbire *to absorb.*

assordare *to deafen; to grow deaf.*

ASSORTIMENTO *assortment.*

assortito *assorted.*

assorto *absorbed.*
> assorto nello studio *absorbed in studying.*

assuefare *to accustom.*

ASSUEFAZIONE *habit, addiction.*
> assuefazione agli stupefacenti *drug addiction.*

ASSUMERE *to assume; to take on.*
> Mi sono assunto questa incombenza. *I took on the task.*

assurdo *absurd.*

asta *lance, spear, pole.*
> vendita all'asta *auction sale.*

astemio *teetotaller.*

ASTENERSI *to abstain.*
> Mi astengo dal bere. *I abstain from drinking.*

astio *hatred.*
> aver astio contro qualcuno *to bear someone a grudge.*

astratto *abstract.*

astronauta *astronaut.*

astronave *spacecraft.*

astuccio *box, case.*

astutamente *cunningly.*

astuto *cunning, astute.*

astuzia *astuteness, cunning, trick.*

ateismo *atheism.*

atleta, m. *athlete.*

atletica *athletics.*

atletico *athletic.*

atmosfera *atmosphere.*

atomico *atomic.*
> bomba atomica *atomic bomb.*

atomo *atom.*

atrio *lobby.*

atroce *atrocious; dreadful.*

attaccapanni *hook; hanger.*

ATTACCARE *to attack; to assail; to attach; to stick; to paste.*

ATTACCO *attack, juncture, connection, touch.*
> attacco elettrico *electric connection (outlet).*
> un'attacco d'influenza *a touch of influenza.*

atteggiamento *attitude, behavior.*

ATTENDERE *to wait; to await; to expect.*
> Bisogna attendere. *We have to wait.*

attenersi *to conform.*

attentato *attempt; crime.*

attento *attentive.*

attenzione, f. *attention.*

atterraggio *landing.*

ATTESA *waiting, expectation.*
> sala d'attesa *waiting room.*

attestare *to testify; to bear witness.*

attico *attic; penthouse.*

attillato *close-fitting, tight.*

attimo *instant, moment.*

attinente *relating to.*

ATTIRARE *to attract; to draw attention.*
> attirare gli squardi *to attract someone's attention (glance).*
> attirarsi *to draw upon oneself.*

ATTITUDINE, f. *disposition, inclination.*

ATTIVITÀ *activity.*
> essere in attività di servizio *to be on active duty.*

attivo *active.*

ATTO *act, deed, certificate.*
> all'atto pratico *in practice.*
> atto di nascita *birth certificate.*
> nell'atto di *in the act of.*
> prendere atto di *to take note of.*
> primo atto *first act.*

attore, m. *actor;* **attrice**, f. *actress.*

ATTORNO *about, around, round.*

ATTRAENTE *attractive, charming.*
ATTRARRE *to attract.*
  attrarr el'attenzione *to attract attention.*
attratto *attracted.*
ATTRAVERSARE *to cross.*
  attraversare la strada *to cross the street.*
  attraversare un fiume a nuoto *to swim across a river.*
  attraversare un paese in automobile *to drive across a country.*
ATTRAVERSO *across, through.*
  Abbiamo trovato uno sbarramento attraverso la strada. *We found a barricade across the road.*
  Siamo passati attraverso lo stretto di Messina. *We passed through the Strait of Messina.*
attrazione, f. *attraction.*
  numero d'attrazione *starring act (theatrical).*
attrezzo *implement, tool.*
ATTRIBUIRE *to attribute.*
attrito *friction.*
attuabile *feasible.*
ATTUALE *actual, real, current, present*
attualità *reality; topic of the day.*
attuare *to carry out.*
attuarsi *to be realized.*
audace *bold, rash.*
audiovisivo *audiovisual.*
audizione, f. *audition.*
Augun! *Congratulations!*
AUGURARE *to wish; to bid.*
  augurare la buona notte *to bid goodnight.*
  Mi auguro di poterlo fare. *I hope to be able to do it.*
augurio *wish, omen.*
  essere di buon augurio *to presage good luck.*
  Auguri di felice Natale. *Wishes for a happy Christmas.*
  Porga i miei auguri a sua moglie. *Extend my wishes to your wife.*
aula *hall, room.*
  aula scolastica *classroom.*
AUMENTARE *to increase; to augment; to raise.*
  aumentare di volume *to increase in volume.*

  aumentare le tasse *to increase the taxes.*
  aumentare lo stipendio *to raise the salary.*
AUMENTO *increase, raise, rise.*
  un aumento del due per cento *a two percent raise.*
aurora *sunrise, dawn.*
  aurora boreale *aurora borealis.*
austero *austere, strict.*
austriaco *Austrian.*
autentico *authentic, real.*
AUTISTA, m. *driver, chauffeur.*
AUTO *car.*
autobiografia *autobiography.*
AUTOBUS, m. *bus.*
autocarro *truck.*
autocorriera *motorcoach.*
automatico *automatic.*
automobile, f. *automobile.*
autonomia *autonomy.*
AUTORE, m. *author.*
autorimessa *garage.*
AUTORITÀ *authority.*
AUTORIZZARE *to authorize.*
autorizzato *authorized.*
  non essere autorizzato a *to be not entitled to; to be not authorized to.*
autorizzazione, f. *authorization.*
autunno *fall, autumn.*
avanguardia *vanguard.*
AVANTI *ahead, before.*
  avanti me *before me.*
  avanti Cristo *before Christ.*
  avantieri *the day before yesterday.*
  d'ora in avanti *from this time forward; from now on.*
  essere molto avanti *to be ahead; to be far advanced.*
  il giorno avanti *the preceding day.*
  Avanti! *Forward! Come in! (in answer to a knock).*
  Il mio orologio è avanti. *My watch is fast.*
avanzamento *advancement.*
avanzare *to advance.*
avanzato *leftover.*
avanzo *remnant, remainder.*
  Ne ho d'avanzo. *I have more than enough.*
avaro, adj. *avaricious; miser.*

avena *oats.*
  farina d'avena *oatmeal.*
AVERE *to have.*
  aver caldo *to be warm.*
  avercela con qualcuno *to bear a*
    grudge against somebody.
  aver dolore a *to feel a pain in.*
  aver fame *to be hungry.*
  aver freddo *to be cold.*
  aver paura *to be afraid.*
  aver ragione *to be right.*
  aver sete *to be thirsty.*
  aver sonno *to be sleepy.*
  aver torto *to be wrong.*
  aver trent' anni *to be thirty years old.*
  Che cosa hai? *What's the matter*
    with you?
aviazione *aviation.*
avo *grandfather.*
  i miei avi *my ancestors.*
avorio *ivory.*
avvelenamento *poisoning.*
avvelenare *to poison.*
avvenente *charming, attractive.*
avvenimento *event, incident.*
AVVENIRE, m. *future.*
  in avvenire *in the future.*
avvenire *to happen.*
avventura *adventure.*
avverbio *adverb.*
avversario *opponent.*
AVVERTIRE *to warn; to caution; to*
    inform.
avviarsi *to set out.*
AVVICINARE *to approach; to draw*
    near.
avvicinarsi *to draw nearer.*
avvillire *to humiliate.*
avvilito *discouraged, humiliated.*
AVVISO *notice, advice, opinion.*
  avviso pubblicitario *poster,*
    advertisement.
  essere dell'avviso *to be of the*
    opinion.
avvocato *lawyer.*
avvolgere *to roll up; to wrap up.*
AZIONE, f. *action; share (stock).*
azionista *shareholder.*
azoto *nitrogen.*
azzardo *hazard, risk.*
  giocare d'azzardo *to gamble.*
azzurro *blue, azure.*

B

babbo *dad, daddy.*
  babbo natale *Santa Claus.*
babbuino *baboon.*
baccano *noise, hubbub.*
bacchetta *rod, baton.*
  bacchetta magica *magic wand.*
baciare *to kiss.*
bacile, m. *washbasin.*
BACIO *kiss.*
baco *worm, beetle.*
  baco da seta *silkworm.*
bacterio *bacterium.*
BADARE *to look after, to tend to; to*
    mind.
  Bada a te! *Beware!*
  Io bado alle mie faccende. *I mind my*
    own business.
  Non ci badare. *Pay no attention.*
baffi, m. pl. *moustache.*
BAGAGLIO *luggage, baggage.*
bagnare *to wet;* **bagnarsi** *to wet*
    oneself; to get soaked.
bagnino *bathing attendant.*
BAGNO *bath.*
  sala da bagno *bathroom.*
  costume da bagno *bathing suit.*
  farsi un bagno *bathe oneself.*
bala *bay.*
balbettare *to stutter; to lisp.*
  balbettare delle scuse *to stammer*
    excuses.
balcone, m. *balcony.*
balena *whale.*
baleno *lightning, flash.*
  È arrivato in un baleno. *He arrived*
    in a flash.
balla *nurse (children's).*
balla *bale.*
BALLARE *to dance.*
ballo *dance, dancing, ball.*
  lezione di ballo *dancing lesson.*
balocco *toy, trifle.*
balsamo *balm, balsam, conditioner.*
balzare *to bound; to start.*
bambagia *cotton (surgical).*
BAMBINA *little girl; child.*
BAMBINO *little boy; child.*
bambola *doll.*
banana *banana.*

banca *bank.*
  biglietto di banca *bank note.*
bancarotta *bankruptcy.*
bancarottierre *bankrupt.*
banchettàre *to banquet; to feast.*
banchiere *banker.*
banco *counter, bench; bank.*
  banco di lavoro *workbench.*
  banco di scuola *school desk.*
Bancomat *automated banking.*
banconota *banknote.*
banda *band, gang.*
bandiera *flag, banner.*
  bandiera a mezz'asta *flag at half-*
    mast.
bar *bar.*
bara *coffin.*
baracca *hut.*
barare *to cheat.*
barattolo *pot, tin.*
barba *beard.*
  farsi la barba; radersi la barba *to*
    shave.
barbabietola *beet.*
barbaro *barbarian, uncivilized.*
barbiere, m. *barber; hairdresser.*
barboso *boring.*
BARCA *boat.*
  barca a remi *rowboat.*
  barca a vela *sailboat.*
barile, m. *barrel.*
  averne a barili *to have a great*
    quantity of (by the barrelful).
baritono *baritone.*
barocco *baroque.*
barzelletta *joke.*
BASE, f. *base, basis.*
  base navale *naval base.*
  in base a *on the basis of.*
basilica *basilica.*
BASSO, adj. *low, short;* n. *base, bass.*
  a bassa voce *in a soft voice.*
  alti e bassi *ups and downs.*
  un' azione bassa *a base deed.*
  basso rilievo *bas-relief.*
BASTARE *to suffice; to be enough.*
  basil dire che *suffice it to say.*
  Basta! *Enough! That will do!*
bastone, m. *stick; cane; club.*
  il bastone della mia vecchiaia *the*
    staff of my old age.
  l'asso di bastoni *the ace of clubs.*

battaglia *battle, fight.*
  campo di battaglia *battlefield.*
battello *boat.*
  battello a vapore *steamboat.*
  battente, m. *leaf of a door;*
    shutter.
  BATTERE *to beat; to strike; to*
    knock.
  battersi a duello *to duel.*
  battere alla porta *to knock at the*
    door.
  battere la grancassa (colloq.) *to*
    advertise; to call attention to (to
    beat the drum).
  senza battere ciglió *without batting*
    an eyelash.
batteri *bacteria.*
BATTERIA, pl. **batterio** *battery.*
  batteria da cucina *set of cooking*
    utensils.
battistero *baptistry.*
battito *beat.*
  battiti del cuore *heartbeats*
battuto *beaten.*
  Mi ha battuto lealmente. *He beat me*
    fairly.
baule, m. *trunk.*
bavero *collar.*
bazar, m. *bazaar.*
beato *happy.*
  Beato te! *Lucky you!*
beiga *Belgian.*
bellezza *beauty.*
  Che bellezza! *How wonderful!*
    (What beauty!)
BELLO *fine, beautiful, handsome.*
benchè *though, although.*
benda *bandage.*
BENE, m. *good, welfare;* adv. *well.*
  beni mobili ed immobili *personal*
    property and real estate.
  per il bene di tutti *for the good of all.*
  voler bene a *to like; to love.*
  fare le cose per bene *to do things*
    well.
  star bene di salute *to be in good*
    health.
  stare abbastanza bene *to be fairly*
    well off.
benedetto *blessed.*
benedire *to bless.*
benedizione, f. *blessing, benediction.*

BENEFICIO *benefit, advantage, profit.*

benessere, m. *comfort, well-being, welfare.*

beni, m. pl. *property.*

benigno *benign.*

benino *fairly well; rather well.*

BENISSIMO *very well; quite well.*
Benissimo! *Fine!*

benna *bucket.*

bensì *but.*

BENVENUTO *welcome.*
Desidero darti il benvenuto. *I wish to welcome you.*

benzina *gasoline.*

BERE *to drink.*
Bevo alla tua salute! *I drink to your health!*

berretto *cap.*

bersaglio *target.*

bestemmia *oath, curse.*

bestia *beast.*

BESTIAME, m. *cattle.*
tanti capi di bestiame *so many head of cattle.*

bevanda *drink.*

BIANCHERIA *linen.*
biancheria da tavola *table linen.*
biancheria personale *lingerie.*

BIANCO *white,* n. & adj.
Mangiare in bianco *to follow a bland diet.*
lasciare in bianco *to leave blank.*

biasimare *to blame; to find fault with.*

bibita *drink.*

bibliotecca *library.*

BICCHIERE, m. *glass.*

bicicletta *bicycle.*
andare in bicicletta *to ride a bicycle.*

bietola *beet.*

bigiotteria *custom jewelry.*

biglietteria *ticket office.*

BIGLIETTO *ticket, note, card.*
biglietto d'ammissione *ticket (admission).*
biglietto di andata e ritorno *round-trip ticket.*
biglietto di banca *bank note.*
biglietto da visita *visiting card.*

bilancia *scales.*

bilanciare *to balance.*

BILANCIO *balance; balance sheet; budget.*

bilancio consuntivo *final balance.*
bilancio dello stato *budget.*
bilancio preventivo *estimate.*
mettere in bilancio *to place in balance.*

binario *track, rail.*

biondo *blond, fair.*

BIRRA *beer.*

bisbigliare *to whisper.*

biscotto *biscuit, cooky.*

bisnonno *great-grandfather.*

BISOGNARE *to be necessary; to have to.*
Bisogna affrettarsi. *We must hurry.*
Bisogna che lo faccia. *He must do it.*
Bisognava saperlo prima. *We should have known sooner.*

BISOGNO *want, need, poverty.*
aver bisogno di *to need.*

bistecca *beefsteak.*
bistecca ai ferri *broiled steak.*

bistecchiera *grill.*

bisticciarsi *to quarrel.*

bivio *crossroads, junction.*

bioccare *to block; to blockade.*

biocco *blockade.*
togliere il blocco *to remove the blockade.*

blu *blue.*

BOCCA *mouth.*
essere di buna bocca *to be easily satisfied.*
bocca del cannone *muzzle.*
In bocca al lupo! *Good luck!*

bocchetta *mouth.*

boccone, m. *mouthful, morsel.*
Mangiamo un boccone. *Let's have a quick snack.*

bolla *bubble.*

bollire *to boil.*

bollito, adj. *boiled;* n. *boiled meat.*

bollo *stamp, seal.*

bomba *bomb.*
a prova di bomba *bombproof.*

bonario *gentle, meek, good-natured.*

BONTÀ *goodness, kindness.*
avere la bontà di *to have the kindness (of).*
bontà d'animo *kindheartedness.*

BORDO *board (naut.); border, margin.*
andare a bordo *to go aboard.*

borghese, adj. & n. m. *civilian, bourgeois, middle class.*

borghesia *bourgeoisie, middle class.*

borgo *village.*

BORSA *purse, bag.*
    borsa di studio *scholarship.*
    borsa nera *black market.*
    Borsa Valori *Stock Exchange.*

borsetta *handbag.*

bosco *woods.*

botte *barrel, cask.*

BOTTEGA *shop.*

bottegaio *shopkeeper.*

BOTTIGLIA *bottle.*

BOTTONE, m. *button.*
    attaccare un bottone *to sew a button.*
    attaccare un bottone a *to buttonhole (somebody).*

bozzetto *sketch; rough model.*

braccialetto *bracelet.*

BRACCIO, m. *braccia,* pl. *arms (of the body).*
    accogliere a braccia aperte *to greet with open arms.*
    aver le braccia legate *to have one's hands tied.*
    bracci *arms (of a stream).*
    braccio di mare *strait.*
    con le braccia incrociate *with folded arms; idle.*
    offrire il braccio *to offer assistance.*
    prendere in braccio *to take in one's arms.*

braciola *cutlet, chop.*

bramare *to covet.*

brano *rag, shread; excerpt.*

brasato *braised.*
    manzo brasato *braised beef.*

BRAVO *clever, skillful, honest, brave, good.*
    Bravo! *Well done!*

bretelle *braces; suspenders.*

BREVE *short, brief.*
    fra breve *shortly; in a little while.*
    in breve *in brief.*
    in breve tempo *in a short time.*

brevetto *patent.*
    ufficio brevetti *patent office.*

brezza *breeze.*

brillante *brilliant, glittering.*

brillare *to sparkle.*

brina *frost.*

brindare *to toast (drink to the health of).*

brindisi m. *a toast.*

brio *spirits, mettle.*

broccato *brocade.*

brodo *broth.*
    Lascialo bollire nel suo brodo. *Let him stew in his own juice.*

bronchite *bronchitis.*

bronzo *bronze.*

BRUCIARE *to burn; to be on fire; to set fire to.*
    bruciarsi *to burn oneself.*

bruciatura *burning, burn, scorch.*

bruma *mist.*

bruno, adj. *dark, brown.*

brutto *ugly, bad.*

buca *hole.*
    buca delle lettere *mailbox.*

bucare *to pierce; to puncture.*

bucato *washing, wash.*
    fare il bucato *to do laundry.*

buccia *skin, peel.*

buco *hole.*

budino *pudding.*

bue *ox.*
    bistecca di bue *beefsteak.*

buffo *comic, funny.*

bugia *falsehood, lie.*
    dire una bugia *to tell a lie.*

bugiardo, m. **bugiarda,** f. *liar.*

BUIO adj. & n. *dark.*
    al buio *in the dark.*
    buio pesto *pitch dark.*
    fare un salto nel buio *to leap into the dark.*
    nel buio della notte *in the dark of night.*
    avere paura del buio *to be afraid of the dark.*

buono, n. *bond, bill; coupon;* adj. *good.*
    buono del tesoro *treasury bond; treasury bill.*
    buono scanto *discount coupon.*
    con le buone *in a kind manner.*
    levarsi di buon ora *to rise early.*
    un pranzo alla buona *a simple meal.*
    Alla buon' ora. *At last.*
    È un buono a nulla. *He's a good-for-nothing.*
    È un poco di buono. *He's not much good.*

burla *trick.*
> fare una burla *to play a trick.*
> per burla *in jest.*

BURRO *butter.*

BUSSARE *to knock.*
> Hanno bussato alla porta. *Someone knocked on the door.*

busta *envelope.*

buttare *to throw.*
> buttare tutto per aria *to upset; to mess up.*
> Buttalo via! *Throw it away!*

C

cabina *cabin, stateroom, dressing room (beach).*
> cabina telefonica *telephone booth.*

cabriolet *convertible.*

cacào *cocoa.*

caccia *hunting, hunt.*
> andare a caccia *to go hunting.*
> cane da caccia *hunting dog.*
> fucile da caccia *hunting rifle.*
> licenza da caccia *game license.*

cacciare *to go hunting.*

cacciatore, m. *hunter.*

cacciavite, m. *screwdriver.*

cachi *khaki.*

CADERE *to fall.*
> cadere dalle nuvole *to be greatly surprised.*
> cadere in ginocchio *to fall to one's knees.*

caduta *fall, downfall.*

caduto *fallen.*

CAFFÈ m. *coffee, cafe.*

caffellatte *latte-style coffee (espresso mixed with hot milk).*

calare *to lower; to let down.*
> calare l'àncora *to drop anchor.*
> al calare del sole *sunset.*

calcagno *heel.*

calcio *kick.*
> dare un calcio *to kick.*
> gioco del calcio *football; soccer.*

calcolare *to calculate.*

calcolatore, m. **calcolatrice,** f. *calculator; computer.*

calcolo *calculation.*

caldaia *boiler.*

CALDO n. *heat, warmth;* adj. *warm.*
> aver caldo *to be warm.*
> ondata di caldo *heat wave.*

calendario *calendar.*

callo *corn (on the toe).*

CALMA *calm, stillness, composure.*

calmare *to calm; to soothe.*

calore, m. *warmth, ardor.*

calunnia *slander, libel.*

calunniare *to libel.*
> to stai calunniando *it libels him.*

calvo *bald.*

CALZA *stocking.*
> fare la calza *to knit.*

calzamaglia *tights.*

calzatura *footwear.*

calzetino *short sock.*

calzino *sock.*

calzolaio *shoemaker.*

calzoleria *shoe store.*

CALZONI *trousers, pants.*

cambiale, f. *bill of exchange; promissory note.*

cambiamento *change.*

cambiare *to change.*
> cambiare idea *to change one's mind.*
> cambiare in meglio *to change for the better.*
> cambiarsi *to change clothes.*

CAMBIO *change.*
> in cambio di *in exchange for.*
> la leva del cambio *gearshift.*
> cambio del giorno *current exchange.*

CAMERA *chamber, room.*
> camera da letto *bedroom.*
> Camera di Commercio *Chamber of Commerce.*

cameriera *maid; waitress.*

cameriere, m. *waiter.*

CAMICIA (camicetta) *shirt.*
> camicia da notte *nightgown.*
> in maniche di camicia *in shirtsleeves.*
> È nato con la camicia. *He was born lucky.*

camino *chimney; fireplace.*

CAMMINARE *to walk.*
> camminare in punta di piedi *to tiptoe.*

camomilla *camomile.*

campagna *country, campaign.*

casa di campagna *country home.*
fare una campagna contraria a *to
    campaign against.*
campana *church bell.*
campanello *bell.*
campanile, m. *church steeple.*
campeggiare *to camp.*
campionario *book of patterns or
    samples; patch.*
campione, m. *sample, champion.*
    campione dei pesi massimi
      heavyweight champion.
    Prendi questo come campione. *Take
      this as a sample.*
campo *field, ground.*
    campo di battaglia *battlefield.*
    campo di gioco *playground.*
camposanto *cemetery.*
CANALE, m. *channel.*
    Canale di Suez *Suez Canal.*
CANCELLARE *to erase; to cancel.*
    cancellare dalla memoria *to forget.*
    cancellare un volo *to cancel a flight.*
cancro *cancer.*
candela *candle.*
CANE, m. **cagna,** f. *dog.*
    non svegliare il cane chi dormi *to let
      sleeping dogs lie.*
cannella *cinnamon.*
cannone, m. *cannon.*
cantare *to sing.*
cantiere, m. *yard.*
    cantiere navale *shipyard.*
canto *song; corner; angle.*
canzone, f. *song.*
capace *able, capable.*
capello *hair.*
    capelli biondi *blond hair.*
    capelli scuri *dark hair.*
    farsi tagliare i capelli *to get a
      haircut.*
    fin sopra i capelli *up to his ears.*
CAPIRE *to understand.*
    capire male *to misunderstand.*
    capirsi a vicenda *to understand each
      other.*
    Mi lasci capir bene. *Let me get
      things straight.*
capitale, f. *capital (city);* m. *capital
    (money);* adj. *main.*
    pena capitale *capital punishment.*
capitano *captain.*

capitolo *chapter.*
capo *head, leader.*
capogiro, *dizziness.*
capolavoro *masterpiece.*
capovolgere *to upset; to overturn.*
    capovolgersi *to capsize.*
cappella *chapel.*
CAPPELLO *hat.*
CAPPOTTO *overcoat.*
cappuccino *espresso with frothed milk.*
cappuccio *hood.*
capra *goat.*
capriccio *whim, fancy, caprice.*
    fare i capricci *to get out of hand.*
capriccioso *capricious, freakish.*
caraffa *carafe.*
CARAMELLA *candy.*
caramente *dearly.*
CARATTERE, m. *character,
    disposition.*
    a caratteri grandi *in bold type.*
    Ha un carattere docile. *He has a
      mild disposition.*
caratteristica *characteristic, feature.*
caratteristico, adj. *characteristic,
    typical.*
CARBONE, m. *coal, carbon.*
    carbone fossile *pit coal.*
    miniera di carbone *coal mine.*
    carta carbone *carbon paper.*
carcere, m. *prison, jail.*
carciofo *artichoke.*
carezza *caress.*
carezzare *to caress.*
CARICARE *to load.*
    caricare l'orologio *to wind one's
      watch.*
    caricare un fucile *to load a gun.*
CARICO *burden, cargo, load, charge.*
    polizza di carico *bill of lading.*
    È arrivato un carico di arance. *A
      load of oranges has arrived.*
    Non ne faccia carico a me. *Don't
      accuse me of it.*
carie *decay; cavity.*
carino *nice, cute, pretty.*
carità *charity.*
caritatevole *charitable.*
carnagione, f. *complexion.*
CARNE, f. *meat, flesh.*
    in carne ed ossa *in flesh and blood.*
CARO *dear, expensive.*

a caro prezzo *dearly.*

mia cara amica *my dear friend.*

Queste scarpe sono troppo care.
These shoes are too expensive.

carrello *cart.*

carriera *career.*

andar di carriera *to walk swiftly.*

possibilità di carriera *career
possibilities.*

carro *truck, wagon, cart.*

Non bisogna mettere il carro avanti
ai buoi. *You shouldn't place the
cart before the horse.*

CARTA *paper.*

carta assorbente *blotter.*

càrte da gioco *playing cards.*

carta da lettere *stationery.*

carta geografica *map.*

carta velina *tissue paper.*

carta di credito *credit card.*

carta igienica *toilet tissue.*

carta d'identità *identity card.*

cartolerìa *stationery store.*

cartolina *postcard.*

CASA *house, home.*

a casa mia *at my house.*

andar di casa in casa *to go from door
to door.*

casa colonica *farmhouse.*

casa di cura *nursing home.*

donna di casa *housewife.*

essere in casa *to be at home.*

casalingo *domestic, household;
homestyle.*

cascare *to fall.*

Non casco il mondo *It's not a big
deal. (The world isn't falling.)*

caseggiato *block; row of houses.*

CASO *case.*

in caso di disgrazia *in case of
accident.*

per puro caso *by mere chance.*

se per caso *if by chance.*

CASSA *case, box; cash register.*

cassa di risparmio *savings bank.*

Pagare alla cassa. *Pay at the register.*

cassaforte, f. *safe.*

cassetta *box, small box.*

cassetta postale *mailbox.*

cassettone, m. *chest of drawers.*

castagna *chestnut.*

CASTELLO *castle.*

castello di poppa *quarterdeck.*

castello di prua *forecastle.*

fare castelli in aria *to build castles in
Spain (in the air).*

castigare *to chastise.*

casuale *casual.*

catasta *stack.*

categorìa *category.*

catena *chain, bondage.*

cattedra *desk, chair.*

cattivo *bad.*

cattolico *Catholic.*

cattura *capture.*

catturare *to capture; to seize.*

CAUSA *cause, reason.*

causa giudiziària *lawsuit.*

per causa mia *on account of me
(because of me).*

Sono arrivati in ritardo a causa del
temporale. *They arrived late
because of the storm.*

CAUSARE *to cause; to be the cause of.*

cauto *prudent, wary.*

cavalcare *to ride horseback.*

cavalleria *chivalry.*

cavallo *horse;* **cavalla** *mare.*

a cavallo *on horseback.*

andare a cavallo *to ride horseback.*

cento cavalli vapore *100 horsepower.*

corse di cavalli *horse races.*

cavare *to excavate; to get.*

cavatappi m. *corkscrew.*

caviglia *ankle.*

cavo, adj. *hollow;* n. *cable.*

cedere *to give up; to cede.*

cedere il posto *to give up one's seat.*

Cedo le armi! *I surrender!*

celebrare *to celebrate.*

celere *rapid, swift.*

celerità *rapidity, swiftness.*

celia *jest, joke.*

cemento *cement.*

cemento armato *reinforced cement.*

celibe, m. *bachelor.*

CENA *supper.*

CENARE *to dine.*

cenere, f. *ash, ashes.*

censimento *census.*

censura *censorship.*

centesimo, adj. *hundredth;* n. *cent; the
hundredth part of.*

centesimo di dollaro *one cent.*

centigrado *centigrade* °C = (°F −32) × 0.555
centimetro *centimeter* = 0.39 in.
cento *hundred.*
    per cento *percent.*
centrale *central.*
centro *center.*
cera *wax, look, aspect.*
    avere brutta cera *to look ill.*
ceramica *ceramics.*
cerca *search, quest.*
    andare in cerca di *to look for.*
CERCARE *to look for; to try.*
    Cercherò di farlo stasera. *I'll try to do it tonight.*
    Cerco mia sorella. *I'm looking for my sister.*
cerchia *circle, sphere.*
cerchio *hoop, circle.*
    formare un cerchio *to form a circle.*
cereale, m. *cereal.*
cerebrale *cerebral.*
cerebroleso *brain-damaged.*
cereo *waxen.*
cerimonia *ceremony.*
cerniera *zipper.*
CERTAMENTE *certainly.*
    Certamente! *Of course!*
certezza *certainty.*
certificato *certificate.*
CERTO *certain, sure.*
    una certa persona *a certain party.*
cervello *brain.*
    senza cervello *brainless.*
CESSARE *to cease.*
cestino *small basket; wastebasket.*
CHE, rel. pron. *that, which, who, whom;* adj. *what, which;* adv. *when.*
    Non c'è di che. *Don't mention it.*
CHI *who, whom.*
    A chi tutto, a chi niente . . . *Some have too much, some too little . . .*
    Chi è? *Who is it?*
    Di chi è questo cappello? *To whom does this hat belong?*
chiacchierare *to chat; to gossip.*
CHIAMARE *to call.*
    chiamare aiuto *to call for help.*
    chiamare al telefono *to telephone.*
    Come si chiama? *What's your name?*
    Lo mando a chiamare. *I'll send for him.*

Mi chiamo Maria. *My name is Mary.*
chiamata *call.*
chiarire *to clarify; to explain.*
    chiarire un dubbio *to dispel a doubt.*
CHIARO, adj. *clear, light, evident;* n. *light, brightness.*
    colore chiaro *light color.*
    Una cosa è chiara. *One thing is evident.*
    È chiaro? *Is it clear?*
    chiaro di luna *moonlight.*
    mettere le cose in chiaro *to explain things; to make things clear.*
chiasso *noise, uproar.*
chiave, f. *key.*
    chiudere a chiave *to lock.*
    chiave inglese *monkey wrench.*
    tener sotto chiave *to keep under lock and key.*
chiedere *to ask.*
    chiedere aiuto *to ask for help.*
    chiedere il permesso di *to request permission to.*
    chiedere in prestito *to borrow.*
    chiedere scusa *to beg pardon.*
chiesa *church.*
    Vado in chiesa. *I'm going to church.*
chilogrammo *kilogram* = 2.204 lbs.
chilometro m. *kilometer.*
chimica *chemistry.*
chimico *chemist.*
china *slope; India ink.*
chinare *to bend.*
chiodo *nail.*
chiostro *cloister.*
chirurgia *surgery.*
chirurgo *surgeon.*
chitarra *guitar.*
CHIUDERE *to close; to shut.*
    chiudere con il catenaccio *to bolt.*
    chiudere la porta a chiave *to lock the door.*
    chiudersi a chiave *to lock oneself in.*
    chiudersi in casa *to shut oneself off (at home).*
chiunque *whoever, whomever, anyone, anybody.*
    chiunque venga *whoever should come.*
    di chiunque sia *whosoever it is.*
chiuso *closed, shut.*
chiusura *closing.*

chiusura lampo *zipper.*

CI adv. *here, there;* pron. *us; to us; each other; one another; it; of it.*
> Ci comprendiamo. *We understand each other.*
> Ci dia la ricevuta. *Give the receipt to us.*
> Ci vede? *Do you see us? Can you see?*
> Non ci penserei nemmeno. *I wouldn't even think of it.*

ciao *hello, hi.*

ciascuno *each; each one.*

cibo *food.*

cicatrice, f. *scar.*

cicatrizzarsi *to heal up.*
> La ferita si sta cicatrizzando. *The wound is healing.*

ciclismo *cycling; biking.*

cicogna *stork.*

cieco *blind.*
> vicolo cieco *blind alley.*

cielo *sky.*

cifra *sum; figure (number).*

ciglio (le ciglia, f. pl.) *eyelash.*
> senza batter ciglio *without blinking.*

ciliegia *cherry.*

cima *top, summit.*
> arrivare in cima alla montagna *to reach the top of the mountain.*

cinema *movies.*

cinghia *strap, belt.*

cinquanta *fifty.*

cinquantesimo *fiftieth.*

cinque *five.*

cinquecento *five hundred.*

cintola *girdle.*

cintura *belt.*

CIÒ *this, that, it.*
> Ciò non importa. *It doesn't matter.*
> Tutto ciò mi preoccupa. *All this worries me.*

cioccolata (cioccolato) *chocolate.*

CIOÈ *that is; namely.*

cipolla *onion.*

cipresso *Cypress.*

cipria *face powder.*

CIRCA *about; as to; concerning.*
> circa cento lire *about a hundred lire.*

circolare *to circulate.*

circolazione, f. *circulation, traffic.*

Circolazione a senso unico *one-way traffic.*
Circolazione vietata *no through traffic.*

circolo *circle.*

circondare *to surround.*

circondato *surrounded.*

circonvallazione *bypass.*

circostanza *circumstance.*

circuito *circuit.*
> corto circuito *short circuit.*

citare *to quote; to sue.*

città *city.*

cittadino *citizen.*

civile *civil; civilized.*

civiltà *civilization.*

CLASSE, f. *class.*

classico *classic.*

clausola *clause.*

cliente, m. *customer.*

clima, m. *climate.*

clinica *hospital; clinic.*

cocchiere, m. *coachman.*

cocomero *watermelon.*

coda *tail.*

codice *code; codex.*

coerente *coherent, consistent.*

COGLIERE *to catch; to seize; to gather.*
> cogliere l'occasione *to take the opportunity.*

cognata *sister-in-law.*

cognato *brother-in-law.*

cognitivo *cognitive.*

cognome, m. *surname.*
> nome e cognome *first and second name.*

coincidenza *coincidence; train connection.*

COLAZIONE, f. *meal.*
> fare colazione *to eat breakfast.*
> prima colazione *breakfast.*
> seconda colazione *lunch.*

colera *cholera.*

colibrì *hummingbird.*

colla *glue.*

collana *necklace.*

collare, m. *collar.*

collega, m. *colleague.*

collegio *college.*

collera *anger, rage.*
> andare in collera *to become angry.*

colletto *collar.*

collezione *collection.*

collo *neck.*
>andare a rotta di collo *to go headlong.*
>Ha un braccio al collo. *His arm is in a sling.*

colloquio *conversation, interview.*
>avere un lungo colloquio con *to have a long conversation with.*
>colloquio di lavoro *job interview.*

colmare *to fill up.*

colonia *colony.*

coloniale *colonial.*

colonizzazione, f. *colonization.*

colonna *column.*

colorare *to color.*

COLORE, m. *color.*
>perdere colore *to fade.*

coloro *they, those.*

colpa *fault.*
>Non dare la colpa a me. *Don't blame me.*
>Non è colpa tua. *It's not your fault.*

colpevole *guilty.*

colpire *to strike; to hit; to hurt.*

COLPO *blow, stroke, shot.*
>colpo di vento *a gust of wind.*
>sparare un colpo *to fire a shot.*
>un colpo alla testa *a blow on the head.*
>un colpo di sole *a sunstroke.*
>Sento dei colpi alla porta. *I hear a knocking at the door.*

coltello *knife.*

colto *educated, learned.*

colui *he; that one.*

comandante, m. *commander.*

comando *command, order.*

comare, f. *godmother.*

COME *as, like, how, as soon as.*
>bella come il sole *as beautiful as the sun.*
>un libro come il mio *a book like mine.*
>Come mi vide, mi venne incontro. *As soon as he saw me, he came toward me.*
>Com' è triste! *How sad it is!*
>Come va? *How goes it? How are you?*

cominciare *to begin.*

comma *paragraph.*

commedia *comedy.*

commerciale *commercial; mercantile.*

commerciare *to trade; to deal.*

COMMERCIO *commerce.*
>Camera di Commercio *Chamber of Commerce.*

commessa, f. **commesso**, m. *clerk.*
>commesso di negozio *salesclerk.*

COMMETTERE *to commit.*

commiato *leave.*

commissione, f. *commission, errand.*

commosso *moved, touched.*

commozione, f. *emotion.*

COMMUOVERE *to move; to touch.*
>commuoversi *to be moved.*

COMODITÀ *comfort.*
>le comodità della propria casa *the comforts of one's own home.*

comodo *comfortable.*

COMPAGNIA *company.*
>compagnia edilizia *construction company.*
>fare compagnia a *to keep someone company.*

compagno, m. **compagna**, f. *companion, mate.*
>compagno di scuola *schoolmate.*

compare, m. *godfather, crony.*

COMPERARE *to buy.*

competente *competent, qualified.*

competere *to compete; to belong.*

compiacenza *obligingness.*

compiangere *to pity; to lament.*

COMPIERE *to accomplish; to fulfill; to perform.*
>compiere il proprio dovere *to do one's duty.*

compito *task.*

compleanno *birthday.*

COMPLETAMENTE *completely.*

COMPLETARE *to complete; to finish.*
>completare gli studi *to finish school.*

completo *complete, full; perfect.*

complicare *to complicate.*
>non complichiamo le cose! *Let's not complicate matters!*

complimento *compliment.*
>fare un complimento a *to compliment someone.*

COMPORRE *to compose; to compound; to consist.*

compositore, m. **compositrice**, f. *composer.*

composizione, f. *composition.*
COMPOSTO *compound, composed, settle.*
  interesse composto *compound interest.*
  Stai composto! *Behave!*
COMPRARE *to buy.*
COMPRENDERE *to understand; to comprise; to include.*
  Non comprendo l'Italiano. *I don't understand Italian.*
  Un pranzo comprende molte pietanze. *A meal consists of many dishes.*
COMPRESO *understood, comprehended, included.*
  tutto compreso *everything included.*
  servizio compreso *service included.*
compromettere *to compromise.*
  compromettersi *to compromise oneself.*
COMPUTER, m. *computer.*
  computer portatile *laptop computer.*
COMUNE, adj. *common, mutual;* m. *town, municipality.*
  di comune accordo *mutually agreed.*
  l'uomo comune *the common man.*
COMUNICARE *to communicate; to inform.*
  Le comunicherò la mia decisione. *I will inform you of my decision.*
COMUNICAZIONE, f. *communication, message.*
  comunicazione telefonica *telephone call.*
  mettere in comunicazione *to put a telephone call through.*
  togliere la comunicazione *to hang up.*
comunità *community.*
  Comunità Economica Europea *European Economic Community.*
COMUNQUE *however; at any rate.*
CON *with; to; by; by means of.*
  con piacere *with pleasure.*
  Con mio grande dolore . . . *To my great sorrow . . .*
concedere *to concede; to grant; to allow.*
  concedere il permesso *to grant permission.*
  Mi conceda un attimo di attenzione. *Please give me your attention.*
concepire *to conceive; to understand.*

CONCERNERE *to concern; to regard.*
  È un affare che non mi concerne. *It's a matter that doesn't concern me.*
concerto *concert.*
concetto *concept.*
conclusione, f. *conclusion.*
  in conclusione *to conclude.*
concluso *concluded.*
concorrente, m. *competitor.*
concorso *competition.*
concreto *concrete, real, actual.*
condannare *to condemn; to blame.*
condire *to season.*
condizionale *conditional.*
condizione, f. *condition.*
  in pessime condizioni *in very bad shape.*
condotta *behavior.*
condurre *to conduct; to lead; to take.*
  condurre all'altare *to marry (to take to the altar).*
  condurre un'azienda *to lead a company.*
condursi *to behave.*
confarsi *to fit; to suit.*
conferenza *lecture, conference.*
conferma *confirmation.*
confermare *to confirm.*
confessare *to confess; to acknowledge; to admit.*
confezionare *to manufacture.*
confezioni *ready-to-wear clothes.*
confidente *confident; trusting.*
confidenza *confidence.*
  essere in confidenza *to be on intimate terms with.*
confine *border, frontier.*
conflitto *conflict; contest.*
confondere *to confuse.*
conforto *comfort; consolation.*
confronto *comparison.*
confusione *confusion.*
congedare *to dismiss.*
congedarsi *to take leave.*
congedo *leave; leave of absence.*
congelato *frozen.*
congiuntivo *subjunctive.*
congiunzione *conjunction.*
congratularsi *to congratulate.*
congratulazione, f. *congratulation.*
  Congratulazioni! *Congratulations!*
congresso *congress.*

coniglio *rabbit.*

connotato *feature.*

CONOSCENZA *knowledge,*
acquaintance.
   essere a conoscenza di una cosa *to*
     have knowledge of something.
   fare la conoscenza di *to make the*
     acquaintance of.
   perdere la conoscenza *to lose*
     consciousness.

CONOSCERE *to know; to meet.*
   Lieto di averla conosciuta *Pleased to*
     have met you.

conosciuto *well known.*

conquistare *to conquer.*

consapevole *aware (of).*

conscio *conscious, aware.*

consegna *delivery.*

consegnare *to deliver; to consign.*

conseguenza *consequence.*

consenso *consent.*

CONSENTIRE *to consent; to allow.*

conservare *to preserve.*

conservativo *conservative.*

conservatore *conservative.*

conservatorio *conservatory.*

considerare *to consider.*

considerazione, f. *consideration.*

considerevole *considerable.*

consigliabile *advisable.*

consigliare *to advise.*

consiglio *advice, counsel.*
   il Consiglio dei Ministri *the Cabinet*
     (of Ministry).

consistere *to consist; to be composed of.*

consolare *to console.*

consolato *consulate.*

consolazione, f. *consolation, solace.*
   trovar consolazione *to find*
     consolation.

console, m. *consul.*

consonante, f. *consonant.*

constare *to consist.*

consultare *to consult.*
   consultar un medico *to consult a*
     doctor.

consumare *to consume; to waste.*

consumo *consumption.*
   per mio uso e consumo *for my*
     private use.

contabile, m. *accountant,*
bookkeeper.

contadino; n. **contadina,** f. *peasant;*
farmer.

CONTANTE, adj. *ready, current.*
   denaro contante *ready cash.*
   in contanti *cash*
   pagare *to pay cash*

CONTARE *to count; to rely; to*
number; to intend.
   Conti pure su di me. *You may count*
     on me.
   Quando conta di partire? *When do*
     you intend leaving?
   Non conta! *It doesn't matter.*

contatto *contact, touch.*

contegno *behavior, conduct.*

contemporaneo *contemporary.*

contenere *to contain; to hold.*
   contenersi *to contain oneself; to*
     restrain oneself.

CONTENTEZZA *happiness, joy.*

contento *glad, pleased.*

contenuto *contents.*

continente, m. *continent.*

continuamente *continuously.*

continuare *to continue; to go on with;*
to keep on.
   Continua a nevicare. *It is still*
     snowing.

continuo *continuous, uninterrupted.*
   una pioggia continua *a constant rain.*

CONTO *account, calculation, bill.*
   chiedere il conto al cameriere *to ask*
     the waiter for the bill.
   chiudere un conto *to close an*
     account.
   conto corrente *current account.*
   conto in banca *bank account.*
   in conto *on account.*
   pagare il conto *to pay the bill.*
   rendere conto di *to account for.*
   rendersi conto *to realize.*
   tener conto di *to take into account.*

contraccambiare *to reciprocate.*

CONTRADDIRE *to contradict.*

contraddizione, f. *contradiction.*

contrariamente *contrarily; on the*
contrary.

contrarietà *contrariety, difficulty,*
disappointment.

CONTRARIO *contrary.*

contrarre *to contract.*

contrattempo *mischance; hitch.*

contratto *contract.*
contravvenzione, f. *infraction, fine.*
contribuire *to contribute.*
contributo *contribution.*
CONTRO *against; in spite of.*
   contro voglia *unwillingly.*
   dire il pro ed il contro *to state the pro and con.*
controllare *to control.*
controllarsi *to control oneself.*
controllo *control.*
controversia *controversy.*
convegno *meeting.*
CONVENIENTE *convenient.*
convenienza *convenience.*
CONVENIRE *to assemble; to admit.*
   Bisogna convenire! *We must admit it!*
convento *convent, monastery.*
conversare *to converse.*
conversazione, f. *conversation.*
convertire *to convert.*
CONVINCERE *to convince.*
convinto *convinced.*
convinzione, f. *conviction.*
coperta *cover; blanket.*
   coperta imbottita *quilt.*
   sotto coperta *below deck.*
coperto adj. *covered, overcast;* n. *cover.*
   al coperto *sheltered.*
   cielo coperto *cloudy sky.*
   mettere un'altro coperto a tavola *to set another place at the table.*
copia *copy.*
   brutta copia *rough copy.*
copiare *to copy; to imitate.*
coppa *goblet.*
COPPIA *couple, a pair.*
   coppia di sposini *a pair of newlyweds.*
copriletto *bedspread.*
coprire *to cover; to drown out.*
coraggio *courage.*
   prendere coraggio *to summon up courage.*
corda *rope, cord.*
   corda vocale *vocal cords.*
   strumento a corda *stringed instrument.*
cordiale *cordial; hearty.*
coreografia *choreography.*
coricarsi *to go to bed; to lie down.*
cornice, f. *frame.*
corno *horn.*

   corno dell'abbondanza *horn of plenty.*
coro *chorus.*
corona *crown.*
   corona di margherite *a wreath of daisies.*
   corona ducale *ducal coronet.*
coronare *to crown.*
   essere coronato dal successo *to be successful.*
CORPO *body, corps.*
corporazione, f. *corporation.*
corredo *equipment, outfit.*
   corredo da sposa *trousseau.*
correggere *to correct.*
CORRENTE, f. *current, stream.*
   corrente d'aria *draft.*
   seguire la corrente *to swim with the tide.*
correntemente *currently, easily.*
   parlare correntemente *to speak fluently.*
CORRERE *to run.*
corretto *correct, proper.*
   agire in modo corretto *to behave properly.*
correzione, f. *correction.*
corridolo *corridor; aisle.*
corriera *coach; bus.*
corriere, m. *messenger.*
corrispondente, m. *correspondent.*
   corrispondente di un giornale *newspaper correspondent.*
corrispondenza *correspondence.*
corrispondere *to correspond; to reciprocate; to pay.*
   la somma corrisposta *the amount paid.*
corrugare *to wrinkle; to corrugate.*
   corrugare la fronte *to frown.*
corruzione, f. *corruption.*
corsa *race; short trip.*
   fare una corsa *to rush; to dash over.*
corsia *ward (hospital).*
corsivo *cursive; italics.*
CORSO *course.*
   l'anno in corso *the present year.*
   nel corso degli eventi *in the course of events.*
   prendere un brutto corso *to take a turn for the worse.*
   un corso universitario *a university course.*

corte, f. *court.*

cortèo *procession.*

cortese *polite, courteous.*

CORTESÌA *politeness, kindness.*

cortile, m. *courtyard, yard.*

CORTO *short, brief.*

   essere a corto di denaro *to be short of money.*

   Taglia corto! *Make it brief! Cut it short!*

COSA *thing.*

   cosa da niente *trifle.*

   prima di ogni altra cosa *first of all.*

   Cos'è successo? *What happened?*

coscia *thigh.*

coscienza *conscience.*

   perdere coscienza *to lose consciousness.*

   riprendere coscienza *to come to one's senses.*

COSI *so, thus.*

   così ebbe fine . . . *and so ended . . .*

   Sono così contenta *I am so happy.*

cosicchè *so that.*

cosmetico *cosmetic.*

cosmico *cosmic; universal.*

cosmonauta *astronaut.*

cosmonave *spaceship.*

costa *coast.*

   sulla costa del Pacifico *on the coast of the Pacific.*

COSTARE *to cost.*

   costi quel che costi *whatever the cost.*

   Costa troppo! *It's too expensive!*

   Quanto costa? *How much is it?*

costata *chop, cutlet.*

   costata di agnello *lamb chop.*

   costata di manzo *beefsteak.*

costituire *to form; to establish.*

costituzione, f. *constitution, foundation.*

   essere di costituzione forte *to be strong.*

costo *cost, price.*

   a costo di *at the risk of.*

   costo di spedizione *shipping cost.*

   ad ogni costo *whatever the cost.*

costola *rib; back; spine (of a book).*

costoro *those people; they.*

costoso *expensive.*

costretto *obliged, compelled.*

costringere *to compel; to force.*

costruire *to build; to construct.*

costruzione, f. *construction.*

costui *this man.*

costume, m. *custom, habit.*

   costume da bagno *bathing suit.*

   di cattivi costumi *of bad habit.*

   È un fatto di costume. *It's a habit.*

cotone, m. *cotton.*

COTTO *cooked.*

   ben cotto *well done.*

   poco cotto *rare.*

   troppo cotto *overcooked.*

cranio *skull.*

cravatta *necktie.*

creare *to create; to establish.*

credere *to believe.*

   credere a *to believe in.*

   Credo che sia vero. *I believe it's true.*

   Non credo! *I don't think so.*

   Non ti credo! *I don't believe you!*

credito *credit.*

   comprare a credito *to buy on credit.*

creditore, m. **creditrice,** f. *creditor.*

crema *cream.*

crepuscolo *twilight, dusk.*

crescere *to grow; to increase; to rear.*

   un figlio cresciuto *a grown son.*

cretino *idiot, fool.*

crimine, m. *crime.*

crisi, f. *crisis.*

   crisi finanziaria *financial crisis.*

   una crisi di nervi *a fit of hysterics; nervous breakdown.*

cristallo *crystal, glass.*

critica *criticism; review.*

criticare *to criticize.*

critico n. *critic;* adj. *critical.*

   un momento critico della sua vita *a difficult period in his (her) life.*

croccante *crisp.*

crocchio *circle, group.*

croce, f. *cross.*

   a occhio e croce *roughly.*

   farsi il segno della croce *to make the sign of the cross.*

crocevia, m. *crossroads.*

crociera *cruise.*

crollare *to collapse.*

cronaca *chronicle, news.*

crosta *crust.*

crostaceo *shellfish.*

crudele *cruel.*

crudo *raw.*

cuccetta *berth.*
CUCCHIAÌNO *teaspoon.*
CUCCHIAIO *tablespoon.*
cucina *kitchen, cooking.*
   occuparsi della cucina *to take care of the cooking.*
cucinare *to cook.*
cucire *to sew.*
   macchina da cucire *sewing machine.*
cucitura *seam.*
CUFFIE *headphones.*
cugino, m. **cugina,** f. *cousin.*
CUI *whom; whose; to whom; which; of which; to which.*
culla *cradle.*
cultura *cultivation, culture, learning.*
   un'uomo di cultura *a man of learning.*
CUOCERE *to cook.*
   cuocere a fuoco lento *to simmer.*
cuoco, m. **cuoca,** f. *cook.*
cuolo *leather.*
CUORE, m. **cuori,** pl. *heart.*
   con tutto il cuore *with all one's heart.*
   prendere a cuore *to take to heart.*
   senza cuore *heartless.*
cupola *dome, cupola.*
CURA *care.*
   essere sotto la cura di un medico *to be under a doctor's care.*
   fare una cosa con cura *to do something carefully.*
   prendersi la cura di *to take the trouble to.*
CURARE *to take care of; to nurse.*
   non curasene *not to mind; not to take heed of.*
curiosità *curiosity.*
   per curiosità *out of curiosity.*
   togliersi la curiosità *to satisfy one's curiosity.*
curioso *curious, odd.*
   una folla di curiosi *a crowd of curious bystanders.*
   un avvenimento molto curioso *a very odd occurrence.*
curriculum vitae *résumé.*
curva *curve, bend.*
cuscino *pillow.*
cuspide *cusp; point.*
custodia *custody; care.*
custodire *to keep; to guard; to take care of.*

cute, f. *skin.*
cuticola *cuticle.*

D

da *from, by, at, to, since.*
   dallo scorso mese *since last month.*
   da lunedi in poi *from Monday on.*
   da quando *since.*
   da quando l'ho conosciuto *from the time I met him.*
   fin dalla prima volta *from the very first time.*
   venire da *to come from.*
   Da dove vieni? *Where do you come from? Where are you coming from?*
   Lo conosco da poco. *I have known him a short while.*
   Vado da Maria. *I'm going to Mary's.*
daccapo *again; once again.*
   Ho dovuto rifare tutto daccapo. *I had to do the whole thing over again.*
   Incominciamo daccapo. *Let's start from the beginning.*
dacchè *since; since when; as.*
daino *deer, suede.*
d'altronde *on the other side; moreover.*
danese *Danish.*
DANNO *damage, injury, harm.*
   a mio danno *to my disadvantage.*
   recare danno a *to cause injury to.*
   risarcire i danni *to indemnify.*
danza *dance.*
dappertutto *everywhere.*
   cercare dappertutto *to search everywhere.*
DARE *to give.*
   dare cattivo esempio *to set a bad example.*
   dare il buongiorno *to say good morning.*
   dare luogo a *to give rise to.*
   dare nell'occhio *to attract attention.*
   darsi a *to devote oneself to.*
   Mi ha dato dell'imbecile. *He called me an imbecile.*
   Mi ha dato un gran da fare. *He caused me a great deal of work.*
   Può darsi! *Perhaps! That might be so!*

Quanti anni mi date? *How old do you think I am?*

Questa finestra da sul giardino. *This window opens onto the garden.*

DATA *date.*

in data del 5 maggio *dated the 5th of May.*

dattilografare *to type.*

dattilografo, m. **dattilografa,** f. *typist.*

dattiloscritto *typed.*

davanti *before; in front of.*

davanzo, d'avanzo *enough of; too much.*

DAVVERO *really, indeed, truly.*

DAZIO *excise duty.*

debito, adj. *due;* n. *debt.*

a tempo debito *in due time.*

Ti sono in debito. *I owe you.*

debole *weak, feeble.*

avere un debole per *to have a weakness for.*

debutto *debut.*

decadente *decadent.*

decadenza *decline, decadence.*

decaffeinato *decaffeinated.*

decedere *to die.*

decenza *decency.*

decidere *to decide.*

decimo *tenth.*

decisamente *decidedly.*

decisione, f. *decision.*

decisivo *decisive.*

una svolta decisiva *a turning point.*

declinare *to decline.*

decollo *takeoff.*

decorare *to decorate.*

decrescere *to reduce.*

DEDICARE *to dedicate.*

dedicarsi *to dedicate oneself.*

dedurre *to subtract; to deduct; to infer.*

definire *to define; to settle.*

definire i termini d'un contratto *to settle the terms of a contract.*

definire una parola *to give the meaning of; to define a word.*

definitivo *definitive, definite.*

DEGNARE *to deem worthy.*

Non ti degno di uno sguardo. *I don't consider you worthy of notice.*

degnarsi *to deign.*

degno *worthy of; deserving.*

degno di fiducia *trustworthy.*

degno di nota *noteworthy.*

deliberare *to deliberate; to resolve upon.*

deliberare a lungo *to deliberate at length.*

deliberatamente *deliberately.*

delicato *delicate.*

delitto *crime.*

deliziare *to delight.*

deliziarsi a *to enjoy.*

delizioso *delightful, delicious.*

deludere *to disappoint; to delude.*

delusione, f. *disappointment.*

denaro *money.*

DENTE, m. *tooth.*

dente del giudizio *wisdom tooth.*

dente per dente *an eye for an eye.*

mal di denti *toothache.*

dentifricio m. *toothpaste.*

dentista, m. *dentist.*

dentro *in, within.*

da dentro *from within.*

in dentro *inward.*

dentatura *teeth.*

denunciare *to denounce.*

deodorante, m. *deodorant.*

deperire *to decline.*

DEPORRE *to lay; to lay down.*

deportare *to deport.*

deposito *deposit.*

depravato *depraved.*

depressione *depression.*

depurare *purify.*

deridere *to ridicule.*

derisione, f. *derision, ridicule.*

derivare *to derive.*

dermatologo *dermatologist.*

derubare *to rob.*

descrivere *to describe.*

descrivere l'accaduto *to describe what happened.*

descrizione, f. *description.*

deserto *desert; wilderness.*

desiderabile *desirable.*

desiderare *to wish; to desire.*

desiderio *desire; wish.*

esprimere un desiderio *to express a desire.*

desinare *to dine.*

desolato *desolate, disconsolate.*

desolazione, f. *desolation.*

DESTARE *to wake; to awaken; to wake up.*

destare sentimenti buoni *to awaken kind feelings.*

destarsi presto al mattino *to wake early in the morning.*

destinare *to assign.*

destinato *destined, appointed.*

destinato ad un glorioso avvenire *destined to have a glorious future.*

l'ora destinata *the appointed hour.*

destinazione, f. *destination.*

arrivare a destinazione *to reach one's destination.*

destino *destiny.*

DESTO *awake; lively.*

Sono desto dalle sette. *I've been awake since seven o'clock.*

DESTRA *right; right side.*

voltare a destra *to turn to the right.*

DESTRO *right, dextrous.*

ambidestro *ambidextrous.*

la mano destra *the right hand.*

determinare *to determine.*

determinazione, f. *determination.*

detersivo *detergent.*

detestare *to hate.*

detrarre *to deduct; to subtract.*

detrimento *detriment.*

dettaglio *detail.*

negoziante dettaglio *retailer.*

vendita al dettaglio *retail.*

DETTARE *to dictate.*

dettare legge *to lay down the law.*

dettare una lettura *to dictate a letter.*

DETTO *said; above mentioned.*

Detto, fatto. *No sooner said than done.*

Non è detto che sia vero! *It is not necessarily true!*

devotissimo *very truly.*

devozione *piety; devoutness.*

DI *of.*

di cattivo umore *in a bad humor.*

di faccia *facing.*

di giorno *in the daytime.*

di male in peggio *from bad to worse.*

scuola di canto *singing school.*

diabete *diabetes.*

diabetico *diabetic.*

diadema *tiara.*

diagnosi *diagnosis.*

dialetto *dialect.*

dialogo *dialogue.*

diamante, m. *diamond.*

diametro *diameter.*

diario *diary, journal.*

diavolo *devil.*

dibattito *debate; discussion.*

dicembre *December.*

DICHIARARE *to declare.*

dichiarare il falso *to make a false declaration.*

dichiararsi *to declare oneself.*

DICHIARAZIONE, f. *declaration.*

diciannove *nineteen.*

diciannovesimo *nineteenth.*

diciassette *seventeen.*

diciassettesimo *seventeenth.*

dlciottesimo *eighteenth.*

diciotto *eighteen.*

didascalico *didactic.*

didascalle *subtitles.*

dieci *ten.*

dieta *diet.*

DIETRO *behind.*

da dietro *from behind.*

di dietro *in back of.*

DIFENDERE *to defend.*

difendere una causa *to defend a case.*

difendersi *to defend oneself.*

difesa *defense.*

legittima difesa *self-defense.*

difetto *defect, flaw.*

difettoso *defective.*

differente *different.*

differenza *difference.*

DIFFICILE *difficult.*

essere difficile da accontentare *to be hard to please.*

difficoltà *difficulty.*

aver difficoltà a *to have difficulty in.*

diffidare *to mistrust.*

diffidenza *distrust, mistrust.*

diffondere *to spread.*

diga *dam.*

digerire *to digest.*

digestione, f. *digestion.*

digiuno *fast.*

essere digiuno di *not to know; to ignore.*

stare a digiuno *to fast.*

DIGNITÀ *dignity.*

dignitoso *dignified.*

dilagare *to overflow.*

dileguarsi *to disappear suddenly.*

dilemma *dilemma.*

diletto *delight.*

diluvio *flood.*
> un diluvio di posta *a flood of mail.*

dimagrire *to grow thin; to slim.*

dimensione, f. *dimension, size.*

DIMENTICARE *to forget.*

dimettere *to dismiss; to remove.*
> dimettersi da una carica *to resign from office.*

diminuire *to diminish.*

diminuzione, f. *reduction.*
> dimettersi da una carica *to resign from office.*

diminuire *to diminish.*

diminuzione, f. *reduction.*
> diminuzione di stipendio *reduction in salary.*

dimissione, f. *resignation.*
> chiedere le dimissioni di *to ask for someone's resignation.*
> dare le dimissioni *to resign.*

dimora *dwelling, residence.*

DIMOSTRARE *demonstrate; to show.*
> dimostrare buon senso *to display good sense.*
> dimostrarsi *to prove oneself.*
> non dimostrare la propria età *not to show one's age.*

dimostrazione, f. *demonstration, display.*
> dimostrazione d'affetto *a display of affection.*

dinamismo *dynamism; energy.*

DINANZI *before; in front of.*
> dinanzi alla legge *in the eyes of the law.*

diniego *denial, refusal.*

DINTORNO *around, round, about.*
> i dintorni *the surrounding area.*
> nei dintorni di *in the general vicinity of; in the neighborhood of.*

dipanare *to wind; to unravel.*

dipartimento *department.*

dipendente, n. & adj. *dependent.*

DIPENDERE *to depend.*
> Dipende da te. *It depends on you.*

dipingere *to paint; to depict.*
> dipinto dal vero *painted from life.*
> Lo ha dipinto come un'eroe. *He depicted him as a hero.*

diplomatico, n. *diplomat;* adj. *diplomatic.*

diplomazìa *diplomacy.*

DIRE *to say; to tell.*
> vale a dire *that is to say.*
> Te l'avevo detto io . . . *I told you . . .*
> Dimmi pure. *Tell me.*
> Come si dice in italiano . . . *How do you say in Italian . . .*
> si dice che . . . *there is a rumor that . . .*
> detto e fatto *said and done.*
> dire il vero *to speak the truth.*
> dire male di qualcuno *to speak ill of someone.*
> per così dire *so as to say.*
> sentire dire *to hear it said; to hear about.*
> Come dice? *What did you say? I beg your pardon.*

direttamente *directly.*

direttissimo *express train.*

diretto *direct, straight.*
> essere diretto a *to be headed toward; to be bound for.*
> treno diretto *a fast train.*
> un appello diretto *a direct appeal.*

direttore, m; **direttrice,** f. *director.*

direzione, f. *direction, management.*
> in direzione giusta *in the right direction.*
> in direzione opposta *in the opposite direction.*
> La direzione dell' impresa è stata affidata a me. *The management of the enterprise was entrusted to me.*

dirigente *executive.*

dirigere *to direct; to manage.*
> dirigere un'azienda *to manage a business.*
> Le sue parole erano dirette a me. *His words were addressed (directed) to me.*

dirigersi *to go toward.*

dirimpetto *opposite; across from.*
> dirimpetto alla banca *opposite the bank.*
> la casa dirimpetto alla mia *the house across from mine.*
> Si sono sedute una dirimpetto all'altra. *They sat face to face.*

DIRITTO, n. *right;* adj. *right, straight, honest.*

diritto di nascita *birthright.*

non avere il diritto di *not to have the right to.*

diritti civili *civil rights.*

diritto privato *private law.*

diritto pubblico *public law.*

diritto comparato *comparative law.*

filosofia del diritto *philosophy of law.*

strada diritta *straight street.*

Vada avanti diritto. *Go straight ahead.*

dirotto *without restraint.*

piangere a dirotto *to cry unrestrainedly.*

piovere a dirotto *to rain in torrents.*

disabile *disabled; handicapped.*

DISACCORDO *disagreement, discord.*

essere in disaccordo con *to disagree with.*

V'è disaccordo fra i due. *There is discord between the two.*

disagio *discomfort.*

sentirsi a disagio *to feel uncomfortable.*

vivere fra i disagi *to live a life of privations.*

disapprovare *to disapprove.*

disappunto *disappointment.*

disastro *disaster, calamity.*

disastroso *disastrous.*

discendente, adj., n. m. & f. *descendant, descending.*

DISCENDERE *to descend; to descend from.*

discendere da una famiglia italiana *to descend from an Italian family.*

discesa *descent, fall.*

I prezzi sono in discesa. *The prices are falling.*

La strada è in discesa. *The street slopes downward.*

dischetto *computer disk.*

disciplina *discipline.*

disciplinato *disciplined, obedient.*

un attore disciplinato *a disciplined actor.*

un bambino disciplinato *an obedient boy.*

disco *disc, record.*

disco sul ghiaccio *ice hockey.*

ascoltare un disco *to listen to a record.*

discordia *discord, dissension.*

discorso *speech, talk.*

fare un lungo discorso *to make a long speech.*

discosto *distant, far.*

poco discosto *not far.*

discoteca *discotheque.*

discreto *discreet, moderate.*

discrezione, f. *discretion.*

discussione, f. *discussion, debate.*

discutere *to discuss; to debate.*

disdegno *disdain; contempt.*

disdire *to annul; to retract.*

disdire un appuntamento *to cancel an appointment.*

DISEGNARE *to draw; to design.*

disegno *drawing, design.*

disfare *to undo.*

disfare il letto *to open (turn down) a bed.*

disfare una cucitura *to rip a seam.*

disfare una valigia *to unpack a valise.*

disfarsi *to get rid of.*

disgelare *to thaw.*

disgelo *thaw.*

DISGRAZIA *misfortune, accident.*

disgustare *to disgust; to shock.*

disgustarsi *to take a dislike to.*

disgusto *disgust, loathing.*

disgustoso *disgusting, loathsome, disagreeable.*

disillusione, f. *disillusion, disenchantment.*

disimpegnare *to disengage; to free.*

disimpegnarsi *to free oneself; to disengage oneself.*

disinteressatamente *disinterestedly, altruistically.*

DISINTERESSE *disinterestedness, unselfishness.*

disinvolto *easy, free, self-possessed.*

disobbedienza *disobedience.*

disobbedire *to disobey.*

disoccupato *unemployed.*

disoccupazione *unemployment.*

DISONESTO *dishonest.*

DISOPRA *on, upon, over, above.*

al disopra di ogni altra cosa *above all else.*

il piano disopra *the upper floor; the floor above.*

Vado disopra. *I'm going upstairs.*

disordine, m. *disorder, confusion.*

disotto *under, below.*

dispari *odd, uneven.*

  numeri dispari *odd numbers.*

disparte *apart.*

  chiamare in disparte *to call aside.*

  tenersi in disparte *to stand aside.*

disperare *to despair.*

  fare disperare *to drive to despair.*

disperato *desperate, hopeless.*

  una misura disperata *a desperate measure.*

  un caso disperato *a hopeless case.*

disperazione, f. *despair.*

disperso *dispersed, scattered.*

  andare disperso *to get lost; to get scattered.*

dispetto *vexation, spite.*

  fare una cosa per dispetto *to do something for spite.*

  fare un dispetto a *to vex someone.*

dispettoso *spiteful.*

dispiacere, m. *sorrow; regret;* v. *to displease.*

  con molto dispiacere *with great sorrow.*

  dare un dispiacere a *to cause sorrow to.*

  Mi dispiace doverti dire. *I'm sorry to have to tell you.*

  Il suo modo d'agire displace a tutti. *His behavior displeases everyone.*

  Non mi dispiace. *I don't dislike it.*

disponibile *available, vacant.*

DISPORRE *to place; to arrange; to dispose of.*

  Disponili in fila. *Place them in a row.*

  Ne puoi disporre come vuoi. *You may dispose of them as you wish.*

DISPOSIZIONE, f. *arrangement, disposition.*

  la disposizione dei fiori *the flower arrangement.*

  Sono a vostra disposizione *I'm at your disposal.*

DISPOSTO *disposed, inclined, willing.*

  disposto in ordine alfabetico *arranged in alphabetical order.*

  Non è disposto agli studi. *He is not inclined to study.*

  Non sono disposto a farlo. *I am not willing to do it.*

dispotico *despotic; tyrannical.*

dispotismo *despotism; tyranny.*

disprezzare *to despise; to hold in contempt.*

disprezzo *contempt.*

disputa *dispute, quarrel.*

dissenso *difference of opinion, dissent.*

dissertazione *dissertation, (academic) thesis.*

dissolvere *to dissolve; to melt.*

distaccare *to detach.*

  distaccarsi *to detach oneself; to come off.*

  Il francobollo si è distaccato dalla busta. *The stamp came off the envelope.*

distacco *detachment, separation.*

  Il distacco fra madre e figlia fu doloroso. *The separation between mother and daughter was painful.*

distante *distant, far away.*

distanza *distance.*

  a grande distanza da *at a great distance from.*

  tenere una persona a distanza *to keep a person at arm's length.*

  Qual'è la distanza fra Roma e Napoli? *What is the distance between Rome and Naples?*

distesa *extent, expanse.*

distinguere *to distinguish.*

  distinguersi *to distinguish oneself.*

distinzione, f. *distinction.*

  fare distinzione fra una cosa e l'altra *to distinguish between one thing and the other.*

  senza distinzione alcuna *without any discrimination.*

distrarre *to distract.*

  distrarre dagli studi *to distract from one's studies.*

  Voglio distrarmi un pò. *I want to relax a little.*

distrazione *absentmindedness, distraction.*

DISTRETTO *district.*

DISTRIBUIRE *to distribute.*

  distribuire la posta *to deliver the mail.*

distribuzione, f. *distribution.*

disturbare *to trouble; to disturb.*

disturbo *trouble, annoyance.*

DISUGUALE *unequal.*

DITO (le dita, f. pl.) *finger.*
  dito del piede *toe.*
DITTA *concern, firm.*
divano *divan, couch, sofa.*
DIVENIRE (diventare) *to become; to grow.*
  diventare pallido *to become pale.*
  diventare pazzo *to go insane.*
  diventare vecchio *to grow old.*
  Siamo diventati amici. *We became friends.*
DIVERSO *different, some, several.*
  da diverso tempo *for some time now.*
  diverse volte *several times.*
  Lui è molto diverso da me. *He is very unlike me.*
divertente *amusing, entertaining.*
divertimento *amusement, recreation.*
divertire *to amuse; to entertain.*
  divertirsi *to amuse oneself; to enjoy oneself.*
dividendo *dividend.*
dividere *to divide; to part; to separate.*
  dividere a metà *to divide in half.*
  Si è diviso da sua moglie. *He separated from his wife.*
divieto *prohibition.*
  Divieto d'Affissione *No Posting.*
  Divieto di Sosta *No Parking.*
divino *divine, splendid.*
divisa *uniform, dress, currency.*
divisione, f. *division.*
divorare *to eat up; to devour.*
divorziare *to divorce.*
divorzio *divorce.*
divulgare *to spread; to broadcast.*
dizionario *dictionary.*
dizione *diction.*
doccia *shower.*
  farsi una doccia *to take a shower.*
docente *teacher, professor.*
docile *docile, submissive.*
documento *document.*
dodicesimo *twelfth.*
dodici *twelve.*
dogana *customs.*
  esente da dogana *duty free.*
doganiere, m. *customhouse officer.*
DOLCE *sweet.*
  acqua dolce *fresh water.*
  dolci *sweets.*
dolcezza *sweetness.*

DOLENTE *sorry, grieved; saddened; painful.*
  Sono dolente di dovervi informare . . . *I am sorry to have to inform you . . .*
DOLERE *to ache; to be grieved; to regret.*
  Gli duole averti fatto male. *He regrets having hurt you.*
  Mi duole la schiena. *My back hurts.*
  Mi duole vederti infelice. *It grieves me to know that you are unhappy.*
dolo *malice.*
DOLORE, m. *pain, ache, sorrow.*
  con molto dolore *with great sorrow.*
  dolor di testa *headache.*
  Ho un dolore alla spalla. *I have a pain in the shoulder.*
dolorosamente *painfully, sorrowfully.*
doloroso *painful.*
doloso *malicious.*
domanda *question.*
  fare domanda *to apply.*
DOMANDARE *to ask; to request.*
  domandare scusa *to beg one's pardon.*
  domandare un piacere *to ask a favor.*
  Mi domando perchè *I wonder why.*
domani *tomorrow.*
domare *to tame.*
DOMATTINA *tomorrow morning.*
domenica *Sunday.*
domestica *maid.*
domestico *domestic, tame; familiar.*
  un animale domestico *a tame animal.*
  lavori domestici *housework.*
domicillo *domicile, residence.*
dominare *to dominate.*
  dominarsi *to control oneself.*
dominio *domain.*
DONARE *to give; to present; to become; to donate.*
  Ha donato il suo patrimonio a istituti di beneficenza. *He donated his inheritance to charitable institutions.*
  Quest' abito non mi dona. *This outfit doesn't look good on me.*
dondolare *to rock; to sway.*
DONNA *woman.*
  donna di casa *housewife.*
  donna di quadri *queen of diamonds.*

donna di servizio *maid.*
prima donna *prima donna (first woman).*

DONO *gift.*
fare dono di *to make a present of.*

DOPO *after.*
dopodomani *the day after tomorrow.*
dopo pranzo *afternoon.*
il giorno dopo *the following day.*
poco dopo *a little later.*

dopotutto *after all.*
doppiaggio *dubbing.*
dopplamente *doubly.*

DOPPIO *double.*
a doppio giro di chiave *double lock.*
a doppio petto *double-breasted.*
pagare il doppio *to pay twice as much:*
un arma a doppio taglio *a double-edged blade.*

DORMIRE *to sleep.*
dormire come un ghiro *to sleep like a log (a top).*

DORSO *back.*

dose, f. *dose.*
una buona dose di giudizio *a great deal of common sense.*
una piccola dose *a small dose.*

dote, f. *dowry; gift; merit.*
dotto *learned.*

DOTTORE *doctor, graduate.*
é dottore in legge *he has a law degree.*

dottoressa *female doctor, graduate.*
dottrina *doctrine.*

DOVE *where.*
Dov'è? *Where is it? Where is he? Where is she?*
Dove siamo *Where are we?*

DOVERE, v. *to be obliged to; to have to; to owe;* n. m. *duty.*
Deve essere tardi. *It must be late.*
Devo andar via. *I must go.*
Dobbiamo partire al più presto. *We must leave at the earliest possible.*
Dovrebbe arrivare da un momento all' altro. *It should arrive any moment.*
credersi in dovere di *to feel obliged to.*
fare il proprio dovere *to do one's duty.*

È mio piacevole dovere . . . *It is my pleasant duty . . .*

DOVUNQUE *wherever, anywhere.*
dovunque volgo lo sguardo *wherever I look.*
seguire dovunque *to follow anywhere.*

DOZZINA *dozen.*
a dozzine *by the dozen.*
mezza dozzina *half-dozen.*

dramma, m. *drama.*
drastico *drastic.*
drenaggio *drainage.*
dritto *straight.*
drizzare *to straighten.*
drizzarsi *to straighten oneself.*
Drizzati! *Stand straight!*
droga *drug.*
drogato *drugged; drug addict.*
dubbio *doubt.*
senza dubbio *doubtless.*
duce, m. *chief.*

DUE *two.*
a due a due *two by two.*
due per volta *two at a time.*
due volte tanto *twice as much.*
tagliare in due *to cut in two.*

duecento *two hundred.*
duaque *then, consequently.*
duomo *cathedral.*
DURANTE *during.*
DURARE *to last; to continue.*
La tempesta dura da parecchio. *The storm has lasted for quite a while.*
Non può durare molto. *It can't last long.*
Tutto dura finchè può. *Everything comes to an end.*

durata *duration.*
di breve durata *of short duration.*
durezza *hardness, harshness.*
DURO *hard.*
dal cuore duro *hard-hearted.*

E

E, ED *and.*
ebanista *cabinet maker*
ebbene *well!*
ebreo *Jew.*

eccedenza *excess.*
eccellente *excellent.*
eccèllere *to excel.*
eccessivamente *excessively.*
eccessivo *excessive.*
ECCETTO *except.*
eccettuare *to except.*
eccezionale *exceptional, unusual.*
    un caldo eccezionale *unusual heat.*
eccezionalmente *exceptionally.*
eccezione, f. *exception.*
    eccezione fatta per *except for.*
    fare eccezione per *to make an exception for.*
    in via di eccezione *as an exception.*
eccitare *to excite.*
eccitazione, f. *excitement.*
ECCO *here, there, that's.*
    ecco fatto *all done.*
    Ecco! *Here!*
    Eccomi! *Here I am!*
eco, f. *echo.*
ecologia *ecology.*
economia *economy.*
    fare economìa *to economize.*
economico *economic, thrity.*
economizzare *to economize.*
edera *ivy.*
edicola *newsstand.*
edificio *building.*
edilizia *building industry.*
èdito *published.*
editore, m. *editor; publisher.*
    casa editrice *publishing house.*
edizione, f. *edition.*
educare *to educate.*
educazione, f. *education.*
effettivo *effective, actual.*
effetto *effect, consequence, impression.*
    effetti personali *personal effects.*
    fare effetto su *to have an effect on.*
    senza effetto *of no effect.*
effettuare *to effect; to put into effect.*
efficace *effective.*
efficiente *efficient; able.*
efficienza *efficiency.*
egoismo *selfishness.*
egoista, m. *selfish; selfish person.*
egregio *exceptional, remarkable.*
eguale *equal.*
    dare eguale importanza *to give the same importance.*

egualità *equality.*
elastico, n. & adj. *elastic.*
elefante, m. *elephant.*
elegante *elegant.*
eleganza *elegance.*
eleggere *to elect; to appoint.*
elementare *elementary.*
elemento *element.*
elemosina *alms.*
elencare *to make a list of.*
elenco *list.*
    elenco telefonico *phone book.*
elettore, m. *elector.*
elettricità *electricity.*
elèttrico *electric.*
    luce elettrica *electric light.*
elevare *to elevate; to raise.*
elezione, f. *election.*
elica *propeller.*
eliminare *to eliminate.*
elogiare *to praise.*
elogio *praise.*
    fare l'elogio di una persona *to sing someone's praises.*
    senza tanti elogi *without much ceremony.*
eludere *to elude; to evade.*
    eludere la sorveglianza *to escape surveillance.*
emancipare *to emancipate; to set free.*
emendamento *amendment.*
emergente *emergent.*
EMERGENZA *emergency.*
emergere *to emerge.*
emesso *given out; put forth.*
emettere *to emit; to send forth.*
emicrania *migraine.*
emigrante, m. & f. *emigrant.*
emigrare *to emigrate.*
emozionante *moving.*
emozione, f. *emotion.*
emporio *market.*
energia *energy.*
    energia atomica *atomic energy.*
    energia solare *solar energy.*
energico *energetic, vigorous.*
enfasi, f. *emphasis.*
enigma, m. *enigma, riddle.*
enorme *enormous.*
enormemente *enormously.*
entrambi *both.*
ENTRARE *to enter; to come in.*

entrare dalla porta *to come in through the door.*
entrare in carica *to take office.*
entrare in vigore *to go into effect.*
Che cosa c'entra? *What does that have to do with it?*
Entrate pure. *Come right in.*
entrata *entrance.*
ENTRO *within, in.*
   entro ventiquattr'ore *within twenty-four hours.*
entusiasmo *enthusiasm.*
entusiastico *enthusiastic.*
enumerare *to enumerate.*
epidermide, f. *skin.*
episodio *episode.*
   un episodio triste della sua vita *a sad episode in his life.*
   un romanzo a episodi *a serial.*
època *era, period.*
EPPURE *yet; and yet; nevertheless.*
   Eppure si muove! *And yet it turns! (Galileo)*
equilibrio *balance.*
   perdere l'equilibrio *to lose one's balance.*
equipaggiamento *equipment.*
equipaggiare *to equip.*
equipaggio *crew.*
equo *equitable, fair.*
ERBA *grass, herb.*
   erbaccia *weed.*
   in erba *in embryo.*
erbivendolo *greengrocer.*
erede, m. & f. *heir.*
eredità *inheritance.*
   lasciare in eredità *to bequeath.*
ereditare *to inherit.*
erigere *to erect; to build.*
   erigere un monumento *to erect a monument.*
   erigersi *to set oneself up as.*
eròe *hero;* **eroina** *heroine.*
eroico *heroic.*
eroina *heroin.*
errato *wrong, incorrect.*
   È errato dire . . . *It is incorrect to say . . .*
errore, m. *error, mistake.*
   errore di stampa *misprint.*
   essere in errore *to be mistaken.*
   per errore *by mistake.*

esagerare *to exaggerate.*
esagerazione, f. *exaggeration.*
esame, m. *examination, inspection.*
   esame di ammissione *entrance exam.*
   superare un esame *to pass an exam.*
ESAMINARE *to examine; to inspect.*
esatto *exact.*
esaudire *to grant.*
   esaudire una richiesta *to grant a request.*
esaurimento *exhaustion.*
   esaurimento nervoso *nervous breakdown.*
esaurire *to exhaust.*
   esaurirsi *to exhaust oneself; to be sold out (theater).*
esausto *exhausted.*
esca *bait.*
esclamare *to exclaim.*
esclamazione, f. *exclamation.*
escludere *to exclude.*
esclusione, f. *exclusion.*
esclusivo *exclusive.*
   rappresentante esclusivo *sole representative.*
escluso *left out.*
esecuzione, f. *execution, performance.*
   mettere un piano in esecuzione *to put a plan into action.*
   un'esecuzione al pianoforte *the performance of a piece of music on the piano.*
eseguire *to execute; to accomplish.*
ESEMPIO *example, instance.*
   dare un cattivo esempio *to set a bad example.*
   per esempio *for instance.*
esequie, f. pl. *funeral.*
esercitare *to exercise; to practice; to exert.*
   esercitare influenza *to exert influence.*
   esercitare una professione *to practice in a given profession.*
   esercitarsi *to train oneself; to exercise.*
esercito *army.*
esercizio *exercise.*
   essere fuori esercizio *to be out of practice.*
   fare degli esercizi *to do some exercises.*
esibire *to exhibit; to show.*

esibirsi in pubblico *to show oneself in public.*

esibizione, f. *exhibition, show.*

esibizione di quadri *a painting exhibition.*

esigenza *demand, need; requirement.*

esiliare *to exile.*

esilio *exile.*

esimere *to exempt.*

esimersi da un impegno *to free oneself of an engagement.*

esistente *existent, existing.*

tutte le creature esistenti sulla terra *all creatures living on earth.*

esistenza *existence.*

un' esistenza monotona *a monotonous existence.*

esitare *to hesitate.*

esitazione, f. *hesitation.*

senza esitazione *unhesitatingly.*

èsito *result.*

L'èsito fu buono. *The result was good.*

Quale fu l'èsito? *What was the result?*

esodo *exodus; flight.*

espandere *to expand.*

espansione, f. *expansion.*

espansivo *expansive.*

espatriare *to immigrate.*

espellere *to expel.*

esperienza *experience.*

esperimento *experiment.*

fare un esperimento *to do an experiment.*

esperto *expert, skilled.*

espiatorio *sacrificial.*

espirare *to exhale.*

esplodere *to explode.*

esplorare *to explore.*

esplorare ogni possibilità *to explore all possibilities.*

esplosione, f. *explosion.*

ESPORRE *to expose; to exhibit.*

ESPORTARE *to export.*

esportazione, f. *exportation.*

esposizion, f. *exhibition.*

espressione, f. *expression.*

espressivo *expressive.*

ESPRESSO *express.*

treno espresso *express train.*

un caffè espresso *an espresso (Italian-style coffee).*

esprimere *to express.*

esprimere i propri sentimenti *to express one's sentiments.*

esprimersi *to express oneself.*

espulsione, f. *expulsion.*

essenza *essence.*

essenziale *essential.*

ESSERE, v. *to be;* n. m. *being, creature.*

essere disposto a *to be willing to.*

essere in cattiva salute *to be in poor health.*

essere in grado di *to be able to.*

essere per; essere sul punto di *to be on the point of; about to.*

essere pronto a *to be ready to.*

se non fosse per te *if it were not for you.*

Che cos' è? *What is it?*

Di chi è questo libro? *Whose book is this?*

Non c' è di che. *You're welcome.*

Può essere. *That may be.*

Quant' è? *How much is it?*

Sia lodato Iddio! *May the Lord be praised!*

un' essere spregievole *a base creature.*

un' essere umano *a human being.*

essiccare *to dry; to dry up.*

EST *east.*

ad est *to the east.*

èstasi, f. *ecstasy.*

ESTATE, f. *summer.*

una notte d'estate *a summer night.*

estatico *ecstatic.*

estendere *to extend.*

estensione, f. *extension, surface.*

esteriore *exterior, outward.*

esteriorità *outward appearance.*

esterno *external, outside.*

ESTERO *foreign.*

all' estero *abroad.*

Ministero degli Esteri *State Department.*

Ministro degli Esteri *Secretary of State.*

esteso *extensive.*

estetica *esthetics.*

estinguere *to extinguish.*

estinto *extinguished, extinct.*

una specie estinta *an extinct species.*

estivo *summery.*

abiti estivi *summer clothes.*

giornata estiva *summer day.*

vacanza estiva *summer vacation.*

estradizione *extradition.*

ESTRANEO *stranger.*

estrarre *to extract; to draw out.*

estratto *extract; certificate.*

estratto di nascita *birth certificate.*

estrazione, f. *extraction, drawing.*

estremamente *extremely.*

estremista *extremist.*

estremo, adj. & n. *extreme.*

L'Estremo Oriente *The Far East.*

estro *inspiration; whim.*

estroverso *extroverted.*

esuberante *exuberant, over-flowery.*

esule *exile.*

ETÀ *age.*

avere la stessa età *to be the same age.*

dimostrare la propria età *to show one's age.*

essere di età maggiore *to be of age.*

mezza età *middle age.*

eternità *eternity.*

Ho atteso un' eternità. *I waited for ages.*

eterno *eternal, everlasting.*

eterogeneo *heterogeneous.*

etica *ethics.*

etichetta *label.*

etimologia *etymology.*

etnico *ethnic.*

etrusco *Etruscan.*

ettogrammo-(etto) *hectogram = 3.52 oz.*

euro, m. *euro (currency).*

EUROPA *Europe.*

europeo *European.*

evadere *to evade; to escape.*

evasione, f. *evasion, escape.*

evasione dal carcere *escape from prison.*

EVENTO *event.*

lieto evento *blessed event.*

eventuale *probable.*

evidente *evident, apparent.*

evidenza *evidence.*

evitabile *avoidable.*

evitare *to avoid.*

evo *epoch; ages.*

Il Medio Evo *the Middle Ages.*

evocare *to evoke.*

evocare tristi memorie *to evoke sad memories.*

evoluto *up-to-date; progressive.*

evoluzione *evolution.*

evolversi *to evolve, to develop.*

EVVIVA *Hurray!*

ex- *ex-.*

ex-combattente *ex-service man.*

ex-moglie *ex-wife.*

extraurbano *suburban.*

F

fa *ago.*

molto tempo fa *a long while ago.*

poco tempo fa *a short while ago.*

fabbrica *factory.*

marchio di fabbrica *trademark.*

fabbricare *to build; to manufacture.*

fabbricato *building.*

tassa sui fabbricati *real estate tax.*

fabbricazione, f. *manufacture.*

faccenda *business matter.*

FACCHINO *porter.*

FACCIA *face.*

avere una faccia tosta *to be impudent; to be bold.*

aver la faccia lunga *to have a long face.*

di faccia *facing.*

faccia a faccia *face to face.*

facciata *facade, front, page.*

la facciata del palazzo *the front of the building.*

la facciata di un libro *the flyleaf of a book.*

FACILE *easy.*

di facili costumi *of easy virtue.*

facile alla collera *easily angered.*

fare le cose troppo facili *to make things too easy.*

FACILITÀ *facility, ease, easiness.*

facilità di parola *fluency of speech.*

facilitare *to facilitate.*

facilmente *easily.*

facoltà *faculty, authority.*

aver facoltá di scelta *to be able to choose.*

nelle sue piene facoltà mentali *completely sane.*

facoltativo *optional.*

facoltoso *wealthy; rich.*

facsimile m. *facsimile, fax.*

fagiolino *string bean.*

fagiolo *bean.*

fagotto *bundle.*
   far fagotto e andare *to pack up and go.*

falciare *to mow; to cut down.*

falco *hawk.*

falegname, m. *carpenter.*

fallimento *failure, bankruptcy.*
   dichiarare fallimento *to declare bankruptcy.*

fallire *to fail; to go bankrupt.*

fallo *fault, defect.*

falò *campfire; bonfire.*

falsare *to alter; to falsify; to distort.*

falso, n. *falsehood;* adj. *false.*
   testimoniare il falso *to bear false witness.*
   moneta falsa *counterfeit.*
   un falso amico *a false friend*

fama *fame, reputation.*
   goder fama di *to have the reputation of.*

FAME, f. *hunger.*
   avere fame *to be hungry.*
   morire di fame *to die of hunger.*

FAMIGLIA *family.*
   rimanere in famiglia *to remain in the family.*

familiare *familiar.*

famoso *famous.*

fanale, m. *headlight.*
   fanale di coda *taillight.*

fanatico, adj. & n. *fanatic, fanatical.*

fanciulla *girl, maid.*

fanciullezza *childhood.*

fanciullo *boy.*

fango *mud.*

fannullone, m. *idler; lazy person.*

fantascienza *science fiction.*

fantasia *fantasy, imagination.*

fantastico *fantastic.*

fantino *jockey.*

FARE *to do; to make.*
   fare bene *to do well (good).*
   fare benzina *to get gas.*
   fare cadere *to let drop; to drop.*
   fare conoscenza *to make acquaintance.*
   fare attenzione *to pay attention.*

fare finta *to make believe.*

fare del surfing sull'Internet *to surf the Net.*

fare il sordo *to pretend to be deaf.*

fare l'avvocato *to be a lawyer.*

fare lo stupido *to be stupid.*

fare presto *to hurry.*

fare una doccia *to take a shower.*

fare una passeggiata *to take a walk.*

fare impazzire *to drive someone crazy.*

fare l'amore con *to make love to.*

fare paura a *to frighten.*

fare piangere *to make somebody cry.*

farsi fare (una cosa) *to have (something) made.*

fare vedere una cosa *to show something.*

Che cosa fai? *What are you doing?*

Fa caldo! *It's warm!*

Fa male! *It hurts!*

Mio fratello si fa tagliare i capelli. *My brother has his hair cut.*

Non fa niente. *It doesn't matter.*

Non sappiamo cosa farci. *We cannot help it.*

Si sta facendo scuro. *It's getting dark.*

farfalla *butterfly.*

farfallino *bow tie; pasta.*

farina *flour.*

faringe *pharynx.*

farmaceutico *pharmaceutical.*

farmacia *drugstore.*

farmacista *druggist.*

farmaco *medicine; drug.*

faro *beacon, lighthouse.*

farsa *farce.*

fascia *girdle.*

fasciare *to bandage; to swathe.*

fascicolo *issue (of a magazine); file.*

fascino *charm.*

fascio *bundle.*

fastidio *trouble, annoyance.*
   Mi da fastidio. *It bothers me.*

fastidioso *troublesome, annoying.*

fata *fairy.*

fatale *fatal.*

fatica *labor, weariness.*

faticare *to labor.*

faticosamente *laboriously; with difficulty.*

fato *fate.*

fattezze, f. pl. *features.*

FATTO *fact, deed, event.* adj. *done, made.*

  È successo un fatto straordinario. *An extraordinary event took place.*

  Non sono fatti vostri. *It's none of your affair.*

  ben fatto *well made; well done.*

  detto fatto *no sooner said than done.*

  fatto su misura *made to order.*

  notte fatta *nighttime.*

  Tutto fatto! *All done!*

fattoria *farm.*

fattorino *messenger.*

  fattorino telegrafico *telegraph messenger.*

fattuale *factual.*

fattura *invoice, bill.*

favella *speech.*

  perdere la favella *to lose one's speech.*

  sciogliere la favella *to loosen one's tongue.*

favola *tale, fable.*

favoloso *fabulous.*

favore, m. *favor.*

  a favore di *in favor of.*

  fare un favore *to do a favor.*

  Per favore. *Please.*

favorire *to favor; to give.*

  Favorisca! *Please, come in.*

  Mi favorisca il burro per piacere. *Please hand me the butter.*

favorito *favorite.*

FAZZOLETTO *handkerchief.*

febbraio *February.*

febbre, f. *fever.*

  aver la febbre *to have a fever.*

  febbre alta *high fever.*

  febbre del fieno *hay fever.*

fecondo *fertile, fruitful.*

FEDE, f. *faith, belief.*

  avere fede in *to have faith in.*

  in buona fede *in good faith.*

  portare la fede al dito *to wear a wedding ring.*

fedele *faithful, true, loyal.*

fedeltà *loyalty.*

federa *pillowcase.*

federale *Federal.*

federazione *federation.*

fegato *liver.*

  aver fegato *to have courage.*

felice *happy.*

felicemente *happily.*

felicità *happiness.*

FEMMINA *female.*

femminile *feminine, womanly.*

  genere femminile *feminine gender.*

femminino *feminine.*

femminismo *feminism.*

femminista *feminist.*

fendere *to cleave; to split.*

fenice *phoenix.*

fenomeno *phenomenon.*

feriale *of work.*

  giorno feriale *weekday, workday.*

FERIRE *to wound.*

  ferirsi *to be wounded.*

ferita *wound.*

  una ferita aperta *an open wound.*

fermaglio *clasp.*

FERMARE *to stop; to fasten.*

  femare un bottone *to fasten a button.*

  fermarsi in aria *to stop in mid-air.*

fermata *stop.*

FERMO *firm, still.*

  con mano ferma *with a firm hand.*

  fermo posta *general delivery.*

  punto fermo *period.*

  stare fermo *to stand still.*

feroce *ferocious, savage.*

ferragosto *August religious holiday.*

ferramenta *hardware.*

ferro *iron, tool.*

  ferro da stiro *iron (for pressing).*

  i ferri del mestiere *the tools of the trade.*

FERROVÌA *railway, railroad.*

  stazione ferroviaria *train station.*

fertile *fertile.*

fertilizzante *fertilizer.*

fervido *fervent, ardent.*

fervore, m. *ardor, fervor.*

festa *feast; holiday party.*

  festa da ballo *dance.*

  fare festa *to make merry.*

festeggiare *to celebrate.*

fetta *slice.*

  tagliare a fette *to slice.*

feudale *feudal.*

FFSS (abbr. of Ferrovie dello Stato) *State railroad.*

fiaba *fable.*

47

fiacco *weary, dull.*
fiàccola *torch.*
fiamma *flame.*
FIAMMIFERO *match.*
fianco *side.*
fiasco *flask, failure.*
    fare fiasco *to be a flop, to be a fiasco.*
    un fiasco di vino *a flask of wine.*
fiatare *to breathe.*
FIATO *breath.*
    bere tutto d'un fiato *to gulp down.*
    Lasciami prendere fiato. *Let me*
        catch my breath.
fibbia *buckle.*
fibra *fiber.*
    fibra cotone *cotton fiber.*
ficcare *to drive in; to set in.*
fico *fig.*
fidanzamento *engagement, betrothal.*
fidanzare *to betroth.*
    fidanzarsi *to become engaged.*
fidanzata *fiancée.*
fidanzato *fiancé.*
fidarsi *to trust.*
    Mi fido di te. *I trust you. I have faith*
        in you.
fidato *trustworthy, faithful.*
fiducia *confidence, trust.*
    un posto di fiducia *a position of trust.*
fiducioso *confident, hopeful.*
fieno *hay.*
fiera *fair; wild beast.*
fierezza *pride.*
fiero *bold, proud.*
fievole *faint; feeble.*
figlia *daughter.*
figliastra *stepdaughter.*
figliastro *stepson.*
figliata *litter.*
FIGLIO *son.*
    essere figlio a *to be the son of.*
figliuolo *son.*
figura *figure, appearance, shape.*
    fare bella figura *to cut a fine figure.*
    Non fa figura. *It doesn't look good.*
fila *line, row.*
    fare la fila *to make the line.*
    in fila *in line.*
filato *yarn.*
    filato di lana *wool yarn.*
    filato pettinato *worsted yarn.*
    filato ritorto *twisted yarn.*

filigrana *filigree.*
film, m. *film.*
filo *thread, blade.*
    dare del filo da torcere *to cause*
        great trouble.
    fil di ferro *wire.*
    filo del discorso *thread of*
        discourse.
    per filo e per segno *in every detail.*
    un filo d'erba *a blade of grass.*
filosofia *philosophy.*
filosofo *philosopher.*
finale *final.*
finanza *finance.*
finanziamento *mortgage.*
finanziario *financial.*
FINCHÈ *till; until; as long as.*
    Bisogna aspettare finchè arrivi. *We*
        must wait until he arrives.
    finchè vivo *as long as I live.*
FINE, f. *end;* m. *purpose;* adj. *fine,*
    thin.
    lieto fine *happy ending.*
    porre fine a *to put an end to.*
    sino alla fine *to the very end.*
    A che fine? *To what purpose?*
    una persona fine *a distinguished*
        person.
FINESTRA *window.*
fingere *to pretend.*
FINIRE *to finish; to end.*
finito *ended; finished.*
FINO A *until; as far as.*
    andare fino a *to go as far as.*
    fino a ieri *up until yesterday.*
    fino a stasera *until tonight.*
finora *till now; to the present moment.*
    Finora non è arrivato nessuno.
        Nobody has arrived yet (until
        now).
finto *false, pretended.*
FIORE, m. *flower.*
    fiore artificiale *artificial flower.*
    nel fiore degli anni *in the prime of*
        life.
    Gli alberi sono in fiore. *The trees are*
        blossoming.
fiorentino *Florentine.*
fiori, f. *clubs (playing cards).*
fiorire *to blossom; to bloom; to*
    flourish.
firma *signature.*

FIRMARE *to sign.*
fischiare *to hiss; to whistle.*
  Mi fischiano gli orecchi. *My ears are buzzing.*
fischio *whistle, hissing.*
fisico, adj. *physical;* n. *body*
fisiologia *physiology.*
fissare *to fix; to fasten; to reserve.*
  fissare con una spilla *to pin; to fasten with a pin.*
  fissare la data *to set the date.*
  fissare qualcuno con lo sguardo *to stare at someone.*
  fissare un posto *to reserve a place.*
  Si è fissato che non gli voglio bene. *He is convinced that I don't care for him.*
fisso *fixed, permanent, steady.*
  a prezzi fissi *at fixed prices.*
  impiego fisso *permanent employment.*
FIUME, m. *river.*
fiuto *scent, smell.*
flotta *fleet.*
fluido, adj. & n. *fluid.*
fluttuare *to fluctuate (economy).*
focolare, m. *hearth, fireside.*
fodera *lining.*
foderare *to line.*
foderato *lined.*
  foderato in pelle *lined in leather.*
foggia *fashion, manner, way.*
FOGLIA *leaf.*
foglio *sheet (of paper).*
fogna *sewer.*
folla *crowd.*
folle *mad, insane.*
follìa *insanity.*
folto *thick.*
  capelli folti *thick hair.*
fondamentale *fundamental.*
fondamento, fondamenta, pl. f. *foundation.*
  senza fondamento *unfounded, groundless.*
fondare *to found.*
fondatore, m. *founder.*
FONDO *bottom, fund.*
  articolo di fondo *leading article (newspaper).*
  da cima a fondo *from top to bottom.*
  fondo cassa *cash fund.*
  in fondo a *at the bottom of.*

  in fondo alla strada *at the end of the street.*
  senza fondi *without funds.*
fonografo *phonograph.*
fontana *fountain.*
fonte, f. *fountain, source.*
  una fonte d'acqua fresca *a spring of fresh water.*
  una fonte di guadagno *a source of income.*
forbici, f. pl. *scissors.*
forcella *hairpin.*
FORCHETTA *fork.*
foresta *forest.*
forestiero *foreigner; stranger.*
forfora *dandruff.*
forma *form, shape.*
  a forma di *shaped like.*
  in forma *in good shape.*
formaggio *cheese.*
formale *formal.*
FORMARE *to form; to mold.*
formazione, f. *formation.*
formica *ant.*
formula *formula.*
fornace, f. *furnace.*
fornaio *baker.*
fornire *to supply; to furnish.*
  fornirsi di tutto *to supply oneself with everything.*
forno *oven.*
  mettere al forno *to put in the oven.*
  forno a microonde *microwave oven.*
FORSE *perhaps, maybe.*
FORTE *strong.*
  correre forte *to run fast.*
  essere forte *to be strong.*
  parlare forte *to speak loudly.*
fortezza *fortress.*
fortuna *fortune, luck.*
  aver fortuna *to be lucky.*
  far fortuna *to make a fortune.*
  per fortuna *fortunately.*
  senza fortuna *without luck.*
fortunato *fortunate, lucky.*
FORZA *strength, force.*
  a forza di *by dint of.*
  farsi forza *to muster one's courage.*
  mettersi in forza *to build up one's strength.*
  per amore o per forza *willing or unwilling.*

per forza *by force.*
forzare *to force; to break open.*
    Ha forzato la porta. *He broke down the door.*
    Non mi forzare a farlo. *Don't force me to do it.*
    Qualcuno ha forzato la serratura. *Someone picked the lock.*
foschia *mist; haze.*
fossa *hole, pit, grave.*
fossile *fossil.*
    carbone fossile *coal.*
fosso *ditch.*
    fare un fosso *to dig a ditch.*
fotografare *to photograph.*
fotografia *photograph, photography.*
    fare una fotografia *to take a photograph.*
    M'interesso di fotografia. *I'm interested in photography.*
FRA *among, between.*
    fra le nuvole *in the clouds.*
    fra moglie e marito *between husband and wife.*
    fra non molto *in a short while.*
    fra una cosa e l'altra *between one thing and the other.*
    trovarsi fra amici *to be among friends.*
fracasso *uproar; noisy quarrel.*
fragile *fragile, frail.*
fragola *strawberry.*
fragrante *fragrant.*
frammento *fragment.*
francese, n. & adj. *French.*
franchezza *frankness; directness.*
franco *frank, open.*
    franco a bordo *free on board.*
    Mi ha parlato franco. *He spoke frankly to me.*
francobollo *stamp, postage.*
frangia *fringe.*
frantumare *to shatter.*
    Questo bicchiere si è frantumato. *This glass is shattered.*
frase, f. *sentence, phrase.*
    frase musicale *a musical phrase.*
frastornato *confused; dazed.*
fratellanza *brotherhood, fraternity.*
FRATELLO *brother.*
frattanto *meanwhile.*
freddamente *coldly.*

freddezza *coolness, indifference.*
FREDDO *cold.*
    aver freddo *to be cold.*
    essere freddo con qualcuno *to be cold toward someone.*
    prendere freddo *to catch cold.*
    Fa freddo. *It's cold.*
fregare *to rub; to cheat (vulg.).*
frenare *to brake; to restrain; to repress.*
    frenare un impulso *to repress an impulse.*
    Ho fatto appena a tempo a frenare. *I applied the brakes just in time.*
    Mi sono frenato a stento. *I was barely able to restrain myself.*
frenesia *frenzy.*
frenetico *frenzied.*
freno *brake.*
    applicare il freno *to apply the brakes.*
    mettere freno a *to restrain.*
    senza freno *unrestrained.*
frequentare *to attend; to frequent.*
    frequentare la scuola *to attend school.*
frequente *frequent.*
freschezza *freshness, coolness.*
fresco, n. *coolness;* adj. *fresh, cool.*
    mettere al fresco *to put in a cool spot.*
    stare al fresco *to stay in a cool place.*
    acqua fresca *fresh water.*
    pesce fresco *fresh fish.*
FRETTA *haste.*
    andar di fretta *to be in a hurry.*
    in fretta *hastily.*
friabile *crumble.*
friggere *to fry.*
frigorifero *refrigerator.*
frittata *omelette.*
fritto *fried.*
frittura *fry.*
    frittura di pesce *fish fry.*
frivolo *frivolous.*
frizzante *sparkling.*
frode, f. *fraud.*
FRONTE, f. *forehead;* m. *front.*
    a fronte alta *with head held high.*
    di fronte a *facing, opposite.*
    fare fronte alle spese *to pay one's expenses.*

frontiera *border; frontier.*
frugare *to search; to poke.*
frusta *whip.*
frustare *to whip.*
frutta *fruit.*
frutto, pl. **frutti** *fruit.*
frutteto *orchard.*
fucile, m. *gun.*
fuscia *fuchsia (color).*
fuga *flight, escape.*
    darsi alla fuga *to take flight.*
fuggire *to run away; to escape.*
fulmine, m. *thunderbolt.*
    un colpo di fulmine *love at first sight*
      (a thunderbolt).
    un fulmine a ciel sereno *a bolt out of*
      the blue.
fumare *to smoke.*
    Vietato fumare! *No smoking!*
fumetti *comics.*
fumo *smoke.*
fune, f. *rope, cable.*
funerale, m. *funeral.*
fungo *mushroom.*
    ai funghi *with mushrooms.*
funivia *cable car.*
funzionare *to work; to function.*
funzione, f. *function.*
fuoco *fire.*
    accendere il fuoco *to light the fire.*
    fuochi artificiali *fireworks.*
FUORCHÈ *except.*
    tutti fuorchè lui *all except him.*
FUORI *out, outside.*
    andar fuori *to go out.*
    .essere fuori di se *to be beside*
      oneself.
    fuoribordo *outboard.*
    fuori mano *out of the way.*
    fuori pericolo *out of danger.*
    fuori uso *out of use.*
furbo *sly, crafty.*
furia *fury, rage.*
    È andato su tutte le furie. *He fell*
      into a rage.
furibondo *raging, furious.*
furto *theft.*
    furto a mano armata *armed robbery.*
fusto *stem; barrel.*
futurismo *futurism.*
futuro, n. & adj. *future.*
    in futuro *in the future.*

gabbia *cage.*
gabbiano *seagull.*
gabinetto *cabinet; toilet.*
gagliardo *vigorous.*
gaiezza *gaiety.*
gaio *cheerful, lighthearted.*
gala *gala.*
galateo *good manners.*
galla (a) *afloat.*
gallerìa *gallery.*
gallina *hen.*
gallo *rooster.*
galoppare *to gallop.*
galoppo *gallop.*
gamba *leg.*
gamberetto *shrimp.*
gambero *crayfish.*
gambo *stalk, stem.*
gancio *hook.*
gara *competition.*
garanzìa *guarantee, security.*
garofano *carnation.*
gas, m. *gas.*
gatto *cat.*
gelare *to freeze.*
gelo *frost.*
gelosìa *jealousy.*
gemello *twin, cufflink.*
gemito *groan.*
gemma *gem.*
generale, n. m. & adj. *general.*
generalmente *generally; in general.*
generazione, f. *generation.*
GENERE, m. *gender, kind.*
    di genere maschile *of masculine*
      gender.
    di ogni genere *of all kinds.*
    generi alimentari *foodstuffs.*
genero *son-in-law.*
generoso *generous.*
genio *genius, taste.*
    Non mi va a genio. *It's not to my*
      liking.
genitori, m. pl. *parents.*
gennaio *January.*
gente, f. *people.*
genti, f. pl. *peoples.*
gentile *kind.*
gentilezza *kindness.*

genuino *genuine.*
geografia *geography.*
geografico *geographical.*
  carta geografica *map.*
geologia *geology.*
geometria *geometry.*
gerente, m. *manager; agent.*
gerenza *management.*
gergo *slang.*
germe, m. *germ, shoot.*
germogliare *to bud; to flower; to sprout.*
gessato *pinstriped.*
gesso *chalk; plaster.*
gesta, f. pl. *deeds.*
gesticolazione *gesticulation.*
gestione, f. *management.*
gestire *to manage.*
gesto *gesture.*
GETTARE *to throw; to fling.*
  gettare via *to throw away.*
  gettarsi *to fling oneself.*
gettone, m. *token.*
ghetto *ghetto.*
ghiaccio *ice.*
ghiaia *gravel.*
ghiandola *gland.*
ghiotto *gluttonous, greedy.*
ghirlanda *garland.*
GIÀ *already.*
  già fatto *already done.*
giacca *jacket.*
giacchè *as, since.*
giacere *to lie (to recline).*
giallo *yellow.*
  giallo d'uovo *egg yolk.*
giapponese *Japanese.*
giardiniere, m. *gardener.*
giardino *garden.*
gigante, m. *giant.*
giglio *lily.*
ginnasio *high school.*
ginnastica *gymnastics.*
ginocchio *knee.*
  in ginocchio *on one's knees.*
giocare *to play.*
  giocare a carte *to play cards.*
giocattolo *toy.*
gioco *game.*
giogo *yoke; summit.*
gioia *joy.*
gioiello *jewel.*
giornalaio *newspaper boy.*

GIORNALE, m. *newspaper.*
  giornale quotidiano *daily newspaper.*
giornallero, adj. *daily.*
giornalismo *journalism.*
giornalista, m. *journalist,*
  newspaperman.
giornalmente, adv. *daily.*
giornata *day.*
  giornata di festa *holiday.*
  giornata lavorativa *workday.*
GIORNO *day.*
  di giorno *in the daytime.*
  giorno per giorno *day by day.*
  il giorno seguente *the following day.*
  un giorno dopo l'altro *day after day.*
giostra *joust; merry-go-round.*
giovane, m. *a young man, a young*
  woman; adj. *young.*
giovanile *youthful.*
giovanòtto *young man.*
giovare *to be useful, to help.*
giovedì *Thursday.*
gioventù, f. *youth.*
giovinezza *youth.*
giramento *turning, revolving.*
  giramento di testa *dizzy spell.*
girare *to turn; to travel.*
  fare girare la testa *to turn one's head.*
  girare intorno a se *to rotate.*
giro *turn, spin.*
  fare il giro del mondo *to go round*
    the world.
  fare un giro intorno al parco *to take*
    a walk around the park.
  in giro *in circulation.*
  un giro d'ispezione *an inspection tour.*
gita *trip, outing.*
GIÙ *down.*
  andare giù per le scale *to go down*
    the stairs.
  camminare su e giù *to pace; to walk*
    up and down.
  su per giù *more or less.*
giubbotto *jacket.*
giudicare *to judge.*
giudice, m. *judge.*
giudizio *judgment, sense.*
  dente del giudizio *wisdom tooth.*
  mettere giudizio *to get wise; to*
    become wiser.
  secondo il giudizio di *according to*
    the judgement of.

giugno *June.*

giungere *to arrive.*
> giungere in fondo *to reach the end.*
> Siamo appena giunti. *We have just arrived.*

giuoco *game.*

giuramento *oath.*
> prestar giuramento *to take an oath.*
> venir meno ad un giuramento *to break an oath.*

giurare *to swear.*

giurisdizionale *jurisdictional.*

giurisprudenza *jurisprudence, law.*

giustamente *justly.*

giustificare *to justify.*

giustificazione, f. *justification.*

giustizia *justice.*
> la mano della giustizia *the arm of justice.*

giusto *right, just.*

GLI 1. m. pl. *the;* 2. *to him.*
> Gli sono grato. *I am grateful to him.*

globo *globe.*

gloria *glory.*

glorioso *glorious.*

gobbo *hunchback.*

goccia *drop.*

goccioiare *to drip.*

GODERE *to enjoy.*
> godere buona salute *to enjoy good health.*
> godersela *to have a good time.*

godimento *enjoyment.*

goffo *awkward.*

GOLA *throat.*
> aver la gola arsa *to be thirsty.*
> aver mal di gola *to have a sore throat.*
> Mi fa gola. *It tempts me.*

gomito *elbow.*

gomma *gum, rubber, tire.*
> una gomm a terra *a flat tire.*

gondola *gondola.*

gonfiare *to inflate.*
> gonfiarsi *to swell.*

gonfio *swollen, inflated.*
> avere il cuore gonfio *to be heavy-hearted.*

gonna *skirt.*
> gonna pantalone *divided skirt.*

governante, f. *governess;* m. *ruler.*

governare *to govern.*

governo *government.*

gradevole *agreeable, pleasant.*
> un gusto gradevole *a pleasant taste.*

gradino *step.*

GRADIRE *to accept; to find agreeable.*
> Gradisca i miei più cordiali saluti.
> *Accept my most cordial greeting.*

grado *degree, extent.*
> cinque gradi sotto zero *five degrees below zero.*
> essere in grado di *to be in a position to.*

graffiare *to scratch.*

granchio *crab.*

GRANDE *great, big.*
> a grandi passi *with long steps; swiftly.*
> a gran velocità *at great speed.*
> farsi grande *to get big; to grow tall.*
> in grande *on a large scale.*

grandezza *greatness.*

grandine, f. *hail.*

grandioso *grand.*

grano *grain, corn.*
> con un grano di sale *with a grain of salt.*
> un grano di sabbia *a grain of sand.*
> un grano d'uva *a grape.*

granturco *corn.*

grappolo *bunch (of grapes).*

grasso, n. *fat, grease;* adj. *greasy.*

grato *grateful.*

grattare *to scratch.*

gratuito *free.*

grave *grave, serious, heavy.*

gravemente *gravely, seriously.*
> Lui è gravemente ammalato. *He is seriously ill.*

grazia *grace, favor.*
> colpo di grazia *final stroke; coup de grace.*
> fare una grazia *to grant a favor.*
> grazie a *thanks to.*

GRAZIE *Thank you.*

grazioso *graceful, pretty.*

gridare *to cry out; to shout.*
> Non c'è bisogno di gridare. *There's no need to shout.*

grido *cry, shout.*

grigio *gray.*

grillo *cricket.*

grosso *big, bulky.*

gruccia *crutch.*

gruppo group.
GUADAGNARE to earn; to gain.
　guadagnare terreno to gain ground.
　guadagnarsi da vivere to earn a
　　livelihood.
　guadagnarsi la stima di qualcuno to
　　earn someone's respect.
　guadagnar tempo to gain time.
guadagno profit, gain.
　guadagno per dividendo earnings
　　per shore.
guaio misfortune, difficulty.
guancia cheek.
　voltare l'altra guancia to turn the
　　other cheek.
guanciale, m. pillow.
guanto glove.
　calzare come un guanto to fit like a
　　glove.
　un paio di guanti a pair of gloves.
GUARDARE to look.
　guardarsi dal to guard against; to
　　refrain from.
　guardarsi negli occhi to stare into
　　each other's eyes.
　senza guardare nessuno in faccia
　　without looking.
　Me ne guarderei bene! I wouldn't
　　dare!
guardaroba, m. wardrobe, cloakroom.
guardia guard.
guardiano watchman, keeper, guard.
　guardiano notturno night watchman.
guarire to recuperate; to get well; to
　cure.
guarnire to trim; to decorate.
guarnito trimmed.
guarnizione, f. trimming.
guastare to spoil.
guerra war.
guida guide, guidebook.
GUIDARE to guide; to drive.
　guidare un' automobile to drive a car.
　Si lasci guidare da me. Allow me to
　　guide you.
guscio shell (egg).
GUSTO taste, relish, liking.
　di buon gusto in good taste.
　gusto amaro bitter taste.
　provare gusto a to take pleasure in.
　una persona di buon gusto a person
　　of good taste.

Non è di suo gusto. It's not to his
　liking.
avere un gusto fine to have good
　taste.

H

haitiano Haitian.
handicappare handicap.
herpes herpes.
hotel, m. hotel.

I

i, m. pl. the.
　i ragazzi the boys.
icona icon.
idea idea.
　cambiare idea to change one's mind.
ideale, n. m. & adj. ideal.
idealismo idealism.
idealista, m. & f. idealist; adj.
　idealistic.
identico identical.
identificare to identify.
idiota, m. & f. idiot; adj. idiotic.
idoneo fit, suitable.
IERI, m. yesterday.
　ieri l'altro the day before yesterday.
　ieri mattina yesterday morning.
　ieri sera last night.
igiene, f. hygiene.
ignobile ignoble.
ignorante ignorant.
ignoranza ignorance.
ignorare to ignore.
ignoto unknown.
　di autore ignoto by an unknown
　　author.
　Milite Ignoto Unknown Soldier.
il, m. sing. the.
illecito illicit, forbidden.
illegale illegal.
illegibile illegible.
illegittimità illegitimacy.
illegittimo illegitimate, unlawful.
illeso uninjured, safe.
illimitato unlimited, endless.

illudere *to deceive.*
> si illuse che il lavoro sarebbe stato facile *he deluded himself into thinking the job would be an easy one.*

illuminare *to light up.*

illusione, f. *illusion.*

illustrare *to illustrate.*

illustrazione, f. *illustration.*

illustre *eminent, renowned.*

imballare *to pack; to wrap.*

imbarazzante *embarrassing.*
> una situazione imbarazzante *an embarrassing situation.*
> imbarazzare *to embarass.*

imbarazzo *embarrassment, difficulty.*
> mettere in imbarazzo *to embarrass.*

imbarcare *to load.*
> imbarcarsi *to embark.*

imbarcare acqua *to ship.*

imbattersi *to meet with.*

imbottire *to stuff; to pad.*

imbottito *quilted.*

imbrattato *dirty.*

imbrogliare *to cheat.*

imbroglio *complication, tangle, trick.*

imbronciato *sullen.*

imbucare *to mail a letter.*

imitare *to imitate.*

imitazione, f. *imitation.*

IMMAGINARE *to imagine.*
> Non riesco ad immaginare. *I can't imagine.*
> Si immagini che . . . ! *Just imagine if . . . !*

immaginario *imaginary.*

immaginazione, f. *imagination.*

immagine, f. *image.*

immedesimarsi *to identify oneself with.*

immediatamente *immediately.*

immediato *immediate.*

immensità *immensity; enormity.*

immenso *huge.*

immettere *to input.*

immigrante, m. & f. *immigrant.*

immigrare *to immigrate.*

imminente *imminent.*

immobilità *immobility.*

immortale *immortal.*

immortalità *immortality.*

impacciare *to impede; to embarrass.*

impacciato *constrained, uneasy.*

impadronirsi *to seize; to take possession of.*

impallidire *to turn pale.*

imparare *to learn.*
> imparare a memoria *to learn by heart.*
> imparare una lingua *to learn a language.*

imparentato *related.*

imparziale *impartial.*

impassibile *impassive.*

impasto *mixture.*

IMPAZIENTE *impatient.*

impazienza *impatience.*
> attendere con impazienza *to look forward to; to await anxiously.*

impedimento *prevention.*

impedire *to hinder; to obstruct.*

impellente *urgent; pressing.*

impazzire *to go crazy.*

IMPEGNARE *to engage; to pawn.*
> impegnare un anello *to pawn a ring.*
> impegnarsi a fare qualcosa *to pledge oneself to do something.*
> Sono già impegnato per quella sera. *I am already engaged for that evening.*

impegno *engagement, obligation.*

impensato *unexpected.*

imperativo *imperative.*

imperatore *emperor.*

imperfetto *imperfect.*

IMPERMEABILE, m. *raincoat;* adj. *waterproof.*

impero *empire.*

impersonale *impersonal.*

impertinente *insolent, impertinent.*

impertinenza *impertinence.*

impeto *vehemence.*

impetuosamente *impetuously.*

impetuoso *impetuous.*
> carattere impetuoso *a violent character.*

impianto *installation, establishment.*

impiccare *to hang.*

impiegare *to employ.*

impiegato, n. *employee;* as adj. *employed.*

impiego *employment.*
> cercare impiego *to look for a job.*

implicare *to involve.*

impolverato *dusty.*

imporre *to impose.*

importante *important.*
importanza *importance.*
  dare importanza a *to attach*
    importance to.
  Non ti dare tanta importanza. *Don't*
    give yourself so many airs.
importare *to matter; to be of*
  consequence.
impossibile *impossible.*
imposta *duty, tax.*
impreparato *unprepared.*
IMPRESA *enterprise, undertaking.*
impressionare *to impress.*
  Non ti impressionare. *Don't be*
    alarmed.
impressione, f. *impression.*
  fare una brutta impressione *to*
    impress unfavorably.
  Non mi ha fatto alcuna
    impressione. *It made no*
    impression on me.
imprevisto (impreveduto), n. & adj.
  unforeseen.
  se tutto procede senza imprevisti *if*
    things proceed without
    complications.
imprigionare *to imprison.*
imprimere *to impress; to stamp.*
improbabile *improbable, unlikely.*
impronta *impression, print.*
improvvisamente *suddenly.*
imprudente *imprudent.*
imprudenza *imprudence.*
impulso *impulse.*
  seguire il proprio impulso *to follow*
    one's instinct.
impurità *impurity.*
imputare *to impute; to accuse.*
IN *in, into.*
  in casa *at home; in the home.*
  In che modo? *In what way?*
inabile *unable.*
inadatto *unsuitable.*
inalterato *unchanged.*
inamidare *to starch.*
inappuntabile *irreproachable.*
inaspettatamente *unexpectedly.*
inaspettato *unexpected.*
inaudito *unheard of.*
inaugurare *to inaugurate; to open.*
inavvertenza *inadvertence.*
incantevole *charming.*

incapacità *inability, incapacity.*
incarcerare *imprison; to jail.*
incarico *task; job.*
incendiare *to set fire to.*
INCENDIO *fire.*
  segnale d'incendio *fire alarm.*
incertezza *uncertainty.*
incerto *uncertain.*
inchiesta *inquiry.*
inchiostro *ink.*
incidente, m. *incident, accident.*
incitare *to incite.*
INCLUDERE *to include.*
incluso *included.*
  tutto incluso *everything included.*
incoerente *inconsistent.*
incolto *uneducated, uncultivated.*
INCOMINCIARE *to begin; to start.*
  incominciando da questo momento
    starting from this moment; from
    this moment on.
incomparabile *incomparable.*
incompatibile *incompatible.*
incompatibilità *incompatibility.*
incompetente, n. m. & adj.
  incompetent.
incompleto *incomplete.*
inconscio *unconscious.*
inconsolabilmente *unconsolably.*
incontentabile *unsatisfiable, exacting.*
INCONTRARE *to meet.*
INCONTRO n. *meeting, encounter,*
  match; **incontro a**, adv. *toward,*
  against.
  un incontro sportivo *a sports match.*
  incontro al vertice *summit.*
  Andiamogli incontro. *Let's go to*
    meet him.
  Mi venne incontro. *He came*
    toward me.
inconveniente, m. *inconvenience;* adj.
  inconvenient.
inconvenienza *inconvenience.*
INCORAGGIARE *to encourage.*
  incoraggiarsi *to take courage.*
incorniciare *to frame.*
incorrere *to incur.*
incosciente *unconscious.*
INCREDIBILE *incredible.*
incrociare *to cross; to cruise; to meet.*
incrocio *crossroads.*
incubo *nightmare.*

incuriosire *to make curious; to entice.*

indebitato *indebted.*

indebolire *to weaken.*
> La malattia lo ha indebolito molto. *His illness has made him very weak.*

indecisione, f. *indecision.*

indeciso *undecided.*

indefinito *undefined.*

indegno *unworthy.*

INDICARE *to indicate; to point out.*
> indicare la strada *to show the way.*

indicativo *indicative.*

INDICE, m. *index finger; index.*

INDIETRO *back.*
> tomare indietro *to go back.*
> volgere lo sguardo indietro *to look back; to look over one's shoulder.*
> Quest' orologio va indietro. *This clock is slow.*

indifferente *indifferent.*
> Mi è del tutto indifferente. *I am completely indifferent to it.*

indifferenza *indifference, unconcern.*

indigeno *domestic, indigenous;* (as noun) *native.*

indigestione *indigestion.*

indignato *indignant.*

indignazione, f. *indignation.*

indimenticabile *unforgettable.*

indipendente *independent.*

indipendentemente *independently.*

indipendenza *independence.*

indirettamente *indirectly.*

indiretto *indirect.*

INDIRIZZARE *to address; to direct.*
> Le sue parole erano indirizzate a tutti. *His words were directed to everyone.*
> Questa lettera non è indirizzata a me. *This letter is not addressed to me.*

indirizzo *address.*

indiscreto *indiscreet.*

indiscrezione, f. *indiscretion.*

individuo *individual* (also adj.).

indivisibile *indivisible.*

indizio *symptom.*

indole *nature; character.*

indolente *indolent.*

indolore *painless.*

indossare *to put on; to wear.*

INDOVINARE *to guess; to imagine.*
> Indovina un po'. *Just guess.*
> Non riesco ad indovinare. *I can't imagine.*

indovinello *enigma, riddle.*

indubbiamente *undoubtedly.*

indugio *delay.*
> Bisogna farlo senza indugio. *It must be done without delay.*

indulgenza *indulgence.*

INDUSTRIA *industry.*

industriale, m. *industrialist;* adj. *industrial.*

industrioso *industrious.*

inesauribile *inexhaustible.*

inesplicabile *inexplicable.*

inevitabile *unavoidable.*

inezia *trifle.*

infallibile *infallible, unfailing.*

infame *infamous.*

infanzia *infancy.*

INFATTI *in fact; in reality.*

infedele *unfaithful.*

infedeltà *infidelity.*

infelice *unhappy.*

infelicità *unhappiness.*

inferiore *inferior.*

inferiorità *inferiority.*
> complesso d'inferiorità *inferiority complex.*

infermiera *nurse.*

infilare *to thread.*

INFINE *at last; after all.*

infinito n. *infinity;* adj. *infinite.*

inflazione *inflation.*

infliggere *to inflict.*

influenzare *to influence.*

influire *to exert influence over.*
> Ha influito sulla mia decisione. *It influenced my decision.*

infondato *unfounded, groundless.*
> una paura infondata *a groundless fear.*

informare *to inform.*
> Mi ha informato dell'accaduto. *He told me what happened.*

informazione, f. *information.*

infrangere *to shatter; to break.*

infuocare *to inflame.*

INFUORI *out; outward, outside of.*
> all'infuori di *except for.*

ingannare *to deceive.*

Inganno il tempo leggendo. *I kill time reading.*

Mi sono ingannato. *I was mistaken.*

inganno *deceit.*

Mi ha tratto in inganno. *He deceived me.*

ingegnere, m. *engineer.*

ingegno *talent, intelligence.*

una persona d'ingegno *a talented person.*

ingenerare *to generate.*

ingente *great; enormous.*

inghiottire *to swallow.*

inginocchiarsi *to kneel.*

INGIÙ *downward, down.*

guardare ingiù *to look down.*

ingiustizia *injustice.*

ingiusto *unjust, unfair.*

inglese *English.*

ingranaggio *gear.*

ingrassare *to become fat; to grease.*

ingratitudine, f. *ingratitude.*

INGRESSO *entrance, admittance.*

porta d'ingresso *entrance door.*

Ingresso Libero. *Free Admittance.*

Vietato l'Ingresso! *No Admittance!*

INGROSSO *wholesale.*

vendere all'ingrosso *to sell wholesale.*

INIZIALE, n. m. & adj. *initial.*

spesa iniziale *initial outlay.*

iniziare *to start; to initiate.*

iniziativa *initiative.*

inizio *beginning.*

dare inizio allo spettacolo *to begin the performance.*

sin dall'inizio *from the beginning.*

innalzare *to raise.*

innamorare *to charm.*

fare innamorare *to cause to fall in love.*

innamorarsi *to fall in love.*

INNANZI *before.*

innanzi tutto *first of all.*

inno *hymn.*

innocente *innocent.*

innocenza *innocence.*

inoltre *besides.*

inosservato *unobserved.*

inquieto *agitated, restless.*

inquietudine, f. *agitation, restlessness.*

insalata *salad.*

insalata condita *salad with dressing.*

insanguinato *bloody.*

insaponare *to soap; to lather.*

INSEGNA *signboard, flag.*

insegna luminosa *neon sign.*

insegnante m. & f. *teacher.*

insegnare *to teach.*

inseguire *to chase.*

insensato *senseless.*

insensibile *insensible.*

inseparabile *inseparable.*

insidia *snare, trap.*

INSIEME *together.*

mettere tutto insieme *to gather; to put everything together.*

nell'insieme *on the whole.*

uscire insieme *to go out together.*

insignificante *insignificant.*

INSINUARE *to insinuate.*

insinuarsi *to insinuate oneself.*

insistenza *insistence.*

INSISTERE *to insist.*

insoddisfatto *dissatisfied.*

insofferente *impatient.*

insolito *unusual.*

insolubile *insoluble.*

INSOMMA *in conclusion; in short; well.*

Ma insomma, che cosa facciamo ora? *Well, what are we going to do now?*

insonne *sleepless.*

insonnia *insomnia.*

insopportabile *unbearable.*

insormontabile *unsurmountable.*

inseperato *unhoped for.*

una gioia insperata *an unhoped-for joy.*

installare *to install.*

Hai installato i nuovi programmi? *Did you install the new programs?*

Si è installato in casa mia. *He installed himself in my home.*

instancabile *untiring.*

INSÙ *up, upward.*

guardare insù *to look upward.*

all'insù *upward.*

andare su e giú *to go up and down.*

insudiciarsi *to become dirty.*

insufficiente *insufficient.*

insufficienza *insufficiency.*

insulare *insular.*

insulso *insipid.*

insuperabile *insuperable.*

intagliare *to carve.*

   legno intagliato *carved wood.*

INTANTO *in the meanwhile; meanwhile.*

intatto *intact.*

integrale *integral.*

intelletto *intellect.*

   di scarso intelletto *of poor intellect.*

   una persona di grande intelletto *a person of great intellect.*

intellettuale, n. m. & f., adj. *intellectual.*

intelligente *intelligent.*

intelligenza *intelligence.*

INTENDERE *to intend; to hear; to understand.*

   Cerchiamo di intenderci. *Let's try to understand one another.*

   Che cosa intende dire? *What do you mean?*

   Non ho inteso bene. *I did not hear well.*

   Non intendo partire. *I do not intend to leave.*

intenerirsi *to become tender; to be moved to tears.*

intenso *intense.*

intenzione, f. *intention.*

   senza intenzione *unintentionally.*

   Non ne ho la minima intenzione. *I don't have the slightest intention.*

interamente *entirely.*

   Non sono interamente convinto. *I am not entirely convinced.*

interdire *to prohibit.*

interessante *interesting.*

interessare *to interest.*

interesse *interest.*

   tassa d'interesse *interest rate.*

   Non è nel mio interesse farlo. *It is not to my advantage to do it.*

interfaccia *interface.*

interiezione *interjection; exclamation.*

interiore, m. *interior; internal.*

intermedio *intermediate.*

intermezzo *interval; interlude.*

interminabile *endless; interminable.*

internazionale *international.*

interno *interior, inside, internal.*

INTERO *entire, whole.*

   il mondo intero *the whole world.*

   per intero *wholly, entirely.*

interporre *to interpose.*

interpretare *to interpret.*

   interpretare male *to misinterpret; to misunderstand.*

interpretazione, f. *interpretation.*

interprete, m. *interpreter.*

interrogare *to question; to ask.*

interrompere *to interrupt.*

interruzione, f. *interruption.*

intervallo *interval.*

   l'intervallo fra un'atto e l'altro *between acts; intermission.*

intervista *interview.*

   fare un intervista a *to interview someone.*

intervistare *to interview.*

intesa *agreement, understanding.*

   secondo la nostra intesa *according to our agreement.*

INTIERO *whole, entire.*

intimazione, f. *order, injunction.*

intimidire *to intimidate; to frighten.*

intimità *intimacy.*

   nell'intimità della propria famiglia *in the intimacy of one's own family.*

intimo *intimate.*

   un'amico intimo *an intimate friend.*

intitolare *to entitle.*

intollerabile *intolerable.*

intollerante *intolerant.*

intolleranza *intolerance.*

intonazione, f. *intonation.*

intorno *around.*

intossicare *to poison.*

intossicazione *poisoning.*

intraprendere *to undertake.*

   intraprendere un viaggio *to embark on a voyage.*

intrattenere *to entertain; to maintain.*

intrigo *plot.*

INTRODURRE *to get in; to put in; to show someone in.*

   introdurre la chiave nella serratura *to put the key in the lock.*

   Si è introdotto in casa mia con una scusa. *He got into my home with an excuse.*

intromettere *to interpose; to interfere with.*

introverso *introverted.*
intùito *intuition.*
inumano *inhuman.*
inumidire *to dampen.*
inutile *useless, unnecessary.*
inutilizzabile *unusable; useless.*
invadente *pushing.*
invadere *to invade.*
invaghirsi *to fall in love, to take a fancy to.*
invariabile *invariable.*
invariabilmente *invariably.*
invasione, f. *invasion.*
invecchiare *to grow old; to age.*
invece *instead.*
inventare *to invent.*
     inventare una scusa *to invent an excuse.*
inventore, m. *inventor.*
invenzione, f. *invention.*
invernale *winter.*
inverno *winter.*
inverosimile *unlikely; improbable.*
inverso *inverted, inverse.*
invertire *to invert.*
investigare *to investigate; to inquire.*
investimento *investment.*
investire *to invest; to collide with; to run down.*
     investire di una carica *to appoint.*
     Fui investito da un'automobile. *I was run down by a car.*
inviare *to send.*
invidiare *to envy.*
INVÌO *shipment, mailing.*
     invìo di merci *shipment of merchandise.*
     l'invìo di posta *the forwarding of mail.*
invisibile *invisible.*
invitare *to invite; to ask.*
invitato *guest.*
INVITO *invitation.*
invocare *to invoke.*
     invocare aiuto *to seek help.*
involontario *involuntary.*
involto *parcel, package.*
involucro *cover; wrapping.*
inzuppare *to soak.*
IO *I.*
iodio *iodine.*
     tintura di iodio *tincture of iodine.*

ipertensione *high blood pressure; hypertension.*
ipocrisia *hypocrisy.*
ipoteca *mortgage.*
IRA *anger, rage.*
     con grande ira *with great anger.*
     Non posso sfogare la mia ira con nessuno. *I can't give vent to my anger with anyone.*
ironia *irony.*
     l'ironia della sorte *the irony of fate.*
irragionevole *unreasonable.*
irreale *unreal.*
irregolare *irregular.*
irreparabile *irreparable.*
irresistibile *irresistible.*
irrestringibile *unshrinkable.*
irrigidire *to stiffen.*
irritare *to irritate.*
     irritarsi per nulla *to get angry over nothing.*
irritazione, f. *irritation.*
ISOLA *island.*
isolare *to isolate.*
isolato *block of houses.*
ispettore, m. *inspector.*
ispezionare *to inspect.*
ispezione, f. *inspection.*
ispirare *to inspire.*
ispirazione, f. *inspiration.*
ISTANTANEA *snapshot.*
istantaneo *instantaneous.*
istante, m. *instant.*
istigare *to instigate.*
istintivo *instinctive.*
istinto *instinct.*
     per istinto *instinctively.*
istituto *institute, institution.*
istituzione, f. *institution, establishment.*
istruire *to instruct; to teach.*
istrulto *educated, learned.*
istruttore, m. *instructor.*
istruzione, f. *education.*
italiano *Italian.*

J

jack *jack; knave.*
jugoslavo *Yugoslavian.*

K

kaki *khaki.*
kilogrammo *kilogram.*
kilowatt *kilowatt.*

L

LA 1. f. sing. *the* (L' *if followed by vowel*); 2. pers. pron. obj. (f. sing. and polite form sing.) *her, it, you.*
   lo la vedo spesso. *I see her often.*
   Vediamo la ragazza sta sera? Sì, la vediamo. *Do we see the girl tonight? Yes, we see her.*
LÀ adv. *there*
LABBRO (labbra, f. pl) *lip.*
   labbro inferiore *lower lip.*
   labbro superiore *upper lip.*
   pendo dalle sue labbra. *I hang on her words.*
labirinto *labyrinth; maze.*
laboratorio *laboratory.*
laborioso *laborous.*
laccio *string, knot.*
lacerare *to tear; to rend.*
lacrima *tear.*
   scoppiare in lacrime *to burst out into tears.*
ladro *thief.*
LAGGIÙ *down there; there below.*
LAGO *lake.*
laguna *lagoon.*
laico n. & adj. *layman; secular.*
lama (lametta) *blade.*
   lama di rasoio *razor blade.*
lamentare *to lament; to regret.*
LAMPADA *lamp.*
lampadario *chandelier.*
lampadina *small lamp.*
   lampadina elettrica *electric bulb.*
   lampadina tascabile *flashlight.*
lampeggiare *to lament; to regret.*
lampo *lightning flash.*
   in un lampo *in a flash.*
lampone *raspberry.*
LANA *wool.*
   vestito di lana *woolen suit.*
lanciare *to hurl.*

languire *to languish.*
languore, m. *languor.*
lanterna *lantern.*
   lanterna magica *magic lantern.*
larghezza *width, breadth.*
   di questa larghezza *this wide.*
LARGO *wide, broad, large.*
   cercare in lungo ed in largo *to seek far and wide.*
   su larga scala *on a big scale.*
   Fate largo! *Make room!*
LASCIARE *to leave; to quit; to let.*
   Ho lasciato detto che sarei tornato alle tre. *I left a message saying I would be back at three.*
   Lasciami stare! *Leave me alone!*
   Mi ha lasciato una fortuna. *He left me a fortune.*
   Ti lascio per sempre. *I'm leaving you forever.*
LASSÙ *up; up there.*
   lassù in cima alla montagna *up there at the top of the mountain.*
   Guarda lassù. *Look up there.*
latino *Latin.*
latitante *fugitive.*
lato *side.*
latta *tin.*
lattaio *milkman.*
LATTE, m. *milk.*
latterìa *diary.*
lattuga *lettuce.*
laurea *degree.*
lavaggio *washing, cleansing.*
lavagna *slate, blackboard.*
lavapiatti *dishwasher.*
LAVARE *to wash.*
   lavarsi *to wash oneself.*
lavastoviglie *dishwasher.*
lavatrice *washing machine.*
lavorare *to work.*
lavoratore, m. lavoratrice, f. *worker.*
lavorazione *manufacture; cultivation.*
   lavorazione a maglia *knitting.*
lavoro *work, job.*
   lavori domestici *housework.*
   lavori forzati *hard labor.*
   lavoro drammatico *play.*
   lavoro eccessivo *overwork.*
LE 1. f. pl. *the;* 2. *them, to you* (sing, polite); *to her.*
leale *loyal.*

lealtà *loyalty.*
leccare *to lick.*
lecito *lawful.*
lega *league.*
legale *legal, lawful.*
legare *to tie; to bind.*
   essere legato da un affetto profondo
    to have a deep affection.
legatura *binding.*
LEGGE, f. *law.*
   approvare una legge *to pass a law.*
   fuori legge *outlaw.*
   invocare una legge *to invoke a law.*
leggenda *legend.*
   La leggenda vuole . . . *The legend
    is . . .*
leggere *to read.*
LEGGERO *light.*
   un peso leggero *a lightweight
    (boxer).*
   Lui prende le cose alla leggera. *He
    takes matters lightly.*
legislazione, f. *legislation.*
legittimità *legitimacy.*
legittimo *legitimate.*
   legittima difesa *self-defense.*
legno *wood.*
   fatto di legno *made of wood.*
legume, m. *vegetable.*
LEI 1. sing. pol. *you;* 2. *her; to her.*
   Noi diamo il libro a lei. *We give her
    the book.*
lentamente *slowly.*
lentezza *slowness; tardiness.*
LENTO *slow.*
lenzuolo (lenzuola, f. pl.) *sheet.*
   cambiare le lenzuola ai letti *to
    change the bed sheets.*
leone, m. *lion.*
   la parte del leone *the lion's share.*
lepre, m. & f. *hare.*
lesbica *lesbian.*
lesso *boiled meat.*
lesto *nimble, quick.*
LETTERA *letter.*
   alla lettera *literally.*
   lettera di presentazione *letter of
    introduction.*
   lettera maiuscola *capital letter.*
   lettera minuscola *small letter.*
   lettera raccomandata *registered letter.*
letterario *literary.*

letteratura *literature.*
LETTO *bed.*
   letto a due piazze *double bed.*
   stanza da letto *bedroom.*
lettura *reading.*
LEVARE *to remove; to take off.*
   farsi levare un dente *to have a tooth
    pulled.*
   levare l'incomodo *to take one's leave.*
   levarsi al mattino *to rise in the
    morning.*
lezione, f. *lesson.*
   dare lezioni di pianoforte *to give
    piano lessons.*
   dare una lezione a *to give a lesson to.*
LÌ adv. *there.*
   Lì per lì non ho saputo cosa
    rispondere. *At that very moment I
    didn't know what to answer.*
   Metti tutto lì. *Put everything there.*
   Stavo lì lì per farlo. *I was just about
    to do it.*
   È lì sotto. *It is under there.*
   Fermo lì! *Stop!*
LI *them.*
   Li vedo benissimo. *I see them clearly.*
libbra *pound.*
liberale *liberal.*
liberare *to free; to liberate.*
   liberarsi *to free oneself.*
   Mi sono liberata da una seccatura. *I
    got rid of a nuisance.*
libero *free.*
libertà *freedom, liberty.*
libraio *bookseller.*
librerìa *bookshop.*
libretto *booklet.*
   libretto degli assegni *checkbook.*
libro *book.*
licenza *license.*
   essere in licenza *to be on leave.*
licenziare *to dismiss; to fire (from a job).*
   Mi sono licenziato. *I resigned. I quit
    my job.*
liceo *secondary school.*
lido *seashore, beach.*
lieto *happy.*
   Molto lieto di conoscervi. *Pleased to
    meet you.*
lieve *light.*
lievito *yeast.*
lima *file.*

limitare *to limit.*
> Se è limitato a un sol bicchiere di vino. *He limited himself to one glass of wine.*

limite, m. *limit, bound.*
> giungere al limite delle proprie forze *to reach the end of one's rope.*
> È arrivato al limite della sua pazienza. *He has reached the end of his patience.*

limonata *lemonade.*

limone, m. *lemon.*
> succo di limone *lemon juice.*

limpido *clear, transparent; pure.*

linea *line.*
> in linea diretta *in direct line.*
> mettersi in linea *to get in line.*
> Linea Aerea *Airline.*
> Linea Ferroviaria *Railway Line.*

LINGUA *tongue; language; idiom.*
> essere sulla lingua di tutti *to be a topic for gossip.*
> lingua madre *native tongue.*
> lingue straniere *foreign languages.*
> parlare bene una lingua *to speak a language well.*
> Il suo nome è sulla punta della mia lingua. *His name is on the tip of my tongue.*

linguaggio *language, speech.*

lino *linen.*
> una tovaglia di lino *a linen towel.*

liquidità *cash flow.*

liquido *liquid.*
> aver denaro liquido *to have ready cash.*

liquore, m. *liquor.*

lirica *lyric.*

lista *menu, list.*

litigare *to quarrel; to argue.*

litorale *coast.*

livello *level.*

LO 1. m. sing. *the;* 2. m. sing. direct obj. pron. *him, it.*
> Io lo chiamo. *I call him.*
> Io lo leggo. *I read it.*

locale *local.*

locazione *lease.*

locomotiva *locomotive.*

lodare *to praise.*
> Sia lodato il cielo! *Heaven be praised!*

logica *logic.*

logico *logical.*
> la soluzione logica *the logical solution.*

lontano *distant, far.*

lordo *dirty, gross.*
> prodotto interno lordo (PIL) *gross domestic product.*

LORO 1. pl. polite pers. pron. subj. *they, you;* 2. pers. pron. obj. *them; to them; you; to you;* 3. pl. polite possessive (undeclinable) *their, theirs; your, yours.*
> Also, *il loro; la loro; i loro; le loro.*
> Vi parlo loro francamente. *I am speaking to you frankly.*
> la loro penna *their pen.*

lotta *struggle; wrestling, fight.*

LOTTARE *to struggle; to fight.*
> lottare contro le avversità *to struggle against adversity.*

LUCE, f. *light.*
> accendere la luce *to turn on the light.*
> alla luce del sole *in the sunlight.*
> luce elettrica *electric light.*
> spegnere la luce *to turn off the light.*
> venire alla luce *to come to light.*

lucidare *to shine; to sparkle.*

luglio *July.*

lui *he.*

lume, m. *light, lamp.*

luminoso *luminous.*

luna *moon.*

lunedì *Monday.*

lunghezza *length.*

LUNGO *long, along.*
> a lungo *for a long time.*
> a lungo andare *in the long run.*
> girare in lungo ed in largo *to wander far and wide.*
> lungo la riva del fiume *along the riverbank.*
> lungo un piede *one foot long.*
> lungo un metro *one meter long.*
> La cosa va per le lunghe. *This matter is taking a long time.*

luogo *place.*

lupo *wolf.*

lusinga *enticement, flattery.*

lusso *luxury.*
> di lusso *luxurious, deluxe.*

Non mi posso permettere il lusso di comprarlo. *I can't permit myself the luxury of buying it.*

lussuoso *luxurious.*

lustrare *to polish.*

farsi lustrare le scarpe *get one's shoes shined.*

lutto *mourning.*

M

MA *but, still, however.*

macchia *spot, stain.*

macchiare *to spot; to stain.*

MACCHINA *machine, engine.*

macchina da cucire *sewing machine.*

macchina da scrivere *typewriter.*

macchina fotografica *camera.*

macedonia *fruit salad.*

macellaio *butcher.*

macellerìa *butchershop.*

macello *slaughter.*

macinare *to grind.*

MADRE, f. *mother.*

madrelingua *native language.*

madreperla *mother of pearl, nacre.*

maestà *majesty.*

maestro *teacher.*

magazzino *warehouse.*

maggio *May.*

maggioranza *majority.*

MAGGIORE *greater, larger, major.*

di maggior importanza *of greater importance.*

fratello maggiore *older brother.*

la maggior parte *the major part.*

maggiore d'età *majority (age).*

stato maggiore *general staff.*

causa di forza maggiore *a case of absolute necessity.*

maggiorenne, m. & f. *of full age.*

magistrato *magistrate, judge.*

maglia *stitch, underwear, sweater.*

lavoro a maglia *knitting.*

magnetòfono *tape recorder.*

magnificenza *magnificence.*

magnifico *magnificent.*

MAGRO *thin, lean.*

MAI *never.*

caso mai *in case.*

mai e poi mai *never ever.*

mai più *never again.*

quando mai *not at all.*

Non si sa mai. *You never can tell.*

Come mai? *How come?*

Meglio tardi che mai. *Better late than never.*

maiale, m. *pig, pork.*

maiuscola *capital.*

lettera maiuscola *capital letter.*

malamente *badly.*

MALATO *ill.*

MALATTÌA *illness.*

essere colto da malattia improvvisa *to become suddenly ill.*

MALE m. *evil, harm;* adv. *badly.*

andare male *to spoil, to be wrong.*

di male in peggio *from bad to worse.*

far male *to harm; to hurt.*

il minore di due mali *the lesser of two evils.*

mal d'orecchio *earache.*

mal d'amore *lovesickness.*

mal di mare *seasickness.*

non c'è male *not too bad.*

Che male fa? *What harm does it do? What harm is there?*

capire male *to misunderstand.*

meno male *so much the better.*

parlare male di *to speak ill of.*

stare male di salute *to be in poor health.*

comportarsi male *to behave badly.*

rimanere male *to feel hurt.*

trattare male *to mistreat.*

È rimasto male. *He was disappointed.*

Gli affari vanno male. *Business is poor.*

maledetto *cursed, damned.*

maleducato *ill-bred.*

malessere *malaise; uneasiness.*

MALGRADO *in spite of; notwithstanding.*

mio malgrado *against my will.*

Malgrado la pioggia siamo usciti. *We went out, the rain notwithstanding.*

Si è alzato malgrado il divieto del dottore. *He got up in spite of the doctor's wishes.*

malìa *charm, enchantment.*

malinconia *melancholy.*
malincuore *unwillingly, reluctantly.*
malinteso *misunderstanding.*
malizia *malice, cunning.*
malizioso *malicious, cunning.*
malsano *unhealthy.*
MALTEMPO *bad weather.*
maltrattare *to ill-treat.*
malumore *ill humor.*
malvagio *wicked.*
mamma *mother.*
MANCANZA *want, lack.*
    in mancanza di meglio *for lack of*
       something better.
    sentire la mancanza *to miss.*
    una grave mancanza *a serious fault.*
MANCARE *to want; to lack; to be*
    absent.
    Lui manca da casa. *He is away from*
       home.
    Essi hanno mancato *They did wrong.*
    Manca del denaro dalla cassaforte.
       Some money is missing from the
       safe.
    Mancano cinque minuti alle nove. *It*
       is five minutes to nine.
    Mancano di tutto. *They lack*
       everything.
    È mancato all'improvviso. *He passed*
       away suddenly.
mancia *tip.*
mancino *left-handed.*
mandare *to send.*
mandorla *almond.*
mandria *herd.*
maneggiare *to handle; to manage.*
MANGIARE *to eat.*
    mangiare con gusto *to eat heartily.*
    mangiarsi il cuore *to eat one's heart*
       out.
    mangiare fuori *to dine out.*
mania *mania; fad; hobby.*
maniaco *maniacal; mad; insane.*
MANICA *sleeve.*
    in maniche di camicia *in shirt*
       sleeves.
    essere di manica larga *to be generous.*
manico *handle.*
    aver il coltello dalla parte del manico
       to hold the knife by the handle.
maniera *manner, way.*
    in questa maniera *this way.*

    in una maniera o nell'altra *in one*
       way or the other.
manifattura *manufacture.*
manifatturiero *manufacturer.*
manifestare *to manifest.*
maniglia *handle.*
    maniglia della porta *door handle.*
MANO, f. *hand.*
    a portata di mano *handy.*
    cambiar di mano *to change hands.*
    dare una mano *to lend a hand.*
    fatto a mano *handmade.*
    fuori mano *out of the way.*
    lavarsi le mani *to wash one's hands.*
    star con le mani in mano *to idle.*
    stretta di mano *handshake.*
    venire alle mani *to come to blows.*
manovra *maneuver.*
mantello *coat, robe.*
MANTENERE *to keep; to maintain.*
    mantenere la parola *to keep one's*
       word.
    mantenere una famiglia *to support a*
       family.
    mantenersi calmo *to keep calm.*
    mantenersi in contatto con *to keep in*
       contact with.
    mantenersi in vita *to stay alive.*
manuale *manual, handbook.*
manutenzione *maintenance.*
manzo *steer.*
    bollito di manzo *boiled beef.*
mappa *map; plan.*
marca *mark, sign; brand.*
marcia *march.*
marciapiede *sidewalk.*
marciare *to march.*
marcire *to rot; to decay.*
MARE, m. *sea.*
    in alto mare *on the high seas.*
    mal di mare *seasickness.*
marèa *tide.*
    alta marèa *high tide.*
    bassa marèa *low tide.*
margherita *daisy.*
margine, m. *margin.*
marina *navy.*
marinaio *sailor.*
marino *marine.*
marionetta *puppet, marionette.*
marito *husband.*
marmellata *marmalade, jam.*

marmo *marble.*

marrone *brown, chestnut.*

martedì *Tuesday.*

   martedì prossimo *next Tuesday.*

   martedì scorso *last Tuesday.*

martello *hammer.*

marzo *March.*

mascella *jaw.*

maschera *mask.*

mascherare *to mask.*

   mascherarsi *to disguise oneself.*

maschile *masculine, male.*

   di genere maschile *of masculine gender.*

   di sesso maschile *of male sex.*

maschio, n. *male, boy;* adj. *manly, virile.*

massa *mass, heap.*

massacro *massacre.*

massaggio *massage.*

massaia *housewife.*

massiccio *massive; solid.*

MASSIMO *greatest.*

   al massimo *at best.*

   arrivare al massimo della gioia *to reach a peak of happiness.*

   peso massimo *heavyweight (boxer).*

masticare *to chew.*

   masticare le parole *to mumble.*

matematica *mathematics.*

materasso *mattress.*

materia *matter, substance.*

materiale, n. m. & adj. *material.*

materno *maternal.*

matita *pencil.*

MATRIMONIO *marriage.*

MATTINA *morning.*

matto *mad, crazy.*

   È diventato matto. *He went mad.*

   Questo bambino mi fa diventare matta. *This child drives me crazy.*

   Vado matto per la musica. *I'm crazy about music.*

   Ho una voglia matta di . . . *I am dying for . . .*

mattone, m. *brick.*

mattonella *tile.*

maturazione *ripening.*

maturità *maturity.*

maturo *mature, ripe.*

   una mela matura *a ripe apple.*

   un'uomo maturo *an aged man.*

mausoleo *mausoleum.*

mazzo *bunch.*

   mazzo di chiavi *bunch of keys.*

   mazzo di fiori *bunch of flowers.*

   mazzo di carte *pack of cards.*

ME *me.*

meccanico, n. *mechanic;* adj. *mechanical.*

medaglia *medal.*

   il rovescio della medaglia *the reverse of the medal.*

medesimo *same, alike.*

   Portiamo la medesima misura. *We wear the same size.*

   Siamo del medisimo parere. *We have the same opinion.*

media *average; mean.*

   una media di *an average of.*

mediante *by means of.*

medicare *to medicate.*

medicina *medicine.*

MEDICO *physician.*

   medico chirurgo *surgeon.*

medievale *medieval.*

MEDIO *middle, medium.*

   di media età *middle-aged.*

   dito medio *middle finger.*

   Appartiene alla classe media. *He belongs to the middle class.*

   Medio Evo *Middle Ages.*

mediocre *mediocre.*

meditare *to meditate.*

meditazione, f. *meditation.*

MEGLIO *better.*

   di bene in meglio *better and better.*

   quanto c'è di meglio *the best there is.*

   sentirsi meglio *to feel better.*

   Ci ho pensato meglio. *I thought it over.*

   Sarebbe meglio partire ora. *It would be better to leave now.*

MELA *apple.*

melanzana *eggplant.*

melodia *melody.*

melodramma *opera; melodrama.*

membro *limb, member;* **membra,** f. pl. *limbs;* **membri,** m. pl. *members.*

   aver le membra stanche *to be tired.*

   membro onorario *honorary member.*

memorabile *memorable.*

memoria *memory.*

   imparare a memoria *to memorize.*

Ho buona memoria. *I have a good memory.*

menare *to lead.*

MENO *less.*

a meno che *unless.*

fare a meno di *to do without.*

meno gente *fewer people.*

più o meno *more or less.*

venir meno ad una promessa *to break a promise.*

Cinque meno tre fanno due. *Five minus three makes two.*

In men che non si dica, tornato. *He came back in no time at all.*

Sono le sette meno dieci. *It's ten minutes to seven.*

Sono meno stanca di te. *I am less tired than you.*

mensile, n. m. *monthly wage;* adj. *monthly.*

mensilmente *once a month.*

menta *mint, peppermint.*

mentale *mental.*

alienazione mentale *insanity.*

MENTE, f. *mind.*

aver in mente di *to intend.*

malato di mente *mentally ill.*

mente sana in corpo sano *sound mind in sound body.*

tenere a mente *to remember.*

Ho un progetto in mente. *I have a project in mind.*

Un pensiero mi è venuto in mente. *A thought occurred to me.*

passare uscire di mente *to forget.*

mentire *to lie.*

mento *chin.*

MENTRE *while, instead.*

Mi ha detto che sarebbe venuto qui, mentre invece è andato da Maria. *He said he was coming here, but instead he went to Mary's.*

Non m'interrompere mentre sto parlando. *Don't interrupt while I'm speaking.*

menu m. *menu.*

menzionare *to mention.*

menzogna *falsehood, untruth, lie.*

meraviglia *wonder, amazement.*

mercante, m. *merchant.*

fare orecchio da mercante *to turn deaf ears.*

mercato *market.*

merce, f. *goods, merchandise.*

mercoledì *Wednesday.*

meridionale *southern.*

meridione *south.*

meritare *to deserve.*

merito *merit, worth.*

rendere merito a *to give credit to.*

una persona di grandi meriti *a person of great merit.*

merietto *lace.*

mescolare *to mix.*

MESE *month.*

il mese in corso *the current month.*

il mese passato *last month.*

il mese scorso *last month.*

il mese che viene *next month.*

il mese entrante *next month.*

il mese prossimo *next month.*

messa *mass.*

messa solenne *solemn mass.*

messaggero *messenger.*

messaggio *message.*

mestiere, m. *trade.*

ognuno al suo mestiere *each to his own trade.*

Non faccio questo mestiere. *This is not my trade.*

Qual'è il suo mestiere? *What is your trade?*

meta *goal; half.*

a metà paga *at half pay.*

a metà prezzo *at half price.*

a metà strada *halfway.*

dividere a metà *to divide in half.*

fare metà per uno *to give each half.*

metodicamente *methodically.*

mètodo *method.*

metro *meter = 39.37 in.*

metropolitana *subway.*

METTERE *to put; to place.*

mettere fine a *to put an end to.*

mettere le cose a posto *to put things in order.*

mettere in libertà *to set free.*

mettere in moto *to set in motion.*

mettere in ordine *to tidy.*

mettersi a *to put oneself to; to begin.*

mezzanotte *midnight.*

mezzo, n. *means; half.*

con mezzi limitati *with limited means.*

per mezzo di *by means of.*

in mezzo a *in the midst of.*

mezz'ora *half an hour.*

un'ora e mezza *one hour and a half.*

mezzogiorno *noon.*

MI *me; to me.*

Mi dai quel libro per piacere? *Will you please give me that book?*

Mi scrivono. *They write to me.*

Mi senti? *Do you hear me?*

mica *not at all.*

microbe *microbe.*

micròfono *microphone.*

miele, m. *honey.*

migliaio, pl. **migliaia** *thousand.*

migliàia di persone *thousands of people.*

miglio *mile.*

migliorare *to better; to improve.*

migliore *better.*

milionario *millionaire.*

milione, m. *million.*

militare, m. *soldier.*

MILLE, pl. *MILA thousand.*

duemila *two thousand.*

minacciare *to threaten.*

minaccioso *menacing, threatening.*

minerale *mineral.*

minestra *soup.*

miniera *mine.*

minimo *minimum.*

il minimo che si possa fare *the least that can be done.*

paga minima *lowest pay.*

ridurre ai minimi termini *to reduce to the lowest terms.*

un minimo di *a minimum of.*

ministero *ministry.*

ministro *minister.*

minoranza *minority.*

minore *less, lesser, minor.*

minore d'età *younger.*

sorella minore *younger sister.*

minorenne, n. m. & f. *minor;* adj. *underage.*

minuscolo *small, tiny.*

minuto *minute.*

Attenda un minuto. *Wait a minute.*

Sono le cinque e dieci minuti. *It's ten minutes past five.*

MIO, mia; miei m. pl.; **mie** f. pl; **il mio; la mìa; i miei; le mie** *my, mine.*

Questo è il mio libro. *This is my book.*

Mia zia è arrivata. *My aunt has arrived.*

miope *nearsighted.*

mira *sight.*

prendere di mira *to aim at.*

miracolo *miracle.*

mirare *to stare at; to aim at.*

miscuglio *mixture.*

miserabile *miserable.*

miserabilmente *miserably.*

misèria *misery, poverty.*

misericordia *mercy.*

mistero *mystery.*

mistura *mixture.*

misura *measure.*

prendere delle misure *to take measures.*

predere le misure *to take measurements.*

passare la misure *to exceed the limit.*

misurare *to measure.*

mite *mild.*

clima mite *temperate climate.*

un carattere mite *a mild character.*

mitragliatrice, f. *machine gun.*

mobile *movable, mobile.*

mobilia *furniture.*

mobilità *mobility.*

mobilitazione, f. *mobilization.*

moda *fashion.*

essere di moda *to be in fashion.*

sfilata di moda *fashion show.*

alta moda *haute couture.*

modella *model.*

modello *pattern, model.*

essere un modello di virtù *to be a model of virtue.*

moderare *to moderate.*

moderare i termini *to keep a civil tongue.*

moderarsi *to moderate oneself.*

moderazione, f. *moderation.*

moderno *modern.*

modèstia *modesty.*

modesto *modest.*

MODO *way, manner.*

a mio modo di vedere *according to my way of thinking.*

in qualche modo *somehow.*

a modo mio *my way.*

per modo di dire *for example.*

in ogni modo *in any case.*

in questo modo *this way; in this manner.*

Non èi modo d'agire. *That's no way to act.*

modulo *form, blank.*

riempire un modulo *to fill out a form.*

MOGLIE *wife.*

chiedere in moglie *to ask in marriage.*

mole, f. *bulk.*

molle *soft.*

mollete, f. pl. *tongs.*

mollica *crumb.*

molliche di pane *crumbs of bread.*

moltiplicare *to multiply.*

MOLTO adj. *much;* **molti** *many;* adv. *very.*

molte persone *many people.*

molti amici *many friends.*

Ho molto lavoro da fare. *I have much work to do.*

Molto bene! *Very good!*

Sono molto stanco. *I am very tired.*

momento *moment.*

da un momento all'altro *any minute.*

in questo momento *right now.*

qualche momento fa *a moment ago.*

monaca *nun.*

monarca, m. *monarch.*

monastero *monastery.*

mondano *worldly.*

mondiale *worldwide.*

MONDO *world.*

andare all'altro mondo *to die.*

caschi il mondo *come what may.*

mettere al mondo *to give birth to.*

venire al mondo *to be born.*

in capo al mondo *to the ends of the world.*

moneta *coin.*

moneta d'argento *silver coin.*

moneta d'oro *gold coin.*

L'ho pagato colla stessa moneta. *I paid him in his own coin.*

Non ha moneta. *She (he) has no change.*

monologo *monologue.*

monotonìa *monotony.*

monotono *monotonous.*

montagna *mountain.*

montare *to go up; to ascend.*

monte, m. *mount, mountain.*

Il matrimonio è andato a monte. *The wedding was called off.*

monte di pietà *pawnbroker.*

monumento *monument, memorial.*

morale adj. *moral;* m. *morale;* n. f *moral, morals.*

Sono un po' giù di morale. *I'm low in spirits.*

morbido *soft.*

mordere *to bite.*

morente *dying.*

morire *to die.*

mormorare *to murmur.*

mormorìo *murmur, murmuring.*

morsicare *to bite.*

morso *bite.*

mortale *mortal.*

mortalità *mortality.*

mortalmente *mortally.*

ferito mortalmente *mortally wounded.*

morte, f. *death.*

morto *dead.*

mosca *fly.*

mossa *movement, gesture.*

mostra *exhibition.*

MOSTRARE *to show; to display.*

mostrare coraggio *to display courage.*

mostrare i denti *to bare one's teeth.*

Cerca di mostrarti più allegra. *Try to appear more cheerful.*

Mi devi mostrare come si fa. *You must show me how it's done.*

motivare *to motivate.*

motivo *motive, reason, tune.*

Non c'è motivo di farlo. *There is no reason to do it.*

moto *motion, impulse.*

di moto proprio *of one's own volition, spontaneously.*

essere sempre in moto *to be constantly on the move.*

mettere in moto l'automobile *to start the car.*

motocicletta *motorcycle.*

motore, m. *motor, engine.*

movimento *movement.*

mucca *cow.*

mucchio *heap, pile.*

Ho un mucchio di corrispondenza da sbrigare. *I have a heap of correspondence to attend to.*

muffa *mold, mustiness.*
mulino *mill.*
mulo n. *mule;* adj. *stubborn.*
multa *fine (penalty).*
municipale *municipal.*
municipalità *municipality.*
municipio *municipality.*
    palazzo del municipio *town hall.*
muovere *to move.*
mura, f. pl. *walls (of a building or city).*
muratore *mason, bricklayer.*
muro *wall.*
muscolare *muscular.*
muscolo *muscle.*
musèo *museum.*
musica *music.*
musicale *musical.*
musicista *musician.*
mutande, f. pl. *shorts (men's), briefs.*
mutandine, f. pl. *panties.*
mutare *to change.*
muto *mute.*
    sordo-muto *deaf-mute.*
mutuo *mutual.*

N

nana *dwarf.*
nanna *sleep (of child).*
    fare la nanna *to sleep.*
napoletano *Neapolitan.*
narice, f. *nostril.*
narrare *to narrate; to tell.*
narrativa *fiction.*
NASCERE *to be born; to originate.*
    far nascere dei sospetti *to give rise*
      to suspicion.
    nascere con la camicia *to be born*
      with a silver spoon in one's mouth.
    nascere morto *to be stillborn.*
    Non so come sia nato questo
      malinteso. *I don't know how this*
      misunderstanding originated.
nàscita *birth.*
    certificato di nascita *birth certificate.*
    controllo delle nascite *birth control.*
NASCONDERE *to hide; to conceal.*
    nascondere la verità *to conceal the*
      truth.
    nascondersi *to hide oneself.*

    Il gattino si è nascosto sotto il letto.
      The kitten hid under the bed.
nascosto *hidden.*
NASO *nose.*
    arricciare il naso *to turn one's nose*
      up at.
    soffiarsi il naso *to blow one's nose.*
nastro *ribbon.*
    nastro adesìvo *adhesive tape.*
    nastro dottilografico *typewriter*
      ribbon.
natale adj. *native;* n. *Christmas.*
    citta natale *native city.*
    la vigilia di Natale *Christmas Eve.*
    Buon Natale! *Merry Christmas.*
nativo, n. & adj. *native.*
nato *child.*
    primo nato *firstborn.*
natura *nature.*
naturale *natural.*
naturalezza *naturalness.*
    con naturalezza *without affectation.*
naturalmente *naturally; of course.*
    Naturalmente! *Naturally!*
navale *naval.*
navata *aisle, nave.*
NAVE, f. *ship.*
    a mezzo nave *by ship.*
    nave a vapore *steamship.*
    nave da carico *cargo ship.*
    nave da guerra *warship.*
    nave mercantile *merchant ship.*
navigare *to navigate.*
navigazione, f. *navigation.*
nazionale *national.*
nazionalità *nationality.*
nazionalizzare *to nationalize.*
nazione, f. *nation.*
    Nazioni Unite. *United Nations.*
NE 1. *of him; about him; of her; about*
    her; of it; about it; of them; about
    them; 2. *from there.*
    Noi ne parliamo spesso. *We often*
      speak of him (of her, of them,
      of it).
    Ne siamo felici. *We are glad about it.*
    Ne sono appena tornato. *I've just*
      returned from there.
NÉ, conj. *neither, nor.*
    Non desidero né l'uno né l'altro. *I*
      wish neither one nor the other.
NEANCHE *not even; not either.*

Non l'ho neanche visto. *I didn't even see him.*

Se tu non esci, non esco neanch'io. *If you don't go out, I won't go out either.*

nebbia *fog.*

necessariamente *necessarily.*

necessario *necessary.*

negare *to deny.*

negativa *negative* (photographic).
dare una negativa a qualcuno *to deny.*

negativo *negative.*

negazione, f. *negation.*

negligenza *negligence.*

negoziante *merchant; dealer.*

negoziare *to negotiate; to transact business.*

negoziazione, f. *negotiation.*

negozio *shop.*

nemico *enemy.*

nemmeno *not even.* See neanche.

neonato *infant, newborn.*

NEPPURE *see neanche.*

nero *black.*
Mar Nero *Black Sea.*
d'umore nero *in a dark humor.*

nervo *nerve.*

nervoso *nervous.*
sistema nervoso *nervous system.*

NESSUNO *nobody; no one; no; anyone.*
in nessun modo *in no way.*
È venuto nessuno? *Did anyone come?*
Non c'è nessuno. *There is no one here.*

neutrale *neutral.*

neutro *neutral.*

neve, f. *snow.*

nevicare *to snow.*
Nevica. *It's snowing.*

nevrotico *neurotic.*

nido *nest.*

NIENTE *nothing.*
Non c'è niente da fare. *Nothing can be done about it.*
Di niente, si figuri. *You're welcome.*
Non posso farci niente. *I can do nothing about it.*
Non fa niente. *It doesn't matter.*

nipote, m. *nephew, grandson;* f. *niece, granddaughter.*

nitidezza *clearness.*

nitido *neat, clear.*

NO *no.*
rispondere di no *to answer no.*
Non sa dite no. *He can't refuse.*

nobile *noble.*

nobiltà *nobility.*

nocciola *hazelnut.*

nocciolo *stone, pit.*
il nocciolo della questione *the very point in question.*

noce, f. *walnut.*

nocivo *harmful; noxious.*

nodo *knot.*
avere un nodo alla gola *to have a lump in one's throat.*
fare un nodo *to make a knot.*

NOI *we.*
noi stessi *ourselves.*

noia *weariness, boredom.*

noioso *tedious, boring.*

noleggiare *to hire.*

NOME, m. *name, noun.*
chiamare per nome *to call by name.*
nome comune *common noun.*
nome di famiglia *family name.*

nomina *appointment.*

nominare *to mention; to appoint.*
Fu nominato ambasciatore. *He was appointed ambassador.*
Ti nominiamo spesso. *We mention you often.*

NON *not.*
Non ne voglio. *I don't want any.*
Non ti sento. *I don't hear you.*

nonna *grandmother.*

nonno *grandfather.*

nono *ninth.*

nonostante *nevertheless.*

NORD, m. *north.*
nord-est *northeast.*
nord-ovest *northwest.*
viaggiare verso nord *to travel north.*
America del Nord *North America.*

norma *rule; norm.*
a norma di legge *according to law.*

normale *normal.*

normalmente *normally.*

nostalgia *nostalgia; homesickness.*

NOSTRO, -a, -i, -e (il nostro; la nostra; i nostri; le nostre) *our, ours.*
il nostro amico *our friend.*
la nostra casa *our home.*

i nostri genitori *our parents.*
le nostre camere *our rooms.*

nota *note.*
degno di nota *noteworthy.*
prendere nota di *to take note of.*

NOTARE *to note; to notice.*
farsi notare *to make oneself conspicuous.*
far notare *to point out.*
Hai notato come Maria si è invecchiata? *Did you notice how Mary has aged?*

notevole *remarkable, considerable.*

notificare *to notify.*

NOTIZIA *news.*
le ultime notizie *the latest news.*
Fammi avere tue notizie. *Let me have news of you.*
Non ho notizie di te da molto tempo. *I haven't heard from you in a long time.*

noto *known; well known.*
Il suo nome è noto a tutti. *Everyone knows his name.*
Lui è una figura nota nel mondo politico. *He is a well-known figure in political circles.*

notorietà *notoriety; fame.*

NOTTE, f. *night.*
a notte inoltrata *in the middle of the night.*
camicia da notte *nightgown.*
di notte *at night.*
mezzanotte *midnight.*

notturno *nocturnal.*

novanta *ninety.*

novantesimo *ninetieth.*

nove *nine.*
nove volte su dieci *nine times out of ten.*

novecento *nine hundred.*

novella *short story; tale.*

novello *new; early.*

novembre *November.*

novità *novelty; latest news.*
una novità assoluta *an absolute novelty.*
Avete sentito la novità? *Have you heard the latest?*

nozione, f. *notion.*

nozze, f. pl. *wedding.*

nube, f. *cloud.*

nubile *unmarried; single (of a woman).*

nuca *nape (of the neck).*

nucleare *nuclear.*
energia nucleare *nuclear energy.*
reactor nucleare *nuclear reactor.*

nudo *naked, bare.*
a piedi nudi *barefoot.*
grande abbastanza da vedersi a occhio nudo *large enough to see with the naked eye.*

nulla *see niente.*

nullo *null, void.*

numerare *to number.*

numero *number.*
numero dispari *odd number.*
numero pari *even number.*

numeroso *numerous.*

nuocere *to harm.*

nuora *daughter-in-law.*

nuotare *to swim.*
nuotare nell'abbondanza *to be well off.*

nuoto *swimming.*
gara di nuoto *swim race.*

nuovo *new.*
di nuovo *again.*

nutrimento *nourishment.*

nutrire *to nourish.*
nutrire un grande affetto per qualcuno *to feel affectionate toward someone.*
nutrire rancore *to bear a grudge.*
Non nutro fiducia in questa impresa. *I have no faith in this enterprise.*
Si dovrebbe nutrire meglio. *He should have better nourishment.*

nutrizione, f. *nutrition, nourishment.*

nuvola *cloud.*
una nuvola di fumo *a cloud of smoke.*
È sempre fra le nuvole. *He's always in the clouds.*

nuvoloso *cloudy.*

nuziale *nuptial.*
marcia nuziale *wedding march.*
velo nuziale *bridal veil.*

O

o, od *(if followed by a vowel) or.*
o uno o l'altro *either one or the other.*

Mi sei amico o nemico? *Are you friend or foe?*

Scegli questo o quello. *Choose one or the other.*

obbediente *obedient.*

obbedienza *obedience.*

obbedire *to obey.*

obbiettivo *aim, purpose, goal; objective.*

obbligare *to obligate; to compel.*

Nessuno ti obbliga a pagare. *No one compels you to pay.*

Sono obbligato a licenziarti. *I am compelled to fire you.*

obbligato *obliged, indebted.*

Le sono molto obbligato. *I am much obliged to you.*

obbligazione, f. *obligation, bond.*

obbligo *obligation.*

obiettare *to object.*

obiettivo *objective.*

obiezione, f. *objection.*

oblio *oblivion, forgetfulness.*

obliquo *oblique, indirect.*

obsoleto *obsolete.*

oca *goose.*

occasionale *occasional.*

occasionalmente *occasionally; by chance.*

occasione, f. *occasion, opportunity.*

cogliere l'occasione *to take the opportunity.*

occhiali, m. pl. *eyeglasses.*

occhiata *glance.*

dare un'occhiata a *to give a glance to.*

occhiello *buttonhole.*

OCCHIO *eye.*

agli occhi del mondo *in the eyes of the world.*

strizzare l'occhio *to wink.*

a perdita d'occhio *as far as the eye can see.*

dare nell'occhio *to attract attention.*

guardare con occhio benigno *to look kindly on.*

tenere d'occhio *to keep one's eye on.*

a occhio nudo *with the naked eye.*

fare gli occhi dolci a qualcuno *to make eyes at someone.*

occidentale, adj. *western;* n. *westerner.*

occidente, m. *west.*

occorrenza *occurrence.*

occorrere *to happen; to be necessary; to occur.*

occupare *to occupy.*

Il mio tempo è occupato con altre cose. *My time is taken up by other things.*

Lei ha occupato il mio posto. *You have occupied my seat.*

Me ne occupo io. *I'll take care of it.*

Occupo il mio tempo studiando l'italiano. *I spend my time studying Italian.*

occupato *engaged, occupied, busy.*

Sono molto occupato questa sera. *I'm very busy this evening.*

La linea telefonica é occupata. *The phone line is busy.*

occupazione, f. *occupation, employment.*

ocèano *ocean.*

odiare *to hate.*

odierno *of today.*

odio *hatred.*

odioso *hateful.*

odorare *to smell.*

odore, m. *smell.*

offendere *to offend.*

offensivo *offensive.*

offensore, m. *offender.*

offerta *offer, offering.*

Ha respinto la mia offerta di denaro. *He refused my offer of money.*

offesa *offense.*

recare offesa a *to give offense to.*

officina *workshop.*

offrire *to offer.*

offuscare *to obscure; to darken.*

oggettivamente *objectively.*

oggettivo *objective.*

oggetto *object.*

OGGI *today.*

da oggi in poi *from today on.*

in data d'oggi *bearing today's date.*

rimandare dall'oggi al domani *to put off from day to day.*

OGNI *every, each.*

ogni settimana *every week.*

Danne uno ad ogni persona presente. *Give one to each person present.*

OGNUNO *everyone, each one.*

Ognuno di noi è libero di fare ciò che vuole. *Each of us is free to do as he wishes.*

olio *oil.*

   olio d'oliva *olive oil.*

   olio di fegato di merluzzo *cod liver oil.*

oliva *olive.*

oliveto *olive grove.*

olocausto *holocaust, sacrifice.*

oltraggio *outrage.*

oltraggiosamente *outrageously.*

oltraggioso *opprobrious.*

OLTRE *beside, beyond.*

   andare oltre i limiti *to go beyond the limits.*

   oltre mare *overseas.*

   Gli ho dato dieci dollari, oltre i cinque che gli avevo già dato. *I gave him ten dollars, besides the five I had already given him.*

omaggio *homage, presentation.*

OMBRA *shadow, shade.*

   all'ombra di un' albero *in the shade of a tree.*

   senza l'ombra di dubbio *without a shadow of doubt.*

ombrello *umbrella.*

omettere *to omit.*

   Il mio nome è stato omesso dalla lista degli invitati. *My name was omitted from the guest list.*

omicidio *murder.*

omosessuale *homosexual.*

oncia *ounce.*

oncologia *oncology.*

onda *wave.*

   andare in onda *to be broadcast.*

ondata *wave, surge.*

   un'ondata di freddo *a cold spell.*

ondulare *to wave.*

   farsi ondulare i capelli *to have one's hair waved.*

ondulazione, f. *waving, undulation.*

onere *burden.*

onesto *honest.*

onorabilità *honorability.*

onorabilmente *honorably.*

onorare *to honor.*

onorario adj. *honorary;* pl. *wages, fee.*

onorato *honored.*

onore, m. *honor.*

aver l'onore di chiedere *to have the honor to request.*

fare onore ai propri impegni *to meet one's obligations.*

in onore di *in honor of.*

parola d'onore *word of honor.*

a onor del vero *to tell the truth.*

onorevole *honorable.*

opaco *opaque.*

opera *opera, work.*

   fare un'opera buona *to do a kind deed.*

   mano d'opera *labor.*

   teatro d'opera *opera house.*

   cantante d'opera *opera singer.*

   un'opera d'arte *a work of art.*

   opera letteraria *literary work.*

operàio *laborer.*

operare *to work.*

   farsi operare *to undergo surgery.*

   Lui opera per il bene di tutti. *He is working for the good of all.*

operazione, f. *operation.*

opinione, f. *opinion.*

   cambiare opinione *to change one's mind.*

   opinione pubblica *public opinion.*

opponente, n. m. *opponent;* adj. *opposing.*

opporre *to oppose.*

   opporre resistenza *to resist.*

   opporre un rifiuto *to refuse.*

   opporsi ad un'idea *to oppose an idea; to declare oneself against an idea.*

opportunista *opportunist.*

opportunità *opportunity, opportuneness.*

   Non mi diede l'opportunità di vederlo. *He didn't give me the opportunity of seeing him.*

   Non ne vedo l'opportunità. *I can't see that it is opportune.*

   cogliere l'opportunità *to seize the opportunity.*

opportuno *opportune.*

   Questo é il momento *opportuno. This is the right time.*

opposizione, f. *opposition.*

opposto *opposite, facing.*

oppressione, f. *oppression.*

oppressivo *oppressive, overwhelming.*

oppressore *oppressor.*
opprimere *to oppress.*
OPPURE *or else.*
opuscolo *pamphlet.*
opzione *option, choice.*
ORA, n. *hour;* adj. *now.*
   fra un'ora *in an hour.*
   le ore lavorative *working hours.*
   ogni ora del giorno *every hour of
     the day.*
   Che ora è? *What time is it?*
   È ora d'andare a casa. *It's time to go
     home.*
   d'ora in poi *from now on.*
   fino ad ora *up until now.*
   ora e per sempre *once and for all.*
   per ora *for the moment.*
   ora di punta *rush hour.*
orafo *goldsmith.*
orale *oral.*
orario, n. *timetable;* adj. *per hour.*
   arrivare in orario *to arrive on time.*
   una velocità oraria di trenta
     chilometri *a speed of thirty
     kilometers per hour.*
oratore, m. *orator.*
orchestra *orchestra.*
   direttore d'orchestra *conductor.*
ordinamento *regulation.*
   ordinamento giuridico *legal
     system.*
ordinare *to order.*
   Ha altro da ordinare? *Do you have
     any further orders?*
   Mi ha ordinato di fare questo lavoro.
     He ordered me to do this work.
   Vuole ordinare la colazione? *Do you
     wish to order breakfast?*
ordinario *ordinary.*
ordinato *orderly.*
ordinazione *order; arrangement;
   prescription (medicine).*
ordine, m. *order.*
   di prim'ordine *first-rate.*
   fino a nuovo ordine *till a change in
     orders occurs.*
   mettere in ordine alfabetico *to put in
     alphabetical order.*
   mettere in ordine una camera *to set a
     room to rights.*
   ordini e contr'ordini *orders and
     counter-orders.*

   per ordine cronologico *in
     chronological order.*
orecchino *earring.*
ORECCHIO *ear.*
   entrare da un orecchio e uscire
     dall'altro *to go in one ear and out
     the other.*
   essere tutto orecchi *to be all ears.*
   fare orecchio da mercante *to make
     believe one doesn't hear.*
   mal d'orecchi *earache.*
   prestare orecchio *to lend an ear.*
   Non ha orecchio per la musica. *He
     has no ear for music.*
orefice *jeweler.*
oreficeria *goldsmith's or jeweler's shop.*
organismo *organism.*
organizzare *to organize.*
organo *organ.*
orgoglio *pride.*
orgoglioso *proud.*
orientale *Eastern, Oriental.*
orientar(si) *to orient oneself.*
oriente, m. *orient, east.*
   l'estremo Oriente *the Far East.*
   il Medio Oriente *the Middle East.*
originale *original.*
originalità *originality.*
origine, f. *origin.*
   dare origine a *to give rise to.*
   di dubbia origine *of dubious origin.*
   di origine italiana *of Italian descent.*
   di umile origine *of humble origin.*
   Come ebbe origine il dissidio? *How
     did the dissension originate?*
   di origine incerta *of uncertain
     origin.*
orizzontale *horizontal.*
orizzonte, m. *horizon.*
orio *border, edge, hem.*
orma *footprint, footmark.*
   Lui segue le orme di suo padre. *He
     is following in his father's
     footsteps.*
ORMAI *now; by now; by this time.*
   Ormai tutto è a posto. *Now
     everything is in order.*
   Sarà già partito ormai. *He has
     probably already left by this time.*
ornamento *ornament.*
ornare *to adorn; to decorate.*
ORO *gold.*

oro a diciotto carati *eighteen-carat gold.*

oro zecchino *pure gold.*

riccioli d'oro *golden ringlets.*

Vale tant'oro quanto pesa. *It is worth its weight in gold.*

Non è tutt' oro quel che luccica. *All that glitters is not gold.*

Non lo farei per tutto l'oro del mondo. *I would not do it for all the money in the world.*

orologiaio *watchmaker.*

orologio *watch.*

caricare l'orologio *to wind the watch.*

Che ora fa il tuo orologio? *What time is it by your watch?*

Il mio orologio fa le quattro e dieci. *According to my watch, it is ten minutes past four.*

Quest' orologio va avanti venti minuti al giorno. *This watch gains twenty minutes a day.*

orribile *horrible.*

orribilmente *horribly.*

orrore, m. *horror.*

Mi fa orrore. *It horrifies me.*

Quel vestito é un orrore. *That dress is awful.*

orso *bear.*

ortaggio *vegetable.*

orto *vegetable garden.*

ortodosso *orthodox.*

ortografia *spelling.*

ortopedico *orthopedics.*

OSARE *to dare.*

Come osi fare una cosa simile? *How dare you do such a thing?*

Non oso chiederlo. *I don't dare ask.*

Sarebbe osare troppo. *That would be going too far.*

osceno *obscene, indecent.*

OSCURARE *to darken; to obscure.*

Il cielo si è improvvisamente oscurato. *The sky darkened suddenly.*

Mi si sta oscurando la vista. *My sight is growing dim.*

oscurità *darkness, obscurity.*

l'oscurità di una notte senza stelle *the darkness of a starless night.*

ospedale, m. *hospital.*

ospitale *hospitable.*

ospitalità *hospitality.*

ospite, m. & f. *guest, host, hostess.*

È stata mia ospite per le vacanze estive. *She was my guest during the summer holidays.*

È un'ospite gradito. *He is a welcome guest.*

I miei ospiti mi hanno gentilmente invitato a tornare a casa loro la settimana prossima. *My hosts have very kindly invited me to return to their home next week.*

osservare *to observe; to notice.*

osservazione, f. *observation, remark.*

Lui ha fatto un'osservazione fuori posto. *He made an uncalled-for remark.*

ossigeno *oxygen.*

OSSO, f. pl. **ossa** *bone.*

in carne e ossa *in the flesh.*

Ho freddo fino alle ossa. *I'm frozen to the bone.*

Mi sento tutte le ossa rotte. *I'm all aches and pains.*

Si è rotto l'osso del collo. *He broke his neck.*

ostacolare *to hinder.*

ostacolare il cammino di qualcuno *to hinder someone's progress.*

ostacolo *obstacle.*

un ostacolo insormontabile *an insurmountable obstacle.*

oste, m. *host, tavern keeper.*

osteria *tavern; inn.*

ostile *hostile.*

forze ostili *hostile forces.*

assumere un atteggiamento ostile *to have a hostile attitude.*

ostilità *hostility.*

ostinato *obstinate.*

ostinazione, f. *obstinacy.*

ostrica *oyster.*

ostruire *to obstruct; to hinder.*

ostruzione, f. *obstruction.*

ottanta *eighty.*

ottantesimo *eightieth.*

ottavo *eighth.*

ottenere *to obtain.*

ottenere il permesso *to obtain permission.*

ottico *optician.*

fibre ottiche *fiber optics.*
ottimismo, n. *optimism;* adj. *optimistic.*
ottimista, m. *optimist.*
ottimo *excellent.*
otto *eight.*
oggi a otto *a week from today.*
ottobre *October.*
ottocento *eight hundred.*
nell' Ottocento *in the nineteenth century.*
ottone, m. *brass.*
ottoni *brass instruments.*
ovale, n. m. & adj. *oval.*
ovatta *wadding.*
ovazione, f. *ovation.*
OVEST, m. *west.*
ad ovest *to the west.*
OVUNQUE *anywhere, everywhere.*
Stiamo cercando ovunque. *We are looking everywhere.*
Ti seguirò ovunque. *I'll follow you anywhere.*
ovviamente *obviously.*
ovvio *obvious.*
ozio *idleness.*
Verrò a trovarti durante le mie ore d'ozio. *I'll come to see you during my leisure hours.*
ozioso *idle, lazy.*

P

pacatezza *calm; calmness.*
pacca *slap; smack on the back.*
pacchetto *packet.*
un pacchetto di sigarette *a pack of cigarettes.*
PACCO *package, parcel.*
spedire come pacco postale *to send by parcel post.*
PACE, f. *peace.*
fare la pace col nemico *to make peace with the enemy.*
giudice di pace *justice of the peace.*
lasciare in pace *to leave alone.*
mettere il cuore in pace *to set one's mind at rest.*
trattato di pace *peace treaty.*
Voglio stare in pace. *I want to live in peace.*

pacificare *to pacify; to appease.*
pacifico *peaceful, pacific.*
Pacifico *Pacific.*
pacifista *pacifist.*
padella *frying pan.*
cadere dalla padella alla brace *to fall out of the frying pan into the fire.*
PADRE *father.*
il Santo Padre *the Holy Father.*
padrona *owner, mistress.*
padrona di casa *landlady.*
PADRONE, m. *landlord, owner.*
essere padrone della situazione *to have the situation well in hand.*
essere padrone di se *to have self-control.*
Sono padrona di fare quello che mi pare e piace. *I am free to do as I choose.*
paesaggio *landscape.*
PAESE, m. *country; land; small town.*
gente di paese *countryfolk.*
il paese dell' abbondanza *the land of plenty.*
paese di montagna *mountain village.*
paese natìo *native land; native town.*
Mi ha mandato a quel paese. *He sent me to the devil.*
Paese che vai, usanza che trovi. *To each country its own customs.*
Siamo del medesimo paese. *We are from the same country.*
paga *pay.*
riscuotere la paga *to collect one's pay.*
pagamento *payment.*
pagamento a rate *payment in installments.*
pagamento in contanti *cash payment.*
PAGARE *to pay.*
da pagarsi alla consegna *C.O.D.*
Quanto mi fa pagare? *How much will you charge me?*
pagato *paid.*
PAGINA *page.*
a piè di pagina *at the foot of the page.*
paglia *straw.*
pagliaccio *clown.*
PAIO, f. pl. **PAIA,** *pair.*
tre paia di guanti *three pairs of gloves.*
un paio di scarpe *a pair of shoes.*
palato *palate.*

palazzo *palace.*
> palazzo municipale *City Hall.*

palco *scaffold, platform, box (theater).*

palcoscenico *stage.*

palesare *to disclose; to reveal.*

palestra *gymnasium.*

palla *ball.*

pallidezza *paleness; pallor.*

pallido *pale.*

pallone, m. *balloon.*

pallore *paleness, pallor.*

palma *palm (bot.).*
> Domenica delle Palme *Palm Sunday.*

palmo *palm (of the hand).*

palo *pole.*
> palo telegrafico *telegraph pole.*
> saltare di palo in frasca *to stray from the point.*

palpebra *eyelid.*

palpitare *to throb.*

palude, f. *marsh.*

panca *bench; long seat.*

panchina *garden bench; low platform.*

pancia *stomach, belly.*

PANE, m. *bread.*
> pane fresco *fresh bread.*
> pane quotidiano *daily bread.*
> pane integrale *whole-grain bread.*
> rendere pane per focaccia *to give tit for tat.*

panetterìa *bakery shop.*

panettiere, m. *baker.*

panettone *"pane Hone" (Milanese cake).*

panificio *bakery.*

pànfilo *yacht.*

panforte *gingerbread (Sienese cake).*

pànico *panic.*

paniere, m. *basket.*
> rompere le uova a nel paniere *to upset one's applecart.*

panificio *bakery.*

panino *roll.*
> panino imbottito (panino ripieno) *sandwich.*

panna *cream.*

pannello *panel.*

PANNO *cloth, clothes.*
> panno di lana *woolen cloth.*
> Non vorrei essere nei tuoi panni. *I wouldn't want to be in your shoes.*

pannocchia *spike; corncob.*

pannolino *diaper.*

panorama, m. *panorama.*

PANTALONI, m. pl. *trousers.*
> pantaloni rigati *striped trousers.*
> pantaloni alla zuava *knickerbockers.*

pantofola *slipper.*

papà *dad, father.*

Papa, n. m. *Pope.*

papavero *poppy.*

pappagallo *parrot.*

parabrezza *windshield.*

paracadute, m. *parachute.*

paradiso *paradise; heaven.*

parafulmine, m. *lightning rod.*

paraggi *vicinity; neighborhood.*

paragonare *to compare.*

paragone, m. *comparison.*
> Non c' è paragone. *There's no comparison.*

paragrafo *paragraph.*

paralisi, f. *paralysis.*

paralizzare *to paralyze.*
> Mi si è paralizzato il braccio. *My arm has become paralyzed.*

parallelo n. & adj. *parallel.*

parata *parade.*

paraurti *bumper.*

paravento *screen, windshield.*

parcheggiare *to park.*

PARCHEGGIO *parking lot.*
> Vietato il parcheggio! *No Parking!*

parco *park.*

parecchio *a good deal of; a good many; several.*
> essere in parecchi *to be several.*
> C'erano parecchie persone. *There were a good many people.*
> L'ho visto parecchio tempo fa. *I saw him a long time ago.*

pareggiare *to equalize; to balance (budget).*

PARENTE, m. & f. *relative, kinsman.*
> Parenti più stretti *next of kin.*
> Lui è senza parenti. *He is without kin.*
> parenti acquisiti *in-laws.*

parentela *relationship, relatives.*

parentesi, f. *parenthesis.*
> fra parentesi *in parenthesis;* (fig.) *by the way.*

PARERE, v. *to seem;* n. m. *opinion, advice, judgment.*
> A quanto pare . . . *It seems . . .*

Mi pare di si. *I think so.*

Mi pare di no. *I don't think so.*

Pare che sia una buona donna. *She seems to be a good woman.*

Ti pare? *Do you think so?*

cambiar parere *to change one's opinion.*

Il mio parere è giusto. *My judgment is correct.*

Sono del parere che . . . *I am of the opinion that . . .*

a parere mio *in my opinion.*

PARETE, f. *wall (interior).*

Questo quadro va appeso alla parete. *This picture is to be hung on the wall.*

PARI, adj. *equal, even, same;* n. m. & f. *peer, equal, par.*

numeri pari *even numbers.*

Cammina di pari passo con me. *He walks at an even pace with me.*

È arrivato in pari tempo. *He arrived at the same time.*

Siamo pari. *We are even.*

sotto la pari *below par.*

Roma non ha pari. *Rome has no equal.*

Sono i pari del Regno Unito. *They are the peers of the United Kingdom.*

a pari condizioni. *under the same conditions.*

parità *parity, equality.*

a parità di fatti *all things being equal.*

parlamento *Parliament.*

Lui è membro del parlamento. *He is a member of Parliament.*

PARLARE *to speak.*

parlare bene *to speak well.*

parlare male di *to speak ill of.*

Di che parlate? *What are you talking about?*

La signora ha fatto parlare di se. *The lady has caused much talk.*

Non se ne parli più. *Let us speak no more about it.*

Parliamo di politica! *Let's talk politics!*

Qui si parla francese. *French is spoken here.*

parmigiano *Parmesan.*

parmigiano reggiano *Parmesan cheese.*

PAROLA *word.*

Chiedo la parola. *I ask to speak.*

Do la mia parola. *I give my word.*

È venuto meno alla parola data. *He broke his word.*

S'è rimangiato le parole. *He ate his words.*

È un gioco di parole. *It is a pun.*

Mi fu tolta la parola. *I was not permitted to speak.*

Non ho parole. *I have no words.*

Ti rivolgo la parola. *I am addressing you.*

parrucca *wig.*

parrucchiere, m. *hairdresser, barber.*

PARTE, f. *part, side, place.*

d'altra parte *on the other hand; on the other side.*

da parte mia *from my point of view; from me.*

da questa parte *on this side; this way.*

la parte del leone *the lion's share.*

parte per parte *bit by bit.*

questa parte del corpo *this part of the body.*

È un caso a parte. *It is a particular case (a thing apart).*

Ha recitato la parte di Otello. *He played the part of Othello.*

Ha messo i libri da parte. *He put the books aside.*

Ha preso la mia parte. *He took my part.*

Ognuno avrà la sua parte. *Each will have his share.*

partecipare *to participate.*

PARTENZA *departure, starting, sailing.*

Ecco il segnale di partenza. *Here is the starting signal.*

La mia partenza fu ritardata. *My departure was delayed.*

La partenza del piroscafo è fissata per le tre. *The sailing of the ship is set for three.*

particolare, adj. *particular, peculiar, special;* n. m. *detail.*

Ogni particolare è corretto. *It is correct in every detail.*

particolarmente *particularly, in particular.*

PARTIRE *to depart; to set sail; to leave.*
  a partire da *beginning from.*
  A che ora bisogna partire? *At what time must we leave?*
PARTITA *game, match.*
  una partita a scacchi *a game of chess.*
  La partita è chiusa. *The question is settled.*
  Questa è la partita decisiva. *This is the deciding game.*
PARTITO *party (political).*
  il partito del lavoro *the labor party.*
  Appartiene al partito d'opposizione. *He belongs to the opposition party.*
  prendere un partito *to make up one's mind.*
parto *childbirth.*
partorire *to give birth to; to deliver; to produce.*
parziale *partial.*
parzialità *partiality.*
parzialmente *partially.*
pascolo *meadow; pasture.*
Pasqua *Easter.*
  giorno di Pasqua *Easter day.*
  vacanze di Pasqua *Easter holidays.*
  vigilia di Pasqua *Easter eve.*
passaggio *passage.*
passaporto *passport.*
  Mettete il visto sul vostro passaporto. *Have your passport stamped.*
PASSARE *to pass.*
  passare attraverso *to pass through.*
  passare il peso *to be overweight.*
  passare per la biblioteca *to stop by the library.*
  passare un esame *to pass an exam.*
  È passato per italiano. *They mistook him for an Italian.*
  M'è passato di mente. *It slipped my mind.*
  Non passate i limiti. *Do not overstep the bounds.*
  Passate, per favore! *Pass through, please.*
  Passiamoci sopra. *Let's dismiss it.*
PASSATO *past; a past time.*
  Conosco il suo passato. *I know his (her) past.*
  Ha messo una pietra sopra il passato. *He let bygones be bygones.*

Il passato non si puo cancellare. *The past cannot be erased.*
PASSEGGERO, n. *passenger, traveler;* adj. *transient, passing.*
  È un malessere passeggero. *It is a passing discomfort.*
PASSEGGIARE *to walk.*
passeggiata *walk, ride.*
passeggio *walk.*
  Andiamo a passeggio. *Let's go for a walk.*
passerella *gangway; runway.*
passero *sparrow.*
passione, f. *passion.*
passivo *passive.*
PASSO *step.*
  passo per passo *step by step.*
  Bisogna fare passi lunghi. *We must take long steps.*
  Essi camminano di pari passo. *They walk at the same pace.*
  Non bisogna fare il passo più lungo della gamba. *We must not be overambitious.*
  Rallentiamo il passo. *Let's slow down our pace.*
  Torniamo sui nostri passi. *Let's retrace our steps.*
PASTA *dough, pasta, pastry.*
pasticceria *pastry shop; candy store.*
pasticcino *cookie.*
pasticcio *pie; bungling piece of work; difficulty.*
  Non voglio mettermi in un pasticcio. *I don't wish to put myself in a difficult position.*
  Questo è un pasticcio. *This is a mess.*
PASTO *meal.*
  pasti compresi *meals included.*
  È un buon vino da pasto. *It is a good table wine.*
  Ho fatto un buon pasto. *I had a good meal.*
PATATA *potato.*
  patate lesse *boiled potatoes.*
  spirito di patata *poor humor (colloq.).*
patema *anxiety; worry.*
patente, f. *patent, diploma, driver's license.*
  Ha preso la patente. *He got his license.*
paternità *paternity; fatherhood.*

paterno *paternal, fatherly.*
  Son tornato alla mia casa paterna. *I returned to my father's home.*
patetico *pathetic.*
patire *to suffer.*
PATRIA *native country.*
  amor di patria *love of one's country.*
  ritornare in patria *to go back to one's country.*
patrimonio *heritage; estate.*
patriota, m. *patriot.*
patriottismo *patriotism.*
pattinagio *skating.*
pattinare *to skate.*
pattino *skate.*
  pattino a rotelle *roller skate.*
PATTO *agreement, term.*
  a nessun patto *on no condition; by no means.*
  a patto che *on condition that.*
  il Patto Atlantico *the Atlantic Pact.*
  Facciamo patti chiari. *Let's make clear terms.*
  Sono venuti a patti. *They came to terms.*
pattumiera *garbage can.*
PAURA *fear, dread, terror, fright.*
  aver paura *to be afraid of.*
pausa *pause, rest.*
PAVIMENTO *pavement, floor.*
paziente, adj. *patient, forbearing;* n. *patient in hospital.*
PAZIENZA *patience.*
  mettere a prova la pazienza *to try the patience.*
  Abbia pazienza! *Have patience!*
  Non perdere la pazienza. *Do not lose your patience.*
  Santa Pazienza! *God give me patience!*
pazzo, adj. *insane, crazy;* n. *madman.*
peccato *sin.*
  Che peccato! *What a pity!*
pecora *sheep.*
peculiare *peculiar.*
pedale, m. *pedal.*
pedata *kick.*
pedone, m. *pedestrian.*
PEGGIO *worse, worst.*
  alla peggio *at the worst.*
  Il peggio è che . . . *The worst of it is . . .*

Va di male in peggio. *It goes from bad to worse.*
peggiore *worse, worst.*
  È il peggiore di tutti. *It is the worst of all.*
pelare *to peel; to strip; to fleece.*
  S'è fatto pelare. *He allowed himself to be fleeced.*
PELLE, f. *skin, rind, leather.*
  rischiare la pelle *to risk one's skin.*
  salvarsi la pelle *to save one's skin.*
  Gli hanno fatto la pelle. *They killed (skinned) him (colloq.).*
  È pelle lucida. *It is patent leather.*
  Ha la pelle dura. *He has a thick skin.*
  Sono guanti di pelle. *They are kid gloves.*
pelliccia *fur.*
  foderato di pelliccia *lined with fur.*
pellicola *film.*
pelo *hair, nap.*
PENA *penalty, punishment; anxiety, pity.*
  a mala pena *hardly, scarcely.*
  Mi fa pena. *I pity him.*
  Vale la pena. *It is worth the trouble.*
pendere *to hang; to hang down; to lean.*
  Pende dalle sue labbra. *He hangs on her words.*
pendìo *the slant; the slope.*
  Scende il pendìo. *He goes down the slope.*
PENETRARE *to penetrate; to get into; to enter.*
penisola *peninsula.*
penitenza *penance, penitence.*
  Fa penitenza per i suoi peccati. *He is doing penance for his sins.*
PENNA *pen, feather, quill.*
  Non sa tenere la penna in mano. *He does not know how to write.*
pennello *paintbrush.*
penoso *painful, difficult.*
PENSARE *to think.*
  Pensa agli affari tuoi. *Mind your own business.*
  Ripensaci. *Think it over.*
PENSIERO *thought, care.*
  È sopra pensiero. *He is worried.*
  Ha molti pensieri. *He has many worries.*
  Muta pensiero facilmente. *He changes his mind easily.*

Non ti dar pensiero. *Don't worry about it.*

Sta in pensiero per qualche cosa. *He is worrying about something.*

pensionato *retired.*

PENSIONE, f. *pension; boarding house.*

Quanto si paga per la pensione completa? *How much does one pay for room and board?*

pensoso *thoughtful; pensive.*

pentimento *repentance.*

pentir(si) *to repent; to regret.*

pentola *pot, kettle.*

penultimo *penultimate; next to last.*

pepe, m. *pepper.*

È pieno di pepe. *He is full of ginger.*

peperone *pepper.*

PER *for; by; through; on account of; owing to; to.*

cinque per cento *five percent.*

per piacere *please.*

per lettera *by correspondence.*

una volta e per sempre *once and for all.*

È partita per Roma. *She left for Rome.*

L'ho fatto per te. *I did it for you.*

Lo mando per posta. *I send it by mail.*

Sarò lì per la fine del mese. *I will be there by the end of the month.*

pera *pear.*

percentuale, f. *percentage.*

percepire *to receive; to get.*

PERCHÈ, adv. *why; because; for; as; that; in order that;* n. *reason.*

Non sa il perchè. *He doesn't know the reason.*

Perchè no? *Why not?*

Senza un perchè *without any reason.*

Lo fa perchè è triste. *He does it because he is sad.*

Lo fa perchè tu non ti spaventi. *He does it so as not to frighten you.*

perciò *therefore, so.*

percorrere *to travel.*

percorso *route.*

PERDERE *to lose; to miss.*

perdere il treno *to miss the train.*

perdere terreno *to lose ground.*

perdersi *to lose oneself; to be spoiled; to go to ruin.*

perdita *loss, waste.*

PERDONARE *to forgive; to pardon; to excuse.*

È un male che non perdona. *It's an incurable disease.*

Perdonate il disturbo. *Excuse the trouble I'm giving.*

PERDONO *forgiveness, pardon.*

Le chiedo perdono. *I ask your forgiveness.*

perduto *lost, ruined, undone.*

perenne *perennial.*

perfetto *perfect.*

PERFEZIONE, f. *perfection, faultlessness.*

Ha raggiunto la perfezione. *He has reached perfection.*

perfino *even.*

PERICOLO *danger.*

Si trova in pericolo di vita. *He is in danger of losing his life.*

pericoloso *dangerous.*

periodico *magazine, periodical.*

periodo *period.*

perla *pearl.*

È una perla di marito. *He is the best of husbands.*

grigioperla *pearl gray.*

permanenza *permanence, stay.*

in permanenza *permanently.*

una lunga permanenza *a long stay.*

PERMESSO *permission, leave, permit, license.*

col vostro permesso *with your permission.*

È permesso. *May I come in?*

permesso di lavoro *work permit.*

permettere *to permit; to allow; to suffer.*

permettersi *to allow oneself; to take the liberty.*

pernottare *to stay overnight.*

PERÒ *but, nevertheless, yet, still.*

perossido *peroxide.*

perseguire *to pursue; to continue.*

perseguitare *to persecute; to harass.*

persistere *to persist.*

PERSONA *person.*

La signora è l'eleganza in persona. *The lady is the personification of elegance.*

Lo conosco di persona. *I know him personally.*

personaggio *character (in a play).*

personale, adj. *personal;* n. m. *staff, personnel.*
  opinione personale *personal opinion.*
  ufficio del personale *personnel department.*
personalità *personality.*
PERSUADERE *to persuade.*
pertinente *pertinent.*
pervenire *to reach.*
perversione *perversion.*
pesante *heavy.*
PESARE *to weigh.*
  Mi pesa sulla coscienza. *It weighs on my conscience.*
  Peso le mie parole. *I weigh my words.*
pesca *fishing; peach.*
  pesca della balena *whaling.*
  andare a pesca *to go fishing.*
pescare *to fish; to find out.*
  Cerco di pescare il significato. *I am trying to find the meaning.*
pescatore, m. *fisherman.*
PESCE, m. *fish.*
  Non è nè carne nè pesce. *He is neither fish nor fowl.*
  Non so che pesce pigliare. *I don't know which way to turn.*
peso *weight.*
pessimo *awful.*
petalo *petal.*
petrollo *oil (petroleum).*
pettegolare *to gossip.*
pettegolo *gossip, tattler.*
pettinare *to comb.*
pettine, m. *comb.*
petto *breast, chest.*
  Ha un bimbo al petto. *She has a child at her breast.*
  giacca a doppio-petto *double-breasted jacket.*
PEZZO *piece.*
  È tutto di un pezzo. *It's all in one piece.*
  L'aspetto da un pezzo. *I've been awaiting him for some time.*
  Lo faccio a pezzi. *I'll break it to pieces.*
PIACERE, n. m. *pleasure;* v. *to like; to be agreeable.*
  a piacere vostro *as you like it.*
  Fammi il piacere . . . *Do me the kindness . . .*

Per piacere. *Please.*
Non ho il piacere di conoscerlo. *I don't have the pleasure of his acquaintance.*
Non mi piace. *I do not like it.*
Piace alle masse. *It is liked by the masses.*
pianeta *planet.*
PIANGERE *to cry; to weep.*
  Mi piange il cuore. *My heart cries.*
  Piange la morte del suo amico. *He mourns the death of his friend.*
PIANO, n. *piano, plane, plan, floor;* adj. *flat, slow;* adv. *slowly; in a low voice, softly.*
  È un piano orizzontale. *It is a horizontal plane.*
  Questo è il mio piano. *This is my plan.*
  Sono al secondo piano. *I am on the third floor.*
pianoforte, m. *piano.*
planta *plant.*
plantare *to plant; to place; to leave, quit, or abandon.*
  Ci piantò *He left us.*
pianterreno *ground floor.*
pianto *weeping, crying.*
pianura *plain.*
piastrella *tile.*
piattaforma *platform.*
piattino *saucer.*
piatto, n. *plate;* adj. *flat.*
PIAZZA *square.*
  piazza del mercato *marketplace.*
  Ha fatto piazza pulita. *He cleared everything away.*
  Ha messo tutto in piazza. *He made everything public.*
picche, f. *spade (playing cards).*
picchiare *to beat; to strike.*
PICCOLO, adj. *little, small;* n. *little boy.*
  da piccolo *as a child.*
PIEDE, m. *foot.*
  prendere piede *to gain ground.*
  Sto in piedi. *I will stand.*
  Tiene il piede in due staffe. *He keeps in with both sides.*
  Vado a piedi. *I will walk there.*
  Vado a piedi nudi. *I go barefoot.*
piega *fold; crease.*

piegare *to fold; to bow; to bend.*
piego *folder.*
pieno *full.*
>in pieno inverno *in the dead of winter.*
>pieno fino all' orlo *full to the brim.*

PIETÀ *mercy, pity, piety, devotion.*
pietanza *dish of food; course.*
pietra *stone.*
pigione, f. *rent.*
pigliare *to take; to catch.*
pigrizia *laziness.*
pigro *lazy.*
pila *pile, battery.*
pillola *pill.*
pilota *pilot.*
pineta *pinewood.*
pinze, f. pl. *tongs.*
pioggia *rain.*
piombatura *filling.*
piombo *lead.*
PIOVERE *to rain.*
>Piove a dirotto. *It is raining heavily.*
>Sta per piovere. *It is about to rain.*

pipa *pipe.*
piroscafo *steamer.*
piscina *swimming pool.*
pisello *green pea.*
pisolino *nap.*
pista *track.*
pittore, m. *painter.*
pittura *painting.*
PIÙ *more, most.*
>a più non posso *to the utmost.*
>mai più *never again.*
>molto di più *much more.*
>per lo più *for the most part.*
>sempre più *more and more.*
>tutt'al più *at the most; at most.*
>La vidi più volte. *I saw her several times.*

piuma *feather.*
piuttosto *rather.*
pizzicare *to pinch; to prick.*
pizzo *lace.*
platea *orchestra seats, audience.*
plurale, m. *plural.*
pneumatico *tire.*
pochino *rather little; very little; short time; little while.*
POCO *little; a short time; a little while.*
>fra poco *in a little while.*
>poco a poco *little by little.*

poco fa *a short while ago.*
podere, m. *farm.*
poderoso *powerful; strong.*
poema, m. *poem.*
poesìa *poetry; short poem.*
poeta, m. *poet.*
POI *then, afterward.*
>da ora in poi *from now on.*
>prima o poi *now or later.*
>E poi? *and then?*

POICHÈ *for, as, since, because.*
polare *polar.*
polenta *corn meal porridge.*
policromo *polychrome.*
politica *politics.*
politico *political, politic.*
polizìa *police.*
poliziotto *policeman.*
pòlizza *policy.*
>pòlizza d'assicurazione contro gl'incendi *fire insurance.*

pòllice *thumb; big toe.*
POLLO *fowl, chicken.*
>pollo arrosto *roast chicken.*
>brodo di pollo *chicken broth.*

polmonite, f. *pneumonia.*
polsino *cuff, wristband.*
polso *wrist.*
poltrona *armchair; (theater) orchestra seat.*
POLVERE, f. *dust, powder.*
>caffè in polvere *ground coffee.*
>polvere da sparo *gun powder.*
>zucchero in polvere *powdered sugar.*
>Gettano la polvere negli occhi della gente. *They throw dust into the eyes of the people.*
>Quando parti l'automobile si alzò una nube di polvere. *A cloud of dust went up as the automobile left.*

pomeriggio *afternoon.*
pomodoro *tomato.*
>salsa di pomodoro *tomato sauce.*

pompelmo *grapefruit.*
pomplere, m. *fireman.*
ponente *west.*
PONTE, m. *bridge.*
>ponte di barche *pontoon bridge.*
>ponte ferroviario *railway bridge.*
>ponte levatoio *drawbridge.*

popolare adj. *popular;* v. *to inhabit.*
popolazione, f. *population, people.*

POPOLO *people, mob.*
porcellana *porcelain.*
porcheria *dirt; filth.*
porcino *edible mushroom.*
porco *pig.*
PORGERE *to give; to offer; to hand.*
  Mi porge la sua mano. *He offers me his hand.*
  Porgimi ascolto. *Listen to me. (Lend me your ears.)*
  Porgo il mio braccio alla signora. *I offer the lady my arm.*
porpora *purple.*
porre *to place; to put.*
PORTA *door.*
  Accompagnalo alla porta. *See him to the door.*
  È entrato dalla porta principale ed è uscito dalla porta secondaria. *He entered by the front door and left by the back door.*
  Si chiude una porta, se ne apre un'altra. *One opportunity is lost, but another presents itself.*
portabagagli *porter.*
portacenere, m. *ashtray.*
portamonete, m. *purse.*
PORTARE *to carry; to bring; to wear; to bear.*
  Il passaporto porta la mia firma. *The passport bears my signature.*
  Il vecchio porta bene gli anni. *The old man carries his years very well.*
  La signora porta bene quel cappotto. *The lady wears that coat well.*
  Porta il documento con te. *Carry the document with you.*
  Porta quest' anello alla signora. *Take (carry) this ring to the lady.*
portata *range.*
  a portata di braccio *within arm's length.*
portatile, adj. *portable;* n. *laptop computer.*
portatore *carrier.*
portavoce *spokesperson.*
portico *porch.*
portinalo *doorman.*
PORTO *harbor, refuge, port, haven.*
  porto affrancato *postage prepaid.*
  È il Capitano di porto. *He is the harbor-master.*

Condusse in porto la sua missione. *He accomplished his mission.*
portone, m. *gate; main entrance.*
porzione *portion; share.*
posare *to place.*
posate *silverware.*
POSITIVO *positive.*
  Cio è positivo. *That's for sure.*
POSIZIONE, f. *position, situation.*
  La casa è in una posizione meravigliosa. *The house is in a wonderful setting.*
  Mi trovo nella posizione di reclamare i miei diritti. *I am in a position to demand my rights.*
POSSEDERE *to own; to possess; to have.*
  Possiede molto denaro e molte buone qualità. *He has much money and many fine qualities.*
possessione, f. *possession, ownership.*
possesso *possession; estate; occupation.*
possessore *owner, proprietor.*
POSSIBILE *possible.*
  Al più presto possibile me ne andrò. *At the earliest possible time I will go.*
possibilità *possibility, power, opportunity.*
  Si presentano diverse possibilità eppur non abbiamo la possibilità di farlo. *Many possibilities present themselves and yet we don't have the power to carry them out.*
POSTA *post, mail, stall, stake.*
  È partito a bella posta. *He left purposely.*
  L'ho ricevuto per posta aerea. *I received it by air mail.*
  Mandalo per posta. *Send it by mail.*
  Parla al direttore delle poste. *Speak to the postmaster.*
  Raddoppiate la posta su questa corsa. *Double your stake on this race.*
  posta elettronica *e-mail.*
POSTALE *postal; of the post.*
  casella postale *post office box.*
  pacco postale *parcel.*
  spese postali *postage.*

timbro postale *postmark.*

ufficio postale *post office.*

vaglia postale *money order.*

posteriore *posterior; subsequent, back.*

posterità *posterity.*

posticipare *to postpone.*

postino *postman.*

POSTO *place, spot, space, situation, post, seat.*

Cambiamo posto. *Let's change seats.*

Ecco un posto libero. *Here is a vacant spot.*

Ho un posto riservato. *I have a reserved seat.*

Mi sento fuori posto qui. *I feel out of place here.*

Non c'è posto per tutti e due. *There is no room for both.*

Prendete i vostri posti. *Take your places (seats).*

Ha trovato un ottimo posto a Milano. *He found a fine position (job) in Milan.*

potabile *drinkable, potable.*

potente *powerful, mighty, influential.*

potenza *power, might.*

POTERE, n. m. *power;* v. *to be able; to be allowed; to be permitted; could; may; might.*

Gli hanno accordato pieni poteri. *They have accorded him full powers.*

Ha il potere di un re. *He has the power of a king.*

Il partito che ora è al potere cercherà di restarci. *The party that is now in power will seek to remain in power.*

Ho tentato a più non posso. *I tried my utmost.*

Non ne posso più. *I can't stand it anymore.*

Non posso farci nulla. *I can't help it.*

Non potei salvarlo perchè non potei parlare. *I could not save him because I was not permitted to speak.*

può darsi; può essere; potrebbe succedere. *It could happen; it might be; it could occur.*

Spero ch'lui possa arrivare, ma potrebbe aver perso il treno. *I*

hope he may arrive, but he might have missed the train.

POVERO *poor, unfortunate, unhappy, humble, late (deceased).*

il mio povero parere *my humble opinion.*

la mia povera sorella *my late sister.*

La nazione è povera di materie prime. *The nation is poor in raw materials.*

povertà *poverty.*

pozzanghera *puddle, pool.*

pozzo *well, tank.*

PRANZO *dinner, meal.*

Ho fatto un buon pranzo. *I had a good meal.*

prassi *use, practice.*

pratica *practice, experience, training.*

Devo fare le pratiche per poter partire. *I must take the necessary steps in order to leave.*

Ha fatto una lunga pratica per diventare avvocato. *He had a long training to become a lawyer.*

Ha molta pratica del suo mestiere. *He knows his job.*

Ho messo in pratica i suoi consigli. *I put your advice into practice.*

La pratica è la migliore maestra. *Practice is the best teacher.*

Mettiamo in pratica le nostre idee. *Let us put our ideas into practice.*

Preferisco la pratica alla teoria. *I prefer practice to theory.*

pratiche *negotiations, dealings.*

pratico *practical, experienced.*

Non sono pràtica di quel luogo. *I do not know that place.*

prato *meadow, grassland.*

precauzione, f. *precaution, care, caution.*

Procedi con molta precauzione. *Proceed with great caution.*

Usa le Dovute Precauzioni! *Use Due Caution!*

precedente, adj. *preceding, previous, former;* n. m. *precedent.*

La sua azione è senza precedenti. *His action is without precedent.*

durante un incontro precedente *during a previous meeting.*

precedenza *priority, yield.*

precedere *to precede; to go before.*
precipizio *precipice.*
> Corre a precipizio. *He runs headlong.*
> Si troverà sull'orlo del precipizio.
> *He will find himself on the edge
> of a precipice.*
preciso *precise, punctual, accurate,
exact.*
> Bisogna trovare il momento preciso.
> *We must find the precise moment.*
> Lui è preciso nei pagamenti. *He is
> punctual in his payments.*
prèdica *sermon, lecture.*
predicare *to preach; to lecture.*
> Lui prèdica bene e razzola male. *He
> does not practice what he
> preaches.*
prefazione *preface.*
preferenza *preference.*
> È chiara la sua preferenza per te. *It's
> obvious that he prefers you.*
preferire *to prefer.*
prefisso *area code; prefix.*
PREGARE *to pray; to request; to beg;
to ask; to invite.*
> Pregate Iddio! *Pray to God!*
> Prego! *Please! (or) You're welcome!*
> Sono pregati di entrare. *Please enter.*
> La prego di considerare. *I beg you to
> consider.*
preghiera *prayer, entreaty, request.*
> Dice le preghiere. *She says her
> prayers.*
> Dopo le mie preghiere, accettò
> l'invito. *After my requests, he
> accepted the invitation.*
> Ho una preghiera da farle. *I have a
> request to make of you.*
pregio *merit, worth, value.*
pregiudizio *prejudice.*
prego *You're welcome.*
preistoria *early history; prehistory.*
preistorico *prehistoric.*
prelevare *to withdraw (money).*
prelibato *exquisite.*
PREMERE *to press; to be urgent (or
pressing).*
> Mi preme molto. *It is of urgent
> importance to me.*
> Non mi preme. *It is of no
> importance to me.*
preminente *preeminent.*

PREMIO *prize, premium.*
> Gli conferirono il primo premio.
> *They conferred first prize on him.*
PREMURA *care; careful attention;
kindness; hurry.*
> Ho molta premura. *I am in a great
> hurry.*
> Ti circonda di premure. *He
> surrounds you with care.*
> Non c'è premura! *There is no hurry.*
> Una madre ha molte premure per il
> suo bambino. *A mother has many
> cares for her child.*
> La ringrazio delle sue premure. *I
> thank you for your kindnesses.*
PRENDERE *to take; to catch; to take
lodgings; to seize.*
> prendere il volo *to take off.*
> Che cosa ti prende? *What is the
> matter with you?*
> Fu preso dal rimorso. *He was
> overtaken with remorse.*
> L'ha preso in parola. *He took him at
> his word.*
> Lo prese per il collo e poi per i
> capelli. *He seized him by the neck
> and then by the hair.*
> Non mi prendo questa libertà. *I will
> not take this liberty.*
> Prende fuoco! *It is catching fire!*
> Prendo il treno delle tre. *I am taking
> the three o'clock train.*
> Prese tutto in considerazione. *He
> took everything into
> consideration.*
> Se la prese col portabagagli. *He put
> the blame on the porter.*
> Se ti prendo! *If I catch you!
> (colloq.).*
> Sto prendendo un raffreddore. *I am
> catching a cold.*
prenotare *to reserve; to book.*
PREPARARE *to prepare.*
> preparare un pasto/un discorso/un
> viaggio *to prepare a meal/a
> speech/a trip.*
> Preparati o farai tardi! *Get ready or
> you'll be late!*
preparasi *to get ready.*
preparazione *preparation.*
preposizione *preposition.*
prepotente *tyrannical, domineering.*

PRESENTARE *to present; to introduce.*

  Lui si presenta bene. *He makes a good impression (presents himself well).*

  Il viaggio presenta delle difficoltà. *The trip presents some difficulties.*

  Mi fu già presentato. *He has already been introduced to me.*

  Presentategli i miei ossequi. *Give him my best regards.*

  Quando si presenta l'occasione, bisogna prenderla. *When the opportunity presents itself, one must take it.*

  Questi problemi si presentano più volte. *These problems occur often.*

presente *present.*

  tempo presente *present time; present tense.*

  tener presente *to bear in mind.*

presenza *presence.*

  fare atto di presenza *to put in an appearance.*

  Non parlò in presenza del presidente. *He did not speak in the presence of the president.*

presidente *president.*

presidenza *presidency.*

pressappoco *approximately.*

pressione *pressure.*

PRESSO *near, by, beside, with.*

  presso la fontana *near the fountain.*

  qui presso *nearby.*

  Indirizza la lettera al Signor Berti, presso il Signor Augusti. *Address the letter to Mr. Berti, in care of Mr. Augusti.*

  Vivo presso mio zio. *I live with my uncle.*

  Lavoro presso una ditta italiana. *I work for an Italian firm.*

PRESTARE *to lend; to give; to offer.*

  prestare attenzione *to pay attention.*

  Lui si presta volentieri. *He offers himself willingly.*

  Non mi presto all'inganno. *I will not consent to this fraud.*

prestito *loan.*

  prendere in (or, a) prestito *to borrow.*

PRESTO *soon, early.*

  al più presto possibile *as soon as possible.*

  Fa presto! *Hurry up!*

  Mi alzo presto. *I get up early.*

  Presto o tardi lo sapremo. *We'll know sooner or later.*

  Si fa presto a dire. *It is easy to say.*

prete *priest.*

pretendere *to pretend; to claim; to exact.*

  Cosa pretendete? *What do you want (claim, exact)?*

  Non bisogna pretendere l'impossibile. *One must not exact the impossible.*

  Pretende d'aver detto il vero. *He claims to have told the truth.*

pretesa *pretension; claim to.*

  Non bisogna considerare la sua pretesa. *We must not consider his claim.*

pretesto *pretext.*

prevedere *to foresee.*

preventivo *estimate.*

prevenzione *prevention.*

previsione *forecast.*

  previsioni metereologiche *weather forecast.*

prezioso *precious.*

PREZZO *price.*

  Il listino dei prezzi da il prezzo all' ingrosso, il prezzo al minuto ed il prezzo netto. *The price list gives the wholesale price, the retail, and the net price.*

  Quella lezione l'ho pagata a caro prezzo. *I learned that lesson the hard way (at a high price).*

prigione, f. *prison.*

PRIMA, n. *first class (in travel); first grade (in school); first performance;* adv. *before, once, formerly, earlier, first.*

  per prima cosa *first.*

  prima di tutto *first of all.*

  Alzati prima. *Get up earlier.*

  Avvisatelo prima di arrivare. *Warn him before arriving.*

  Non sono più quella di prima. *I am no longer my former self.*

  Prima o poi ci arriveremo. *Sooner or later we'll get there.*

Questa era prima una chiesa e poi una cattedrale. *This was first a church and then a cathedral.*

Siamo più nemici di prima. *We are more enemies than we were.*

primavera *spring, springtime.*

È nella primavera della sua vita. *He is in the springtime (prime) of his life.*

PRIMO *first.*

Arrivò primo. *He arrived first.*

È il primo della classe. *He is the best in the class.*

È il primo della fila. *He is the first in line.*

Fu il primo a partire. *He was the first to leave.*

Ritornerà al primo del mese. *He will return the first of the month.*

principale, adj. *principal, chief, main;* n. m. *principal, employer, master.*

principalmente *chiefly, mainly.*

principe, m. *prince.*

principiante *beginner.*

PRINCIPIO *beginning, principle.*

dal principio alla fine *from beginning to end.*

È questione di principio. *It's a matter of principle.*

privare *to deprive.*

Mi sono privato di tutto. *I deprived myself of everything.*

Non mi privi del piacere. *Don't deprive me of the pleasure.*

PRIVATO *private.*

privo *devoid; lacking in.*

privo di mezzi finanziari *lacking financial means.*

privo di senso comune *devoid of common sense.*

Sono privo di sue notizie da due mesi. *I haven't heard from him in two months.*

pro *profit, advantage, benefit.*

a pro di *for the benefit of.*

A che pro? *What for?*

il pro ed il contro *the pros and cons.*

probabile *probable, likely.*

Non è probabile ch'io venga questa sera. *I am not likely to come tonight.*

probabilmente *probably.*

Probabilmente verrò. *I'll probably come.*

problema, m. *problem.*

un problema di carattere personale *a personal problem.*

PROCEDERE v. *to proceed; to go on;* m. *conduct, passing.*

Il lavoro procede molto lentamente. *The work is going on very slowly.*

La neve ci impedisce di procedere. *The snow makes it impossible for us to proceed.*

Procediamo con calma. *Let us proceed calmly.*

col procedere degli anni *with the passing years.*

procedura *procedure.*

procedura legale *legal procedure.*

processo *process, trial.*

processo per assassinio *murder trial.*

prodigare *to lavish.*

Mi ha prodigato le sue cure con affetto. *He lavished his cares on me affectionately.*

prodigioso *prodigious.*

PRODOTTO *product.*

prodotti agricoli *agricultural products.*

PRODURRE *to produce; to cause.*

produrre una reazione *to cause a reaction.*

Lui produce articoli di lusso. *He produces luxury items.*

produzione, f. *production.*

professionale *professional.*

professione, f. *profession.*

professore, m. *professor.*

profilo *profile; sketch, outline.*

profitto *profit, benefit.*

profondo *deep, profound.*

a notte profonda *in the deep of night.*

cadere in sonno profondo *to fall into a deep sleep.*

profondo rispetto *profound respect.*

profugo *refugee.*

profumare *to perfume.*

profumarsi *to put perfume on.*

profumato *scented, sweet-smelling.*

profumo *perfume.*

progettare *to project; to make plans.*

progetto *plan.*
  aver in mente un progetto *to have a plan in mind.*
  fare progetti *to make plans.*

programma, m. *program.*
  programma di videoscrittura *word processor.*
  in programma *on the program.*

progredire *to make progress.*

progresso *progress.*
  Lui sta facendo grandi progressi negli studi. *He is making great progress in his studies.*

proibire *to forbid; to prohibit.*
  È proibito l'ingresso. *No admittance.*
  Mia madre mi ha proibito di uscire questa sera. *My mother has forbidden me to go out tonight.*

prolettare *to project.*

proiezione *projection.*

prole, f. *descent, offspring.*

prolungare *to prolong.*

promessa *promise.*
  fare una promessa *to make a promise.*
  venire meno ad una promessa *to break a promise.*

promettere *to promise.*
  prometto di scriverti spesso. *I promise I'll write often.*

prominente *prominent.*
  Lui è una figura prominente nel mondo scientifico. *He is a prominent figure in the world of science.*

prominenza *prominence.*

promotore *promoter, organizer.*

promozione *promotion.*

promuovere *to promote; to further.*

pronipote m. & f. *great-grandchild.*

pronome, m. *pronoun.*

prontezza *readiness, promptness.*
  prontezza di spirito *presence of mind.*

pronto *Hello! (answering phone);* adj. *ready, prompt.*
  in attesa di una sua pronta risposta *awaiting your prompt reply.*
  Siamo pronti! *We are ready!*

pronuncia *pronunciation.*

pronunciare *to pronounce; to utter.*

  Rimase lì senza pronunciare parola. *He just stayed there without saying a word.*
  pronunciare bene *to pronounce well, to have good diction.*

propaganda *advertising.*
  far molta propaganda *to advertise well.*

proporre *to propose.*

proporzionale *proportional.*

proporzione, f. *proportion.*
  fuori proporzione *out of proportion.*

PROPOSITO *purpose, intention.*
  a proposito *by the way.*
  cattivi propositi *with bad intentions.*
  di proposito *on purpose.*
  A che proposito te ne ha parlato? *How come he spoke to you about it?*

proposta *proposal, proposition.*

proprietà *property, ownership.*
  La casa è di sua proprietà. *The house is hers.*
  Questo libro è proprietà mia. *This book is my property.*

proprietario *proprietor, owner.*

PROPRIO, adj. *own; one's own;* adv. *just, exactly.*
  la propria casa *one's own home.*
  nome proprio *proper noun.*
  Veste con un gusto che le è proprio. *She dresses with a taste that is all her own.*
  proprio in questo momento *at this very moment.*
  proprio mentre *just as.*
  proprio ora *just now.*
  È proprio come dico io. *It is exactly as I say.*
  Proprio! *Exactly!*

proroga *extension.*

prosa *prose.*

prosciutto *ham.*

proseguire *to go on; to continue.*
  Da Napoli proseguimmo per Roma. *From Naples we went on to Rome.*

prosperità *prosperity.*

prospero *prosperous.*

prospettiva *perspective, prospect.*

prossimità *proximity.*
  in prossimità *in the vicinity of.*

PROSSIMO *next, near.*
in un prossimo futuro *in the near future.*
la settimana prossima *next week.*
Siamo prossimi a partire. *We are about to go.*
protagonista *protagonist; main character.*
PROTEGGERE *to protect; to safeguard.*
Ognuno cerca di proteggere i propri interessi. *Everyone tries to protect his own interests.*
Ti protegga Iddio! *May God protect you!*
protesta *protest, protestation.*
fare protesta *to protest; to make a protest.*
protestare *to protest.*
protestare contro *to protest against.*
protettivo *protective.*
protetto *protected.*
protezione, f. *protection.*
PROVA *proof, rehearsal, trial.*
fare una prova *to try; to rehearse.*
fino a prova contraria *till there is proof to the contrary.*
fornire le prove *to furnish evidence.*
Ha dato prova di coraggio. *He gave proof of courage.*
prova generale *dress rehearsal (theater).*
provare *to prove; to try; to rehearse.*
provare la verità *to prove the truth.*
Vogliamo provare questa scena? *Shall we rehearse this scene?*
Voglio provare a farlo. *I want to try to do it.*
provenienza *origin, source.*
provenire *to originate; to come from.*
proverbio *proverb, saying.*
come dice il proverbio *as the saying goes.*
provincia *province.*
provinciale *provincial.*
provocare *to provoke.*
provvedere *to provide; to supply.*
Bisogna provvedere ai bisognosi. *We must provide for the needy.*
Siamo provvisti di tutto il necessario. *We have provided ourselves with all the necessities.*

provvidenza *providence.*
Divina Provvidenza *Divine Providence.*
provvidenziale *providential.*
provvisoriamente *temporarily.*
provvisorio *temporary.*
condizioni provvisorie *temporary conditions.*
in via provvisoria *temporarily.*
provvista *supply.*
Abbiamo un' ottima provvista di viveri in casa. *We have ample supply of foodstuffs in the house.*
prudente *prudent, wise.*
Non credo sia prudente uscire di casa con questo temporale. *I don't think it is wise to go out in this storm.*
prudenza *prudence, wisdom.*
dimostrare prudenza *to display prudence.*
PUBBLICARE *to publish.*
pubblicazione *publication.*
pubblicità *advertising.*
pubblico, n. *audience, public;* adj. *public.*
esibirsi in pubblico *to appear in public.*
Il pubblico lo applaudì calorosamente. *The audience applauded him warmly.*
giardino pubblico *park; public garden.*
pugno *fist, punch.*
dare un pugno *to punch.*
di proprio pugno *in one's own handwriting.*
fare a pugni *to fight.*
stringere i pugni *to clench one's fists.*
pulce, f. *flea.*
pulcino *chick.*
PULIRE *to clean.*
pulirsi *to clean oneself.*
pulito *clean.*
con la coscienza pulita *with a clear conscience.*
pulizia *cleanliness.*
fare la pulizìa *to do the cleaning.*
pulsante *buzzer.*
PUNGERE *to prick; to sting.*
Mi ha punto un' ape. *A bee stung me.*

91

Mi sono punta un dito con una spilla. *I pricked my finger with a pin.*

punire *to punish.*

punizione, f. *punishment.*

subire una punizione *to endure punishment.*

PUNTA *point, tip.*

fare la punta ad una matita *to sharpen a pencil.*

Cammino in punta di piedi per non fare rumore. *I'm tiptoeing so as not to make noise.*

Il suo nome è sulla punta della mia lingua. *His name is on the tip of my tongue.*

punteggiatura *punctuation.*

punteggio *score.*

puntino *dot, point.*

mettere i puntini sulle i *to get things straight.*

punto *stitch, point.*

alle tre in punto *at three o'clock sharp.*

due punti *colon.*

di punto in bianco *all of a sudden.*

fino a un certo punto *to a certain extent.*

punto di partenza *point of departure.*

punto di vista *point of view.*

punto e virgola *semicolon.*

punto fermo *period.*

venire al punto *to come to the point.*

puntuale *punctual.*

puntualità *punctuality.*

puntura *injection; insect bite.*

purchè *provided that.*

PURE *also, too.*

Andiamo pure noi. *We are going too.*

Venga pure! *Do come!*

puro *pure, mere.*

acqua pura *pure water.*

per puro caso *by mere chance.*

PURTROPPO *unfortunately.*

Q

QUÀ *here.*

Vieni quà! *Come here!*

quaderno *notebook.*

quadrato, n. & adj. *square.*

quadri, m. *diamond (playing cards).*

quadro *square picture, painting.*

A quale parete vuole che appenda questo quadro? *On which wall do you want this picture hung?*

QUAGGIÙ *here below; down here.*

Guarda quaggiù, in fondo alla pagina. *Look down here, at the bottom of the page.*

Ti aspetto quaggiù, ai piedi della scala. *I'll wait for you here below, at the foot of the stairs.*

qualche *some, any.*

qualcheduno *someone, somebody.*

qualcuno *somebody, someone, anybody.*

QUALE *which, who, whom.*

Quale scegli? *Which do you choose?*

Le persone alle quali hai esteso l'invito sono arrivate. *The people to whom you have extended an invitation have arrived.*

qualificare *to qualify.*

qualificato *qualified.*

qualità *quality.*

qualsìasi *any.*

qualunque *whatever, any.*

QUANDO *when, while.*

da quando *since.*

di quando in quando *from time to time.*

quando mai *whenever.*

Quando sei arrivato? *When did you arrive?*

Ti scrissi quand'ero in Italia. *I wrote you while I was in Italy.*

quantità *quantity.*

QUANTO,-A,-I,-E *how much; how many; as many as.*

quanto prima *in a short while.*

Quanti ne abbiamo oggi? *What is today's date?*

Quanti ne vuole? *How many do you want?*

Quanto mi fa pagare? *How much will you charge me?*

Quanto tempo? *How long?*

quaranta *forty.*

quarantesimo *fortieth.*

quaresima *Lent.*

quartiere, m. *quarters, lodging,*
   neighborhood.
   quartier generale *headquarters.*
quarto *fourth, quarter, half pint.*
   tre quarti *three-fourths.*
   un quarto di vino *quarter-liter (half*
     pint) of wine.
   un quarto d'ora *a quarter of an hour.*
QUASI *almost.*
QUASSÙ *up here.*
quattordicesimo *fourteenth.*
quattordici *fourteen.*
quattro *four.*
quattrocento *four hundred.*
   nel Quattrocento *in the fifteenth*
     century.
quattromila *four thousand.*
quello *that one; that.*
   Mi dia quello. *Give me that one.*
   Quel libro mi appartiene. *That book*
     belongs to me.
questione, f. *question, argument.*
questo *this; this one.*
   Questo non è affare mio. *This is*
     none of my business.
questura *police station.*
QUI *here; in this place.*
   Qui non c'è nessuno. *There is no*
     one here.
   Vieni qui! *Come here!*
quietare *to calm, to quiet.*
   quietarsi *to become calm; to become*
     quiet.
quiete, f. *quiet, tranquillity, stillness.*
quieto *quiet, calm, still.*
   star quieto *to be still; to be quiet.*
QUINDI *therefore.*
quindicesimo *fifteenth.*
quindici *fifteen.*
quindicimila *fifteen thousand.*
quintale, m. *one hundred kilograms in*
   weight.
   Ho un quintale di lavoro da fare. *I*
     have a tremendous amount of
     work to do.
quinte *backstage; (theater) wings.*
quinto, adj. *fifth;* n. *one-fifth.*
quota *share.*
quotare *to assess; to quote (prices).*
quotazione *quotation (of prices).*
quotidiano *daily.*
   giornale quotidiano *daily paper.*

R

rabbia *rage, ire.*
rabbino *rabbi.*
rabbioso *irate, wrathful.*
racchetta *racket.*
racchia *unattractive girl; dog.*
racchiudere *to contain; to enclose.*
raccogliere *to gather; to collect.*
raccolta *collection.*
raccolto *harvest.*
raccomandare *to recommend.*
   lettera raccomandata *registered letter.*
   raccomandarsi a *to appeal to.*
raccomandazione *recommendation.*
raccontare *to tell; to narrate.*
   Mi ha raccontato la storia della sua
     vita. *He told me the story of his*
     life.
racconto *story, tale.*
raddoicire *to sweeten.*
raddoppiare *to double.*
   Gli hanno raddoppiato lo stipendio.
     They doubled his salary.
raddrizzare *to straighten.*
radere *to shave.*
   farsi radere la barba *to get a shave.*
radice, f. *root, origin.*
radio, f. *radio;* m. *radium.*
radiografia *X ray.*
rado *rare.*
   di rado *seldom.*
raffinare *to refine.*
   una persona raffinata *a refined*
     person.
raffinatezza *refinement.*
raffreddare *to cool; to chill.*
   raffreddarsi *to catch cold.*
raffreddore, m. *cold.*
ragazza *girl.*
   nome da ragazza *maiden name.*
RAGAZZO *boy; young man.*
raggiante *radiant.*
   La sposa era raggiante. *The bride*
     was radiant.
raggio *ray.*
   un raggio di sole *a ray of sunshine.*
raggiungere *to reach; to arrive; to*
   catch up with.
   raggiungere una destinazione *to*
     reach a destination.

raggiungere una meta *to reach a goal.*

Era partito prima di me ma l'ho raggiunto. *He had left before me but I caught up with him.*

ragionare *to reason; to discuss logically.*

Ognuno ragiona a modo proprio. *Each person reasons in his own way.*

Lui non ragiona. *He is not logical; he has lost his reason.*

RAGIONE, f. *reason.*

a ragione del vero *in truth.*

a torto o a ragione *right or wrong.*

aver ragione *to be right.*

senza ragione *without reason.*

Ho le mie buone ragioni. *I have my good reasons.*

Non ha nessuna ragione di farlo. *He has no reason to do it.*

ragionevole *reasonable.*

ragionevolmente *reasonably.*

ragioniere, m. *bookkeeper.*

ragno *spider.*

RAGÙ *meat sauce.*

rallegrare *to cheer; to make happy.*

Me ne rallegro! *I am happy about it!*

Si è rallegrato con me. *He extended his felicitations to me. He congratulated me.*

rallentare *to loosen; to slow down.*

rallentare la stretta *to lessen the grip.*

rallentare la velocità *to reduce speed.*

rame, m. *copper.*

rammaricar(si) *to grieve.*

rammentare *to remember.*

Me ne rammento perfettamente. *I remember perfectly well.*

ramo *branch.*

in ogni ramo della scienza *in every branch of science.*

ramo d'albero *branch of a tree.*

rana *frog.*

rancore, m. *resentment.*

serbar rancore a *to bear a grudge against.*

rannuvolarsi *to cloud over; to darken.*

Il cielo si rannuvola. *The sky is clouding.*

Si è rannuvolato in viso. *His expression darkened.*

RAPIDO *rapid, speedy.*

dare uno sguardo rapido *to give a quick glance.*

treno rapido *express train.*

rapportare *to report; to repeat.*

Non è bello rapportare tutto ciò che si vede e si sente. *It is not nice to repeat everything one sees and hears.*

rapporto *report.*

Mi ha mandato un rapporto sul lavoro compiuto. *He sent me a report on the completed work.*

rappresentante, m. *representative.*

rappresentare *to represent.*

rappresentazione, f. *representation, performance.*

È la prima rappresentazione di questa commedia. *This is the first performance of this play.*

raramente *rarely.*

raro *rare; uncommon.*

raso *satin.*

rasòio *razor.*

lametta da rasòio *razor blade.*

rassegna *exhibit; show.*

rassegnazione, f. *self-resignation, resignation.*

rasserenarsi *to clear up (weather).*

rassicurare *to reassure.*

rassicurarsi *to reassure oneself.*

rassicurazione, f. *reassurance.*

rassomiglianza *resemblance.*

rastrello *rake.*

rata *installment.*

ratificare *to ratify.*

rattristare *to sadden.*

rauco *hoarse.*

ravioli *ravioli.*

razionale *rational.*

razione, f. *ration.*

razza *race.*

razziale *racial.*

razzismo *racism.*

razzista *racist.*

razzo *rocket.*

re *king.*

reagire *to react.*

reale *royal, real.*

nella vita reale *in real life.*

in casa reale *the Royal House.*

un avvenimento reale *a true happening.*

REALIZZARE *to fulfill, to carry out.*

   realizzare un progetto *to carry out a project.*

realizzazione *fulfillment.*

   realizzazione personale *personal gratification.*

realmente *really.*

reato *crime.*

reazionario *reactionary.*

reazione, f. *reaction.*

recapitare *to deliver.*

recapito *address.*

recare *to bring.*

recensione *review.*

recensire *to review (a play, a book, a performance).*

recente *recent.*

recinto *enclosure.*

recipiente, m. *receptacle.*

reciproco *reciprocal.*

recitare *to recite; to play.*

   recitare la parte di Amleto *to play the part of Hamlet.*

reclamo *complain.*

recluta *recruit.*

redattore *reporter.*

redazione, f. *editor's office.*

reddito *revenue; income.*

redigere *to draft; to compose.*

   redigere un contratto *to draw up a contract.*

redimere *to redeem.*

reduce, m. *veteran.*

referenza *reference, information.*

regalare *to make a present.*

regalo *gift, present.*

   fare un regalo a *to give a present to.*

regata *regatta, boat race.*

reggere *to support, to hold.*

reggiseno *brassiere, bra.*

regia *directory (movie, TV).*

regime *regime, regimen.*

regina *queen.*

regionale *regional.*

regione, f. *region.*

regista *director (movie, theater).*

registrare *to register; to record.*

registratore magnètico, m. *tape recorder.*

registrazione, f. *registration, recording.*

registro *book, register.*

regno *realm, kingdom.*

regola *rule, regulation.*

   secondo la regola *according to regulations.*

   L'eccezione conferma la regola. *The exception proves the rule.*

regolamento *rule, regulation.*

regolare, adj. *regular;* v. *to regulate.*

   regolare un conto *to pay a bill.*

   regolarsi *to behave.*

regolarmente *regularly.*

relativamente *relatively.*

relativo, adj. *relative.*

relazione, f. *report, relationship.*

   fare una relazione *to make a report.*

   Non c'è relazione fra una cosa e l'altra. *There's no relation between one thing and the other.*

religione, f. *religion.*

religioso *religious.*

remare *to row.*

remo *oar.*

remoto *remote.*

rendere *to render; to make; to return.*

   rendere bene per male *to render good for evil.*

   rendere grazie *to thank.*

   rendere infelice *to make unhappy.*

   Mi ha reso il libro. *He returned the book to me.*

   Questo lavoro non rende molto. *There is little return for this work.*

rene, m. *kidney.*

reparto *department.*

   capo reparto *department head.*

repressione, f. *repression.*

reprimere *to repress.*

   reprimere uno sbadiglio *to stifle a yawn.*

   Non riesco a reprimere le lacrime. *I can't hold back the tears.*

repubblica *republic.*

reputazione, f. *reputation.*

   godere di un ottima reputazione *to have a good reputation.*

resa *surrender.*

residente, adj. & n.m. *resident.*

residenza *residence.*

   cambiamento di residenza *change of address.*

resistente *resistant.*

resistenza *resistance, endurance.*

resistere *to resist; to withstand.*
> resistere alla prova *to withstand the test.*
> resistere all'avversità *to resist against adversity.*

respingere *to drive back; to reject.*
> essere respinto ad un esame *to fail an exam.*
> Ha respinto la mia domanda. *He rejected my application.*

respirare *to breathe; to take a breath.*
> respirare a pieni polmoni *to take a deep breath.*

respiro *breath.*
> avere il respiro corto *to be out of breath.*
> trattenere il respiro *to hold one's breath.*

responsabile *responsible.*

responsabilità *responsibility.*

RESTARE *to remain; to stay.*
> restare a pranzo *to stay for dinner.*
> restare indietro *to lag behind.*
> Non restano che due giorni alla partenza. *There are only two days left before our departure.*

restaurare *to restore.*

restauro *restoration.*
> il restauro della Cappella Sistina *the Sistine Chapel restoration.*

restituire *to give back; to return.*
> Devo restituire questo libro. *I must return this book.*

RESTO *remainder, rest, change.*
> Il resto del lavoro lo finisco io. *I will finish the remainder of the work.*
> Il resto non conta. *The rest is of no matter.*
> Potete tenere il resto. *You may keep the change.*

restringere *to contract; to shrink.*

rete f. *net.*
> cadere in una rete *to fall into a trap.*
> rete da tennis *tennis net.*

retro *back.*

retrocedere *to go back; to retreat.*

retta *straight line; attention.*
> dare retta a *to listen to.*

rettangolo *rectangle.*

rettificare *to rectify.*

revisionare *to revise.*

revisione *revision.*

rialzare *to lift up again; to rise.*
> rialzare i prezzi *to raise the prices.*

riassunto *summary.*

ribalta *footlight.*

ribasso *decline, reduction.*

ribelle, m. *rebel.*

ribellione, f. *rebellion.*

ricambiare *to reciprocate; to return.*

ricamo *embroidery.*

ricavo *revenue.*
> ricavi netti consolidati *consolidated net revenues.*

ricchezza *wealth.*

riccio *curl, lock (of hair).*

ricco *rich, wealthy.*

ricerca *research, demand.*
> andare alla ricerca di *to go in search of.*

ricercare *to search for; to investigate.*

RICETTA *prescription, recipe.*
> Porta questa ricetta al farmacista. *Take this prescription to the druggist.*
> Questa è la ricetta per fare il ragù. *This is the recipe for making sauce.*

RICEVERE *to receive.*
> ricevere ospiti *to receive guests.*
> ricevere posta *to receive mail.*

ricevimento *reception.*

ricevitore, m. *receiver.*
> staccare il ricevitore *to lift the receiver.*

ricevuta *receipt.*

richiedente, m. *applicant.*

RICHIEDERE *to request; to ask again; to require.*
> Ho richiesto i soldi che mi deve. *I asked for the money he owes me.*
> Il signor Alberti richiede l'onore ... *Mr. Alberti requests the honor ...*
> Questo lavoro richiede tutto il mio tempo. *This work requires all of my time.*

RICHIESTA *request, application.*
> dietro richiesta di ... *at the request of ...*
> fare richiesta d'ammissione *to apply for admission.*

riciciaggio *recycling.*

riciciare *to recycle.*

ricominciare *to recommence; to start again.*

RICOMPENSA *reward, recompense.*

ricompensare *to reward; to recompense.*
È stato ampiamente ricompensato. *He was amply rewarded.*

riconciliare *to reconcile.*

riconciliazione, f. *reconciliation.*

riconoscente *grateful, thankful.*

riconoscere *to recognize; to admit.*
riconoscere i propri torti *to admit one's fault.*
L'ho riconosciuto subito. *I recognized him immediately.*

ricoprire *to cover.*
ricoprire un carica *to hold an office.*

RICORDARE *to remember.*
Non me ne ricordo. *I don't remember it.*
Per quanto ricordo. *As far as I remember.*

RICORDO *memory, remembrance, recollection.*
Ho un vago ricordo dei miei primi anni. *I have a vague recollection of my first years.*
Lo terrò per ricordo. *I'll keep it as a remembrance.*

ricorrente *recurrent.*

ricorrere *to apply to; to report.*

ricostruire *to rebuild.*

ricoverare *to shelter; to give shelter.*
ricoverare in ospedale *to admit to the hospital.*
ricoverarsi *to take shelter; to take refuge.*

ricovero *shelter.*

ricreare *to recreate; to entertain.*

RICUPERO *recovery, salvage.*
capacità di ricupero *power of recovery.*

RIDERE *to laugh.*

ridicolo *ridiculous.*

ridotto *reduced.*
mal ridotto *in poor shape.*
prezzo ridotto *reduced price.*

RIDURRE *to reduce.*
ridurre le spese *to cut down expenses.*

riduzione, f. *reduction.*

RIEMPIRE *to fill.*
riempire una bottiglia *to fill a bottle.*
riempire un modulo *to fill out a blank.*
riempirsi *to fill up; to stuff oneself.*
vederti mi riempie di gioia *seeing you fills me with joy.*

rientrare *to come in again; to be included.*

rifare *to remake; to restore.*

riferimento *reference.*

riferire *to report; to relate.*
Mi ha riferito quanto è accaduto. *He told me what happened.*
Non mi riferivo a lui. *I was not referring to him.*

RIFIUTARE *to refuse; to decline.*
Ha rifiutato d'accompagnarmi. *He refused to accompany me.*
Sono costretto a rifiutare l'invito. *I am obliged to decline the invitation.*

rifiuto *refusal, waste.*

riflessione, f. *reflection, consideration.*
dopo matura riflessione *upon further consideration.*

riflessivo *thoughtful; reflective.*

riflesso *reflection.*
Ho visto il mio riflesso nello specchio. *I saw my reflection in the mirror.*

riflettere *to reflect; to think.*
La luna riflette i raggi del sole. *The moon reflects the sun's rays.*
Ho riflettuto bene prima di decidere. *I thought at length before making up my mind.*

riforma *reform.*

riformare *to reform.*

rifugio *refuge, shelter.*

RIGA *line, row, ruler.*
farsi la riga nei capelli *to make a part in one's hair.*
in riga *in a row.*
scrivere poche righe *to write a few lines.*
stoffa a righe *striped material.*

rigido *rigid.*

rigoroso *rigorous.*

RIGUARDO *regard, respect.*
per riguardo a *out of respect for.*

senza riguardo *without regard.*

Sotto questo riguardo ha perfettamente ragione. *In this respect he is perfectly right.*

rilasciare *to leave; to issue; to free.*

rilassare *to slacken.*

rilassarsi *to relax; to become lax.*

rilegare *to bind (a book).*

rilegato in pelle *a leather-bound book.*

rileggere *to reread.*

rilevare *to point out; to perceive; to learn.*

RILIEVO *relief.*

basso rilievo *bas-relief.*

mettere in rilievo *to point out; to emphasize.*

riluttante *reluctant.*

riluttanza *reluctance.*

con riluttanza *reluctantly.*

rimandare *to send back; to postpone.*

Bisogna rimandare questo appuntamento. *We must postpone this appointment.*

Gli ho rimandato il libro che mi aveva prestato. *I sent back the book he lent me.*

RIMANERE *to remain; to stay.*

Rimane poco tempo. *Little time remains.*

rimanere male *to be disappointed.*

Siamo rimasti fuori casa per due giorni. *We stayed away from home for two days.*

rimborsare *to repay.*

rimedio *remedy.*

Non c'è rimedio. *There is nothing to be done about it.*

RIMETTERE *to put back; to put again; to remit; to lose.*

Favorite rimettere la somma di . . . *Please remit the sum of . . .*

Ho rimesso parecchio in questo affare. *I lost quite a good deal in this business affair.*

Ho rimesso tutto a posto. *I put everything back in place.*

rimodernare *to modernize.*

rimorso *remorse.*

rimpiangere *to regret.*

rimproverare *to reproach; to scold.*

rimprovero *reproach, reprimand.*

RIMUOVERE *to remove; to dismiss.*

rinascimento *rebirth.*

Rinascimento *Renaissance.*

rinascita *rebirth; Renaissance.*

rincarare *to raise.*

rincarare i prezzi *to raise prices.*

rincorrere *to pursue.*

rincrescimento *regret.*

rinforzo *reinforcement.*

rinfrescare *to cool; to refresh.*

rinfrescarsi *to refresh oneself.*

rinfresco *refreshment.*

ringraziamento *thanks, thanksgiving.*

RINGRAZIARE *to thank.*

RIPARARE *to repair; to mend.*

riparazione, f. *repair, reparation.*

RIPARO *shelter.*

a riparo da *sheltered from.*

ripartire *to divide; to share.*

ripassare *to look over again.*

ripetere *to repeat.*

ripetizione, f. *repetition.*

ripieno *stuffed; stuffing.*

tacchino ripieno *stuffed turkey.*

RIPOSARE *to rest.*

riposo *rest.*

riprodurre *to reproduce.*

riproduzione *reproduction.*

Riproduzione vietata. *All rights reserved.*

risata *laugh, laughter.*

riscaldamento *heater.*

riscaldare *to warm; to heat.*

rischiare *to risk.*

rischio *risk.*

riscontrare *to check; to find.*

riserbo *discretion, secrecy.*

RISO *rice; laughter.*

riso amaro *bitter laughter.*

riso con piselli *rice with peas.*

risoluto *determined, resolute.*

risoluzione, f. *resolution.*

prendere una risoluzione *to resolve, to decide.*

risorgere *to rise again.*

RISPARMIARE *to save.*

risparmiare tempo *to save time.*

risparmio *saving.*

cassa di risparmio *savings bank.*

RISPETTARE *to respect.*

rispettare le leggi *to respect the laws.*

rispetto *respect.*

RISPETTOSO *respectful.*

RISPONDERE *to answer.*
> rispondere ad una lettera *to answer a letter.*
> rispondere al telefono *to answer the telephone.*

RISPOSTA *answer, reply.*

ristorante, m. *restaurant.*

ristretto *contracted, narrow, limited.*

risultare *to result.*
> risultarne *to result from.*

risultato *result.*

RISVEGLIARE *to awaken; to reawaken.*

risvolto *lapel.*

RITARDARE *to delay; to be late.*

ritardo *delay.*
> essere in ritardo *to be late.*

ritegno *discretion, reservedness.*

ritirare *to withdraw.*
> andare a ritirare un pacco *to go and pick up a package.*

ritmo *rhythm.*

RITORNARE *to return; to go back to.*
> tornare a casa *to come back home.*
> Non ritornero più. *I will never go back.*

RITORNO *return.*
> Attendo con ansia il tuo ritorno. *I anxiously await your return.*
> Sarò di ritorno alle cinque. *I will be back at five.*

RITRATTO *portrait.*
> Questo è un mio ritratto fatto due anni fa. *This is a portrait of me taken two years ago.*

ritrovare *to find.*

ritrovo *club.*

ritto *straight.*

riunlone *meeting.*

riunire *to reunite.*

RIUSCIRE *to succeed; to be able.*
> Non riesco a farlo. *I am not able to do it.*
> È riuscito a far fortuna. *He succeeded in making a fortune.*

rivale, adj. & n.m. *rival.*

rivedere *to see again; to review.*

rivelare *to reveal.*

rivenditore, m. *merchant.*

rivolgere *to turn; to address.*

rivoluzionare *to revolutionize.*

rivoluzione, f. *revolution.*

roba *things, goods, stuff.*

robusto *robust.*

rocca *fortress.*

roccia *rock.*

romanico *Romanesque; Romance (language).*

romano, adj. & n. *Roman.*

romanticismo *romanticism.*

romantico *romantic.*

romanzo *novel.*
> lingue romanze *Romance languages.*

ROMPERE *to break.*
> rompere relazioni con *to break off with.*
> Ho rotto un bicchiere. *I broke a glass.*

rondine, f. *swallow.*

ronzare *to hum; to buzz.*

rosa, n. & adj. *rose*

roseo *rosy; pink.*

rosone *rose window.*

rossetto *lipstick.*

rosso *red.*
> veder rosso *to see red.*

rossore, m. *redness.*
> Il rossore le salì alle guance. *She blushed.*

rotale *railroad track.*

ròtolo *roll, scroll.*

ROTONDO *round.*

rotta *course, rout.*

rotto *broken.*

rottura *break; fracture.*

rovesciare *to overthrow; to pour.*

rovescio, n. & adj. *reverse.*
> il rovescio della medaglia *the other side of the medal.*
> Si è messo il vestito a rovescio. *He put his suit on wrong side out.*

rovina *ruin.*

ROVINARE *to ruin.*

rozzo *rough, coarse.*

rubare *to steal.*
> Ha rubato un orologio. *He stole a watch.*

rubinetto *faucet.*

ruga *wrinkle.*

ruggine, f. *rust.*

rugiada *dew.*

RUMORE, m. *noise.*

far rumore *to make noise.*
rumoroso *noisy.*
ruolo *role.*
RUOTA *wheel.*
rurale *rural.*
ruscello *stream.*
russare *to snore.*
russo, adj. & n. *Russian.*
rustico *rustic.*
ruvido *rough.*

S

sabato *Saturday.*
sabbatico *sabbatical.*
sabbia *sand.*
sabbioso *sandy.*
sacco *bag, sack.*
sacrificare *to sacrifice.*
sacrilegio *sacrilege.*
sacro *sacred.*
  l'osso sacro *sacrum.*
saggezza *wisdom.*
saggio *wise.*
SALA *hall.*
  sala da ballo *ballroom.*
  sala da pranzo *dining room.*
  sala d'aspetto *waiting room.*
  sala operatoria *operating room.*
salame *salami.*
salare *to salt.*
salario *wage.*
salassare *to bleed; to fleece; to soak.*
salato *salty.*
saldo *firm, balanced.*
SALE, m. *salt.*
  aver sale in zucca *to have good
    sense (colloq.).*
salire *to go up.*
  salire le scale *to go up the stairs.*
  salir su per la montagna *to climb up
    the hill.*
salita *ascent, ascension, slope.*
  Questa strada è in salita. *This street
    is on an incline.*
salotto *parlor.*
salsa *sauce.*
salsiccia *sausage.*
SALTARE *to jump; to jump over; to
  skip.*

saltare di palo in frasca *to stray from
    the subject.*
  saltare fuori *to pop up.*
  saltare giù dal letto *to jump out of
    bed.*
  Bisogna saltare questo fosso. *We
    have to jump over this hurdle
    (ditch).*
  Ha saltato una pagina intera. *He
    skipped a whole page.*
  Non ti far saltare la mosca al naso.
    Don't get angry (colloq.).
SALTO *jump.*
  fare un salto nel buio *to take a
    risk.*
  Faccio un salto a casa di mia madre.
    *I'll take a quick run over to my
    mother's house.*
salumeria *delicatessen.*
SALUTARE *to salute; to greet.*
  Ci siamo salutati alla stazione. *We
    said good-bye at the station.*
  Mi ha salutato con un cenno della
    mano. *He waved to me.*
  Mi ha salutato freddamente. *He
    greeted me coldly.*
salute, f. *health.*
saluto *greetings.*
salvagente, m. *life preserver.*
SALVARE *to save.*
  salvare le apparenze *to keep up
    appearances.*
  Mi ha salvato dalla rovina. *He saved
    me from ruin.*
  salvare con rome *to save as
    (computer).*
salvezza *salvation, safety.*
SALVO *safe; save for; except for.*
  sano e salvo *safe and sound.*
  trarre in salvo *to conduct to safety;
    to save.*
  Salvo possibile cambiamenti, tutto
    rimane come stabilito. *Save for
    possible changes, everything
    remains as planned.*
sanabile *curable.*
sanare *to cure; to make well.*
sandalo *sandal.*
sangue, m. *blood.*
  a sangue freddo *in cold blood.*
  dare il proprio sangue *to give one's
    life.*

dello stesso sangue *related; of the same family.*

versare sangue *to shed blood.*

Il riso fa buon sangue. *Laughter is the best medicine.*

sanguinare *to bleed.*

Mi sanguina il cuore al pensiero. *My heart bleeds at the thought.*

sanitario *sanitary.*

leggi sanitarie *sanitary laws.*

SANO *sound, healthy, whole.*

di principi sani *of sound principles.*

di sana pianta *entirely.*

sano di corpo e di mente *sound in mind and body.*

un'uomo sano *a healthy man.*

santo, n. *saint;* adj. *saintly.*

santuario *sanctuary.*

SAPERE, n.m. *learning, erudition;* v. *to know.*

saperia lunga *to be clever, to know a thing or two.*

Sa il fatto suo. *He knows his trade.*

sapienza *knowledge.*

sapone, m. *soap.*

saponetta *face soap.*

SAPORE, m. *flavor, taste; relish.*

saporito *flavorful.*

sardina *sardine.*

sarta *dressmaker.*

sarto *tailor.*

sartorìa *tailor shop; boutique.*

sasso *small stone; pebble.*

Lui ha un cuore di sasso. *He is hard-hearted.*

Siamo rimasti di sasso. *We stood amazed.*

sassolino *pebble.*

satellite, m. *satellite.*

SAZIARE *to satiate; to satisfy.*

saziare la fame *to satisfy hunger.*

saziare la sete *to quench thirst.*

saziarsi di *to fill oneself with.*

sazio *satiated, satisfied.*

sbadato *needless, inadvertent.*

sbadigliare *to yawn.*

sbadiglio *yawn.*

sbagliare *to mistake; to miscalculate.*

SBAGLIO *error.*

sbalordire *to amaze; to astonish.*

sbalzare *to thrust; to bounce.*

sbalzo (balzo) *bounce.*

cogliere la palla al balzo *to catch a ball on the bounce; to take advantage of an opportunity.*

sbarazzar(si) *to get rid of.*

sbarcare *to disembark; to go ashore.*

sbarcare il lunario *to make ends meet.*

sbarrare *to bar; to obstruct.*

sbattere *to slam; to toss.*

Ha sbattuto la porta e se n' è andato. *He slammed the door and left.*

sbiadito *faded.*

sbilanciare *to throw off balance.*

sbottonare *to unbutton.*

sbrigare *to dispatch; to expedite.*

sbucciare *to peel; to skin.*

scacchiera *chessboard.*

scadere *to expire.*

scala *stairway, stairs.*

scala a chiocciola *spiral staircase.*

scala mobile *escalator.*

su vasta scala *on a large scale.*

scalare *to climb.*

scaldare *to warm; to heat.*

scaldarsi *to warm oneself; to get excited.*

scalo *call, landing place.*

scaltro *astute, clever.*

scalzo *barefooted.*

scambiare *to exchange.*

scambio *exchange.*

scamiciato *jumper.*

scamosciato *suede.*

scampagnata *picnic.*

scampare *to escape from danger.*

Dio ce ne scampi e liberi! *Heaven preserve us!*

scamparla bella *to have a narrow escape.*

scappare *to run away; to escape.*

SCARICARE *to unload.*

scaricare una nave *to unload a ship.*

scaricare un fucile *to unload a gun; to fire all the rounds of a gun.*

scarico *unloaded.*

SCARPA *shoe.*

scarpa da tennis *tennis shoe.*

scarso *scarce, lacking.*

di scarso valore *of little value.*

scartare *to reject; to discard; to unwrap.*

scarto *reject.*

SCATOLA *box.*
  cibo in scatola *canned food.*
scavare *to dig; to dig up; to excavate.*
  andare a scavare *to try and find out.*
  scavare la propria fossa *to be the cause of one's own ruin.*
SCEGLIERE *to choose.*
scelto *chosen.*
scena *scene.*
  andare in scena *to be performed.*
SCENDERE *to descend.*
  Scendo subito! *I'll be right down!*
scheda *card.*
scheletro *skeleton.*
schema *scheme; outline.*
schermo *screen.*
scherzare *to jest; to joke.*
scherzo *joke, jest.*
  fare un brutto scherzo *to pull a prank.*
  uno scherzo di cattivo gusto *a joke in poor taste.*
schiaffo *slap, box.*
  Le ha presso a schiaffi. *He boxed his ears.*
schiena *back.*
  Ho un dolore alla schiena. *I have a pain in my back.*
schiuma *froth, foam.*
schizzo *sketch, splash.*
sci *ski.*
sciagura *misfortune, ill luck.*
sciare *to ski.*
sciarpa *scarf.*
scienza *science.*
scimmia *monkey.*
sciocchezza *nonsense.*
  fare una sciocchezza *to do something silly.*
sciocco *silly, stupid.*
SCIOGLIERE *to untie; to melt; to release.*
  sciogliere da una promessa *to release from a promise.*
  sciogliere la neve *to melt snow.*
  sciogliere un nodo *to untie a knot.*
  sciogliere il Parlamento *to dissolve the Parliament.*
sciolto *loose, untied.*
sciopero *strike.*
sciroppo *syrup.*
SCIUPARE *to spoil; to damage; to waste.*

  sciupare il tempo inutilmente *to waste time.*
  Mi ha sciupato tutto il vestito. *He spoiled my dress completely.*
scivolare *to slip; to glide.*
scogliera *cliff.*
scoglio *rock.*
scoiattolo *squirrel.*
scolaro *pupil, student.*
scoliato *low-necked.*
scollatura *neckline.*
  scollatura a V *V neck.*
  scollatura rotonda *round neck.*
scolorire *to fade; to lose color.*
scomodare *to inconvenience.*
scomodo *uncomfortable, inconvenient.*
scompaginare *to upset; to disrupt.*
SCOMPARIRE *to disappear; to vanish.*
scompartimento *division, compartment.*
sconfiggere *to defeat.*
sconfitta *defeat.*
sconosciuto, adj. *unknown;* n. *stranger.*
scontento *dissatisfied.*
sconto *discount.*
scontrino *check, ticket.*
scontro *collision.*
sconvolgere *to upset.*
sconvolto *upset.*
SCOPA *broom.*
scopare *to sweep.*
scoperta *discovery.*
scoperto *uncovered.*
SCOPO *aim, intent, scope.*
  lo scopo della mia vita *my aim in life.*
  A che scopo? *To what intent?*
scoppiare *to burst; to explode.*
SCOPRIRE *to discover; to uncover.*
scoraggiare *to discourage.*
scorcio *end, finale.*
scordare *to forget.*
  scordarsi di fare qualcosa *to forget to do something.*
scorrere *to flow.*
scorretto *incorrect, improper.*
scorrevole *fluent.*
scorso *last, past.*
scortese *impolite, rude.*
scorza *peel.*
  scorza d'arancia *orange peel.*

scossa *shake, shock.*

scottare *to burn; to scald.*

scrittore, m. **scrittrice,** f. *writer.*

scrittura *writing.*

scrivania *desk.*

SCRIVERE *to write; to spell.*

scucire *to rip (a seam).*

SCUOLA *school.*
    frequentare la scuola *to go to school; to attend school.*

scuotere *to shake.*

scurire *to darken.*

scuro *dark (in color).*
    verde scuro *dark green.*

scusa *excuse.*
    far le scuse *to excuse oneself.*

scusare *to excuse.*

scusato *forgiven; excused.*
    Scusi (*or* mi scusi). *Excuse me.*

sdegno *indignation.*

sdraiare *to lay.*
    sdraiarsi *to lie; to lie down.*

SE *if; of it, from it, for it.*
    anche se *even if.*
    come se *as if.*
    se posso *if I can.*
    se vuoi *if you wish.*
    Se ne liberò. *He got rid of it.*
    Se ne pentì. *She was sorry for it.*

SÈ *her, him, them, herself, himself, themselves.*
    Lui è fuori di sè. *He has no control of himself.*
    Essi pensano solo a sè. *They think only of themselves.*
    un uomo che si è fatto da sè *a self-made man.*
    Maria non sta in sè dalla gioia. *Mary is beside herself with joy.*

seccare *to dry; to bother.*

seccato *bored; angry.*

secchio *pail.*

secco *dry.*

sècolo *century.*

secondo, n. & adj. *second;* adv. *according to.*
    secondo me *in my opinion.*

sedano *celery.*

SEDERE *to sit.*
    sedersi a tavola *to sit at the table.*

SEDIA *chair.*

sedicesimo *sixteenth.*

sedici *sixteen.*

sedile *seat.*

seducente *seductive.*

seduto *seated.*

sega *saw.*

SEGNO *sign, indication.*
    dare segni di vita *to give signs of life.*
    perdere il segno *to lose one's place in a book.*
    È buon segno. *It's a good sign.*

segretaria, f. *secretary.*

segretario, m. *secretary.*

segreteria *secretary's office.*
    segreteria telefonica *answering machine.*

segreto, n. & adj. *secret.*

seguente *following, ensuing.*
    Lui ha fatto la seguente dichiarazione. *He made the following statement.*

seguire *to follow.*

sei *six.*

seicento *six hundred.*

seimila *six thousand.*

selezione *selection.*

selvaggio *wild.*

selvatichezza *wildness; unsociableness.*

semaforo *traffic light.*

SEMBRARE *to seem.*
    Lui sembra impazzito. *He seems to be insane.*
    Mi sembra strano. *It seems strange to me.*
    Sembra impossibile! *It seems impossible!*

seme, m. *seed.*

semi-, prefix *half-, semi-*
    semicerchio *semicircle.*
    semifinale *semifinal.*

seminare *to sow.*

semolino *semolina.*

semplice *simple, easy.*

semplicità *simplicity, easiness.*

SEMPRE *always.*
    per sempre *forever.*

senno *sense.*

sensibile *sensitive, impressionable.*

SENSO *sense, meaning.*
    espressione a doppio senso *an ambiguous expression.*
    senso unico *one-way (street).*

usare un po'di buon senso *to use common sense.*

sentenza *judgment.*

sentimentale *sentimental.*

SENTIRE *to hear; to feel.*

non sentire dolore *to feel no pain.*

sentire freddo *to feel cold.*

sentire odore *to smell.*

sentire rimorso *to feel remorse.*

Come si sente? *How do you feel?*

Con tutto questo rumore non riesco a sentire niente. *With all this noise, I can't hear a thing.*

Mi sento bene. *I feel well.*

Sentite! *Hear!*

SENZA *without.*

senza considerazione *inconsiderately, inconsiderate.*

senza dire nulla *without saying a word.*

senza di me *without me.*

senza dar fastidio a nessuno *without bothering anyone.*

senz'altro *right away; of course.*

SEPARARE *to separate; to part.*

la distanza che ci separa *the distance that separates us.*

separarsi da *to separate from.*

Ci siamo separati a malincuore. *We parted reluctantly.*

SEPARATO *separate.*

separazione, f. *separation, parting.*

sepolto *buried.*

seppellire *to bury.*

SERA *evening, night.*

Buona sera. *Good evening.*

SERATA *evening.*

Passeremo una serata in compagnia. *We will spend the evening in company.*

serenamente *serenely.*

sereno *serene, clear.*

una giornata serena *a clear day.*

serie, f. *series.*

una serie di articoli *a series of articles.*

serio *serious, grave.*

sul serio *seriously.*

serpente, m. *snake, serpent.*

serpente a sonagli *rattlesnake.*

serra *greenhouse, hothouse.*

SERRARE *to close; to shut.*

con i pugni serrati *with clenched fists.*

serrare le file *to close ranks.*

serratura *lock.*

SERVIRE *to serve.*

A che serve? *What is it used for?*

In che cosa la posso servire? *What can I do for you?*

Non mi serve nulla. *I don't need anything.*

Non serve! *It's of no use!*

Potete servire il pranzo. *You may serve dinner.*

Vuole che le serva la carne? *Shall I serve you the meat?*

SERVIZIO *service, set.*

Servizio compreso *Service included.*

fuori servizio *off duty.*

in servizio *on duty.*

rendere un servizio a *to render a service.*

servizio da tavola *dinner set; dinner service.*

servizio militare *military service.*

il servizio è pessimo in quest'albergo. *The service is very poor in this hotel.*

servizio compreso *service included.*

sessanta *sixty.*

sessantesimo *sixtieth.*

sesto *sixth.*

seta *silk.*

seta cruda *a lightweight silk fabric.*

seta greggia *raw silk.*

seta lavata *washed silk.*

SETE, f. *thirst.*

avere sete *to be thirsty.*

settanta *seventy.*

settantesimo *seventieth.*

sette *seven.*

settecento *seven hundred.*

nel Settecento *in the eighteenth century.*

settembre, m. *September.*

settentrionale, adj. *northern;* n.m. *northerner.*

Italia settentrionale *northern Italy.*

SETTIMANA *week.*

di settimana in settimana *from week to week.*

fra una settimana *in a week.*

la settimana prossima (entrante) *next week.*

una settimana fa *a week ago.*
due settimane *a fortnight.*
settimanale, adj. & n.m. *weekly.*
  un settimanale *a weekly*
    publication.
settimo *seventh.*
settore, m. *sector.*
severamente *severely.*
severo *severe, strict.*
sezione, f. *section.*
sfacciato *saucy; impudent; glaring.*
sfarzo *pomp, magnificence.*
  fare le cose con sfarzo *to do things*
    in grand style.
sfarzoso *gorgeous, magnificent.*
sfasciare *to remove the bandages; to*
    break into pieces.
sfavorevole *unfavorable.*
sfavorevolmente *unfavorably.*
sfera *sphere.*
  la sfera dell'orologio *the face of the*
    clock.
sfida *challenge.*
sfidare *to challenge; to dare.*
  sfidare le intemperie *to face (to*
    challenge) the inclemency of the
    weather (the storms).
  Sfido io! *Of course!*
  Ti sfido a farlo. *I dare you to do it.*
sfiducia *distrust.*
  Nutro una grande sfiducia verso di
    lui. *I distrust him very much.*
sfilare *to unthread; to unstring (beads);*
    to slip off.
  sfilare le scarpe *to slip off shoes.*
sfilata *parade.*
  sfilata di moda *fashion show.*
sfinire *to exhaust; to wear down.*
  Mi sento sfinito. *I feel exhausted.*
  Questo lavoro mi ha sfinito. *This*
    work has exhausted me.
sfogare *to vent; to give vent to.*
  sfogarsi con *to confide in.*
  Ha sfogato la sua ira su di me. *He*
    vented his wrath on me.
sfoggiare *to show off; to make a display.*
sfondo *background.*
sfortuna *bad luck; misfortune.*
  per mia sfortuna *unfortunately for*
    me.
  La sfortuna lo perseguita. *Misfortune*
    dogs his footsteps.

sfortunatamente *unfortunately.*
sfortunato *unlucky.*
  sfortunato al giuoco *unlucky at cards*
    (at games).
  sfortunato in amore *unlucky in love.*
sforzare *to strain; to force.*
  sforzarsi *to strain oneself; to try*
    hard.
SFORZO *effort.*
  fare uno sforzo *to make an effort.*
  senza sforzo *without effort.*
  Non mi costa sforzo. *It is no effort*
    to me.
sfrattare *to dispossess; to evict.*
sfratto *eviction.*
sfrontato *shameless, bold.*
sfruttamento *exploitation.*
sfruttare *to exploit, to take*
    advantage of.
  sfruttare al massimo *to exploit fully;*
    to get the most out of.
sfuggire *to run away; to escape.*
sgabello *stool.*
sganciare *to unfasten; to release.*
sgarbatamente *rudely.*
sgarbato *rude.*
  Mi ha trattato in maniera molto
    sgarbata. *He treated me with*
    great rudeness.
sgarbo *rudeness; act of rudeness.*
  fare uno sgarbo a qualcuno *to be*
    rude toward someone; to commit
    an act of rudeness toward
    someone.
sgelare *to melt; to thaw.*
sgocciolare *to trickle.*
sgombrare *to clear; to clear out of.*
sgombro *clear, free.*
  La stanza è sgombra. *The room is*
    free.
sgomento *dismay.*
sgonfiare *to deflate.*
  Si è sgonfiata una gomma dell'
    automobile. *The car has a flat tire.*
sgonfio *deflated; not swollen.*
sgorgare *to gush out; to overflow.*
sgradevole *unpleasant, disagreeable.*
sgradito *unpleasant, disagreeable,*
    unwelcome.
sgranchire *to stretch.*
  sgranchirsi le gambe *to stretch one's*
    legs.

SGRIDARE to scold; to reprimand.

sgridata scolding.

Mi ha fatto una sgridata per nulla. *He gave me a scolding over nothing.*

sgualcire to rumple.

Questa veste è tutta sgualcita. *This dress is all wrinkled.*

SGUARDO look, glance.

con sguardo severo *with a stern look.*

dare uno sguardo a *to glance at.*

Mi ha lanciato uno sguardo di sottecchi. *He glanced at me furtively.*

sgusciare to shell; to slip away.

sgusciare dalle mani *to slip out of one's hands; to slip away.*

sgusciare i piselli *to shell the peas.*

SI oneself, himself, herself, itself, themselves, we, they, one; one another; each other.

Non si è sempre contenti. *We are not always glad.*

Si dice che . . . *They say (it is said) that . . .*

Si è messo a piovere. *It has started to rain.*

Si è messo a sedere. *He sat (himself) down.*

Si sono divertiti. *They enjoyed themselves.*

Si sono finalmente rivisti. *They finally saw each other again.*

SÌ, adv. yes.

dire di sì *to say yes.*

Mi pare di sì. *I think so.*

Sì davvero! *Yes indeed!*

sia . . . sia whether . . . or . . .

sia che ti piaccia, sia che non ti piaccia *whether you like it or not.*

sibilare to hiss.

sibilo hiss, hissing.

il sibilo del vento *the hissing of the wind.*

sicchè so; so that.

Sicchè hai deciso di venire? *So you've decided to come?*

siccome as; inasmuch as.

Siccome era già partito, non ho potuto dargli il tuo messaggio. *Inasmuch as he had already left,*

I wasn't able to give him your message.

siciliano, adj. & n. Sicilian.

sicuramente certainly, surely.

Verrà sicuramente. *He will surely come.*

sicurezza safety, security.

per maggior sicurezza *for greater safety.*

rasòio di sicurezza *safety razor.*

spilla di sicurezza *safety pin.*

sicuro safe, secure, sure.

essere sicuro di *to be sure of.*

mettersi al sicuro *to place oneself in safety.*

Sicuro! *Certainly!*

siepe, f. hedge.

sigaretta cigarette.

sigaro cigar.

sigillare to seal.

sigillo seal (on letter, etc.).

significante significant.

significare to mean; to signify.

Che cosa intendeva significare con quel gesto? *What did you wish to signify with that gesture?*

Che cosa significa questa parola? *What does this word mean?*

Che significa tutto ciò? *What is the meaning of all this?*

significato meaning, significance.

SIGNORA Mrs.; lady.

È una vera signora. *She is a real lady.*

SIGNORE, m. Mr.; gentleman.

Questo signore desidera vederla. *This gentleman wishes to see you.*

Signor Rossi *Mr. Rossi.*

signorile gentlemanly, ladylike.

signorilità distinction.

signorilmente refinedly.

SIGNORINA Miss; young lady.

SILENZIO silence.

silenziosamente silently.

silenzioso silent.

sillaba syllable.

simboleggiare to symbolize.

simbolico symbolic.

simbolo symbol.

similarità similarity.

SIMILE like, similar, such.

il tuo simile *your neighbor; your fellow creature.*
Non ho mai visto una cosa simile. *I've never seen such a thing.*
Questa borsetta è simile alla mia. *This handbag is like mine.*
simmetrìa *symmetry.*
simmetrico *symmetrical.*
simpatìa *liking.*
aver simpatìa per *to have a liking for.*
simpatico *nice, pleasant.*
riuscire simpatico *to be liked.*
simposio *symposium.*
simulare *to feign; to pretend.*
simultaneamente *simultaneously.*
simultaneo *simultaneous.*
sinagoga *synagogue.*
sinceramente *sincerely, truly.*
SINCERO *sincere, candid.*
un amicizia sincera *a sincere friendship.*
Dammi la tua sincera opinione. *Give me your candid opinion.*
sindacato *labor union.*
sindaco *mayor.*
sinfonìa *symphony.*
singhiozzare *to sob.*
Si è messa a singhiozzare. *She started to sob. She burst into sobs.*
singhiozzo *sob, hiccup.*
Ho il singhiozzo. *I have the hiccups.*
singolare *singular, peculiar.*
singolo *single; individual.*
SINISTRA *left hand, left.*
voltare a sinistra *to turn to the left.*
sinistro *left, sinister.*
lato sinistro *left side.*
Quell'uomo ha un'aspetto sinistro. *That man has a sinister look.*
sinonimo, adj. *synonymous;* n. *synonym.*
sintassi *syntax.*
sintesi *synthesis.*
siatetico *synthetic; concise.*
sìatomo *symptom.*
sipario *curtain.*
siringa *syringe.*
SISTEMA, m. *system.*
sistema nervoso *nervous system.*
sistema solare *solar system.*

sistenare *to arrange; to settle.*
sistemarsi *to settle; to settle down.*
sistematico *systematic.*
sistemazione *accommodation.*
situazione, f. *situation, position.*
siacciare *to unfasten.*
sieale *disloyal, unfair.*
siealmente *unfairly; disloyally.*
slealtà *disloyalty.*
slegare *to unbind.*
slitta *sleigh, sled.*
slogare *to dislocate.*
slogarsi una caviglia *to sprain an ankle.*
smacchiare *to remove stains from; to clean.*
smacchiatura *cleaning.*
smagliante *shining, dazzling.*
smalto *enamel.*
SMARRIRE *to lose.*
smarrirsi *to lose one's way.*
smarrito *lost, bewildered.*
smemorato *forgetful.*
smentire *to belie; to deny.*
smeraldo *emerald.*
SMETTERE *to stop.*
Smettila! *Stop it!*
Smetto di lavorare alle sei. *I stop working at six.*
SMONTARE *to dismount; to get out; to take apart.*
È smontato da cavallo. *He dismounted from his horse.*
Ho dovuto smontare l'orologio. *I had to take the clock apart.*
smorto *pale, dull.*
snello *slender.*
sobborgo *suburb.*
soccorrere *to help.*
SOCCORSO *help, aid, succor.*
chiedere soccorso *to ask for help.*
prestare i primi soccorsi *to render first aid.*
pronto soccorso *first aid.*
società di mutuo soccorso *mutual aid society.*
sociale *social.*
socialismo *socialism.*
società *society, company.*
in società con *in partnership with.*
società anonima *joint stock company.*
società per azioni *limited company.*

socievole *sociable, companionable.*

SOCIO *associate, partner, member.*

socio in affari *business associate.*

Siamo tutti e due soci del medesimo circolo. *We are both members of the same club.*

soddisfacente *satisfactory.*

soddisfacentemente *satisfactorily.*

soddisfare *to satisfy.*

soddisfatto *satisfied.*

soddisfazione, f. *satisfaction.*

con mia grande soddisfazione *to my great satisfaction.*

sodo *solid, substantial.*

dormir sodo *to sleep soundly.*

uovo sodo *hard-boiled egg.*

sofà m. *sofa.*

sofferente *suffering, unwell.*

sofferenza *suffering, pain.*

sofferto *suffered, endured.*

SOFFIARE *to blow.*

soffiarsi il naso *to blow one's nose.*

SOFFICE *soft.*

soffio *puff, breath.*

in un soffio *in a moment.*

senza un soffio d'aria *without a breath of air.*

un soffio di vapore *a puff of steam.*

un soffio di vento *a breeze.*

soffitta *garret, attic.*

soffitto *ceiling.*

soffocamento, f. *suffocation.*

Morì per soffocamento durante un incendio. *He suffocated during a fire.*

soffocante *suffocating, oppressive.*

SOFFOCARE *to choke; to suffocate; to smother; to stifle.*

SOFFRIRE *to suffer; to bear.*

Lui soffre di mal di cuore. *He is suffering from heart trouble.*

Non posso soffrire quella gente. *I can't bear those people.*

Se non ti concedi un po' di riposo, la tua salute ne soffrirà. *If you don't get some rest, your health will suffer.*

sofisticato *sophisticated.*

soggettivamente *subjectively.*

soggettivo *subjective.*

SOGGETTO *subject.*

essere soggetto a *to be subject to.*

un pessimo soggetto *a very bad specimen (of humanity).*

soggezione, f. *uneasiness, awe, embarrassment.*

Lui mi fa soggezione. *He makes me uneasy.*

Provo soggezione a parlarne. *It embarrasses me to speak of it.*

soggiornare *to sojourn; to reside.*

soggiorno *stay, sojourn.*

Il nostro soggiorno a Parigi durerà due settimane. *Our stay in Paris will be two weeks long.*

soglia *threshold.*

sogliola *sole (fish).*

SOGNARE *to dream, to fancy.*

sognatore, m. *dreamer.*

sogno *dream.*

neanche per sogno *by no means.*

SOLAMENTE *only, merely.*

Se potessi solamente vederla! *If I could only see her!*

solare *solar.*

luce solare *sunlight.*

SOLDATO *soldier.*

fare il soldato *to be a soldier.*

soldo *cent.*

Non vale un soldo. *It isn't worth a penny.*

SOLE, m. *sun.*

bagno di sole *sunbath.*

raggio di sole *ray of sun.*

solenne *solemn.*

solidarietà *solidarity.*

solido *solid, substantial.*

solitario *solitary.*

SOLITO *usual.*

contro il mio solito *contrary to my custom.*

più presto del solito *earlier than usual.*

sollecitare *to hasten; to entreat.*

sollecito *prompt, speedy, solicitous.*

una risposta sollecita *a prompt reply.*

solleticare *to tickle.*

SOLLEVARE *to lift; to raise; to comfort.*

sollevare gli occhi *to life one's eyes.*

sollevare una nuvola di polvere *to raise a cloud of dust.*

sollevare un peso *to lift a weight.*

Mi solleva il pensiero del tuo prossimo ritorno. *I am comforted by the thought of your impending return.*

Molte voci si sollevarono in protesta. *Many voices were raised in protest.*

sollevato *lifted, raised; in good spirits.*

sollievo *relief, comfort.*

SOLO *alone, only.*

Sono completamente sola al mondo. *I am completely alone in the world.*

Sono i soli rimasti. *They are the only ones left.*

SOLTANTO *only.*

Eravamo soltanto in due. *We were only two.*

soluzione, f. *solution.*

somiglianza *resemblance.*

SOMIGLIARE *to resemble.*

SOMMA *sum, amount.*

fare una somma *to make an addition; to add; to total.*

sommare *to add.*

sommesso *subdued.*

sommità *summit, top.*

sommo *greatest, highest, supreme.*

sommossa *rising, riot.*

sonnambulo *sleepwalker.*

sonnecchiare *to doze.*

sonnellino *nap.*

SONNO *sleep.*

aver sonno *to be sleepy.*

malattia del sonno *sleeping sickness.*

sonno leggero *light sleep.*

sonno profondo *deep sleep.*

sontuoso *sumptuous.*

sopportare *to bear.*

soppressione, f. *suppression.*

soppresso *suppressed, abolished.*

sopprimere *to suppress; to abolish.*

SOPRA *on; on top of; above.*

al piano di sopra *on the floor above.*

andare di sopra *to go upstairs.*

sopra zero *above zero.*

Posa quel libro sopra il tavolo. *Put that book on the table.*

sopracciglio, m.pl. **sopraccigli** f.pl. **sopracciglia** *eyebrow.*

soprannome, m. *nickname.*

sopraffare *to overwhelm.*

soprano *soprano.*

soprassalto *start, jolt.*

svegliarsi di soprassalto *to wake with a start.*

soprattutto *above all.*

sopravvivere *to survive; to remain in existence.*

sopravvivere a *to outlive.*

sordità *deafness.*

SORDO *deaf.*

fare il sordo *to turn a deaf ear.*

sondo da un orecchio *deaf in one ear.*

sordomnto *deaf-mute.*

sorella *sister.*

SORGENTE, f. *spring, source.*

sorgente di ricchezza *a source of wealth.*

una sorgente d' acqua minerale *a mineral spring.*

sorgere, v. & n.m. *to rise; to arise.*

al sorgere del sole *at sunrise.*

far sorgere dei dubbi *to give rise to doubt.*

È sorto un malinteso. *A misunderstanding arose.*

sormontabile *surmountable.*

sormontare *to surmount; to overcome.*

Abbiamo sormontato tutti gli ostacoli. *We have surmounted all the obstacles.*

Non riesce a sormontare le difficoltà della vita. *He can't succeed in overcoming life's difficulties.*

sormione *sly, sneaking.*

gatto sornione *tabby cat.*

sorpassare *to surpass.*

La produzione di quest'anno ha sorpassato quella dell'anno precedente. *This year's production surpassed last year's.*

sorpassato *surpassed, old-fashioned, outdated.*

È un'usanza sorpassata. *It's an outdated custom.*

sorprendente *surprising, astonishing.*

SORPRENDERE *to surprise.*

sorprendersi *to be surprised.*

sorpresi in flagrante *caught in the act.*

La tua condotta mi sorprende. *Your behavior surprises me.*

Siamo stati sorpresi da una tempesta. *We were overtaken by a storm.*

SORPRESA *surprise.*

  con mia grande sorpresa *much to my surprise.*

  di sorpresa *by surprise.*

  fare una sorpresa a *to surprise.*

  cogliere di sorpresa *to take by surprise; to catch someone unawares.*

sorpreso *surprised, astonished.*

  Siamo tutti molto sorpresi. *We are all very surprised.*

  Sono rimasta sorpresa nel sentire. *I was surprised to hear it.*

SORRIDERE *to smile.*

  La fortuna mi sorride. *Fortune smiles on me.*

SORRISO *smile.*

  con sorriso amaro *with a bitter smile.*

  fare un sorriso a *to smile at.*

sorso *sip, gulp.*

  tutto d'un sorso *all in a gulp.*

  un sorso d'acqua *a sip of water; a drop of water.*

sorta *kind, lot.*

  di ogni sorta *of all kinds; all kinds of.*

SORTE, f. *lot, destiny, fate.*

  le sorti del paese *the destiny of the country.*

  tirare a sorte *to draw lots.*

  La sorte gli fu avversa. *Fate was against him.*

sorveglianza *superintendence, watch, surveillance.*

  sotto sorveglianza *under surveillance.*

sorvegliare *to oversee; to watch; to watch over.*

  sorvegliare i lavori *to oversee the work.*

sorvolare *to fly over; to pass over.*

  L'aereo ha sorvolato la mia casa. *The plane flew over my house.*

  Sorvoliamo questi dettagli di poca importanza. *Let's pass over these unimportant details.*

sospendere *to suspend; to adjourn; to hang.*

  Bisogna sospendere i lavori. *The work must be stopped.*

  La seduta fu sospesa. *The meeting was adjourned.*

sospeso *suspended, hung.*

  con animo sospeso *with anxious mind.*

  sospeso ad un chiodo *hanging on a nail.*

  sospeso in aria *hanging in mid-air.*

  tener in sospeso *to keep in suspense.*

SOSPETTARE *to suspect.*

  Non sospettavo di nulla. *I suspected nothing.*

sospetto *suspicion.*

  fare sorgere dei sospetti *to create suspicion.*

  sotto sospetto di *on suspicion of.*

sospettosamente *suspiciously.*

sospettoso *suspicious.*

sospirare *to sigh.*

sospiro *sigh.*

  sospiro di sollievo *a sigh of relief.*

SOSTA *halt, stay.*

  fare una sosta breve *to stop for a short while.*

  senza sosta *without pause; without stops.*

  Divieto di Sosta *No Parking.*

sostanza *substance.*

  dare sostanza a *to give substance to.*

  in sostanza *on the whole.*

sostanziale *substantial.*

sostanzialmente *substantially.*

sostare *to stay; to stop.*

sostegno *support, mainstay.*

  senza sostegno alcuno *completely without support.*

  a sostegno delle sue teorie *in support of his theories.*

SOSTENERE *to support; to sustain; to hold up; to maintain.*

  Io sostengo il contrario. *I maintain the contrary.*

  sostenere una conversazione in italiano *to carry on a conversation in Italian.*

sostenuto *sustained, played, tolerated.*

SOSTITUIRE *to substitute; to replace; to take the place of.*

  essere sostituito da *to be replaced by.*

sostituto *substitute.*

sostituzione, f. *substitution, replacement.*

  Mi hanno dato questo paio di guanti in sostituzione di quelli difettosi. *They gave me this pair of gloves in place of the defective ones.*

SOTTANA *skirt.*
sotterfugio *subterfuge.*
sotterraneo *underground.*
sotterrare *to bury.*
sottile *subtle, thin.*
  sottile ironia *subtle irony.*
sottintendere *to understand.*
sottinteso, n. *inuendo;* adj. *understood,*
  implied.
SOTTO *under.*
  al di sotto di *below; beneath.*
  sotto acqua *underwater.*
  sotto forma di *in the shape of; in the*
    guise of.
  sotto l'influenza di *under the*
    influence of.
  sottosopra *upside down.*
  sotto sospetto *under suspicion.*
  sotto terra *underground.*
  sotto zero *below zero.*
sottocchio *under or before one's eyes.*
sottolineare *to underline.*
sottomesso *submissive, subdued.*
sottomettere *to submit; to subdue.*
sottoporre *to submit to; to place under.*
sottoscritto, adj. *signed;* n. *undersigned.*
sottoscrivere *to sign.*
  sottoscrivere a *to subscribe to.*
sottoscrizione *subscription.*
sottosopra *upside-down.*
sottoveste *undergarment.*
SOTTOVOCE *in a whisper.*
SOTTRARRE *to subtract; to steal.*
  sottrarsi a *to get out of; to avoid.*
sottrazione, f. *subtraction, theft.*
SOVENTE *often, frequently.*
sovrana (sovrano) *sovereign.*
sovrapporre *to superimpose.*
sovrastare *to dominate; to stand above.*
sovvertire *to overthrow.*
spaccare *to cleave; to split.*
  spaccare la legna *to chop wood.*
spaccio *shop.*
  spaccio di sale e tabacchi *tobacco*
    and salt shop.
spada *sword.*
spaghetti, m.pl. *spaghetti.*
spagnolo, n. & adj. *Spanish, Spaniard.*
spago *string.*
spalancare *to throw open.*
  spalancare la porta *to throw open the*
    door.

spalancato *wide open.*
  finestra spalancata *wide-open*
    window.
spaiato *unmatched.*
SPALLA *shoulder.*
  scrollare le spalle *to shrug one's*
    shoulders.
spalliera *back (of a chair); backrest.*
spalmare *to spread.*
  spalmare il burro sul pane *to spread*
    butter on the bread.
sparare *to shoot; to fire.*
sparecchiare *to clear away.*
  Ho sparecchiato la tavola. *I cleared*
    the table.
SPARGERE *to spread; to shed.*
  spargere sangue *to shed blood.*
  La notizia si è sparsa rapidamente.
    The news was spread quickly.
SPARIRE *to disappear; to vanish.*
sparizione, f. *disappearance.*
sparso *scattered.*
spasimo *spasm.*
spassionato *dispassionate, impartial.*
  giudizio spassionato *impartial*
    judgment.
spasso *amusement; fun.*
  andare a spasso *to go out for a walk.*
spavaldo, adj. *bold, defiant;* n. *braggart.*
SPAVENTARE *to frighten.*
  spaventarsi *to become frightened.*
spavento *fright, terror, fear.*
  provare spavento *to feel fear.*
spaventoso *frightening, fearful.*
SPAZIO *space.*
  nello spazio di un giorno *in a day's*
    time.
  spazio bianco *blank space.*
  Non c'è spazio. *There is no room.*
spazioso *spacious, broad.*
spazzaneve, m. *snowplow.*
spazzare *to sweep; to sweep away.*
spazzatura *trash.*
SPAZZOLA *brush.*
spazzolino *small brush.*
  spazzolino da denti *toothbrush.*
SPECCHIO *mirror.*
SPECIALE *special.*
specialista, m. *specialist.*
specialità *specialty.*
  la specialità della casa *the specialty*
    of the house.

specialmente *specially, especially.*

specie, f. *species, kind, sort.*
  di ogni specie *of every kind.*

specificare *to specify.*

specifico *specific.*

speculare *to speculate.*

speculatore, m. *speculator.*

speculazione, f. *speculation.*

SPEDIRE *to send; to mail.*
  Ho già spedito la lettera. *I have
    already mailed (sent) the letter.*

spedizione, f. *shipment.*

SPEGNERE *to extinguish; to blow out.*
  spegnere la luce *to turn off the light.*
  spegnersi *to die.*

spellare *to skin.*

SPENDERE *to spend.*
  Chi più spende meno spende. *The
    best is always the cheapest. (Who
    spends more, spends less.)*

spensieratamente *thoughtlessly,
  lightheartedly.*

spensierato *lighthearted; without
  cares; happy-go-lucky.*

spento *extinguished.*
  a luce spenta *with the lights out.*
  uno sguardo spento *a lifeless
    expression.*

SPERANZA *hope.*
  perdere ogni speranza *to lose all
    hope.*
  senza speranza *hopeless.*

SPERARE *to hope.*
  sperare in vano *to hope in vain.*
  Spero di vederti domani. *I hope to
    see you tomorrow.*

SPESA *expense, expenditure.*
  a spese mie *at my expense.*
  fare spesa *to go shopping; to do the
    shopping.*
  fare là spesa *to go to the grocery
    store.*
  Si tratta di una spesa troppo grande.
    It's too great an expense.

SPESSO, adj. *thick, dense;* adv. *often.*
  Ci vediamo spesso. *We see each
    other often.*

spessore, m. *thickness.*

spettabile *respectable.*

spettacolare *spectacular.*

SPETTACOLO *spectacle,
  performance, sight.*

spettacolo di gala *gala performance.*
  uno spettacolo triste *a sad sight.*
  Lui ha dato spettacolo di sè. *He
    made a spectacle of himself.*

spettare *to belong; to be one's duty.*
  Spetta a te decidere. *It's up to you to
    decide.*

spettatore, m. **spettatrice,** f.
  spectator.

spettro *ghost, specter.*

spezie, f. pl. *spices.*

spezzar(si) *to break.*
  Mi si spezza il cuore. *My heart is
    breaking.*
  Si è spezzato. *It broke.*

spiacente *sorry.*
  Sono spiacente di fare . . . *I'm sorry
    for doing . . .*

spiacere *to displease; to be
  disagreeable; to be sorry for; to
  regret.*

spiacevole *unpleasant.*

spiacevolmente *unpleasantly.*

SPIAGGIA *shore, beach.*

spiantato *uprooted, ruined, broke.*

spiccato *detached, pronounced,
  marked.*

spicchio *segment, clove.*

spicciare *to dispatch.*
  spicciarsi *to hurry.*

spicciolo *small.*
  avere spiccioli *to have change.*
  moneta spicciola *small change.*

spiedo *spit.*
  allo spiedo *on the spit.*

SPIEGARE *to explain; to unfold.*
  spiegare le ali *to spread out; to try
    one's wings; to unfold one's
    wings.*
  Spiegami che cosa significa questa
    parola. *Explain the meaning of
    this word.*

spiegazione, f. *explanation.*

spietato *merciless, pitiless.*

spiga *ear.*
  spiga di grano *ear of corn.*

spigliato *easy, frank.*

spigolo *corner, angle, edge.*

SPILLA *pin, brooch.*
  cuscinetto per spille *pincushion.*
  spilla di diamanti *diamond brooch.*
  spilla da balia *safety pin.*

spilla di sicurezza *safety pin.*
spilorcio *miserly, stingy.*
spina *thorn; plug.*
    spina dorsale *spinal column.*
spinaci, m. pl. *spinach.*
SPINGERE *to push; to drive.*
    spingersi *to drive oneself; to push forward.*
    Non spingere! *Don't push!*
    Sono stata spinta a farlo. *I was driven to do it.*
spinoso *thorny.*
    un problema spinoso *a thorny problem.*
spinta *push, shove.*
    dare una spinta *to shove; to give a push forward.*
spintome, m. *violent push.*
spiraglio *opening, airhole.*
SPIRITO *spirit, ghost, wit.*
    senza spirito *without spirit.*
    un uomo di spirito *a witty man.*
spiritoso *witty.*
spirituale *spiritual.*
splendente *shining, resplendent.*
splendere *to shine.*
splendidamente *splendidly.*
splendido *splendid.*
splendore, m. *splendor.*
spogliare *to undress; to strip.*
    spogliarsi *to undress oneself.*
spogliatoio *dressing room.*
spolverare *to dust.*
sponda *bank (of a river).*
spontaneamente *spontaneously.*
spontaneità *spontaneity, spontaneousness.*
spontaneo *spontaneous.*
SPORCARE *to dirty.*
    sporcarsi *to get dirty; to become dirty.*
sporcizia *dirt.*
sporco *dirty.*
sporgente *protruding.*
    denti sporgenti *protruding teeth.*
sporgere *to put out; to stretch out; to lean out.*
    Si è sporto dalla finestra. *He leaned out the window.*
    Ha sporto la mano dal finestrino dell'automobile. *He put his hand out of the car window.*

sportello *window, booth.*
    sportello dei biglietti *ticket window.*
SPOSA *bride.*
sposalizio *wedding.*
sposare *to marry.*
    sposarsi *to get married.*
sposo *groom.*
spossato *weary, fatigued.*
spostare *to move; to shift.*
    Si è spostato da un paese all'altro. *He moved from one country to the other.*
    Sposta quel libro dall'altra parte del tavolo. *Shift that book to the other side of the table.*
sprecare *to waste.*
spreco *waste.*
spregevole *despicable.*
spremere *to squeeze; to wring out.*
    spremere un arancia *to squeeze an orange.*
spremuta *squeezing.*
    una spremuta d'arancia *freshly squeezed orange juice.*
sprofondare *to sink; to collapse.*
sproporzionatamente *disproportionately.*
sproporzionato *disproportionate.*
sproporzione *disproportion.*
sproposito *mistake, blunder.*
spugna *sponge.*
spuma *foam, lather.*
spumante *sparkling wine.*
spumeggiante *sparkling.*
spuntare *to appear; to break through.*
spuntino *snack.*
    fare uno spuntino *to have a snack.*
sputare *to spit.*
squadra *team.*
squalifica *disqualification.*
squallido *squalid; miserable.*
squalo *shark.*
squillibrio *lack of balance.*
    squilibrio mentale *mental unbalance.*
squillare *to resound; to ring.*
squisitamente *exquisitely.*
squisito *exquisite.*
sradicare *to uproot.*
sregolato *disordered, irregular.*
stàbile *stable, steady.*
stabilimento *factory, establishment.*
stabilire *to establish; to settle.*

Si è stabilito in Italia. *He settled in Italy.*

Stabiliamo prima dove ci incontreremo. *Let's settle first where we are going to meet.*

stabilità *stability.*

stabilizzare *to stabilize.*

staccare *to detach.*

staccarsi da *to part from.*

stadio *stadium.*

staffa *stirrup.*

Ha perduto le staffe. *He lost his temper. (He lost his stirrups.)*

stagionale *seasonal.*

stagione, f. *season.*

stagnante *stagnant.*

stagnare *to cover with tin; to stop (the flow of a liquid); to be stagnant.*

Le acque stagnano. *The waters are stagnant.*

stagno *pond.*

stagnola *tinfoil.*

stalla *stable.*

stampa *print, press.*

errore di stampa *misprint.*

libertà di stampa *freedom of the press.*

stampante, m. *printer.*

stampare *to print.*

stampatello *block letters.*

STANCARE *to tire.*

stancarsi *to get tired.*

stanchezza *tiredness.*

stanco *tired.*

STANOTTE *tonight.*

STANZA *room, chamber.*

prendere una stanza in albergo *to take a room in a hotel.*

prenotare una stanza d'albergo *to reserve a room at a hotel.*

stanza da letto *bedroom.*

Si Affitta Stanza *Room for Rent.*

STARE *to stay.*

non stare in se *to be beside oneself.*

stare a sentire *to listen to.*

stare attento *to be careful.*

stare bene *to feel well.*

stare in piedi *to stand up.*

Che cosa stai facendo? *What are you doing?*

Come stanno le cose? *How do things stand?*

Lasciami stare! *Let me be!*

Stai quì finchè torno. *Stay here till I come back.*

Sto preparando il pranzo. *I'm preparing dinner.*

starnutire *to sneeze.*

starnuto *sneeze.*

STASERA *this evening; tonight.*

statale adj. *state.*

impiegato statale *state employee.*

STATO *state.*

affari di stato *affairs of state.*

in cattivo stato *in bad shape; in poor condition.*

Gli Stati Uniti *The United States.*

Lo stato della sua salute mi preoccupa. *The state of his health worries me.*

Questo stato di cose non può durare. *This state of affairs cannot last.*

statua *statue.*

STAZIONE, f. *station.*

stazione balneare *beach resort; seaside resort.*

stazione climatica *health resort.*

stazione ferroviaria *railroad station.*

STELLA *star.*

portare alle stelle *to praise someone to the skies.*

stellato *starry, star-studded.*

stelo *stem, stalk.*

stemma, m. *emblem; coat of arms.*

stendere *to stretch out.*

stendere un contratto *to draw up a contract.*

Mi ha steso la mano. *He offered his hand.*

stento *difficulty, fatigue.*

STESSO, n. *self, selves;* adj. *same.*

lui stesso *himself.*

essa stessa *herself.*

me stessa *myself, I.*

noi stessi *ourselves.*

dello stesso sangue *of the same blood; kindred.*

sempre lo stesso *always the same.*

stesura *drafting; drawing up (a document).*

stile, m. *style.*

stima *esteem, evaluation.*

degno di stima *worthy of esteem.*

fare una stima *to evaluate; to make an appraisal.*

stimare *to appraise; to consider; to esteem.*
> Ho fatto stimare il mio anello. *I had my ring appraised.*

stimolante *stimulating.*

stimolare *to stimulate.*
> L'odore d'arrosto stimola il mio appetito. *The smell of roast whets (stimulates) my appetite.*

stipendio *salary, wage.*

STIRARE *to iron.*
> far stirare *to have ironed.*

stirar(si) *to stretch.*

stivale, m. *boot.*

stizza *grudge, pique.*

stoffa *material, fabric.*
> fatto di stoffa buona *made with good material.*

stolto *foolish, silly.*

stomaco *stomach.*
> mal di stomaco *stomachache.*

stonato *out of tune.*

stordire *to stun.*

stordite *dizzy.*

STORIA *story, tale, history.*
> raccontare una storia *to tell a story.*
> La storia insegna . . . *history teaches us . . .*

storico, adj. *historical;* n. *historian.*

storto *crooked.*

stoviglie *dishes.*

stracciare *to tear.*

straccio *rag.*
> carta straccia *wrapping paper; wastepaper.*

STRADA *street, road.*
> farsi strada *to make headway; to get on.*
> per strada *on the road.*
> strada di campagna *country road.*
> strada facendo *on the way.*
> strada maestra *main street.*
> È sulla mia strada. *It's on my way.*
> Non mi ha detto che strada prendere. *He did not tell me which road to take.*

stranezza *strangeness; oddness.*

STRANIERO, adj. *foreign;* n. *foreigner.*
> Lui parla una lingua straniera. *He speaks a foreign language.*

strano *strange, queer, odd.*

> Mi sembra strano. *It seems strange to me.*

straordinario *extraordinary.*

strapazzo *overwork, disorder.*

strappare *to snatch; to tear.*

strappo *pull; tear.*
> fare uno strappo alla regola *to make an exception to the rule.*

strato *layer.*
> strato su strato *layer upon layer.*
> uno strato di pòlvere *a layer of dust.*

stravolgere *to distort.*

stravolto *altered, troubled.*

strega *witch.*

stregare *to bewitch.*

strepito *noise.*

STRETTA *grasp, grip, hold.*
> rallentare la stretta *to relax the grip.*
> una stretta di mano *handshake.*

STRETTO, adj. *narrow; tight;* n. *strait.*
> La strada è molto stretta. *The street is very narrow.*
> Lo Stretto di Messina *The Strait of Messina.*
> Questo vestito è troppo stretto per me. *This dress is too tight for me.*

stridente *shrill, sharp.*

stridere *to screech; to shriek.*

strillare *to scream; to shout.*

strillo *cry, shriek.*

STRINGERE *to tighten.*
> far stringere i freni *to have the brakes tightened.*
> stringere amicizia con *to make friends with.*
> stringere la mano *to shake hands.*
> Il tempo stringe. *Time presses; time is drawing short.*

striscia *strip, stripe.*
> a strisce *striped.*

strisciare *to creep; to slide.*

strizzare *to wring out; to squeeze.*
> strizzare i panni *to wring clothes out.*
> strizzare un occhio *to wink.*

strofinare *to rub.*
> strofinarsi *to rub oneself.*

strumento *tool, implement, instrument.*

studente, m. **studentessa,** f. *student.*

STUDIARE *to study.*

studio *study.*

stufa *stove.*

stufare *to stew.*
> stufarsi *to grow weary (colloq.).*

stufato *stew.*

stufo *weary, tired.*

stupendo *stupendous.*

stupidamente *stupidly.*

stupido, adj. *stupid;* n. *fool.*

stupire *to astonish.*
> stupirsi *to be astonished.*

stupore, m. *astonishment, stupor.*

stuzzicadenti *toothpick.*

SU *up, above, on.*
> andar su per le scale *to go up the stairs.*
> sulla panca *on the bench.*
> sullo scaffale *on the shelf.*
> su per giù *more or less.*
> più su *further up.*

subacqueo *underwater.*

subire *to endure; to feel.*

SUBITO *immediately; at once.*
> subito dopo *right after.*
> subito prima *just before.*
> Bisogna farlo subito. *It must be done right away.*
> Torno subito. *I'll be right back.*
> Vieni subito! *Come quickly!*

sublime *sublime.*

SUCCEDERE *to happen; to follow.*
> Che cosa è successo? *What happened?*
> La calma succede alla tempesta. *Calm follows the storm.*

successione, f. *succession.*

successivamente *successively.*

successivo *successive, following.*
> la settimana successiva *the following week.*

successo *success.*
> aver successo *to be successful.*

successore, m. *successor.*

SUCCHIARE *to suck.*

succo *juice.*

succursale, f. *branch; branch office; subsidiary.*

SUD, m. *south.*
> a sud di *south of.*
> sud-est *southeast.*
> sud-ovest *southwest.*

sudare *to perspire; to sweat.*

suddetto *above mentioned.*

suddito *subject.*

sudicio *dirty.*

sudore, m. *perspiration, sweat.*

sufficiente *sufficient.*

sufficienza *sufficient quantity.*
> a sufficienza *more than enough.*

suggerire *to suggest; to prompt.*

sughero *cork.*

sugo *juice, gravy.*
> sugo di pomodoro *tomato sauce.*

suicidio *suicide.*

SUO, sua, suoi, sue (il suo; la sua; i suoi; le sue) *his, her, its, your (polite).*
> la sua maestra *his teacher; her teacher.*
> suo padre *his father; her father.*
> Metti questo libro al posto suo. *Put this book in its place.*
> Vive coi suoi. *He lives with his parents (family).*

SUOCERA *mother-in-law.*

SUOCERO *father-in-law.*

suola *sole (of shoes).*

suolo *soil, ground.*
> il patrio suolo *native soil.*
> cadere al suolo *to fall to the ground.*

SUONARE *to sound; to ring; to play.*
> suonare il campanello *to ring the bell.*
> suonare il pianoforte *to play the piano.*
> suonare l'allarme *to sound the alarm.*

SUONO *sound.*
> a suon di *to the tune of.*

suora *nun, sister.*

SUPERARE *to surpass; to excel; to exceed.*
> superare gli esami *to pass one's examinations.*
> superare in numero *to surpass in number.*
> Mi supera per talento. *He has greater talent than I.*

superbo *proud.*

superficiale *superficial.*

superficie, f. *surface.*

superfluo *superfluous.*

superiore, adj. & n.m. *superior.*

superiorità *superiority.*

superlativo *superlative.*

supermercato *supermarket.*

superstite *surviving.*
superstizione, f. *superstition.*
suppergiù *approximately, about.*
supporre *to suppose.*
supposizione, f. *supposition.*
supposto *supposed.*
supremazia *supremacy.*
supremo *supreme.*
    la Corte Suprema *the Supreme
      Court.*
suscettibile *susceptible, touchy.*
suscettibilità *susceptibility.*
    offendere la suscettibilità di *to hurt
      the feelings of.*
suscitare *to rouse; to provoke; to give
    rise to.*
    suscitare l'ira di qualcuno *to rouse
      someone's anger.*
    suscitare uno scandalo *to provoke a
      scandal.*
sussurrare *to murmur; to mutter; to
    whisper.*
suvvia *Come on!*
svagare *to distract.*
    Mi voglio svagare un po'. *I want to
      amuse myself (distract myself) a
      little.*
svago *amusement, recreation; fun.*
svalutare *to devalue; to depreciate.*
svalutazione *depreciation.*
SVANIRE *to vanish.*
svanito *vanished.*
svantaggio *disadvantage.*
svasato *A-line.*
svedese *Swedish.*
SVEGLIA *alarm clock.*
SVEGLIARE *to wake.*
svegliar(si) *to wake up.*
sveglio *awake, alert, quick-witted.*
    È una ragazza molto sveglia. *She is
      a very bright girl.*
    Sono sveglio dalle sette di questa
      mattina. *I've been awake since
      seven this morning.*
svelare *to reveal.*
    svelare un segreto *to reveal a secret.*
sveltezza *quickness.*
svelto *quick, rapid, swift.*
    Bisogna agire alla svelta. *We must
      act quickly.*
svenire *to faint.*
sventura *misfortune.*

sventurato *unfortunate, unlucky.*
svenuto *fainted.*
svestire *to undress.*
    svestirsi *to undress oneself.*
sviare *to mislead; to lead astray.*
sviluppo *development, growth.*
svista *oversight.*
    Fu una svista da parte mia. *It was an
      oversight on my part.*
svitare *to unscrew.*
svizzero, adj. & n. *Swiss.*
svogliato *indifferent; lazy.*
svolgere *to develop; to unfold.*
svolta *turn; turning point.*

T

tabaccàio *tobacco shop owner.*
tabaccheria *tobacco store.*
tabacco *tobacco.*
tabella *list; table; schedule.*
tacchino *turkey.*
tacco *heel.*
taccuino *notebook.*
TACERE *to be silent.*
    far tacere *to silence.*
tacitamente *silently, tacitly.*
tacito *tacit, silent.*
taciturno *taciturn.*
taffeta *taffeta.*
taglia *size, ransom.*
    della stessa taglia *of the same size.*
tagliacarte, m. *paper knife.*
TAGLIARE *to cut; to slash.*
    essere tagliato per *to be cut out for.*
    farsi tagliare i capelli *to get a
      haircut.*
    tagliare i panni addosso a *to speak
      ill of.*
tagliatelle, f. *noodles.*
tagliente *cutting, sharp.*
taglio *cut.*
    Il taglio di questo vestito non mi sta
      bene. *The cut of this suit is not
      good for me.*
talco *talc.*
TALE *such.*
    di uno splendore tale *of such
      splendor.*
    il signor Tal dei Tali *Mr. So-and-So.*

quel tale *that person.*
tale e quale *exactly the same.*
talento *talent, intelligence.*
tallone, m. *heel.*
talmente *so; so much.*
talvolta *sometimes.*
tamburo *drum.*
tana *den, lair.*
tangibile *tangible.*
tangibilmente *tangibly.*
TANTO *so; so much.*
   di tanto in tanto *from time to time.*
   ogni tanto *every so often.*
   tanto meglio *so much the better.*
   tanto per cominciare *to begin with.*
   tanto quanto *as much as.*
   una volta tanto *once in a while.*
   Si vogliono tanto bene. *They love
     each other so much.*
tappa *halting place.*
   a piccole tappe *in small stretches.*
tappare *to stop; to stop up; to cork.*
   tappare una bottiglia *to cork a bottle.*
tappeto *rug, carpet.*
tappezzeria *tapestry, wallpaper.*
tappe *stopper, cork.*
TARDARE *to delay; to be late.*
   Non tardare per pranzo. *Don't be
     late for lunch.*
   Non tarderanno molto a venire. *They
     will not be very late coming.*
TARDI *late.*
   fare tardi *to be late.*
   meglio tardi che mai *better late than
     never.*
   presto o tardi *sooner or later.*
   Si sta facendo tardi. *It's getting late.*
targa *plate, nameplate.*
   targa dell' automobile *license plate.*
tariffa *rate, tariff.*
tarma *moth.*
tartaruga *tortoise, turtle.*
tartina *canapé.*
tasca *pocket.*
taschino *breast pocket.*
tassa *tax, duty.*
   tassa d'ammissione *entrance fee.*
   tassa sul reddito *income tax.*
tassare *to tax.*
tassativo *positive, explicit.*
tassì, m. *taxi.*
tasso *rate.*

   tasso di cambio *rate of exchange.*
   tasso d'interesse *rate of interest.*
tastiera *keyboard.*
tasto *key (of musical instruments).*
tattica *tactics.*
   seguire la tattica sbagliata *to go
     about things in the wrong
     manner.*
TAVOLA *table, board, plank.*
   apparecchiare la tavola *to set the
     table.*
   sparecchiare la tavola *to clear the
     table.*
   una tavola di legno *a wooden board.*
tavoletta *tablet; bar.*
   una tavoletta di cioccolato *a bar of
     chocolate.*
TAZZA *cup.*
   tazza da tè *teacup.*
   tazza di tè *cup of tea.*
te, sing. *you.*
   Parlo di te. *I am speaking of you.*
tè, m. *tea.*
teatrale *theatrical.*
TEATRO *theater.*
tecnica *technique.*
tecnicamente *technically.*
tecnico, adj. *technical;* n. *technician.*
tecnologia *technology.*
tedesco, n. & adj. *German.*
tegame, m. *pan.*
tegola *tile.*
telera *teapot.*
tela *cloth, linen; canvas.*
   olio su tela *oil on canvas.*
telecamara *video camera.*
telcomando *remote control.*
telecomunicazioni *telecommunication.*
telefonare *to telephone.*
telefonata *telephone call.*
   telefonata a carico del destinatario
     collect call.
telefonicamente *by telephone.*
telefonico *telephonic.*
   cabina telefonica *telephone booth.*
   elenco telefonico *telephone book.*
telefonista, m. & f. *telephone operator.*
telefono *telephone.*
   telefono portatile *cordless phone.*
telegiornale *TV news.*
telegrafare *to telegraph; to wire.*
telegrafia *telegraphy.*

telegraficamente *telegraphically.*
telegrafico *telegraphic.*
   ufficio telegrafico *telegraph office.*
telegrafista, m. & f. *telegraph operator.*
telègrafo *telegraph.*
telegramma *telegram, wire, cable.*
telepatìa *telepathy.*
   telepatìa mentale *mental telepathy.*
telescòpio *telescope.*
telescrivente, f. *tape machine.*
televisione, f. *television.*
telex *telex machine.*
tema, m. *theme.*
temerarie *rash.*
TEMERE *to fear; to be afraid; to dread.*
   Non temo nulla. *I fear nothing.*
temibile *dreadful.*
temperante *temperate, sober, tempering.*
temperatura *temperature.*
temperino *penknife.*
tempesta *storm, tempest.*
   una tempesta in un bicchier d'acqua *a tempest in a teapot.*
tempestivo *timely.*
tempestoso *tempestuous.*
   mare tempestoso *stormy sea.*
tempia *temple (side of head).*
tempio *temple (cathedral).*
TEMPO *weather.*
   cattivo tempo *bad weather.*
   di questi tempi *in these times.*
   nello stesso tempo *at the same time.*
   perdere tempo *to lose time.*
   tempo fa *some time ago.*
   tempo presente *present tense.*
   Che tempo fa? *How is the weather?*
   Chi ha tempo non aspetti tempo. *Never put off till tomorrow what can be done today.*
   Da quanto tempo non ci vediamo! *How long it has been since we've seen each other!*
   È tempo di . . . *It's time to . . .*
temporale, m. *storm.*
temporaneamente *temporarily.*
temporaneo *temporary.*
tenace *tenacious, persevering.*
tenacemente *tenaciously.*
tenacia *tenaciousness.*

tenda *tent, curtain.*
tendenza *tendency.*
tendere *to tend to; to stretch out; to hold out.*
tenebre *darkness.*
tenente, m. *lieutenant.*
teneramente *tenderly.*
TENERE *to keep; to hold.*
   tenere a mente *to remember; to keep in mind.*
   tenere compagnìa a *to keep someone company.*
   tenere d'occhio *to keep an eye on.*
   tenere gli occhi aperti *to keep one's eyes open.*
   tenere il broncio verso *to keep a grudge against.*
   tenersi a destra *to keep to the right.*
   tenersi in contatto con *to keep in contact with.*
   Non ci tengo. *I don't care about it.*
tenerezza *tenderness.*
tenero *tender, affectionate.*
tenore, m. *tenor; way.*
   tenore di vita *way of life.*
tensione, f. *tension.*
   tensione nervosa *nervous tension.*
TENTARE *to attempt.*
tentativo *attempt, endeavor.*
tentazione, f. *temptation.*
   resistere alla tentazione *to resist temptation.*
tentennare *to sway; to hesitate.*
teoria *theory.*
teppismo *hooliganism.*
terme, f. pl. *hot springs.*
TERMINARE *to finish; to end.*
   Appena ho terminato questo lavoro, ti raggiungo. *I'll join you as soon as I finish this work.*
termine, m. *term, limit, boundary.*
   allo scadere del termine fissato *at the end of the established term.*
   aver termine *to end.*
   fissare un termine *to fix a date; to set a date.*
   porre termine a *to put an end to.*
   ridurre ai minimi termini *to reduce to the lowest terms.*
   secondo i termini stabiliti in precedenza *according to the terms previously agreed to.*

termòmetro *thermometer.*
termos, m. *thermos bottle.*
termosifone, m. *radiator (heating).*
TERRA *earth.*
    cader per terra *to fall to the ground.*
    per terra *on the ground.*
    scendere a terra *to go ashore.*
    terra madre *motherland; native land.*
    terra nativa *native land.*
terrazza *balcony, terrace.*
terreno, adj. *earthly;* n. *earth.*
    a pian terreno *on the ground floor.*
    perdere terreno *to lose ground.*
terribile *terrible.*
terribilmente *terribly.*
territorio *territory.*
terrore, m. *terror.*
terrorismo *terrorism.*
terrorizzare *to terrorize.*
TERZA *third.*
    fare la terza elementare *to be in the third grade in elementary school.*
    mettere in terza *to shift into high gear.*
    viaggiare in terza *to travel third class.*
TERZO, adj. & n. *third.*
teso *stretched out; tightened.*
tesoro *treasure.*
tessera *card, ticket.*
tessile *textiles.*
tessuto *cloth, fabric.*
TESTA *head.*
    alla testa di *at the head of.*
    giramento di testa *dizzy spell.*
    mal di testa *headache.*
    perdere la testa *to lose one's head.*
testamento *will; testament.*
testardaggine, f. *stubbornness.*
testardamente *stubbornly.*
teste, m. & f. *witness.*
testimone, m. & f. *witness.*
    testimone oculare *eyewitness.*
testimonianza *testimony.*
testimoniare *to witness.*
testo *text.*
    libro di testo *textbook.*
testuale *exact, precise.*
    le mie testuali parole *my very words.*
tetro *gloomy, dismal.*
TETTO *roof.*

TI *you, to you; yourself.*
    Che cosa ti ha detto? *What did he tell you?*
    Questo libro ti appartiene. *This book belongs to you.*
    Ti sei guardato allo specchio? *Did you look at yourself in the mirror?*
tiepido *tepid, lukewarm.*
tifone, m. *typhoon.*
tifoso *fan, supporter; typhus patient.*
    un tifoso di pugilato *boxing fan.*
tigre, f. *tiger, tigress.*
timbro *stamp.*
    timbro postale *postmark.*
timidamente *timidly.*
timidezza *timidity, shyness.*
timido *timid, shy.*
TIMORE, m. *fear.*
    aver timore di *to be afraid of.*
    per timore di *for fear of.*
timpano *eardrum.*
tingere *to dye; to tint.*
    tingere di nero *to dye black.*
    tingersi i capelli *to dye one's hair.*
tinta *dye.*
    a forti tinte *sensational.*
tinto *dyed.*
tintore, m. *dyer.*
tipicamente *typically.*
tipico *typical.*
tipo *type.*
tiranno *tyrant.*
TIRARE *to draw; to pull.*
    tirare a scherma *to fence.*
    tirare a sorte *to draw lots.*
    tirare avanti *to keep going.*
    tirare un colpo *to fire a shot.*
    tirare per le lunghe *to go on and on.*
    tirarsi da parte *to stand aside.*
    tirarsi indietro *to draw back.*
    una carrozza tirata da quattro cavalli *a coach drawn by four horses.*
tiro *trick.*
tirocinio *apprenticeship.*
titolo *title.*
titubante *hesitant, irresolute.*
titubanza *hesitancy, irresoluteness.*
titubare *to hesitate; to waver.*
TOCCARE *to touch.*
    toccare il cuore *to touch one's heart.*

toccare sul vivo *to touch a sore spot.*

A chi tocca? *Whose turn is it?*

Mi tocca rifare la strada. *I have to retrace my footsteps.*

TOGLIERE *to take; to take off; to remove.*

togliere di mano *to snatch.*

togliersi di mezzo *to get out of the way.*

togliersi il cappello ed il cappotto *to remove one's hat and coat.*

togliersi la vita *to commit suicide.*

tollerabile *tolerable.*

tollerante *tolerant.*

tolleranza *tolerance.*

tomba *grave, tomb.*

tonalità *tonality.*

tondo *round.*

cifra tonda *round sum.*

dire chiaro e tondo *to speak plainly.*

tonico n. & adj. *tonic.*

tonnellata *ton.*

tonno *tuna.*

tono *tone, tint.*

con tono aspro *with a sharp tone.*

Non permetto che mi si parli in quel tono di voce. *I will not be spoken to in that tone of voice.*

tonsilla *tonsil.*

tonsillite, f. *tonsillitis.*

topazio *topaz.*

topo *mouse.*

Topolino *Mickey Mouse (little mouse).*

torbido *muddy; not clear.*

torcere *to twist.*

torcia *torch, brand.*

torciollo *stiff neck.*

tormenta *blizzard.*

tormentare *to torment.*

tormentarsi *to torment oneself; to worry.*

tormento *torment, torture.*

TORNARE *to return.*

tornare a casa *to come home.*

tornare in se *to come to one's senses.*

tornare sui propri passi *to retrace one's footsteps.*

Il conto non torna. *The account is incorrect.*

Torna indietro! *Come back!*

tornèo *tournament.*

toro *bull.*

torre, f. *tower.*

Torre di Pisa *the Tower of Pisa (the Leaning Tower).*

torrente, m. *torrent, stream.*

torrido *torrid; burning.*

torrione *large tower; castle keep.*

torrone *nougat.*

torso *trunk, torso.*

torta *cake, pastry.*

torta di frutta *pie.*

tortellini *stuffed macaroni.*

TORTO *wrong.*

a torto o a ragione *right or wrong.*

aver torto *to be wrong.*

essere dalla parte del torto *to be in the wrong.*

fare un torto a *to wrong someone.*

tortuoso *tortuous, winding.*

tortura *torture, pain.*

tosse *cough.*

tosse convulsiva *whooping cough.*

un colpo di tosse *a coughing fit; a coughing spell.*

Ho la tosse. *I have a cough.*

tossico *toxic.*

TOSSIRE *to cough.*

tostare *to toast.*

pane tostato *toasted bread.*

tosto, adj. *hard;* adv. *soon.*

aver la faccia tosta *to have cheek; to be impudent.*

totale, adj. & n. m. *total.*

totalità *totality, whole.*

totalmente *totally.*

TOVAGLIA *tablecloth.*

tovagliolo *napkin.*

traballare *to stagger; to reel.*

traboccare *to overflow.*

traccia *trace, track, trail.*

mettersi sulle tracce di *to follow the trail of.*

perdere le tracce di *to lose track of.*

seguire la traccia di *to follow the track of.*

Non ne rimane neppure una traccia. *There is not a trace of it left.*

tracciare *to trace; to mark out; to draw.*

tracciare una linea *to make a line.*

tradimento *betrayal, treason.*
  colpevole di alto tradimento *guilty of high treason.*
TRADIRE *to betray; to deceive; to be unfaithful to.*
  tradire la propria moglie *to be unfaithful to one's wife.*
  tradirsi *to betray oneself; to give oneself away.*
  Lui ha tradito la patria. *He betrayed his country.*
  La sua espressione tradiva il suo terrore. *Her expression betrayed her terror.*
traditore, m. **traditrice,** f. *traitor.*
tradizionale *traditional.*
tradizione *tradition.*
traducibile *translatable.*
tradurre *to translate.*
  tradurre dall' italiano all'inglese *to translate from Italian to English.*
traduttore, m. **traduttrice,** f. *translator.*
traduzione, f. *translation.*
trafficante *dealer; trafficker.*
trafficare *to trade; to traffic.*
traffico *traffic.*
tragedia *tragedy.*
traghetto *ferry, ferryboat.*
tragicamente *tragically.*
tragico, adj. *tragic;* n. *tragedian.*
tragicomico *tragicomic.*
tragitto *journey, passage.*
traiettoria *trajectory.*
trainare *to haul; to drag.*
tralasciare *to leave out; to omit.*
  senza tralasciare nulla *without leaving anything out.*
tralucere *to be transparent; to shine through.*
tram, m. *trolley car.*
trama *plot.*
tramandare *to hand down.*
  Questa usanza fu tramandata da padre in figlio. *This custom was handed down from father to son.*
tramite *through.*
  tramite un'agenzia *through an agency.*
TRAMONTARE *to go down; to set; to fade.*
  al tramontar del sole *at sundown.*

  La sua gloria non tramonterà mai. *His glory will never fade.*
tramonto *setting.*
  tramonto del sole *sunset.*
trampolino *springboard.*
tramutare *to transmute; to turn.*
  La sua gioia si è tramutata in dolore. *His joy turned to sorrow.*
tranello *trap, snare.*
  tendere un tranello *to trap; to ensnare.*
TRANNE *save, but, except.*
  tutti tranne uno *all save one; all but one.*
  Ha invitato tutti tranne Maria. *She invited everyone except Mary.*
tranquillamente *peacefully.*
tranquillità *tranquility, peace.*
tranquillizzare *to quiet; to calm.*
  tranquillizzarsi *to calm down; to calm oneself.*
tranquillo *peaceful.*
  mare tranquillo *a calm sea.*
  Lasciami tranquillo. *Leave me in peace.*
transazione, f. *transaction.*
transigere *to yield; to come to terms.*
  Su questioni di denaro io non transigo. *On financial matters I do not yield.*
transitare *to pass through.*
  Molte persone transitano per questa strada. *Many people pass through this street.*
trànsito *transit.*
  La merce è in trànsito. *The merchandise is in transit.*
  Vietato il Trànsito! *No Through Traffic!*
transitorio *transitory, temporary.*
transizione, f. *transition.*
tranvia, m. *streetcar; trolley car.*
trapiantare *to transplant; to migrate.*
trapianto *graft.*
trappola *trap, snare.*
  cadere in trappola *to be caught in a trap.*
trapunta *quilt.*
trarre *to draw; to draw out.*
  trarre in inganno *to deceive.*
  trarre ispirazione da *to draw inspiration from.*

trarre vantaggio da *to benefit from.*
trarsi in disparte *to draw aside.*
trasalire *to start.*
   Un rumore improvviso mi ha fatto
   trasalire. *A sudden noise made*
   me start (startled me).
trasandato *careless.*
trascinare *to drag.*
   trascinare per terra *to drag about the*
   floor.
   trascinarsi *to drag oneself.*
trascorrere *to spend; to pass.*
   trascorrere il tempo leggendo *to*
   spend the time reading.
   Abbiamo trascorso un' estate
   meravigliosa in campagna. *We*
   spent a marvelous summer in the
   country.
   Sono trascorsi molti anni dall' ultima
   volta che lo vidi. *Many years*
   have gone by since the last time I
   saw him.
trascrivere *transcribe.*
trascrizione *transcription.*
trascurabile *negligible.*
TRASCURARE *to neglect.*
   trascurare il proprio dovere *to*
   neglect one's duties.
   trascurarsi *to neglect oneself.*
trascuratamente *carelessly.*
trascuratezza *carelessness, neglect.*
trascurato *careless.*
trasferimento *transfer.*
trasferire *to transfer.*
   trasferirsi *to move.*
   Fu trasferito da una città all' altra.
   He was transferred from one city
   to the other.
trasformare *to transform.*
   trasformarsi *to transform oneself.*
trasformazione, f. *transformation.*
trasfusione, f. *transfusion.*
   trasfusione di sangue *blood*
   transfusion.
trasgredire *to transgress.*
traslato *metaphor.*
traslocare *to move; to change address.*
trasloco *removal.*
   furgone per traslochi *moving van.*
trasmettere *to transmit.*
   trasmettere per radio *to broadcast.*
trasmettitore, m. *transmitter.*

trasmissione, f. *transmission,*
   broadcast.
trasognato *dreamy; lost in reverie; lost*
   in daydreams.
trasparente *transparent.*
trasparenza *transparency.*
trasparire *to shine through; to be*
   transparent.
traspirare *to perspire.*
traspirazione, f. *perspiration.*
trasportare *to transport; to convey.*
   trasportare per mare *to transport*
   by sea.
   trasportare per terra *to transport by*
   land.
trasportate *transported.*
trasporto *transportation, transport.*
   Non vi sono mezzi di trasporto.
   There is no means of
   conveyance.
trasversale *transversal.*
trasvolare *to fly across; to fly.*
trasvolata *flight.*
tratta *draft.*
   pagare una tratta *to pay a draft.*
   tratta bancaria *bank draft.*
trattabile *tractable, treatable.*
trattamento *treatment.*
TRATTARE *to treat; to deal (with).*
   trattare bene *to treat well.*
   trattare male *to treat badly.*
   trattare un argomento *to deal with a*
   subject.
   trattarsi *to be a question of.*
   Di che si tratta? *What is it all about?*
   Si tratta della prossima festa. *It's*
   about the coming party.
trattative, f. pl. *negotiations.*
   condurre a termine le trattative *to*
   carry out negotiations.
   essere in trattative *to be negotiating.*
   Abbiamo dovuto interrompere le
   trattative. *Negotiations had to be*
   interrupted.
trattato *treaty.*
   trattato di pace *peace treaty.*
TRATTENERE *to withold; to restrain;*
   to keep.
   trattenere il respiro *to hold one's*
   breath.
   trattenere le lacrime *to restrain one's*
   tears.

Mi dispiace non potermi trattenere
più a lungo con voi. *I'm sorry I
can't stay with you any longer.*

Riesco a stento a trattenermi. *I can
hardly restrain myself.*

Si è trattenuta la somma che gli
dovevo. *He withheld the sum I
owed him.*

trattenimento *entertainment.*

Vorrei organizzare un piccolo
trattenimento in casa mia domani
sera. *I would like to organize a
small party at my house
tomorrow night.*

trattenuta *deduction.*

trattiso *hyphen, dash.*

TRATTO *stroke, gesture.*

a grandi tratti *by leaps and bounds.*

tutto d'un tratto *all of a sudden.*

un tratto signorile *very refined
manners.*

un tratto di strada *partway.*

trattore, m. *tractor.*

trattoria *restaurant; eating place.*

travaglio *labor, toil, anxiety.*

travatura *beams.*

trave, f. *beam, rafter.*

traversa *side street; crossroad.*

TRAVERSARE *to cross.*

traversare una strada *to cross a
street.*

traversata *crossing.*

traverso *cross; adverse.*

andare di traverso *to go the wrong
way.*

di traverso *sideways, askance.*

travestimento *disguise.*

travestire *to disguise.*

travestitismo *transvestism; cross-
dressing.*

travisare *to distort; to misrepresent.*

Lui ha travisato completamente i
fatti. *He completely distorted the
facts.*

travolgere *to sweep away.*

TRE *three.*

treccia *braid.*

portare le treccie *to wear one's hair
in braids.*

trecento *three hundred.*

tredicesimo, n. & adj. *thirteenth.*

tredici *thirteen.*

tregua *truce.*

senza tregua *unrelentingly.*

TREMARE *to tremble; to shake.*

tremar di freddo *to shiver with cold.*

tremar di paura *to shake with fear.*

tremarella *trembling.*

aver la tremarella *to have the shakes.*

tremendamente *tremendously.*

tremendo *terrible, awful.*

trèmito *trembling, tremble.*

TRENO *train.*

perdere il treno *to miss the train.*

prendere il treno *to take the train.*

treno direttissimo, treno expresso
express train, intercity train.

treno rapido *fast train.*

treno merci *freight train.*

trenta *thirty.*

trentesimo *thirtieth.*

trepidante *anxious, apprehensive,
trembling.*

triangolare *triangular.*

triangolo *triangle.*

tribolare *to trouble; to worry; to suffer.*

tribolazione, f. *worry, suffering,
tribulation.*

tribù, f. *tribe.*

tribunale, m. *tribunal, court.*

tributare *to give; to render.*

tributare omaggio *to pay homage.*

tributario *tributary.*

tributo *tribute.*

triciclo *tricycle.*

trifoglio *clover.*

trimestrale *quarterly.*

trio *trio.*

trionfale *triumphal.*

trionfalmente *triumphantly.*

trionfante *triumphant.*

trionfare *to triumph.*

trionfare di *to triumph over.*

trionfare sui nemici *to triumph over
enemies.*

trionfo *triumph.*

triplice *threefold.*

triplo *triple.*

trippa *tripe.*

trisillabo *trisyllable.*

TRISTE *sad, sorrowful.*

uno sguardo triste *a sad look.*

tristemente *sadly, sorrowfully.*

tristezza *sadness, sorrow.*

tritacarne, m. *meat grinder.*
tritare *to mince; to hash.*
trito *trite, common.*
trittico *triptych.*
triviale *trivial, vulgar.*
trivialità *triviality.*
trivialmente *trivially; vulgarly.*
trofèo *trophy.*
tromba *trumpet.*
troncare *to cut off; to break off.*
tronco *trunk (tree).*
trono *throne.*
tropicale *tropical.*
TROPPO *too; too much.*
   parlare troppo *to talk too much.*
   troppi *too many.*
   troppo forte *too loud; too strong.*
   troppo spesso *too often.*
trota *trout.*
trottare *to trot.*
trotto *trot.*
   mettere a trotto *to put to a trot.*
TROVARE *to find.*
   Trovo che . . . *I think that . . .*
   trovarsi come a casa propria *to feel*
     at home.
   Come l'hai trovato? *How did you*
     find it?
   Come ti trovi qui? *How do you feel*
     here?
   Mi trovo molto bene, grazie. *I feel*
     quite well, thank you.
   Ti verrò a trovare. *I'll come to*
     see you.
trovata *invention, contrivance,*
   expedient.
truccare *to make someone up; to apply*
   makeup.
   truccarsi *to make oneself up.*
   truccarsi da pagliaccio *to make*
     oneself up as a clown.
trucco *trick, makeup.*
   Questo è un trucco. *This is a trick.*
truffa *swindle.*
truffare *to cheat; to swindle.*
truffatore, m. *cheat, cheater, swindler.*
truppa *troop.*
TU fam. sing. *you.*
tubatura *piping; plumbing pipes.*
tubercolosi, f. *tuberculosis.*
tubetto *small tube; tube paint.*
tubo *pipe, tube.*

tubo del gas *gas pipe.*
tubo di scarico *exhaust pipe.*
tubolare *tubular.*
tuffare *to plunge.*
   tuffarsi *to dive.*
tuffata *dive.*
tuffo *dive.*
   sentire un tuffo al cuore *to feel one's*
     heart skip a beat.
tulipano *tulip.*
tumulto *tumult, uproar.*
tumultuoso *tumultuous.*
TUO, tua, tuoi, tue (il tuo; la tua; i
   tuoi; le tue) *your, yours.*
   Il tuo libro è qui. *Your book is here.*
   Questo libro è tuo. *This book is*
     yours.
tuono *thunder.*
tuorlo *yolk.*
turacciolo *cork.*
turare *to stop; to cork; to fill.*
   turarsi gli orecchi *to stop one's*
     ears.
turbamento *agitation, commotion.*
turbante, m. *turban.*
turbare *to trouble; to disturb; to*
   agitate.
   turbarsi *to become agitated.*
   Questo pensiero mi turba molto.
     This thought disturbs me a great
     deal.
turbato *troubled, agitated.*
   avere un aria turbata *to have a*
     troubled air.
turbine, m. *hurricane, whirlwind.*
   un turbine sabbia *a whirl of sand.*
turbolento *turbulent, troubled.*
turbolenza *turbulence.*
turchese, f. *turquoise.*
turchino *dark blue.*
turismo *touring*
turista, m. *tourist.*
turistico, adj. *touring, tourist.*
   classe turistica *tourist class.*
turno *turn.*
   essere di turno *to be on duty.*
   lavorare a turni *to work by turns.*
   medico di turno *doctor on duty.*
tuta, m. *overalls.*
tutela *tutelage, guardianship.*
   sotto la tutela di *under the*
     wardship of.

tutelare *to protect; to defend.*
tutore, m. *guardian, protector.*
TUTTAVIA *still, yet, however, nevertheless.*
  Non lo vedo da molti anni, tuttavìa credo che lo riconoscerei subito. *I haven't seen him in many years, yet I think I would recognize him right away.*
TUTTO *all, whole, every.*
  del tutto *quite, completely.*
  essere tutti d'accordo *to be all in agreement.*
  in tutto e per tutto *all and for all.*
  tutte le sere *every night.*
  tutti i giorni *every day.*
  tutti insieme *all together.*
  tutto ciò che *all that.*
  tutto fatto *all done.*
  tutto il giorno *all day.*
  tutto il mondo *all the world; the whole world.*
  Essa conosce tutta la mia famiglia. *She knows my whole family.*
  tutti e due *both.*
  tutte le volte che *every time.*
  tutto quello che *whatever.*

U

ubbidiente *obedient.*
ubbidire *to obey.*
ubicazione *site; location.*
ubriacare *to make drunk; to intoxicate.*
  ubriacarsi *to become drunk; to become intoxicated.*
ubriacatura *intoxication.*
  postumi di una ubriacatura *hangover.*
  prendere un'ubriacatura per qualcuno *to have a crush on someone.*
ubriachezza *drunkenness, intoxication.*
  in stato di ubriachezza *in a drunken state.*
ubriaco *drunk, inebriated.*
UCCELLO *bird.*
  uccello di mal augurio *bird of ill omen.*
  uccelli di passo *birds of passage.*
UCCIDERE *to kill; to slay.*

  uccidersi *to commit suicide; to kill oneself.*
uccisione, f. *killing, murder.*
ucciso *killed, slain.*
uccisore, m. *killer.*
udibile *audible.*
udienza *audience, hearing.*
  chiedere un'udienza *to ask an audience.*
  L'udienza è rinviata. *Court is adjourned.*
UDIRE *to hear.*
  Non ho udito bene. *I didn't hear well.*
  Odo un rumore strano. *I hear a strange noise.*
udito *hearing.*
  aver l'undito fine *to have a good hearing.*
uditore, m. **uditrice,** f. *hearer, listener.*
uditorio, adj. *auditory;* n. *audience.*
ufficiale, n. m. *official, officer;* adj. *official.*
  ufficiale della marina *navy officer.*
  comunicato ufficiale *official communiqué.*
  L'Italiano è la lingua ufficiale dell'Italia. *Italian is the official language in Italy.*
ufficiare *to officiate.*
UFFICIO *office.*
  d'ufficio *officially.*
  ufficio postale *post office.*
  ufficio telegrafico *telegraphic office.*
uguale *equal, same.*
  Dividilo in parti uguali. *Divide it in equal parts.*
  Il prezzo dei due abiti è uguale. *The price of the two dresses is the same.*
  La legge è uguale per tutti. *The law is the same for everyone.*
uguaglianza *equality.*
uguagliare *to equal.*
  Nessuna ti uguaglia in bellezza. *No one equals you in beauty.*
ugualmente *equally; all the same.*
  Devi essere ugualmente gentile con tutti. *You must be equally courteous with everyone.*
  Preferirei restare in casa questa sera, ma dovrò uscire ugualmente. *I*

would prefer to remain at home
this evening, but I will have to go
out all the same.

ùlcera *ulcer.*

ulteriore *further, ulterior.*

Ti darò ulteriori informazioni
domani. *I will give you further
information tomorrow.*

ulteriormente *ulteriorly; later on.*

ultimamente *ultimately.*

ultimare *to finish; to complete.*

I lavori furono ultimati soltanto ieri.
*The work was completed only
yesterday.*

ultimato *finished, completed.*

a lavoro ultimato *upon completion of
the work.*

ultimatum *ultimatum.*

ÙLTIMO *latest, last.*

le ùltime notizie *the latest news.*

l'ultima volta che ci siamo visti *the
last time we saw each other.*

ùltima moda *latest fashion.*

Fui l'ùltima ad arrivare. *I was the
last to arrive.*

ultravioletto *ultraviolet.*

uluato (ùlulo) *howl, howling.*

ululare *to howl.*

Il vento ùlula. *The wind is howling.*

umanamente *humanly, humanely.*

trattare umanamente *to treat
humanely.*

Non è umanamente possibile. *It is
not humanly possible.*

umanità, f. *humanity, humankind,
humaneness.*

umanitario *humanitarian.*

umanizzare *to humanize.*

umanizzarsi *to become humane.*

umano *human, humane.*

la natura umana *human nature.*

ogni essere umano *every human
being.*

umidità *humidity, dampness, moisture.*

l'umidità dell'aria *the humidity of
the air.*

ùmido *damp, moist.*

tempo caldo ùmido *muggy weather.*

carne in ùmido *meat stew.*

ùmile *humble.*

di ùmile origine *of humble origin; of
humble birth.*

umiliante *humiliating, mortifying.*

umiliare *to humiliate; to mortify.*

umiliarsi *to humble oneself.*

umiliato *humbled, humiliated.*

umiliaxione, f. *humiliation.*

umiltà *humility, humbleness.*

umilmente *humbly.*

UMORE, m. *humor, temper.*

di cattivo umore *bad-tempered,
moody.*

d'umore nero *in a bad humor.*

di buon umore *in a good mood.*

umorismo *humor.*

Non è il caso di fare dell' umorismo.
It's not a matter to joke about.

avere il senso dell' umorismo *to
have a sense of humor.*

umorista, m. *humorist.*

umoristico *humorous.*

un *see UNO.*

unanime *unanimous.*

unanimemente *unanimously.*

unanimità *unanimity.*

all'unanimità *unanimously.*

uncinetto *crochet hook.*

lavoro all'uncinetto *crochet.*

undicesimo, n. & adj. *eleventh.*

undici *eleven.*

ungere *to grease; to smear.*

ùngere le ruote *to oil the wheels; to
make things go more smoothly.*

unghie *nail, hoof.*

le ùnghie del cavallo *the horse's
hooves.*

pulirsi le ùnghie *to clean one's
nails.*

spazzolino da ùnghie *nail brush.*

unguento *unguent, ointment.*

unicamente *only, solely.*

UNICO *only, sole, unique.*

figlio ùnico *only son.*

l'ùnico motivo della mia visita *the
sole reason for my visit.*

Ha un talento ùnico al mondo. *He
has a unique talent.*

l'unica copia esistente *the only
existing copy.*

unificare *to unify.*

unificazione, f. *unification.*

uniformare *to conform.*

Mi sono uniformato ai suoi voleri. *I
complied with his wishes.*

uniforme, n. f. *uniform;* adj. *uniform.*
  indossare l'uniforme *to don the uniform.*
uniformità *uniformity.*
unione, f. *union.*
UNIRE *to unite; to join; to enclose.*
  unire in matrimonio *to join in marriage.*
  Mi sono unito a lui in questa impresa. *I joined him in this endeavor.*
  In questa mia lettera unisco una fotografia del mio bambino. *I am enclosing in my letter a photograph of my baby.*
unìsono *unison, harmony.*
  Hanno risposto tutti all'unìsono. *They all answered in unison.*
unità *unity.*
unitario, adj. *unit.*
  prezzo unitario *unit price.*
unito *united.*
universale *universal.*
universalità *universality.*
universalmente *universally.*
università *university.*
universitario, adj. *of a university;* n. *university student.*
universo, adj. *universe;* adj. *universal.*
UNO (UN, UNA, UN') *one, a, an, someone.*
  l'un l'altro *each other; one another.*
  una ragazza *a girl; one girl.*
  un' idea *an idea; one idea.*
  uno ad uno *one by one.*
  uno alla volta *one at a time.*
  uno dopo l'altro *one after the other.*
  uno sciocco *a fool; one fool.*
  un ragazzo *a boy; one boy.*
  Ne desidero uno di qualità migliore. *I want one of better quality.*
  Uno mi ha detto . . . *Someone told me . . .*
  Uno non sa mai quando può succedere una disgrazia. *One never knows when an accident might happen.*
ùnto *greasy; oily; dirty.*
untuoso *oily, unctuous.*

unzione, f. *unction.*
UOMO *man.*
  un bell'uomo *a handsome man.*
  un uomo d'affari *a businessman.*
  un uomo di mezz'età *a middle-aged man.*
  un uomo di parola *a man of his word.*
UOVO *egg.*
  le uova *eggs.*
  uovo fresco *fresh egg.*
  uovo sodo *hard-boiled egg.*
  Meglio un' uovo oggi, che una gallina domani. *A bird in the hand is worth two in the bush.*
uragano *hurricane.*
urbanistica *urban planning.*
urbano *urban, urbane.*
urgente *urgent.*
  aver bisogno urgente *to have urgent need.*
urgentemente *urgently.*
urgenza *urgency.*
  Il medico è stato chiamato d'urgenza. *The doctor was called in a hurry.*
  in caso d'urgenza *in an emergency.*
ùrgere *to be urgent.*
  Ùrge la sua presenza. *Your presence is urgently needed.*
uriare *to shout; to howl.*
urlo *shout, cry.*
urna *urn.*
urtante *irritating.*
urtare *to knock against; to annoy.*
  Ho urtato contro lo stipite della porta. *I knocked against the doorpost.*
  Mi ùrta il suo modo di fare. *His manner irritates me.*
urto *push, shove.*
USANZA *usage, custom.*
  un'usanza antica *an old custom.*
  un'usanza comune *a common custom.*
  secondo l'usanza *according to custom.*
USARE *to use; to make use of.*
  usare giudizio *to use common sense; to exercise judgment.*
  I cappelli a larghe falde si usano molto quest'anno. *Wide-brimmed*

hats are very fashionable this
year.

Mia madre usava raccontarmi delle
favole. *My mother used to tell me
fairy stories.*

Posso usare la sua penna per un
momento? *May I use your pen
for a moment?*

usato *second-hand, used, usual.*
mobili usati *second-hand
furniture.*
non più usato *obsolete.*
più dell'usato *more than usual.*

usciere, m. *usher, bailiff,
receptionist.*

ùscio *door.*
sull'ùscio di casa *on the doorstep.*

USCIRE *to go out; to come out.*
Desidero uscire da questa situazione
penosa. *I wish to get out of this
unhappy situation.*

Esco di casa ogni mattina alle otto. *I
leave the house (go out of the
house) every morning at eight.*

La Signora esce questa sera? *Is the
lady going out this evening? Will
the lady be out this evening?*

Usciamo a fare una passeggiata!
Let's go out for a walk!

USCITA *coming out; getting out; exit;
outlay.*
uscita di sicurezza *emergency exit.*
Dov'è l'uscita del palazzo? *Where is
the exit of the building?*
Gli attori furono applauditi alla loro
uscita. *The actors were
applauded upon coming out.*
Le uscite sono grandi e le entrate
sono piccole. *The expenditures
are great and the income is
small.*
Non abbiamo via d'uscita. *We have
no avenue of escape.*

USO *use, custom.*
fare uso di *to make use of.*
pagare per l'uso di *to pay for the use
of.*
fuori uso *off duty.*

usuale *usual, customary.*

usualmente *usually, generally.*

usufruire *to take advantage of; to
benefit by.*

Usufruisco soltanto degli interessi
sul capitale. *I benefit only by the
interest on the capital.*

usura *usury, wear.*
usura del materiale *wear and tear of
material.*
resistere all'usura del tempo *to
withstand attrition.*

utensile, m. *utensil.*
utensili di cucina *kitchen utensils.*

utente *user; consumer.*
gli utenti del telefono *telephone
users.*

UTILE *useful; income.*
l'ùtile ed il dilettevole *business and
pleasure.*

utilità *utility, usefulness.*
È un oggetto bello, ma non ha
utilità. *It is a beautiful object, but
it is of no use.*

utilizzare *to utilize.*

utilmente *usefully, profitably.*

uva *grapes.*
un grappolo d'uva *a bunch of
grapes.*
uva passa *raisins.*

vacante *vacant, empty.*

VACANZA *vacation, holiday.*
Dove passa le vacanze di Natale?
*Where are you spending the
Christmas holidays?*

vacca *cow.*

vaccinare *to vaccinate.*

vaccinazione, f. *vaccination.*

vaccino *vaccine.*

vacillante *vacillating, wavering,
hesitating.*

vacillare *to vacillate; to waver; to
hesitate.*

vagabondo *vagabond, wanderer;
bum.*

vagamente *vaguely.*
rispondere vagamente *to answer in a
vague manner.*

vagante *wandering, rambling.*

vagare *to wander; to ramble.*

vagire *to whimper.*

Il neonato vagiva nella sua culla. *The
infant was whimpering in his
cradle.*

vagito *whimper.*

vaglia, m. *postal money order; check.*

vagliare *to sift; to consider.*
vagliare una proposta *to consider a
proposal.*

vago *vague; lovely, desirous.*
una vaga fanciulla *a lovely girl.*
vago di gloria *desirous of glory.*
Ne ho una vaga idea. *I have a vague
idea of it.*

vagone, m. *truck, van, car (of train).*
vagone ristorante *dining car.*
vagone letto *sleeping car.*

valanga *avalanche.*
È scesa una valanga di neve. *An
avalanche of snow came down.*

valente *clever; of worth.*

VALERE *to be worth.*
vale a dire *that is to say; namely.*
A che vale? *What good is it?*
La salute vale più del denaro. *Health
is worth more than wealth.*
Mi sono valso dei miei diritti. *I took
advantage of my rights.*
Non vale la pena parlarne. *It isn't
worth speaking of.*
Per quanto tempo vale questo
biglietto? *How long is this ticket
good?*
Questo diamante vale diversi
milioni. *This diamond is worth
several millions.*

valevole *good, usable, effective.*
È un rimedio valevole. *It is an
effective remedy.*
Il biglietto è valevole per dieci giorni.
The ticket is good for ten days.

valicare *to pass over; to cross.*
Bisognerà valicare i monti, per
giungere al nostro paese. *We'll
have to cross the mountains
before arriving in our country.*

validamente *validly.*

validità *validity.*

valido *valid, strong.*
Lui ha una mente valida. *He has an
untiring mind.*
Questo contratto non è valido. *This
contract is not valid.*

valigerìa *luggage shop.*

valigia *suitcase.*

vallata (valle) f. *valley.*
scendere a valle *to go downhill.*

VALORE, m. *value, valor.*
secondo il valore che lui dà alle sue
parole *according to the value
(meaning) he gives his words.*
È un' artista di gran valore. *He is a
great artist.*
Il valore di queste gemme è
inestimabile. *The value of these
gems is inestimable.*
I valori morali sono molto cambiati
negli ultimi decenni. *Moral
values have changed a great deal
in the last decades.*

valorizzare *to increase in value.*

valorizzazione *improvement.*

valorosamente *bravely, valiantly.*
Hanno combattuto valorosamente.
They fought valiantly.

valoroso *brave, valiant.*

valuta *value; monetary value; currency.*
norme valutarie *currency
regulations.*
valuta estera *foreign currency.*

VALUTARE *to appraise; to estimate.*
Sarà difficile valutare il tempo che ci
vorrà per finire questo lavoro. *It
will be difficult to estimate the
time it will take to finish this
work.*
Valutò l'anello cento mila lire. *He
appraised the ring at one
hundred thousand lire.*
valutare le possibilità *to consider the
possibilities.*

valutazione, f. *estimate, appraisal.*

valvola *valve.*
valvola di sicurezza *safety valve.*

valzer, m. *waltz.*
Vuol ballare questo valzer con me?
Will you dance this waltz with me?

vampata *sudden wave of intense heat;
passion; flush.*

vanamente *vainly; in vain.*
Decantava vanamente le proprie
virtù. *He was vainly extolling his
own virtues.*
Ti ho atteso vanamente. *I waited for
you in vain.*

vandalismo *vandalism.*

vandalo *vandal.*

vaneggiamento *raving.*

vaneggiare *to rave.*

vanesio *vain; conceited.*

vanga *spade.*

vangare *to dig; to turn over the earth.*

Vangelo *Gospel.*

vaniglia *vanilla.*

vanità *vanity.*

vanitoso *vain; conceited.*

vano, n. *room;* adj. *vain, useless, empty.*

  un appartamento di quattro vani *a four-room apartment.*

  È perito nel vano tentativo di salvare sua figlia dalle fiamme. *He died trying vainly to save his daughter from the fire.*

VANTAGGIO *advantage, odds.*

  Lui ha il vantaggio su di me. *He has the advantage over me.*

  Mi ha dato dieci punti di vantaggio. *He gave me a ten-point advantage over him.*

vantaggioso *advantageous.*

VANTARE *to boast of; to boast.*

  vantarsi *to brag.*

  Lui ha agito male e se ne vanta. *He behaved poorly and he brags about it.*

  Lui vanta le sue ricchezze. *He boasts about his wealth.*

vanto *honor, merit.*

  Lui si dava vanto dei suoi successi. *He was priding himself on his successes.*

vanvera (a) *at random; without thought.*

  parlare a vanvera *to talk nonsense.*

vaporare *to evaporate.*

vaporazione, f. *evaporation.*

vapore, m. *vapor, steam.*

  bagno a vapore *steam bath (Turkish bath).*

  battello a vapore *steamship.*

vaporetto *steamboat.*

vaporizzare *to vaporize.*

vaporizzatore, m. *vaporizer.*

vaporoso *vaporous, vague.*

varare *to launch.*

  varare una nave *to launch a ship.*

  varare una norma *to pass a law.*

varcare *to cross; to go beyond.*

  varcare la soglia di casa *to cross the threshold.*

  varcare una frontiera *to pass a frontier.*

  Essa ha varcato la soglia dei quarant'anni. *She has passed her fortieth year.*

varco *passage, way.*

  aspettare al varco *to be in wait for.*

  aprirsi un varco *to clear a path.*

variabile *variable, changeable.*

  Il suo umore è variabile. *His mood is changeable.*

variante *variant; modification.*

  una variante dialettale *a dialectal variant.*

variare *to vary.*

  tanto per variare *just for a change.*

  La temperatura varia da una stanza all'altra. *The temperature varies from room to room.*

variato *varied, various.*

variazione, f. *variation, change.*

varicella *chicken pox.*

varietà *variety.*

  teatro dì varietà *music hall; vaudeville house.*

vario *various, different, several.*

  Ho da fare varie cose. *I have various things to do.*

  Gli è successo varie volte. *It has happened to him several different times.*

variopinto *multicolored.*

vasca *basin, tub.*

  vasca da bagno *bathtub.*

  vasca di marmo *marble basin.*

  vasca per pesci *fish pond.*

vaselina *vaseline.*

vaso, m. *pot, vase, jar.*

  vaso da fiori *flowerpot.*

vassòlo *tray.*

vastità *vastness.*

vasto *wide, vast.*

  le vaste distese dell' ovest *the vast plains of the West.*

Vaticano *Vatican.*

ve *there.*

  Ve ne sono due. *There are two.*

vecchiaia *old age.*

pensioni per la vecchiàia *old-age pensions.*

VECCHIO, adj. *old;* n. *old man.*

i vecchi *the aged.*

Il vecchio camminava a stento. *The old man could hardly walk.*

Questo vestito è troppo vecchio per essere messo. *This suit is too old to wear.*

vece, f. *stead.*

fare le veci di *to act as.*

Vai tu in vece mia. *You go in my place.*

VEDERE *to see.*

dare a vedere *to make one believe.*

essere ben visto *to be popular; to be well liked.*

Il bimbo ha visto la luce il 3 marzo, 1956. *The child was born March 3, 1956.*

Lo vidi tre settimane fa. *I saw him three weeks ago.*

Non mi può vedere. *He can't see me.*

Non ne vedo la necessità. *I don't see the necessity of it.*

Non si fa vedere da un pezzo. *He hasn't shown up for some time.*

Non vedo l'ora di finire. *I can hardly wait to finish.*

Non vedo l'ora di vederti. *I'm looking forward to seeing you.*

vedetta *lookout, watch.*

far da vedetta *to act as lookout.*

vedette f. *star; starlet; performer.*

vedova *widow.*

vedovo *widower.*

VEDUTA *view.*

Da questa finestra c'è un ottima veduta del mare. *From this window there is a lovely view of the sea.*

Ognuno ha le proprie vedute. *Everyone has his own views.*

una persona di larghe vedute *an open-minded person.*

vegtale, adj. & n. m. *vegetable.*

vegetare *to vegetate.*

vegetariano, n. & adj. *vegetarian.*

vegetazione, f. *vegetation.*

vègeto *strong, vigorous.*

vivo e vègeto *hale and hearty.*

veglia *waking; watch; evening party.*

fare la veglia *to keep vigil.*

fra veglia e sonno *between slumber and waking.*

VEGLIARE *to sit up; to remain awake.*

vegliare un ammalato *to sit up with a patient; to watch over a patient.*

veìcolo *vehicle.*

vela *sail.*

barca a vela *sailboat.*

Tutto procede a gonfie vele. *Everything is going very well.*

velare *to veil.*

velatamente *covertly.*

velato *veiled.*

con voce velata *in a disguised voice.*

una velata minaccia *a veiled threat.*

veleno *poison.*

velenoso *poisonous, venomous.*

velìvolo *airplane.*

velleità *vain ambition.*

vellutato *velvety.*

velluto *velvet.*

Velluto a coste *corduroy.*

velo *veil.*

stendere un velo sopra *to draw a veil over.*

veloce *swift, rapid.*

velocemente *swiftly, rapidly.*

Il tempo scorre velocemente. *Time goes quickly.*

velocità *velocity, speed.*

ad una velocità media di *at an average speed of.*

a grande velocità *at great speed.*

a tutta velocità *at full speed.*

la velocità del suono *the speed of sound.*

vena *vein.*

essere in vena *to be in the mood.*

vena artistica *an artistic vein.*

venale *venal.*

venalità *venality.*

venatorio *of hunting.*

stagione venatoria *hunting season.*

vendemmia *grape harvest.*

vendemmiare *to harvest grapes.*

VENDERE *to sell.*

vendere a buon mercato *to sell cheap.*

vendere all' ingrosso *to sell wholesale.*

vendere al minuto *to sell retail.*
vendere bene *to sell at a good price;
to sell well.*
vendetta *revenge; vengeance.*
vendibile *saleable.*
vendicare *to avenge.*
vendicativo *revengeful.*
vendita *sale.*
in vendita *on sale.*
vendita all' asta *sale by auction.*
venditore, m. *seller.*
venditore ambulante *peddler.*
venduto *sold.*
venerabile *venerable.*
venerabilità *venerability.*
venerare *to venerate; to revere.*
venerazione, f. *veneration.*
venerdì *Friday.*
veneziano, adj. & n. *Venetian.*
veniente *coming, next.*
la settimana veniente *the coming
week.*
VENIRE *to come.*
venir bene *to turn out well.*
venire ai fatti *to get down to facts.*
venire alle mani *to come to blows.*
venire meno *to faint.*
venire meno ad una promessa *to
break a promise.*
Lui viene da famiglia umile. *He
comes from a humble family.*
Mi è venuta un' idea! *I just got an
idea!*
Mi venne in aiuto. *He came to my
aid.*
Mi venne incontro. *He came to
meet me.*
Non mi viene in mente il suo nome.
I can't remember his name.
Vieni su! *Come up!*
ventaglio *fan.*
ventata *gust; rush of wind.*
una ventata di freddo *a gust of cold
air.*
ventesimo, n. & adj. *twentieth.*
venti *twenty.*
venticello *light wind; breeze.*
ventilare *to ventilate.*
ventilare una stanza *to air a room.*
ventilato *airy, ventilated.*
ventilatore, m. *ventilator.*
ventilazione, f. *ventilation.*

ventina *about twenty.*
una ventina di persone *about twenty
people.*
VENTO *wind.*
farsi vento *to fan oneself.*
parlare al vento *to talk into deaf
ears.*
vento contrario *contrary wind.*
vento favorevole *fair wind.*
Tira vento. *It's windy.*
ventoso *windy.*
ventrìloquo *ventriloquist.*
ventura *luck, fortune.*
andare alla ventura *to trust to
chance.*
augurare buona ventura *to wish good
luck.*
per mia buona ventura *luckily for me.*
venturo *next, future, coming.*
la settimana ventura *next week.*
le generazioni venture *the coming
generations; the future
generations.*
venturoso *lucky, fortunate.*
venusto *beautiful, lovely, handsome.*
VENUTA *coming, arrival.*
La sua venuta fu una sorpresa per
tutti. *His coming was a surprise
to everyone.*
verace *veracious, true.*
veramente *truly, really.*
Mi ha fatto veramente piacere. *I was
really pleased.*
Veramente? *Really?*
veranda *veranda.*
verbale, n. m. *minutes;* adj. *verbal.*
leggere il verbale *to read the
minutes.*
verbo *verb.*
VERDE *green.*
essere al verde *to be penniless.*
verde bottiglia *green bottle.*
verdechiaro *light green.*
verdecupo *dark green.*
verdetto *verdict.*
verdura *verdure, vegetables, greens.*
Fa bene mangiare un po' di verdura.
*It is good for one to eat some
vegetables.*
minestra di verdura *vegetable soup.*
vergogna *shame, disgrace.*
vergognarsi *to be ashamed.*

vergognosamente *shamefully.*

vergognoso *shameful.*

verifica *inspection, examination.*
   verifica dei conti *inspection of the accounts.*
   verifica dei passaporti *examination of passports.*

verificare *to verify; to inspect.*
   verificarsi *to occur; to happen.*
   Si è verificato un increscioso incidente. *An unfortunate incident happened.*

verismo *realism.*

VERITÀ *truth.*
   dire la verità *to tell the truth.*
   in verità *in truth.*
   la verità dei fatti *the truth of the matter.*

veritiero *truthful.*

verme, m. *worm.*

vermiglio *vermilion, red.*

vermut, m. *vermouth.*

vernacolo *vernacular, dialect.*

vernice, f. *varnish.*

verniciare *to varnish.*

VERO, n. *truth;* adj. *true.*
   a dire il vero *to tell the truth.*
   Non c'è una parola di vero in quanto mi ha raccontato. *There isn't a word of truth in what he told me.*
   Non è vero. *It's not true.*
   Venite con noi, è vero? *You are coming with us, isn't that so?*

verosimile *likely, probable.*

VERSARE *to pour; to spill; to shed.*
   versare lacrime *to shed tears.*
   versare una somma *to pay a sum.*
   versare un bicchiere d'acqua *to pour a glass of water.*
   Si è versato il caffè addosso. *He spilled the coffee over himself.*

versatile *versatile.*

versatilità *versatility.*

versione, f. *version.*
   versione in italiano *Italian version; Italian translation.*
   una versione nuova *a new version.*
   Ognuno mi ha dato una versione diversa dell' accaduto. *Everyone gave me a different version of what happened.*

VERSO, n. *verse, line;* adv. *toward.*
   per un verso o per l'altro *one way or the other.*
   scrivere dei versi *to write verses (poetry).*
   versi sciolti *blank verse.*
   Questo dramma è scritto in versi. *This drama is written in verse.*
   verso la fine del mese *toward the end of the month.*
   verso nord *northward.*
   Lui viene verso di me. *He is coming toward me.*

vertenza *quarrel, question.*
   risolvere una vertenza *to settle a quarrel.*

verticale *vertical.*

verticalmente *vertically.*

vertice *top; summit; top.*
   conferenza al vertice *summit conference.*

vertigine, f. *dizzy spell; dizziness.*

vertiginoso *dizzy.*
   un altezza vertiginosa *a dizzy height.*

vèscovo *bishop.*

vespa *wasp.*

vespaio *wasps' nest.*

vestaglia *dressing gown.*

VESTE, f. *dress, gown.*
   in veste di *in the guise of.*
   veste da camera *dressing gown.*
   veste da sposa *bridal gown.*

vestiarie *clothes.*

vestibolo *hall.*

vestigio (vestigia) *trace, vestige.*

VESTIRE *to dress.*
   vestire bene *to dress well.*
   vestirsi *to dress oneself.*

VESTITO *suit, dress.*
   vestito da sera *evening gown.*

veterano *veteran.*

veterinario, adj. *veterinary;* n. *veterinarian.*

veto *veto.*

vetràio *glass blower; glazier.*

vetrata *glass door; glass window.*
   vetrata di chiesa *stained glass window.*

vetreria *glassworks.*

vetrina *shop window.*

VETRO *glass.*
   vetro colorato *stained glass.*

vetta *summit, top.*

vettevaglie, f. pl. *food provisions.*

vettura *carriage, coach.*
   l'ultima vettura *the last coach.*
   In vettura! *All aboard!*

vetturino *driver, cabbie.*

vezzo *charm, coaxing.*

VI adv. *there;* pron. pl. *you; to you.*
   Non ho desiderio di andarvi. *I don't wish to go there.*
   Vi andrò se potrò: *I'll go there if I can.*
   Vi restituirò il libro domani. *I will give the book back to you tomorrow.*
   Vi rivedo con piacere. *I am pleased to see you again.*

VIA, n. *street, road, way;* adv. *away, off.*
   in via *on the way.*
   la via più breve *the shortest way.*
   per via di *by way of.*
   Via Veneto *Veneto Street.*
   andar via *to go away.*
   e così via *and so forth.*
   mandar via *to send away.*

viabilità *road condition.*

viaggette *trip.*

VIAGGIARE *to travel.*
   viaggiare in prima classe *to travel first class.*

viaggiatore, m. **viaggiatrice,** f. *traveler, passenger.*

VIAGGIO *journey, voyage.*
   essere in viaggio *to be traveling; to be on the way.*
   fare un viaggio *to take a voyage; to take a trip.*
   mettersi in viaggio *to set out; to start out.*
   Buon viaggio! *Happy journey! Bon Voyage!*

viale, m. *avenue.*
   viali alberati *tree-lined avenues.*

viandante, m. *passerby, pedestrian.*

viavai *coming and going; hustle and bustle.*
   C'è un viavai continuo in questa casa. *There is a continuous hustle and bustle in this house.*

vibrare *to vibrate.*
   vibrare un colpo *to strike a blow.*

vicario *substitute; deputy.*

vice *vice.*
   vicepresidente *vice president.*
   vicedirettore *assistant director.*

vicenda *vicissitude, event.*
   a vicenda *in turn.*
   le vicende della vita *the vicissitudes of life.*
   volersi bene a vicenda *to love one another.*

vicendevole *mutual.*

vicendevolmente *mutually, reciprocally.*

viceversa *vice versa; on the contrary.*
   Se viceversa vuole rimanere qui, faccia pure. *If on the other hand you prefer to remain here, do so.*

vicinanza *nearness, proximity, vicinity, neighborhood.*
   essere in vicinanza di *to be close to; to be approaching.*
   La mia casa è nelle vicinanze della sua. *My home is near his.*
   La sua vicinanza è un gran conforto per me. *His nearness is a great comfort to me.*

vicinato *neighborhood.*

vicino, n. *neighbor;* adj. & adv. *near.*
   La mia vicina mi ha salutato dalla finestra. *My neighbor greeted me from the window.*
   vicino casa mia *near my home.*
   Siamo vicini alla fine del lavoro. *We are close to the end of the work.*

vicolo *lane.*

video cassetta *video cassette.*

videodisco *videodisc.*

video registratore *VCR.*

VIETARE *to forbid; to prohibit.*
   Il medico mi ha vietato di fumare. *The doctor has forbidden me to smoke.*

VIETATO *forbidden, prohibited.*
   Vietato l'Ingresso! *No Admittance!*
   Vietato Fumare! *No Smoking!*
   Vietata la Sosta! *No Parking!*

vigente *in force.*
   leggi vigenti *laws in force.*
   norme vigenti *current regulations.*

vigere *to be in force.*
   Questa legge vige ancora. *This law is still in force.*

vigilante *vigilant.*

vigilanza *vigilance.*

vigilare *to watch over; to guard.*

vigile, m. *policeman.*
   vigile del fuoco *fireman.*

vigilia *eve, vigil.*
   la vigilia di capodanno *New Year's Eve.*
   la vigilia di Natale *Christmas Eve.*

vigliacco *coward.*

vigna *vineyard.*

vigneto *vineyard.*

vignetta *vignette, cartoon.*

vigore, m. *vigor, strength.*
   con vigore instancabile *with untiring strength.*
   in pieno vigore *in full strength.*
   Questa legge non è ancora in vigore. *This law is not in force yet.*

vigorosamente *vigorously.*

vigoroso *vigorous, strong.*

vile *low, mean, cowardly.*

villa *villa; country house.*

villaggio *village.*

villanamente *rudely, roughly.*

villanìa *rudeness.*

villano *unrefined man; peasant.*

villeggiatura *holiday, country vacation.*
   luogo di villeggiatura *vacation spot.*

villino *cottage.*

vilmente *in a cowardly or mean manner.*

viltà *cowardice.*

vincente, adj. *winning;* n. *winner.*
   il numero vincente *the winning number.*
   Il vincente riceverà un premio. *The winner will receive a prize.*

VINCERE *to win; to overcome; to get the better of.*
   vincere una battaglia *to win a battle.*
   vinto dalla stanchezza *overcome by fatigue.*
   Non voglio lasciarmi vincere dalla collera. *I don't want to let my anger get the better of me.*

vincita *win; winnings.*

vincitore, m. **vincitrice,** f. *winner.*

vincolare *to bind.*
   vincolarsi *to bind oneself.*

vincolo *tie, bind.*
   vincolo di sangue *blood tie.*

VINO *wine.*
   vino bianco *white wine.*
   vino leggero *light wine.*
   vino rosso *red wine.*
   vino spumante *sparkling wine.*

VINTO *won, overcome, conquered.*
   darsi per vinto *to give up; to give in.*
   È un uomo vinto dalle sventure. *He is a man who has been overcome by misfortune.*
   Non te la do vinta. *I won't let you have your own way.*

viola n. & adj. (invariable) *violet.*

violare *to violate.*

violazione, f. *violation.*

violentemente *violently.*

violento *violent.*

violenza *violence.*

violinista, m. *violinist.*

violino *violin.*

vipera *viper.*

virgola *comma.*
   punto e virgola *semicolon.*

virgolette, f. pl. *quotation marks.*

virile *manly, virile.*

virilmente *manfully.*

virtù, f. *virtue.*
   in virtù di *in virtue of.*

virtuale *virtual.*

virtuoso *virtuous.*

virus, m. *virus.*

visibile *visible.*

visibilità *visibility.*

visibilmente *visibly.*

visione, f. *vision.*
   prendere visione di *to examine.*
   prima visione *premiere.*

VISITA *visit.*
   biglietto da visita *visiting card.*
   fare una visita a *to pay a visit to.*
   farsi fare una visita medica *to submit to a medical examination.*

VISITARE *to visit; to call on somebody.*
   visitare un amico *to visit a friend.*

visivo *visual.*

VISO *face.*

visone, m. *mink.*
   una pelliccia di visone *a mink coat.*

vispo *lively.*
   un bimbo vispo *a lively child (boy).*

VISTA *sight, view.*

a prima vista *at first sight*.
aver la vista buona *to have good eyesight*.
aver la vista corta *to be nearsighted*.
conoscere di vista *to know by sight*.
in vista *in sight*.
perdere di vista *to lose sight of*.
punto di vista *point of view*.
una vista panoramica *a panoramic view*.

visto, m. *visa*.
vistoso *showy, gaudy*.
visuale *view*.
VITA *life; waist*.
essere corta di vita *to be short-waisted*.
essere lunga di vita *to be long-waisted*.
intormo alla vita *around the waist*.
in vita *alive*.
pieno di vita *full of life*.

vitale *vital*.
vitalità *vitality*.
vitamina *vitamin*.
vite, f. *screw, vine*.
vitello *calf*.
cotoletta di vitello *veal cutlet*.
fegato di vitello *calves' liver*.

vittima *victim*.
VITTO *food*.
vitto e alloggio *food and lodging*.
Il prezzo della camera comprende anche il vitto. *The price of the room includes meals.*

vittoria *victory*.
vittoriosamente *victoriously*.
vittorioso *victorious*.
viva *horray! long live!*
vivace *lively, vivacious*.
vivacemente *vivaciously*.
vivacità *vivacity, liveliness*.
vivaio *nursery*.
vivamente *keenly, deeply*.
vivanda *food*.
vivente *living*.
Non ho parenti viventi. *I have no living relatives.*

VIVERE *to live*.
Lui vive alla giornata. *He lives from hand to mouth.*

modo di vivere *way of life*.
viveri, m. pl. *victuals; food supplies*.
vivido *vivid*.
VIVO *alive, living, vivid*.
argento vivo *quicksilver, mercury*.
con suo vivo dispiacere *with great sorrow on his part*.
I miei genitori sono ancora vivi. *My parents are still alive.*
un vivo ricordo *a vivid memory*.

viziare *to spoil*.
viziato *spoiled*.
vizio *fault, vice*.
vocabolario *vocabulary; dictionary*.
vocabolo *word, term*.
vocale, adj. *vocal*; n. f. *vowel*.
corde vocali *vocal cords*.
vocazione *vocation*.
VOCE, f. *voice*.
abbassare la voce *to lower one's voice*.
alzar la voce *to shout*.
a voce alta *in a loud voice*.
a voce bassa *in a low voice*.
Corre voce che . . . *There is a rumor that . . .*

voga *fashion, vogue*.
essere in voga *to be in fashion*.
vogare *to row*.
VOGLIA *wish, desire*.
Hai voglia di fare una passeggiata? *Do you feel like going for a walk?*
Non ho voglia di uscire questa sera. *I don't wish to go out this evening.*

VOI pl. familiar, also formal *you*.
volante, n. m. *wheel*; adj. *flying*.
Ero al volante è avvenuto lo scontro. *I was at the wheel when the crash occurred.*

VOLARE *to fly*.
volare via *to fly away*.
volata *flight*.
Faccio una volata a casa. *I rush home.*

volente *willing*.
volente o nolente *willing or not*.
volentieri *willingly*.
mal volentieri *unwillingly*.
volere, n. m. *will*; v. *to want; to wish*.
il volere di Dio *the will of God*.
il volere del popolo *the will of the people*.

Volere è potere. *Where there's a will, there's a way.*

voglia o non voglia *whether he wishes or not.*

voler dire *to mean.*

Non voglio mangiare ora. *I don't want to eat now.*

Vorrei riposare un po'. *I would like to rest a while.*

volgare *vulgar.*

volgarità *vulgarity.*

volgarmente *vulgarly.*

VOLGERE *to turn.*

volgere al termine *to come to an end; to draw to a close.*

volgere gli occhi insù *to look up.*

volgere lo sguardo intorno *to look about; to look around.*

volgere le spalle a *to turn one's back to.*

volo *flight.*

volo (al) *right away.*

volontà *will.*

di spontanea volontà *of one's free will.*

le ultime volontà del defunto *the last will of the deceased.*

volontariamente *voluntarily.*

volontario *voluntary.*

volpe, f. *fox.*

volpe argentata *silver fox.*

volpone, m. *old fox.*

VOLTA *time.*

di volta in volta *from time to time.*

due per volta *two at a time.*

la prossima volta *next time.*

qualche volta *sometimes.*

questa volta *this time.*

una alla volta *one at a time.*

una volta per sempre *once and for all.*

C'era una volta . . . *Once upon a time . . .*

VOLTARE *to turn.*

voltare a destra *to turn to the right.*

voltare una pagina *to turn a page.*

voltarsi *to turn around.*

voltato *turned.*

Gli occhi di tutti erano voltati verso di lui. *All eyes were turned toward him.*

volto *face.*

volume, m. *volume.*

vongola *clam.*

VOSTRO, -a, -i, -e (il vostro; la vostra; i vostri; le vostre) *your, yours.*

il vostro amico *your friend.*

vostro padre *your father.*

Questo libro è il vostro. *This book is yours.*

votare *to vote.*

votato *consecrated.*

voto *vow, vote.*

dare il proprio voto a *to cast one's vote for.*

fare un voto *to make a vow.*

vulcano *volcano.*

vulnerabile *vulnerable.*

vulnerabilità *vulnerability.*

vuotare *to empty.*

vuotare il sacco *to get something off one's chest (to empty the sack).*

vuoto, n. *emptiness; empty space; vacuum;* adj. *empty.*

andare a vuoto *to come to nothing.*

a tasche vuote *with empty pockets; penniless.*

Non posso andare a mani vuote. *I can't go empty-handed.*

Questo fiasco è vuoto. *This bottle is empty.*

W

water *toilet bowl.*

whisky *whiskey.*

X

xerografia *xerography.*

xilofono *xylophone.*

Y

yankee *Yankee.*

yuppismo *yuppie culture.*

Z

zabaglione, m. *eggnog.*
zafferano *saffron.*
zaffiro *sapphire.*
zàino *knapsack, pack; backpack.*
   con lo zaino in spalla *with the
      backpack on his back.*
zampa *paw.*
zampillare *to gush; to spring.*
   La fontana zampillava. *The fountain
      was gushing.*
zampillo *jet, squirt, stream.*
zanna *tusk, fang.*
zanzara *mosquito.*
zappa *hoe.*
zappare *to hoe; to dig.*
zàttera *raft.*
zebra *zebra.*
zebrato *zebra-striped.*
zecca *mint; tick.*
   nuovo di zecca *brand-new.*
zèffiro *breeze.*
zelante *zealous.*
zelo *zeal.*
zènzero *ginger.*
zeppo *full.*
   Questa valigia è piena zeppa.
      The suitcase is quite full.
zero *zero.*
   sopra zero *above zero.*
   sotto zero *below zero.*
zeta *z.*
   dall'A alla Z *from start to
      finish.*
ZIA *aunt.*
zibellino *sable.*
zigomo *cheekbone.*
   aver gli zigomi alti *to have high
      cheekbones.*
zimarra *robe; gown.*
zimbello *laughingstock.*

   essere lo zimbello *to be the
      laughingstock.*
zinco *zinc.*
zingaro *gypsy.*
ZIO *uncle.*
zitella *old maid.*
zittire *to hiss, to boo.*
ZITTO *silent.*
   stare zitto *to keep quiet.*
   Zitto! *Quiet!*
zoccolo *wooden shoe; hoof.*
   gli zoccoli del cavallo *the horse's
      hooves.*
zodìaco *zodiac.*
zolfo *sulphur.*
zolla *clod, sod.*
zolletta *lump (of sugar).*
zona *zone.*
zoo *zoo.*
zoologìa *zoology.*
zoològico *zoological.*
   giardino zoologico *zoo.*
zoppicare *to limp.*
zoppo *lame.*
   essere zoppo *to be lame.*
   sedia zoppa *wobbly chair.*
zucca *pumpkin, pate.*
   aver la zucca pelata *to be bald-
      headed.*
   aver sale in zucca *to be sensible.*
   semi di zucca *pumpkin seeds.*
zuccherare *to sugar; to sweeten.*
zuccherato *sugared, sweetened.*
ZUCCHERO *sugar.*
   due zollette di zucchero *two lumps
      of sugar.*
   zucchero di canna *cane sugar.*
   zucchero in pólvere *powdered sugar.*
zucchino *squash.*
zuccone, m. *blockhead.*
zufolare *to whistle; to hiss.*
zuppa *soup.*
zuppiera *tureen, bowl.*

GLOSSARY OF PROPER NAMES

Adriana *Adriane.*
Alberto *Albert.*
Alessandro *Alexander.*
Alfredo *Alfred.*
Alice *Alice.*
Andrèa *Andrew.*
Anita *Anita.*
Antonio *Anthony.*
Arnoldo *Arnold.*
Arrigo *Harry.*
Arturo *Arthur.*

Beatrice *Beatrice.*
Bianca *Blanche.*

Carlo *Charles.*
Carlotta *Charlotte.*
Carolina *Carol.*
Caterina *Katherine.*

Daniele *Daniel.*
Davide *David.*
Donato *Donald.*

Edmondo *Edmund.*
Edoardo *Edward.*
Eleanora *Eleanor.*
Elizabetta *Elizabeth.*
Enrico *Henry.*
Evelina *Evelyn.*

Federico *Frederick.*
Ferdinando *Ferdinand.*
Francesca *Frances.*
Francesco *Francis.*

Gabriele *Gabriel.*
Gianna *Jean, Jane.*

Gilberto *Gilbert.*
Giorgio *George.*
Giovanna *Joan.*
Giovanni *John.*
Giuditta *Judith.*
Giulia *Julia.*
Giuliano *Julian.*
Giuseppe *Joseph.*
Gregorio *Gregory.*
Guglielmo *William.*
Guido *Guy.*

Irene *Irene.*
Isabella *Isabel.*

Liliana *Lillian.*
Lorenzo *Lawrence.*
Lucìa *Lucy.*
Luigi *Lewis, Louis.*
Luisa *Louise.*

Marco *Mark.*
Marìa *Mary.*
Maurizio *Maurice.*
Michele *Michael.*

Paolo *Paul.*
Pietro *Peter.*

Raffaele *Raphael.*
Raimondo *Raymond.*
Riccardo *Richard.*
Roberto *Robert.*
Rosa *Rose.*

Silvia *Sylvia.*

Teresa *Theresa.*
Tommaso *Thomas.*

Vincenzo *Vincent.*
Viviana *Vivian.*

GLOSSARY OF
GEOGRAPHICAL NAMES

Adriatico *Adriatic.*
Africa *Africa.*
America *America.*
   America del Nord *North America.*
   America del Sud *South America.*
   America Centrale *Central America.*
Argentina *Argentina.*
Asia *Asia.*
Atlantico *Atlantic.*
Australia *Australia.*
Austria *Austria.*

Belgio *Belgium.*
Bermunde f. pl. *Bermuda.*
Bolivia *Bolivia.*
Bosnia-Erzegovina *Bosnia-Herzegovina.*
Brasile m. *Brazil.*
Brusselles *Brussels.*

Canadà *Canada.*
Cile m. *Chile.*
Cina *China.*
Colombia *Colombia.*
Confederacione Stati Independenti *Commonwealth of Independent States*
Corea *Korea.*
Costa Rica *Costa Rica.*
Cuba *Cuba.*

Danimarca *Denmark.*
Dover *Dover.*

Ecuador *Ecuador.*
Egitto *Egypt.*
Europa *Europe.*

Finlandia *Finland.*
Firenze *Florence.*
Francia *France.*

Galles *Wales.*
Germania *Germany.*
Genova *Genoa.*
Giappone *Japan.*
Ginevra *Geneva.*

Gran Bretagna *Great Britain.*
Grecia *Greece.*
Guatemala *Guatemala.*

Il Salvador *El Salvador.*
India *India.*
Inghilterra *England.*
Iraq m. *Iraq.*
Irianda *Ireland.*
Islanda *Iceland.*
Israele m. *Israel.*
Italia *Italy.*

Lisbona *Lisbon.*
Londra *London.*

Messico *Mexico.*
Milano *Milan.*
Mosca *Moscow.*

Napoli *Naples.*
Nicaragua m. *Nicaragua.*
Norvegia *Norway.*
Nuova Zelanda *New Zealand.*

Olanda *Holland.*
Onduras *Honduras.*

Pacifico *Pacific.*
Padova *Padua.*
Paraguay *Paraguay.*
Perù *Peru.*
Parigi *Paris.*
Polonia *Poland.*
Portogalio *Portugal.*
Porto Rico *Puerto Rico.*

Reno *Rhine.*
Repubblica Ceca *Czech Republic.*
Repubblica Dominicana *Dominican Republic.*
Roma *Rome.*
Rumania *Rumania.*
Russia *Russia.*

Sardegna *Sardinia.*
Scozia *Scotland.*
Siberia *Siberia.*
Sicilia *Sicily.*
Slovachia *Slovakia.*
Sorrento *Sorrento.*
Spagna *Spain.*
Stati Uniti *United States.*

Sud Africa *South Africa.*
Svezia *Sweden.*
Svizzera *Switzerland.*

Toscana *Tuscany.*
Turchia *Turkey.*

Ungheria *Hungary.*

Venezia *Venice.*
Venezuela m. *Venezuela.*
Vesuvio *Vesuvius.*
Vienna *Vienna.*

English-Italian

A

a, an uno, un, una, un'.

abandon (to) abbandonare.

abbreviate (to) abbreviare.

abbreviation abbreviazione, f.

abdicate (to) abdicare.

ability abilità, talento.

able (adj.) abile, capace.

able (to be) potere; essere capace di; avere la forza di.

aboard a bordo.

abolish (to) abolire.

abortion aborto provocato.

about circa; a proposito di *(with reference to);* in giro *(in circulation).*
    about the end of the month verso la fine del mese.
    What's it about? Di che si tratta?

above sopra; in alto.
    above all soprattutto.

abroad all' estero.

absence assenza.

absent assente, distratto.

absentminded distratto.

absolute assoluto.

absorb (to) assorbire.

abstain (to) astenersi.
    to abstain from astenersi dal.

abstract astratto.

absurd assurdo, ridicolo.

abundance abbondanza.

abundant abbondante.

abuse abuso.

abuse (to) abusare, insultare.

academy accademia.

accelerate (to) accelerare.

accelerator acceleratore, m.

accent accento.

accent (to) accentare, accentuare.

accept (to) accettare.

accident accidente, m.; incidente, m.

accidental accidentale, casuale.

accidentally accidentalmente.

accommodate (to) accomodare, adottare.

accommodation accomodamento; alloggio *(lodging);* sistemazione.

accompany (to) accompagnare.

accomplish (to) compi(e)re, finire, perfezionare.

accord accordo.

according to secondo.

account conto; resoconto; relazione, f. *(report).*
    on account of a causa di.

accuracy esattezza, accuratezza.

accurate esatto.

accuse (to) accusare.

accustom (to) abituare, abituarsi a.

ace asso.

ache dolore, m.
    headache mal di testa.

achieve (to) compiere; raggiungere.

achievement compimento, successo.

acid acido.

acknowledge (to) riconoscere, convenire.

acoustics acustica.

acquaintance conoscenza.
    to make someone's acquaintance fare la conoscenza di qualcuno.

acquire (to) acquistare.

across attraverso.

act atto, legge, decreto.

act (to) agire; rappresentare *(represent).*
    to act as fare da.

action azione, f.

active attivo.

activity attività.

actor attore.

actual reale, vero.

acute acuto.

adapt (to) adattare.

add (to) aggiungere; fare la somma; addizionare; sommare.

addition addizione, f.
    in addition to oltre a.

additive additivo.

address indirizzo *(street, location);* recapito; discorso *(speech).*

address (to) indirizzare.
    to address oneself to rivolgersi a.

adequate sufficiente, adeguato.

adhesive tape nastro adesivo.

adjective aggettivo.

adjoining vicino, confinante.
    adjoining rooms stanze contigue.

administer (to) amministrare.

administration amministrazione, f.; governo.

admiral ammiraglio.

admiration ammirazione, f.

admire (to) ammirare.

admission ammissione, f.

    ticket of admission biglietto d'ingresso.

admit (to) riconoscere, ammettere, contenere.

admittance ammissione, f.; permesso d'entrare.

    Free admittance Entrata libera.

    No admittance Vietato l'ingresso.

adopt (to) addottare.

    adopted child figlio adottivo.

adorn (to) ornare.

adorned adorno.

adult adulto.

adultery adulterio.

advance progresso, avanzata, a conto.

    in advance in anticipo.

advance (to) progredire.

advantage vantaggio.

adventure avventura, speculazione, rischio.

adverb avverbio.

advertise (to) fare pubblicità; avvisare.

advertisement avviso; annuncio pubblicitario.

advertising pubblicità.

advice consiglio.

    to take someone's advice seguire il consiglio di qualcuno.

advise (to) consigliare.

aesthetics estetica.

affair affare, m.; relazione amorosa.

affect (to) influire, concernere, riguardare, ostentare.

affected affettato, studiato.

affection affezione, f.; affetto.

affectionate affettuoso.

affirm (to) affermare.

afloat a galla.

    to be afloat galleggiare.

afraid pauroso, intimorito.

after dopo; in seguito; più tardi.

after all dopotutto.

afternoon pomeriggio; dopo pranzo.

afterward dopo.

again di nuovo.

    never again mai più.

against contro.

age epoca; età *(of a person)*, periodo.

    of age maggiorenne.

    underage minorenne.

age (to) invecchiare.

agency agenzia.

agent agente, rappresentante, m.

aggravate (to) aggravare, esasperare.

aggressor aggressore.

agile agile.

ago fa.

    five years ago cinque anni fa.

    long ago molto tempo fa.

agree (to) consentire; essere d'accordo.

agreeable convenevole, ameno.

agreed inteso, d'accordo.

agreement patto, accordo.

    as by agreement come si è convenuto.

agricultural agricolo.

agriculture agricoltura.

ahead in avanti.

    to get ahead of oltrepassare.

aid assistenza, aiuto.

aid (to) assistere, aiutare.

    first aid pronto soccorso.

aim mira, fine, m., intento.

aim (to) prendere di mira; mirare.

air aria.

    by air per via aerea.

airmail posta aerea.

airplane aeroplano.

air raid incursione aerea.

aisle corridoio; passaggio; navata *(of a church).*

alarm allarme, m.

alarm (to) allarmare; dare l'allarme.

alarm clock sveglia.

albumen albume.

alcoholic alcolico.

alien straniero.

alienation alienazione.

alike simile.

alive vivo.

    more dead than alive più morto che vivo.

all (n.) tutto; (adj.) tutto, tutta, tutti, tutte.

    all day tutto il giorno.

allow (to) permettere.

allowed permesso.

ally alleato.

almost quasi.

alone solo.

along lungo.

aloud ad alta voce.

also anche.

alter (to) alternare, cambiare.

alternate (to) alternare.
alternately a vicenda; alternamente.
although benchè, sebbene.
altitude altitudine, f.
always sempre.
amaze (to) stupire.
amazed (to be) essere sorpreso; essere stupefatto.
amazement stupore, m.
ambassador ambasciatore, m.
ambitious ambizioso.
amend (to) correggere, modificare.
amends riparazione, f.
amendment emendamento.
American americano.
among fra; nel mezzo.
amount somma.
amount (to) ammontare.
ample ampio, vasto.
amuse (to) intrattenere, divertire.
amusement intrattenimento, divertimento; spasso.
amusing divertente.
analogy analogia.
analyze (to) analizzare.
anarchy anarchia.
anatomy anatomia.
ancestor antenato.
anchor àncora.
ancient antico.
and e.
anecdote aneddoto.
angel angelo.
anger collera, rabbia.
angry arrabbiato, irato, collerico.
    to get angry arrabbiarsi, adirarsi; accaldarsi.
animal animale, m.
animate (to) animare.
ankle caviglia.
annex (to) annettere.
annexed annesso.
annihilate (to) annientare.
anniversary anniversario.
announce (to) annunciare.
announcement annuncio.
announcer annunciatore, annunciatrice.
annoy infastidire, disturbare, contrariare.
annual annuale, annuo.
annul (to) annullare.
anonymous anonimo.
another un altro, un'altra.

    in another hour un'ora più tardi.
answer risposta.
answer (to) rispondere.
answering machine segretaria telefonica.
anterior anteriore.
antibiotic antibiotico.
anticipate (to) anticipare.
antique antico.
antiques dealer antiquario.
anxiety ansia.
anxious ansioso; desideroso *(eager)*.
any qualunque, qualche, del.
anybody chiunque, qualcuno.
anyhow comunque.
anyone chiunque, qualcuno.
anything qualunque cosa; qualche cosa.
anyway in qualunque modo.
anywhere dovunque.
apart a parte.
apartment appartamento.
apiece ciascuno; per uno; a testa.
apologize (to) scusarsi.
apparel abbiglia mento.
apparent evidente.
appeal (to) rivolgersi a; ricorrere a.
appear (to) apparire.
appearance aspetto; apparizione, esteriorità, f.
appease (to) placare.
appendix appendice, f.
appetite appetito.
applaud (to) applaudire.
applause applauso.
apple mela.
application domanda; richiesta *(request);* assiduità *(diligence).*
apply (to) essere adatto *(to be suitable);* sollecitare *(to apply for);* rivolgersi a *(to apply to).*
appoint (to) nominare, stabilire.
appointment appuntamento; nomina *(to a position),* por domanda.
appreciate (to) apprezzare.
appreciation apprezzamento.
approach (to) avvicinare, accostare.
appropriate appropriato, adatto.
approval approvazione, f.
approve (to) approvare.
apricot albicocca.
April aprile.
apron grembiule, m.
arbitrary arbitrario.

arcade arcata, portico, galleria.
archaeology archeologia.
architect architetto.
architecture architettura.
ardent ardente.
arduous arduo; difficile.
area area, spazio.
argue (to) discutere, litigare.
argument discussione, f.; argomento.
arise (to) levarsi, sorgere.
arm braccio; braccia, f. pl.
    arm in arm a braccetto.
armchair poltrona.
armistice armistizio.
arms reduction riduzione degli
    armamenti.
army esercito.
around in giro *(in circulation);*
    intorno a.
arouse (to) svegliare, sollevare, aizzare.
arrange (to) aggiustare, assettare,
    stabilire.
arrangement disposizione, f.; accordo
    (agreement).
arrest arresto, cattura.
arrest (to) arrestare, catturare.
arrival arrivo.
arrive (to) arrivare.
arsenal arsenale.
art arte, f.
    Fine Arts Belle Arti, f.
artery arteria.
artichoke carciofo.
article articolo, oggetto.
artificial artificiale.
artist artista, m & f.
artistic artistico.
as come *(like);* mentre *(while).*
    as . . . as . . . così . . . come . . .
    as it were per così dire.
    as little as tanto poco quanto.
    as long as finchè.
    as much altrettanto.
    as much . . . as . . . tanto . . .
      quanto . . .
ascertain (to) constatare.
ash cenere, f.
ashamed vergognoso.
    to be ashamed of aver vergogna di.
ashtray portacenere, m.
aside a parte.
ask (to) chiedere, domandare.

    to ask a question fare una domanda.
asleep addormentato.
    to fall asleep addormentarsi.
asphalt asfalto.
asphyxia asfissia.
aspire (to) aspirare.
aspirin aspirina.
assault assalto.
assemble (to) riunire.
assembly assemblea.
assign (to) assegnare, destinare.
assist (to) assistere, aiutare.
assistance assistenza, soccorso.
associate socio.
associate (to) associare.
assume (to) assumere.
assurance sicurezza.
    self-assurance confidenza in se
      stesso.
assure (to) assicurare.
astonish (to) stupire.
astounded stupefatto.
astounding stupefacente.
astronaut astronauta.
at a.
    at first in principio; dapprima.
    at last finalmente.
    at once immediatamente, subito.
    at the same time nello stesso
      tempo.
atheism ateismo.
athlete atleta, m.
athletic atletico.
athletics sports, m. pl.
atmosphere atmosfera.
atom atomo.
atrocious atroce.
attach (to) attaccare, aderire (a).
attack assalto, attacco.
attack (to) assalire, attaccare,
    aggredire.
attain (to) ottenere, conseguire,
    raggiungere.
attempt tentativo, attentato.
attempt (to) tentare.
attend (to) assistere, frequentare.
    to attend to occuparsi di.
attention attenzione, f.
attic soffitta.
attitude atteggiamento.
attorney avvocato.
attract (to) attirare.

attraction attrazione, f.; attrattiva.
attractive affascinante, interessante.
auction asta.
audience udienza, uditorio.
audiovisual audiovisivo.
August agosto.
aunt zia.
author autore, m.
authority autorità.
authorize (to) autorizzare.
automated banking Bancomat.
automatic automatico.
automobile automobile, f.; vettura.
autonomy autonomia.
autumn autunno.
available utilizzabile, disponibile.
average media, f.; medio (adj.).
aviation aviazione.
avoid (to) evitare.
avoidable evitabile.
awake sveglio.
awake (to be) essere sveglio.
awaken (to) svegliare, destare.
award premio.
away assente, lontano.
  to go away andar via.
awful spaventoso.
awhile per qualche tempo.
awkward goffo.

baby bambino, m. bambina, f.
back (n.) dorso (in body); spalliera (of piece of furniture); fondo (of room or place); (adv.) indietro; di dietro; posteriore; retro.
  to be back essere di ritorno.
background sfondo.
backward indietro.
bacon pancetta.
bacteria batteri.
bad cattivo; guasto (spoiled).
badge segno, insegna.
badly male.
bag sacco, borsa.
baker panettiere, fornaio.
bakery panetterìa, panificio.
balance equilibrio; saldo.
balance (to) pareggiare.

bald calvo.
ball palla; ballo (dance).
balloon pallone, m.
balsam balsamo.
banana banana.
band orchestra, banda.
bandage benda.
banister balaustrata.
bank banca; sponda (river); argine.
  bank account deposito in banca.
banknote biglietto di banca.
bankruptcy bancarotta, fallimento.
  to go bankrupt fallire.
banquet banchetto.
banquet (to) banchettare.
baptistry battistero.
bar bar, m.; tavoletta; barra.
barbaric barbaro.
barber barbiere, m.; parrucchiere, m.
barbershop barbiere.
bare nudo.
bargain affare, m.
barge barchetta.
baritone baritono.
barn capanna, granaio.
baroque barocco.
barrel barile, m.
barren sterile, arido.
base fondamento.
bashful timido.
basin bacino, catinella.
basket paniere, m.; canestro; cesto.
bas-relief bassorilievo.
bath bagno.
  to take a bath fare un bagno.
bathe (to) bagnare.
  bathing suit costume da bagno, m.
bathrobe accappatoio.
bathtub vasca.
battle battaglia.
be (to) essere.
  to be ahead essere in capo.
  to be hungry avere fame.
  to be right avere ragione.
  to be sleepy avere sonno.
  to be sorry dispiacersene.
  to be thirsty avere sete.
  to be wrong avere torto.
  to be tired sentirsi stanco.
beach spiaggia.
beaming raggiante.
bean fagiuolo.

bear (to) sostenere; soffrire con rassegnazione *(morally);* sopportare.

bearer portatore.

beat (to) battere; sbattere.

beautiful bello.

beauty bellezza.

because perchè.

    because of a causa di.

become (to) diventare.

    to become accustomed abituarsi.

becoming confacente.

bed letto.

bedclothes coperte, f. pl.

bedroom camera da letto.

bedspread copriletto.

beef manzo.

beer birra.

beet bietola.

before prima; davanti; prima che.

    the day before la vigilia.

beg (to) mendicare.

beggar mendicante, m. & f.

begin (to) incominciare.

beginner principiante.

beginning principio, inizio.

behave (to) comportarsi, condursi.

behavior condotta; maniere, f. pl.

behind di dietro; dietro a.

Belgian belga, m.

belief credenza, opinione, f.

believe (to) credere.

bell campana, campanello.

belly pancia.

belong (to) appartenere; essere di.

below di sotto; in basso.

belt cintura.

beltway circonvallazione.

bench panca, panchina.

bend (to) piegare, curvare.

beneath al di sotto; inferiore a.

benefit beneficio, vantaggio.

benefit (to) beneficare, giovare.

benign benigno.

beside presso; accanto a.

besides a parte; inoltre.

best il migliore; il meglio.

bet scommessa.

bet (to) scommettere.

betray (to) tradire.

better migliore, meglio.

between fra.

beyond oltre; al di là.

bicycle bicicletta.

bid offerta.

big grande.

bill conto.

    to pay the bill pagare il conto.

    bill of fare menu, m.; lista.

    bill-posting affissione.

billion miliardo, m.

bind (to) legare; rilegare.

bird uccello.

birth nascita.

birthday compleanno.

biscuit biscotto.

bishop vescovo.

bit pezzetto.

    a bit un po'.

bite morsicatura; boccone; m.

bite (to) mordere.

bitter amaro.

bitterness amarezza.

black nero, negro.

blackbird merlo.

blade lama; lametta *(razor)*.

blame colpa, biasimo.

blame (to) incolpare.

blank (n.) modulo *(form);* (adj.) in bianco.

blanket coperta.

bleach decolorante.

bleed (to) sanguinare.

bless (to) benedire.

blessing benedizione, f.

blind (n.) tendina *(for window);* (adj.) cieco.

blind (to) accecare.

block blocco; isolato *(a city block).*

block (to) ostacolare, sbarrare.

blood sangue m.

blouse camicia, camicetta.

blow colpo, botta.

blow (to) soffiare.

blue blu, azzurro, turchino.

blush rossore, m.

blush (to) arrossire.

board vitto e alloggio *(food and lodging);* asse, f. *(plank).*

boarding house pensione, f.

boast (to) vantare.

boat barca, battello.

    sailboat barca a vela.

    rowboat barca a remi.

boil (to) bollire.

boiler caldaia.

bold ardito.

bomb bomba.
    atomic bomb bomba atomica.
bond legame, m., obbligazione.
bone osso.
book libro.
booklet libretto.
bookseller libraio.
bookstore librerìa.
border frontiera, confine.
boring noioso; barboso.
born (to be) nascere.
borrow (to) pigliare in prestito.
both ambedue, entrambi.
bother noia.
bother (to) annoiare.
    Don't bother. Non disturbatevi.
bottle bottiglia.
bottle opener apribottiglie.
bottom (n.) fondo; (adj.) ultimo; in
    fondo.
bounce (to) saltare.
boundary limite, m.; confine, m.
boundless sconfinato, illimitato.
bowl scodella.
box scatola.
boy ragazzo.
bra reggiseno.
bracelet braccialetto.
braid treccia.
brain cervello.
braised brasato.
brake freno.
branch ramo; succursale, f. *(business)*.
brand marca, marchio.
brassiere reggiseno, m.
brave coraggioso, bravo.
bread pane, m.
break (to) rompere.
    to break out irrompere.
breakfast colazione, f.
    to have breakfast far colazione.
breast petto.
breast pocket taschino.
breath soffio, respiro.
breathe (to) respirare.
breeze brezza.
bribe (to) corrompere.
brick mattone, m.
bride sposa.
bridge ponte, m.
brief breve.
bright chiaro, vivo.
brighten (to) brillare.

brilliant brillante; smagliante.
bring (to) portare, condurre; apportare.
    to bring together avvicinare.
    to bring up educare.
British inglese, britannico.
broad largo.
brocade broccato.
broil (to) arrostire.
    broiled sulla graticola.
broken rotto.
bronchitis bronchite.
bronze bronzo.
brook ruscello.
broom scopa.
brother fratello.
brotherhood fratellanza.
brother-in-law cognato.
brown marrone.
bruise (to) ammaccare.
brush spazzola.
brute bruto, animale.
bubble bolla.
buckle fibbia.
bud bocciolo.
budget bilancio.
buffet buffet.
build (to) costruire, fabbricare.
building construzione, f.; palazzo,
    edificio.
bulletin bollettino.
bumper paraurti.
bunch mazzo, gruppo.
bundle pacco.
burden onere.
burn (to) bruciare.
burst eruzione, f.; scoppio.
burst (to) scoppiare.
bury (to) seppellire.
bus autobus, m.
bush cespuglio, macchia.
business affare, m.; commercio.
businessman uomo d'affari;
    commerciante *(dealer)*.
busy occupato.
busy (to) affaccendarsi.
but ma.
butcher macellaio.
butcher shop macellerìa.
butter burro.
button bottone, m.
buy (to) comprare.
buyer compratore, m.
by per, a.

by and by più in là; fra poco.
by day di giorno.
by then allora.

C

cab tassì, m.
cabbage cavolo.
cab driver autista, m.
cabinet gabinetto, armadio.
cable car funivia.
cage gabbia.
cake torta.
    cake of soap pezzo di sapone.
calculate (to) calcolare.
calculation calcolo.
calendar calendario.
calf vitello.
call chiamata, visita, grido.
call (to) chiamare.
    to call back richiamare.
    to call forth evocare.
    to call out gridare.
    to call on someone visitare.
calm sereno.
camera macchina fotografica.
camomile camomilla.
camp campo.
camp (to) accampare.
campfire falò.
can scatola, latta.
can (to be able) potere.
cancel (to) annullare.
candidate candidato.
candle candela.
candy caramella.
can opener apriscatole.
cap berretto.
capacity capacità.
capital (n.) capitale, f. *(city);* capitale,
    m. *(money);* (adj.) capitale,
    principale; eccellente.
capricious capriccioso.
captain capitano.
captive prigioniero.
capture (to) catturare.
car automobile, f.; vettura *(wagon).*
carafe caraffa.
carbon paper carta copiativa.
card carta; biglietto; scheda.

    game of cards partita a carte.
care cura.
    in care of presso *(on a letter).*
    take care of prendere cura di.
care (to) curare.
    to care for amare.
    to care to desiderare.
    I don't care. Non me ne curo.
career carriera.
careful cauto, attento.
careless incauto, trascurato.
cares noie, f. pl.
carpenter falegname, m.
carpet tappeto.
carrier portatore.
carry (to) portare.
carry out (to) eseguire; attuare,
    realizzare.
cart carrello.
carve (to) tagliare, scolpire.
case caso; recipiente, m. *(container);*
    cassa *or* cassetta *(box).*
    in that case in tal caso.
cash contanti, m. pl.
cash (to) incassare.
cash flow liquidità.
cashier cassiere, m.
cask fusto.
cast (to) gettare *(throw).*
castle castello.
casual casuale, fortuito.
cat gatto.
catch (to) afferrare.
category categorìa.
cathedral cattedrale, duomo.
Catholic cattolico.
cattle bestiame, m.
cause causa.
cause (to) causare.
cavity carie, cavità.
cease (to) cessare.
ceiling soffitto.
celebrate (to) celebrare, proclamare.
cellar cantina.
cement cemento.
cemetery cimitero.
censorship censura.
census censimento.
cent centesimo.
center centro.
centigrade centigrado.
central centrale.

century secolo.
ceramics ceramica.
cereal cereale, m.
cerebral cerebrale.
ceremony cerimonia.
certain certo.
certainty certezza.
certificate certificato, atto.
   birth certificate atto di nascita.
chain catena.
chain (to) incatenare.
chair sedia.
chairman presidente, m.
chalk gesso.
challenge sfida.
challenge (to) sfidare.
champagne champagne, m.
champion campione, m.
chance caso, azzardo, sorte, f.
   to take a chance correre il rischio.
chandelier lampadario.
change cambiamento; trasformazione;
   resto *(money)*.
change (to) cambiare.
chapel cappella.
chapter capitolo.
character carattere, m.; personaggio *(in*
   a play).
characteristic caratteristica.
charge (to) far pagare; mettere a carico
   di; accusare *(to accuse)*.
charitable caritatevole.
charity carità.
charm fascino.
charm (to) affascinare.
charming affascinante.
chase (to) inseguire.
chat (to) chiacchierare.
cheap a buon mercato.
cheat (to) ingannare, truffare, barare.
check freno; assegno *(bank)*.
check (to) verificare *(verify);* reprimere
   (hold back).
cheek guancia.
cheer (to) rallegrare, acclamare,
   rianimare.
cheerful allegro.
cheese formaggio.
chemical sostanza chimica.
chemist chimico.
cherish (to) amare teneramente.
cherry ciliegia.

chest petto *(body);* cassa *(box)*.
   chest of drawers stipo; armadio.
chestnut castagna.
chew (to) masticare.
chicken pollo.
chief (n.) capo; (adj.) principale.
child bambino, bambina, fanciullo,
   fanciulla.
childbirth parto.
chimney camino; focolare, m. *(hearth)*.
chin mento.
china porcellana.
chip scheggia.
chivalry cavalleria, cortesia.
chocolate cioccolato.
choice scelta; (adj.) scelto.
choir coro.
cholera colera.
choke (to) strangolare, soffocare.
choose (to) scegliere.
chop braciola *(cut of meat)*.
choreography coreografia.
Christian cristiano (n. & adj.).
Christmas Natale.
   Christmas Eve Vigilia di Natale.
   Merry Christmas! Buon Natale!
chronicle cronaca.
church chiesa.
cigar sigaro.
cinnamon cannella.
circle cerchio.
circular rotondo.
circulation circolazione, f.
circumstances circostanze, f. pl.
citizen cittadino.
city città.
city hall municipio.
civil civile.
civilization civilizzazione, f.; civiltà.
civilize (to) civilizzare, incivilire.
claim diritto, reclamo.
claim (to) reclamare, affermare.
clam vongola.
clamor clamore, m.; strepito.
clap (to) applaudire, battere le mani.
class classe, f.
classic classico.
classified advertisement annuncio.
classify (to) classificare.
clause clausola.
clean pulito.
clean (to) pulire.

    (to) dry clean pulire a secco.
cleanliness pulizia.
clear chiaro, limpido.
clear (to) schiarire.
    (to) clear up rasserenarsi.
clearly chiaramente.
clerk commesso.
clever scaltro.
cliff scogliera.
climate clima, m.
climb (to) arrampicare; scalare.
clip (to) attaccare, appuntare.
cloak mantello.
clock orologio.
cloister chiostro.
close vicino *(near)*.
close (to) chiudere.
closed chiuso.
closet armadio a muro, stanzino,
    ripostiglio.
cloth stoffa.
clothe (to) vestire.
clothes vestiti, indumenti,
    abbigliamento.
cloud nuvola.
cloudy nuvoloso.
clover trifoglio.
clown pagliaccio.
club circolo *(organization);* bastoni, f.
    (playing cards).
coach corriera, carrozza.
coal carbone, m.
coarse ruvido.
coast costa, litorale.
coat cappotto *(overcoat).*
cocoa cacào.
code codice, m.
coffee caffè, m.
    coffee with cream caffè con panna.
coffin bara.
cognitive cognitivo.
coin moneta.
cold freddo.
    to be cold aver freddo; far freddo
    (weather).
coldness freddezza.
collaborate (to) collaborare.
collar collare, m.; colletto.
collect (to) raccogliere.
collection collezione, f.; raccolta.
collective collettivo.
college università.
colonial coloniale.

colony colonia.
color colore, m.
color (to) colorare.
column colonna.
comb pettine, m.
comb (to) pettinare.
combination combinazione, f.
combine (to) combinare.
come (to) venire.
    to come about accadere.
    to come back ritornare.
    to come by passare per.
    to come down scendere.
    to come for venire a prendere.
    to come in entrare.
    to come out uscire.
comedy commedia.
comet cometa.
comfort conforto, agio.
comfort (to) consolare, rassicurare.
comfortable confortevole.
comics fumetti.
comma virgola.
command comando.
command (to) comandare.
commander comandante, m.
commerce commercio.
commercial commerciale, pubblicità.
commission commissione, f.
commit (to) commettere.
common comune.
communicate (to) comunicare.
communication comunicazione, f.
community comunità.
compact disk compact.
companion compagno, compagna.
company compagnià *(firm);* invitati
    (guests).
compare (to) paragonare, confrontare.
comparison paragone, m.; confronto.
compete (to) competere.
competent competente, abile.
competition competizione, f.;
    concorrenza.
complain (to) lamentarsi.
complaint lagnanza; reclamo.
complete completo.
complex complesso (n. & adj.).
complexion carnagione, f.
complicate (to) complicare.
complicated complicato.
compliment complimento.
compose (to) comporre.

composer compositore, m.
composition composizione, f.
comprehend (to) comprendere, includere.
compromise compromesso.
compromise (to) compromettere.
computer computer, m.
conceive (to) concepire, immaginare.
concentrate (to) concentrare.
concept concetto.
concern ditta *(business);* ansietà *(anxiety).*
concern (to) concernere, riguardare.
concert concerto.
conclusion conclusione, f.; fine, f.
concrete (adj.) concreto.
condemn (to) condannare.
condense (to) condensare.
condition condizione, f.
conditional condizionale.
conditioner balsamo.
conduct condotta.
conduct (to) condurre, dirigere.
conductor conduttore, m.; direttore, m.; controllare.
confess (to) confessare.
confession confessione, f.
confidence confidenza, fiolucia.
confident confidente, sicuro.
confidential confidenziale.
confirm (to) confermare.
confirmation conferma.
conflict conflitto.
confusion confusione.
congratulate (to) congratulare.
congratulation congratulazione, f.
congress congresso.
conjunction congiunzione.
connect (to) unire.
connection connessione, f.; relazione, f.
conquer (to) conquistare.
conquest conquista.
conscience coscienza.
conscientious coscienzioso, scrupoloso.
conscious conscio, consapevole.
consent consenso.
consent (to) acconsentire.
consequence conseguenza.
conservative conservativo, conservatore.
conservatory conservatorio.
consider (to) considerare.
considerable considerabile.

consideration considerazione, f.
consist (to) consistere, constare.
consistent consistente; coerente.
console (to) consolare.
constant costante.
constitute costituire.
constitution costituzione, f.
constitutional costituzionale.
construct (to) costruire.
consul console, m.
contagious contagioso.
contain (to) contenere.
container recipiente, m.
contemporary contemporaneo.
contend (to) contendere, affermare, sostenere.
content (to) accontentare.
content (to be) essere contento.
contents contenuto.
continent continente, m.
continual continuo.
continue (to) continuare.
continuously continuamente.
contraceptive anticoncezionale.
contract contratto.
contract (to) contrattare.
contractor appaltatore, fornitore.
contradict (to) contraddire, smentire.
contradiction contraddizione, f.
contradictory contraddittorio.
contrary (n.) contrario, cocciuto; (adj.) contrario.
    on the contrary contrariamente; al contrario.
    contrary to contrario a.
contrast contrasto.
contrast (to) contrastare.
contribute (to) contribuire.
contribution contributo.
control controllo; potere, m. *(power or ability).*
    remote control telecomando.
control (to) controllare.
controversy controversia.
convenience convenienza, vantaggio.
    at your convenience a vostro commodo.
convenient conveniente, comodo.
convent convento.
convention convenzione, f.; congresso.
conversation conversazione, f.
converse (to) conversare.
convert (to) convertire.

convict (to) condannare.
conviction convinzione, f.
convince (to) convincere.
cook cuoco, cuoca.
cook (to) cucinare.
cool fresco.
cool (to) rinfrescare, raffreddarsi.
copy copia, articolo, testo.
copy (to) copiare.
cork sughero.
cork (to) tappare, turare.
corkscrew cavatappi, m.
corn grano.
corncob pannocchia.
corner angolo, spigolo.
corporation corporazione, f.
correct corretto, giusto.
    Am I correct? Ho ragione?
correct (to) correggere.
correction correzione, f.
correspond (to) corrispondere.
correspondence corrispondenza.
correspondent corrispondente, m. & f.
corresponding corrispondente.
corrupt corrotto.
corruption corruzione, f.
cosmetic cosmetico.
cosmic cosmico.
cost prezzo, costo.
    at any cost a qualunque costo.
cost (to) costare.
costume costume, m.
cottage capanna.
cotton cotone, m. *(cotton thread, material);* ovatta *(wadding).*
couch divano.
cough tosse, f.
cough (to) tossire.
count conte, m. *(title);* conto, m. *(computation, reckoning).*
count (to) contare.
counter banco *(store).*
countess contessa.
countless innumerevole.
country campagna; patria *(fatherland).*
country house casa di campagna.
countryman compatriota; contadino *(farmer).*
couple coppia.
courage coraggio.
course corso.
    of course naturalmente; s'intende.

court corte, f., tribunale, m. *(of law).*
courteous cortese.
courtesy cortesia.
courtship corte, f.
courtyard cortile, m.
cousin cugino, cugina.
cover coperchio, *(lid);* coperta *(for a bed).*
cover (to) coprire; ricoprire; fare la cronaca.
cow mucca, vacca.
co-worker collega, m. & f.
crack fessura.
crack (to) crepare, fendere.
cradle culla.
craftsman artigiano.
craftsmanship artigianato.
crash scontro, fracasso.
crash (to) fracassare.
crazy folle, pazzo.
cream crema.
crease piega.
create (to) creare.
creature creatura.
credit credito, fiducia, riputazione.
creditor creditore, m.
cricket grillo.
crime delitto.
criminal (n. & adj.) delinquente, m.
crisis crisi, f.
crisp croccante.
critic critico.
criticism critica.
crooked storto; disonesto *(morally).*
crop raccolta.
cross (n.) croce, f.; (adj.) adirato; di cattivo umore.
cross (to) traversare.
crossing passaggio.
crossroads bivio, crocevia, m.
crouch (to) appiattarsi.
crow corvo.
crowd folla.
crowd (to) affollare, ingombrare.
cruel crudele.
cruelty crudeltà.
cruise crociera.
crumb mollica, briciola.
crumble (to) sgretolarsi.
crust crosta.
crutch gruccia, stampella.
cry grido.

cry (to) piangere.
   to cry out gridare.
crypt cripta.
cuff polsino.
cunning scaltrezza.
cup tazza.
cure cura.
cure (to) curare.
curiosity curiosità.
curious curioso, struno.
curl riccio.
curl (to) arricciare.
current (n.) corrente, f.; (adj.) corrente;
   in corso.
cursive corsivo.
curtain tendina; sipario (theater).
curve curva.
curved arcuato.
cushion cuscino.
cusp cuspide.
custody custodia, arresto.
custom usanza; clientela.
   custom jewelry bigiotteria.
customary abituale.
customer cliente, m. & f.
customhouse dogana.
customs official doganiere, m.
cut taglio.
   cut and paste taglia e incolla.
cut (to) tagliare.
cuticle cuticola.
cycle ciclo.
cycling ciclismo.
cypress cipresso.
Cyprus Cipro.

D

dad, daddy papà, babbo.
dagger pugnale, m.
daily quotidiano.
dainty delicato.
dairy latteria.
   dairy products latticini, m. pl.
dam diga.
damage danno.
damage (to) danneggiare.
damp umido.
dance danza.
dance (to) ballare, danzare.

danger pericolo.
dangerous pericoloso.
dark buio; oscuro; scuro (color).
darkness oscurità; tenebre.
dash (to) precipitarsi.
date data, scadenaza.
date (to) datare.
daughter figlia.
daughter-in-law nuora.
dawn alba.
day giorno.
   all day tutto il giorno.
   the day after tomorrow dopo
      domani; l'indomani, m.
   the day before il giorno prima.
   the day before yesterday avantieri;
      ieri l'altro.
dazzle (to) abbagliare.
dazzling abbagliante, smagliante.
dead morto, morta.
deaf sordo (also deaf person).
deafen (to) assordare.
   deaf-mute sordomuto, sordomuta.
deal affare, m.
deal (to) fare affari con; commerciare.
dealer mercante, m.; venditore, m.;
   negoziante.
dear caro.
death morte, f.
debatable discutibile.
debate discussione, f.; dibattito.
debate (to) discutere.
debris rovine, f. pl.
debt debito.
debtor debitore, m.
debut debutto.
decadent decadente.
decaffeinated decaffeinato.
decanter caraffa.
decay decadenza; carie (tooth).
decay (to) decadere, appassire.
deceased defunto.
deceit inganno.
deceive (to) ingannare, illudere.
December dicembre.
decent decente.
decide (to) decidere.
decidedly decisamente.
decision decisione, f.
decisive decisivo.
deck ponte, m.
declare (to) dichiarare.

decline decadenza, abbassamento.
decline (to) declinare.
decorate (to) decorare.
decrease diminuzione, f.
decrease (to) diminuire.
decree decreto.
dedicate (to) dedicare.
deed atto.
deep profondo.
deer cervo.
defeat sconfitta.
defeat (to) sconfiggere.
defect difetto.
defend (to) difendere.
defense diffesa.
defiance sfida, disfida.
define (to) definire.
definite definitivo, preciso.
defy (to) sfidare.
degree grado; laurea.
delay ritardo.
delay (to) ritardare.
delegate delegato.
delegate (to) delegare.
deliberate deliberato.
deliberate (to) deliberare.
deliberately deliberatamente.
delicacy delicatezza, ghiottoneria.
delicate delicato.
delicious delizioso.
delight delizia, compiacimento.
delight (to) dilettare.
deliver (to) recapitare, consegnare;
    partorire.
deliverance liberazione, f.
delivery liberazione, f.; consegna
    (package).
delude illudere.
demand domanda, richiesta.
demand (to) domandare, richiedere.
demonstrate (to) dimonstrare.
demonstration dimostrazione, f.
denial diniego, rifiuto.
denounce (to) denunziare.
dense denso.
density densità.
dental dentale.
dentifrice dentifricio.
dentist dentista, m.
dentures dentatura.
deny (to) negare, refiutare.
department dipartimento, reparto.
depend (to) dipendere.

dependence dipendenza.
dependent (adj.) dipendente.
deplore (to) deplorare.
deport (to) deportare.
deposit deposito.
deposit (to) depositare.
depot deposito.
depress (to) deprimere.
depression depressione, f.
deprive (to) privare.
depth profondità.
derive (to) derivare.
dermatologist dermatologo.
descend (to) discendere, scendere.
descent discesa.
describe (to) descrivere.
description descrizione, f.
desert deserto.
desert (to) abbandonare.
deserve (to) meritare.
design disegno.
    interior design arredamento.
design (to) disegnare *(to draw)*.
designed (for) destinato a.
designer stilista.
desirable desiderabile.
desire desiderio.
desire (to) desiderare.
desirous desideroso.
desk serivanìa.
desolate desolato.
desolation desolazione, f.
despair disperazione, f.
despair (to) disperare.
desperate disperato.
despise (to) disprezzare; sdegnare.
despite malgrado.
despondent abbattuto.
dessert frutta e dolci.
destine (to) destinare.
destiny destino.
destitute indigente.
destroy (to) distruggere.
destruction distruzione, f.
detach (to) staccare, separare.
detail dettaglio, particolare, m.
detain (to) trattenere.
detect (to) notare.
detergent detersivo; detergente.
determination determinazione, f.
determine (to) determinare, fissare,
    stabilire.
detest (to) detestare.

detour svolta.

detract from (to) detrarre, denigrare.

detriment detrimento.

devaluation svalutazione.

devalue (to) svalutare.

develop (to) sviluppare.

development sviluppo.

device espediente, apparecchio.

devil diavolo.

devise (to) immaginare.

devoid of privo di.

devote (to) dedicare.

devour (to) divorare.

devoutness devozione.

dew rugiada.

diabetes diabete.

diabetic diabetico.

diagnosis diagnosi.

dial quadrante *(clock)*.

dialect dialetto.

dialogue dialogo.

diameter diametro.

diamond diamante, m.; quadri, m. pl. *(playing cards)*.

diaper pannolino.

diary diario.

dictate (to) dettare.

diction dizione

dictionary dizionario, vocabolario.

didactic didattico.

die (to) morire.

diet dieta.

differ (to) differire.

difference differenza.

different diverso.

difficult difficile.

difficulty difficoltà.

dig (to) scavare.

digest (to) digerire.

dignity dignità.

dilemma dilemma.

dim oscuro, annebbiato, debole.

dimension dimensione, f.

diminish (to) diminuire.

dine (to) pranzare.

dinner pranzo.

dip (to) immergere, intingere.

diplomacy diplomazìa.

diplomat diplomatico.

direct (to) dirigere.

direction direzione, f.; senso; regia.

   in all directions in tutte le direzioni.

director direttore, m.; regista.

directory elenco, rubrica.

dirt sudiciume, m.

dirty sudicio, sporco.

disability incapacità.

disabled incapacitato; disabile.

disadvantage svantaggio.

disagree (to) differire; non essere d'accordo.

disagreeable contrario, sgradevole.

disagreement differenza, disaccordo.

disappear (to) sparire.

disappearance sparizione, f.; scomparsa.

disappoint (to) deludere l'aspettativa di.

disappointment disappunto.

disapprove (to) disapprovare.

disaster disastro.

disastrous disastroso.

discharge congedo *(from army or a position)*; scarica *(of a gun)*.

discharge (to) congedare *(military)*; licenziare *(from a position)*; scaricare *(firearm)*.

discipline disciplina.

disclaim (to) negare, rinunziare.

disclose (to) svelare, palesare.

disclosure rivelazione, f.; palesamento.

discomfort disagio.

discontent malcontento.

discontented scontento.

discontinue (to) cessare.

discord discordia, dissenso, dissidio.

discotheque discoteca.

discount sconto.

discourage (to) scoraggiare.

discouragement scoraggiamento.

discover (to) scoprire.

discovery scoperta.

discreet discreto.

discretion discrezione, f.

discuss (to) discutere.

discussion discussione, f.

disdain sdegno.

disdain (to) disdegnare.

disease malattìa.

disgrace vergogna, disonore, m.

disguise travestimento.

   in disguise travestito.

disgust disgusto.

disgusted disgustato.

disgusting schifoso, disgustoso.

dish piatto.

dishes stoviglie.

dishonest disonesto.
dishwasher lavastoviglie, lavapiatti.
disk disco; dischetto *(computer)*.
dislike avversione, f.; antipatìa.
dislike (to) sentire avversione; sentire antipatìa; non amare.
dismiss (to) congedare, licenziare.
dismissal congedo.
disobey (to) disobbedire.
disorder disordine, m.
dispense (to) dispensare, distribuire.
display esposizione, f.
display (to) esporre, mostrare.
displease (to) dispiacere.
disposal disposizione, f.; vendita *(sale)*.
dispose (to) disporre.
disproportion sproporzione.
dispute disputa, contesa.
dispute (to) disputare, contestare.
disqualification squalifica.
dissatisfied scontento, insoddisfatto.
dissertation dissertazione.
dissolve (to) dissolvere, disfare.
distance distanza.
distant lontano, distante.
distinct distinto, chiaro.
distinction distinzione, f.; signorilità.
distinguish (to) distinguere.
distort (to) distorcere, deformare.
distract (to) distrarre.
distress afflizione, f.; affanno, imbarazzo.
distress (to) affliggere.
distribute (to) distribuire.
distribution distribuzione, f.
district quartiere, m.
distrust sfiducia.
distrust (to) non aver fiducia.
disturb (to) disturbare.
disturbance disturbo, disordine, m.
ditch fosso.
dive (to) tuffarsi.
divide (to) dividere, separare.
divine divino.
division divisione, f.
divorce divorzio.
divorce (to) divorziare.
dizziness vertigine, f., capogiro.
dizzy stordito.
do (to) fare.
    to do again rifare.

dock darsena.
doctor dottore, m.
doctrine dottrina.
document documento.
dog cane, m.
dome cupola.
domestic domestico.
dominate (to) dominare; sovrastare.
door porta.
    next door la porta accanto.
doorman portinaio.
dose dose, f.
dot punto; puntino.
double doppio.
doubt dubbio.
doubt (to) dubitare.
doubtful dubbioso.
doubtless senza dubbio.
dough pasta.
down giù; in basso.
downward in giù.
dozen dozzina.
draft corrente, f. *(air);* leva *(military);* cambiale, f. *(bank).*
draft (to) reclutare *(military);* fare la pianta *(make a plan).*
drag (to) strascinare.
drain (to) scolare.
drainage drenaggio.
drama dramma, m.
draw (to) disegnare.
    to draw back indietreggiare.
drawback svantaggio.
drawer tiretto, cassetto.
drawing room salone, m.
dread terrore, m.; paura.
dread (to) temere.
dreaded terribile, formidabile.
dream sogno.
dream (to) sognare.
dreamer sognatore, m.
dress abito, vestito, veste, f.
dress (to) vestirsi, vestire.
drink bevanda.
drink (to) bere.
drinkable potabile.
drip (to) sgocciolare.
drive (to) guidare *(car);* spingere *(to force or induce).*
    disk drive unità a disco.
driver conducente, m.
    driver's license patente.

drop goccia *(of water);* caduta *(a fall).*
drop (to) lasciare cadere.
drown (to) annegare.
drug droga.
drug addict drogato.
druggist farmacista, m.
drugstore farmacia.
drum tamburo.
drunk ubriaco, ebbro.
dry asciutto, secco.
dry (to) asciugare, seccare.
dryness aridità.
dubbing doppiaggio.
duchess duchessa.
due dovuto.
duke duca, m.
dull fosco *(color);* ottuso *(stupid).*
dumb stupido *(stupid).*
during durante.
dust polvere, f.
dust (to) spolverare.
dusty polveroso.
duty dazio *(customs tolls);* dovere *(obligation).*
    duty-free esente da dogama.
dwarf f. nana.
dwell (to) dimorare, abitare.
dwelling dimora, abitazione, f.
dye tintura.
dye (to) tingere.

each ciascuno, ciascuna, ogni.
    each other si; ci; l'un l'altro.
    each time ogni volta.
eager ansioso; desideroso di.
eagle aquila.
ear orecchio.
early presto; di buon'ora.
earn (to) guadagnare.
earnest zelante, fervido, sincero.
earth terra.
ease agio.
ease (to) alleviare, mitigare.
easily facilmente.
east est, m.; oriente, m.
Easter Pasqua.
eastern orientale.

easy facile.
eat (to) mangiare.
echo eco, m. & f.
ecology ecologia.
economical economico.
economize (to) fare delle economìe; economizzare.
economy economìa.
ecstatic estatico.
edge bordo, orlo; spigolo.
edition edizione, f.
editor editore, m.; redattore, m.
editorial articolo di fondo; (adj.) editoriale.
education educazione, f.; istruzione, f.
effect effetto.
effect (to) effettuare, compiere.
effective efficace.
efficiency efficienza.
efficient efficiente.
effort sforzo.
egg uovo.
    hard-boiled egg uovo sodo.
    scrambled eggs uova strapazzate.
eggplant melanzana.
egoism egoismo.
eight otto.
eighteen diciotto.
eighteenth diciottesimo.
eighth ottavo.
eightieth ottantesimo.
eighty ottanta.
either . . . or . . . sia . . . che . . .
    either . . . or . . . o . . . o . . .
    either one l'uno o l'altro.
    either one of the two ognuno dei due.
elastic (n. & adj.) elastico.
elbow gomito.
elder anziano, maggiore.
elderly anziano.
eldest il più anziano; il maggiore.
elect scegliere, eleggere.
election elezione, f.
elector elettore, m.
electric(al) elettrico.
electricity elettricità.
elegant elegante.
element elemento, fattore, m.
elementary elementare.
elephant elefante, m.
elevator ascensore, m.

eleven undici.
eleventh undicesimo.
eliminate (to) eliminare.
eloquence eloquenza.
eloquent eloquente.
else altro.
  or else altrimenti.
  someone else qualche altro.
elsewhere altrove.
elude (to) eludere.
e-mail e-mail, posta elettronica.
emancipate (to) emancipare.
embark (to) imbarcare, imbarcarsi.
embarrass (to) imbarazzare.
embarrassing imbarazzante.
embarrassment imbarazzo.
embassy ambasciata.
embody (to) incarnare.
embroider (to) ricamare.
embroidery ricamo.
emerge (to) emergere.
emergency emergenza.
eminent eminente, illustre.
emotion emozione, f.
emperor imperatore.
emphasis enfasi, f.
emphasize (to) accentuare.
emphatic enfatico.
empire impero.
employ (to) impiegare.
employee impiegato.
employer datore di lavoro, m.
employment impiego.
empty vuoto.
empty (to) vuotare.
enable (to) rendere abile; mettere in
  condizione di.
enamel smalto.
enclose (to) rinchiudere.
enclosed rinchiuso.
encourage (to) incoraggiare.
encouragement incoraggiamento.
end fine, f.
end (to) finire.
endeavor sforzo, tentativo.
endeavor (to) tentare; sforzarsi di.
endorse (to) firmare *(a check)*;
  sottoscrivere a *(an idea)*.
endure (to) durare *(last)*; sopportare
  (bear).
enemy nemico, nemica.
energetic energico.
energy energia.

  solar energy energia solare.
enforce (to) imporre.
engage (to) impegnare.
engagement impegno *(social)*;
  fidanzamento *(romantic)*.
engine macchina, motore, m.
engineer ingegnere, m.; macchinista,
  m. *(railway)*.
English (n. & adj.) inglese.
engrave (to) intagliare.
enjoy (to) godere.
enjoyment godimento.
enlarge (to) ingrandire.
enlist (to) arruolare, arruolarsi.
enormous enorme.
enough abbastanza.
  Enough! Basta!
enrich (to) arricchire.
enter (to) entrare.
enterprise impresa.
enterprising intraprendente.
entertain (to) intrattenere.
entertainment intrattenimento.
enthusiasm entusiasmo.
enthusiastic entusiasta.
entire intero.
entitle (to) intitolare *(title)*; dare diritto
  di *(give the right to)*.
entrance entrata.
entrust (to) affidare.
enumerate (to) enumerare.
envelope busta.
envious invidioso.
envy invidia.
episode episodio.
equal uguale.
equal (to) uguagliare.
equality uguaglianza.
equilibrium equilibrio.
equip (to) fornire; equipaggiare *(ship,
  army)*.
equipment fornimento;
  equipaggiamento *(army)*.
equity equità.
era era.
erase (to) cancellare.
eraser gomma.
erect diritto, eretto.
erect (to) erigere.
err (to) errare.
errand commissione, f.
error errore, m.
escalator scala mobile.

escape fuga.
escape (to) fuggire.
escort scorta *(military);* guida.
escort (to) scortare, accompagnare.
especially specialmente.
espirare to exhale.
essay composizione, f. *(school);*
    tentativo *(attempt).*
essence essenza.
essential essenziale.
establish (to) stabilire.
establishment stabilimento.
estate beni, m. pl.; proprietà,
    patrimonio.
esteem stima.
esteem (to) stimare.
esthetic estetico.
estimate valutazione, f.; preventivo.
estimate (to) valutare.
estimation valutazione, f.; stima.
eternal eterno.
eternity eternità.
ethics etica.
ethnic etnico.
Etruscan etrusco.
etymology etimologia.
euro euro, *m.*
European (n. & adj.) europeo.
evade (to) evadere.
evasion evasione, f.
eve vigilia.
    on the eve of la vigilia di.
even (adj.) pari, uguale; (adv.) anche.
evening sera, serata.
    tomorrow evening domani sera.
    yesterday evening ieri sera.
    Good evening! Buona sera!
event avvenimento.
ever sempre.
every ogni.
everybody tutti, tutte.
everyone ognuno, ognuna.
everything tutto.
everywhere ovunque, dappertutto.
evidence evidenza.
evident evidente.
evil (n.) male, m.; (adj.) cattivo.
evoke (to) evocare.
evolution evoluzione.
evolve (to) evolvere.
exact preciso.
exaggerate (to) esagerare.
exaggeration esagerazione, f.

exalt (to) esaltare.
exaltation esaltazione, f.
examination esame, m.
    to take an examination fare un
        esame.
examine (to) esaminare.
example esempio.
exceed (to) eccedere, oltrepassare.
excel (to) eccellere.
excellence eccellenza.
excellent eccellente.
except eccetto, salvo.
except (to) eccettuare.
exception eccezione, f.; strappo.
exceptional eccezionale.
exceptionally eccezionalmente.
excess eccesso.
exchange cambio; scambio.
excite (to) eccitare.
    to get excited accalorarsi.
excitement eccitamento.
exclaim (to) esclamare.
exclamation esclamazione, f.
exclamation point punto
    esclamativo.
exclude (to) escludere.
exclusive esclusivo.
excursion escursione, f.
excuse scusa.
excuse (to) scusare.
    Excuse me. Mi scusi.
execute (to) eseguire *(to carry out);*
    giustiziare *(a prisoner).*
execution esecuzione, f.
exempt esente.
exercise esercizio.
exercise (to) esercitare, esercitarsi.
exert (to) adoprarsi.
exertion sforzo.
exhaust (to) sfinire, esaurire.
exhaustion esaurimento.
exhibit (to) esibire.
exhibition esibizione, f.; mostra;
    rassegna.
exile esilio; esule.
exile (to) esiliare.
exist (to) esistere.
existence esistenza.
exit uscita.
exodus esodo.
expand (to) espandere.
expansion espansione, f.
expansive espansivo.

expect (to) attendere, aspettare, aspettarsi.
expectation aspettativa.
expedition spedizione, f.
expel (to) espellere.
expense spesa.
expensive costoso, caro.
experience esperienza.
experience (to) provare.
experiment esperimento.
expert esperto.
expire (to) spirare, morire.
explain (to) spiegare.
explanation spiegazione, f.
explode (to) esplodere.
exploit gesta, f. pl.
exploit (to) sfruttare.
explore (to) esplorare.
explosion esplosione, f.
export esportazione, f.
export (to) esportare.
expose (to) esporre.
express (n. & adj.) espresso.
express (to) esprimere.
expression espressione, f.
expressive espressivo.
expulsion espulsione, f.
exquisite squisito.
extend (to) estendere.
extensive estensivo.
extent estensione, f.; limite, m.
   to some extent fino ad un certo
      punto.
exterior esteriore.
exterminate (to) sterminare.
external esteriore.
extinct estinto.
extinction estinzione, f.
extinguish (to) estinguere.
extra in più; supplementare.
extract estratto.
extract (to) estrarre.
extradition estradizione.
extraordinary straordinario.
extravagance stravaganza.
extravagant stravagante.
extreme estremo.
extremely estremamente.
extremist estremista.
extremity estremità.
extroverted estroverso.
eye occhio.

eyebrow sopracciglio.
eyeglasses occhiali, m. pl.
eyelash ciglio, pl. ciglia.
eyelid palpebra.

F

fable favola.
fabric stoffa, tessuto.
face viso, faccia.
face (to) affrontare.
facilitate (to) facilitare.
facility facilità.
facsimile facsimile.
fact fatto.
   in fact infatti.
factory fabbrica.
factual fattuale.
faculty facoltà.
fade (to) sbiadire.
fail fallo, mancanza.
   without fail senz' altro; senza
      fallo.
fail (to) fallire, mancare.
faint fievole *(sound, voice)*; debole;
   fioco.
faint (to) svenire.
fair giusto; equo; biondo *(blond)*.
faith fede. f.
faithful fedele.
faithfulness fedeltà.
fall caduta; cascata *(of water)*.
fall (to) cadere.
false falso.
fame fama, reputazione, f.; notorietà.
familiar noto.
family famiglia.
famine carestìa.
famous famoso.
fan ventaglio.
   electric fan ventilatore elettrico.
fancy fantasia, capriccio.
fantastic fantastico.
far lontano.
   far away molto lontano.
farce farsa.
fare prezzo della corsa, tariffa.
farm fattoria, podere, m.
farmer agricoltore, m.
farming agricoltura.

farther più lontano.
farthest il più lontano.
fashion moda.
    old-fashioned passato di moda;
      fuori di moda.
fashionable di moda.
fashion show sfilata di moda.
fast veloce, fisso, rapido.
fasten (to) attaccare; allacciare.
fat grasso (noun & adj.).
fatal fatale.
fate destino.
father padre, m.
father-in-law suocero.
faucet rubinetto.
fault colpa.
favor favore, m.; cortesia.
favor (to) favorire, preferire.
favorable favorevole.
favorite favorito (noun & adj.).
fax facsimile.
fax machine facsimile.
fear timore, m.; paura.
    to be afraid aver paura.
fearless intrepido.
feasible attuabile.
feather piuma.
feature caratteristica, lineamento.
February febbraio.
federal federale.
federation federazione.
fee onorario, paga.
feeble debole; fievole.
feed (to) nutrire.
feel (to) sentire; tastare *(to touch)*.
    to feel well sentirsi bene.
feeling sensibilità, sentimento.
fellow compagno, camerata, m.
fellowship compagnia, società.
female femmina.
feminine femminile.
feminism femminismo.
feminist femminista.
fence siepe, f.; chiusura, steccato.
fencing scherma.
fender parafango.
ferocious feroce.
ferry chiatta.
    ferryboat nave-traghetto.
fertile fertile.
fertilize (to) fertilizzare.
fertilizer fertilizzante, m.

fervent fervente.
fervor fervore, m.
festival festa, festival.
fetch (to) andare a cercare.
feudal feudale.
fever febbre, f.
few pochi, poche, m. & f. pl.
fiber fibra.
fiber optics fibre ottiche.
fiction romanzo, narrativa.
field campo, ambito.
fierce violento.
fiery focoso.
fifteen quindici.
fifteenth quindicesimo.
fifth quinto.
fiftieth cinquantesimo.
fifty cinquanta.
fig fico; pl. fichi.
fight lotta.
fight (to) lottare, combattere.
figure forma *(form);* cifra *(number).*
file lima *(tool);* fascicolo *(papers).*
file (to) archiviare.
filigree filigrana.
fill (to) riempire.
film pellicola.
filthy sudicio.
final finale.
finance finanza.
financial relativo alle finanze;
    finanziario.
find (to) trovare, ritrovare.
    to find out scoprire.
fine (n.) multa, contravvenzione; (adj.)
    fine *(not coarse);* bello.
    Fine! Bene!
finger dito.
finish (to) terminare, completare, finire.
fire fuoco, incendio.
firearms armi da fuoco.
fireplace focolare, m.
firm (n.) ditta; (adj.) fermo, fisso.
first (adj.) primo; (adv.) prima.
    for the first time per la prima volta.
    at first dapprima; da principio.
fish pesce, m.
fish (to) pescare.
fisherman pescatore, m.
fist pugno.
fit (n.) attacco; crisi, f. *(illness);* (adj.)
    idoneo, capace.

fit (to) essere idoneo; essere della stessa misura.
fitness convenienza; attitudine, f.; proporzione, f.
five cinque.
fix (to) accomodare, aggiustare.
flag bandiera.
flame fiamma.
flank fianco, lato.
flash baleno.
flashlight lampadina tascabile; pila.
flat (n.) bemolle, m. *(in music);* (adj.) piatto, piano.
flatter (to) adulare.
flattery adulazione, f.
flavor gusto.
fleet flotta.
flesh carne, f.
flexibility flessibilità.
flexible flessibile.
flight volo *(in air);* fuga *(escape).*
fling (to) gettare.
flint pietra focaia.
float (to) galleggiare.
flood inondazione, f.
flood (to) inondare.
floor pavimento.
Florentine fiorentino.
flourish (to) prosperare.
flow (to) scorrere.
flower fiore, m.
    flower bed aiunola.
fluctuate (to) fluttuare *(economy).*
fluent scorrevole.
    He is fluent in Italian. Parla correntemente l'Italiano.
fluid fluido.
fly mosca.
fly (to) volare.
foam schiuma.
foam (to) fare la schiuma.
fog nebbia.
fold piega.
fold (to) piegare.
foliage fogliame, m.
follow (to) seguire.
following seguente.
fond (to be) sentire tenerezza; affezionarsi.
fondness tenerezza.
food nutrimento, cibo.
fool sciocco (noun & adj.).
foolish sciocco.

foot piede, m.
footstep passo.
for per.
    for example per esempio.
    for the first time per la prima volta.
    for the most part per la maggior parte.
    for the present per il momento.
forbid (to) vietare.
force forza.
force (to) obbligare.
ford guado.
forecast previsione.
foreground primo piano.
forehead fronte, f.
foreign straniero.
foreigner straniero, forestiero.
forest foresta.
forget (to) dimenticare.
forgetfulness oblio, dimenticanza.
forgive (to) perdonare.
forgiveness perdono.
fork forchetta.
form forma.
form (to) formare.
formal formale.
formation formazione, f.
former precedente.
formerly precedentemente.
formula formula.
forsake (to) abbandonare.
fort forte, m.
fortieth quarantesimo.
fortress rocca, fortezza.
fortunate fortunato.
fortunately fortunatamente.
fortune fortuna.
forty quaranta.
forward avanti.
forward (to) spedire *(goods, letters).*
fossil fossile.
foster (to) nutrire, proteggere.
found trovato.
found (to) fondare.
foundation fondazione, f. *(society or order);* fondamento *(base).*
founder fondatore, m.
fountain fontana.
four quattro.
fourteen quattordici.
fourteenth quattordicesimo.
fourth quarto.
fowl uccello, pollo.

fox volpe, f.
fragment frammento.
fragrance fragranza, profumo.
fragrant fragrante, profumato.
frail fragile.
frame cornice, f.
frame (to) incorniciare.
frank franco.
frankness franchezza.
free libero *(without restraint);* gratuito *(at no cost).*
free (to) liberare.
freedom libertà.
freeze (to) gelare.
freight merce, f.; carico.
freight train treno merci.
French (n. & adj.) francese.
frenzy frenesia.
    frenzied frenetico.
frequent frequente.
frequently frequentemente.
fresh fresco.
friction frizione, f.
Friday venerdì.
friend amico, amica.
    to be friends with essere in buoni rapporti.
friendly amichevole.
friendship amicizia.
frieze fregio.
frighten (to) spaventare.
frightening spaventoso.
fringe frangia.
frivolity frivolezza.
frog rana.
from da.
front davanti.
    in front of davanti a.
frontier frontiera.
frost brina.
fruit frutto, frutta.
fruit salad macedonia.
fry (to) friggere.
frying pan padella.
fuchsia fucsia *(color).*
fuel combustibile, m.
fugitive fuggitivo, latitante.
fulfill (to) adempire, realizzare.
fulfillment realizzazione, adempimento.
full pieno.
fully pienamente.
fun divertimento; spasso.
    to have fun divertirsi.

function funzione, f.
function (to) funzionare.
fund fondo.
fundamental fondamentale.
funds fondi, m. pl.
funny buffo.
fur pelliccia *(coat).*
furious furioso, frenetico, violento.
furnace fornace, f.
furnish (to) fornire *(provide);* ammobiliare *(a house),* arredare.
furnishings arredamento.
furniture mobilia.
furrow solco, fosso.
further più lontano; ulteriore.
fury furia.
fuse miccia, fusibile.
future futuro, avvenire.
    in the future nel futuro.
futurism futurismo.

gain guadagno.
gain (to) guadagnare.
gallant galante, valoroso, cavalleresco.
gallery galleria.
gallop (to) galoppare.
gamble (to) giocare.
game partita; gioco.
gang banda.
gangplank passerella.
garage rimessa, autorimessa.
garbage rifiuti, m. pl.
garden giardino, orto.
gardener giardiniere, m.
garlic aglio.
gas benzina *(for car);* gas *(chemical).*
gate cancello.
gather (to) raccogliere, riunire.
gathering riunione, f.
gaudy vistosa, appariscente, di cauttivo gusto.
gay gay *(homosexual).*
gem gemma.
gender genere, m.
general (n. & adj.) generale
generality generalità.
generalize (to) generalizzare.
generation generazione, f.

generosity generosità.
generous generoso.
genius genio.
gentle gentile, garbato, calmo.
gentleman gentiluomo, signore.
   Gentlemen. Signori.
   Ladies and gentlemen. Signore e
    signori.
gentleness gentilezza.
genuine genuino, autentico.
geographical geografico.
geography geografia.
geology geologia.
geometry geometria.
germ germe, m.
German (n. & adj.) tedesco.
germane pertinente, relativo.
gesture gesto.
get (to) ottenere, diventare *(become)*.
   Get down! Scenda! Scendete!
    Scendi!
   Get up! Si alzi! Alzatevi! Alzati!
giant gigante, m.
gift dono; talento *(talent)*.
gifted dotato; con talento *(talented)*.
girdle fascia.
girl fanciulla; ragazza.
give (to) dare, donare.
   to give back restituire, rendere.
   to give up abbandonare.
glad felice.
gladly volentieri.
glance (to) intravedere; dare un'
   occhiata; gettare uno sguardo.
gland ghiandola.
glass bicchiere, m.; vetro.
   glasses occhiali, m. pl.
glitter splendore, m.
glitter (to) splendere, brillare.
globe globo.
gloomy lugubre, fosco.
glorious glorioso.
glory gloria.
glove guanto.
go (to) andare.
   to go away partire.
   to go back ritornare.
   to go down discendere.
   to go forward avanzare.
   to go out uscire.
   to go to bed coricarsi.
   to go to sleep addormentarsi.

   to go up salire.
   to go with accompagnare.
goal meta, scopo, fine; rete *(soccer)*.
goblet calice, coppa.
God Dio.
gold oro.
golden d'oro.
goldsmith orefice, orafo.
good buono.
   Good! Bene!
   Good afternoon. Buon
    pomeriggio.
   Good evening. Buona sera.
   Good morning. Buongiorno.
   Good night. Buona sera; buona
    notte.
good-bye arrivederci, addio.
goodness bontà.
goods merce, f.
goodwill buona volontà.
goose oca.
gossip pettegolezzo.
gossip (to) pettegolare.
govern (to) governare, controllare,
   dominare.
gothic gottico; rosso, barbarico.
   gothic novel romanzo dell'orrore.
governess governante, f.
government governo.
grace grazia.
graceful grazioso.
grade grado, voto.
grain grano.
grammar grammatica.
   grammar school scuola
    elementare.
grand grandioso, imponente,
   splendido.
   Grand! Magnifico!
grandchild nipote, m. & f.
granddaughter nipote, f.
grandfather nonno.
grandmother nonna.
grandson nipote, m.
grant concessione, f.; dono.
grant (to) concedere, accordare.
   Granted! D'accordo!
grape uva.
grapefruit pompelmo.
grapevine vite.
grasp (to) afferrare *(seize)*;
   comprendere *(understand)*.

grass erba.
grateful riconoscente, grato.
gratitude riconoscenza, gratitudine, f.
gratuity mancia, gratifica.
grave (n.) tomba; (adj.) grave, serio.
gravel ghiaia.
graveyard cimitero.
gray grigio.
grease grasso.
great grande *(person);* enorme *(size);*
    lungo *(time).*
greatness grandezza.
greedy avido.
green verde.
greet (to) salutare.
greeting saluto.
grief pena.
grieve (to) penare.
grin (to) sogghignare.
grind (to) macinare.
groan gemito.
groan (to) gemere.
grocer venditore di generi alimentari.
grocery store negozio di generi
    alimentari.
groom sposo.
gross grosso; lordo.
    gross domestic product prodotto
        interno lordo.
ground terra.
ground floor pianterreno.
group gruppo.
group (to) raggruppare.
grouping raggruppamento.
grow (to) crescere.
growth crescita.
grudge rancore, m.
    hold a grudge against volerne a.
guard guardia.
guard (to) fare le guardia a.
guardian tutore, amministratore,
    curatore.
guess congettura.
guess (to) indovinare.
guest invitato.
guide guida.
guilt colpa.
guilty colpevole.
gum gengiva *(of the teeth);* gomma (da
    masticare) *(for chewing).*
gun fucile, m.; schioppo.
gush getto.

gymnasium palestra.
gymnastics ginnastica.

H

habit abitudine, f.
    to be in the habit of aver
        l'abitudine di.
habitual abituale.
hail grandine, f.
hair capelli.
hairdo pettinatura.
hairdresser parrucchiere, m.
hair dryer asciugacapelli.
hairpin forcina.
half (n.) metà; (adj.) mezzo.
half hour mezz'ora.
hall sala, corridoio.
ham prosciutto.
hammer martello.
hand mano, f.
    handmade fatto a mano.
hand (to) consegnare, passare.
handbag borsetta.
handbook manuale.
handful manata.
handkerchief fazzoletto.
handle manico.
handle (to) maneggiare, toccare.
handsome bello.
handy destro, abile *(person);*
    conveniente *(thing).*
hang (to) appendere.
hanger attaccapanni *(clothes).*
happen (to) succedere, avvenire.
happening avvenimento, accaduto.
happiness felicità.
happy felice.
harbor porto *(ship);* rifugio *(refuge).*
hard difficile *(difficult);* duro *(not soft).*
harden (to) indurire.
hardly appena.
hardness durezza.
hardship privazione, f.
hardware chincaglia.
hardware store chincaglierìa.
hare lepre, m & f.
harlequin arlecchino.
harm male, m.; danno.
harm (to) nuocere; fare del male a.

harmful nocivo.

harmless innocuo.

harmonious armonioso.

harmonize (to) armonizzare.

harmony armonia.

harsh aspro.

harvest raccolto.

harvest (to) vendemmiare *(grapes)*.

haste fretta.

hasten (to) affrettarsi.

hat cappello.

hate odio.

hate (to) odiare, dispiacere.

hateful odioso.

hatred odio.

haughty altero.

have (to) avere.

haven asilo, rifugio.

hay fieno.

haze bruma.

he lui, egli.

head testa; capo *(leader or chief)*.

headache mal di testa.

headphones cuffie.

headlights anabbaglianti.

heal (to) guarire; cicatrizzarsi *(a wound)*.

health salute, f.

health food alimenti dietetici.

healthy sano.

heap mucchio.

heap up (to) ammucchiare.

hear (to) udire, sentire.

    to hear from ricevere notizie da.

hearing udito; udienza.

heart cuore, m; cuori, m. pl. *(playing cards)*.

    by heart a memoria.

heat calore.

heat (to) scaldare.

heater scaldatore, riscaldatore, calorifero.

heating riscaldamento.

heaven cielo.

heavy pesante.

hedge siepe, f.

heed (to) badare.

heel calcagno, tallone, m.

height altezza.

heir erede, m. & f.

hello ciao.

helm elmo, timone.

help aiuto, soccorso.

help (to) aiutare, soccorrere.

    I cannot help it. Non ci posso nulla.

helper aiutante, m.; assistente, m.

helpful utile.

hem orlo.

hen gallina.

henceforth d'ora in poi.

her (pron.) lei, la, le; (adj.) il suo; la sua; i suoi; le sue.

    to her a lei.

herb erba.

herd branco, mandra, gregge, m.

here qui.

    Here! Ecco! Tenga! Tenete! Tieni!

herewith con ciò.

hero eroe, m.; protagonista, m. *(theater)*.

heroine eroina.

herring aringa.

hers il suo; la sua; i suoi; le sue.

herself se stessa; ella stessa.

hesitant esitante.

heterogeneous eterogeneo.

hide (to) nascondere; nascondersi *(oneself)*.

hideous mostruoso.

high alto.

higher più in alto.

hijack (to) dirottare.

hill collina.

him (pron.) lui, lo, gli.

    to him a lui.

himself se stesso; lui stesso.

hinder (to) ostacolare.

hinge cardine, m.

hint allusione, f.; accenno.

hint (to) alludere.

hip fianco.

hire (to) affittare; moleggiare; prendere in servizio *(person)*.

his il suo; la sua; i suoi; le sue.

hiss (to) sibilare; fischiare *(a play)*.

historian storico.

historic storico.

history storia.

hitch contrattempo.

hoarse rauco.

hoe zappa.

hold presa.

hold (to) tenere.

    to hold back trattenere.

holder possessore.

hole buco.

holiday giorno di festa.

holiness santità.
hollow vuoto.
holocaust olocausto.
holy santo.
homage omaggio.
home casa.
    at home a casa.
hometown città nativa.
homosexual omosessuale.
honest onesto.
honesty onestà.
honey miele, m.
honeymoon luna di miele.
honor onore, m.
honor (to) onorare.
honorable onorevole.
hood cappuccio.
hoof zoccolo.
hook gancio.
hook (to) agganciare.
hope speranza.
hope (to) sperare.
hopeful fiducioso.
hopeless disperato.
horizon orizzonte, m.
horizontal orizzontale.
horn tromba *(musical);* corno
    (animal).
horrible orribile.
horror orrore, m.
horse cavallo.
horseback (on) a cavallo.
hosiery calze.
hospitable ospitale.
hospital ospedale, m.
host ospite, m.
hostess ostessa, padrona di casa.
hostile ostile.
hot caldo.
    to get hot accaldarsi.
hotel albergo.
hour ora.
house casa.
housekeeper massaia.
housemaid donna di servizio.
how come.
    how long quanto tempo.
    how many quanti, quante.
    how much quanto.
    how often quante volte.
    however comunque.
    How are you? Come sta? Come
      state? Come stai?

    How beautiful! Com' è bello!
howl ululato, ululo.
howl (to) ululare.
human umano.
humane umano.
humanity umanità.
humble umile.
humid umido.
humiliate (to) umiliare.
humility umiltà.
humor umore, m.; stato d'animo.
hundred cento.
hundredth centesimo.
hunger fame, f.
hungry (to be) aver fame.
hunt caccia.
hunt (to) andare a caccia.
hunter cacciatore, m.
hurrah! viva! evviva!
hurricane uragano.
hurry fretta.
    to be in a hurry aver fretta.
hurry (to) affrettarsi.
hurt (to) dolere, far male, offendere, far
    dispiacere.
    It hurts. Mi fa male. (Mi duole.)
husband marito.
hypertension ipertensione.
hyphen trattino.
hypocrisy ipocrisìa.
hypocrite ipocrita, m.
hypothesis ipotesi, f.

I

I io.
ice ghiaccio.
ice cream gelato.
icon icona.
icy ghiacciato.
idea idea.
ideal (n. & adj.) ideale, m.
idealism idealismo.
idealist idealista, m. & f.
identical identico.
identity identità.
idiom idioma, frase idiomatica.
idiot idiota (n. & adj.); cretino, sciocco.
idle pigro, inattivo.
idleness ozio.
idol idolo.

if se.
ignoble ignobile.
ignorance ignoranza.
ignorant ignorante.
ignore (to) ignorare, trascurare.
ill malato.
    to become ill ammalarsi.
illegible illeggibile.
illegitimacy illegittimità.
illegitimate illegittimo.
illicit illecito.
illness malattìa.
illusion illusione, f.
illustrate (to) illustrare.
illustration illustrazione, f.
image immagine, f.
imaginary immaginario.
imagination immaginazione, f.
imagine (to) immaginare.
imitate (to) imitare.
imitation imitazione, f.
immediate immediato.
immediately immediatamente.
imminent imminente.
immobility immobilità.
immoral immorale.
immorality immoralità.
immortal immortale.
immortality immortalità.
impartial imparziale.
impassive impassibile.
impatience impazienza.
impatient impaziente.
imperative imperativo.
imperfect imperfetto.
impersonal impersonale.
impertinence impertinenza.
impertinent impertinente.
impetuosity impetuosità.
impetuous impetuoso.
impious empio, irreligioso.
import importanza, valore.
import (to) importare.
importance importanza.
    of the utmost importance della
      massima importanza.
important importante.
importation importazione.
imposing imponente.
impossible impossibile.
impress (to) imprimere.
impression impressione, f.

    to be under the impression that
      avere l'impressione che.
imprison (to) imprigionare.
improbable improbabile; inverosimile.
improve (to) migliorare, approfittare.
improvement miglioramento.
improvise (to) improvvisare.
imprudence imprudenza.
imprudent imprudente.
impudent sfacciato, impudente.
impulse impulso, slancio.
impure impuro.
in in, dentro.
inadequate inadeguato.
inaugurate (to) inaugurare.
incapable incapace, inabile.
incapacity incapacità.
inch pollice, m.
incident incidente, m.
include (to) includere, comprendere.
included incluso.
income rendita, entrata.
    income tax imposta sul reddito.
incomparable incomparabile.
incompatible incompatibile.
incompetent incompetente.
incomplete incompleto.
incomprehensible incomprensibile.
inconsistent incoerente.
inconvenience inconveniente, m.;
    disturbo, scomodità.
inconvenient inconveniente, incomodo.
incorrect non corretto, scorretto.
increase aumento.
increase (to) aumentare.
incredible incredibile.
indebted indebitato, obbligato.
indecision indecisione, f.
indecisive indecisivo, indeciso.
indeed infatti.
independence indipendenza.
independent indipendente.
index indice, m.
index finger indice, m.
indicate (to) indicare.
indicative indicativo.
indifference indifferenza.
indifferent indifferente, mediocre,
    scadente.
indigestion indigestione.
indignant indignato.
indignation indignazione, f.

indirect indiretto.
indirectly indirettamente.
indiscretion indiscrezione, f.; imprudenza.
indispensable indispensabile.
indisposition malessere; indisposizione.
individual (n.) individuo; (adj.) individuale, particolare.
indivisible indivisibile.
indolence indolenza.
indolent indolente.
indoors in casa; dentro.
    to go indoors rientrare.
induce (to) indurre.
induct (to) iniziare, installare.
indulge (to) favorire; concedere; essere indulgente, tollerare.
indulgence indulgenza.
indulgent indulgente.
industrial industriale.
industrious industrioso.
industry industria.
ineffective inefficace.
inexhaustible inesauribile.
inexplicable inesplicabile.
inexpressible inesprimibile.
infallible infallibile.
infamous infame.
infancy infanzia, minore età.
infant neonato, m.; neonata, f.
infantry fanteria.
infection infezione, f.
infer (to) inferire, dedurre.
inference deduzione, inferenza, f.
inferior inferiore.
infernal infernale.
infinite infinito.
infinity infinità.
inflict (to) infliggere.
influence influenza.
influence (to) influenzare.
inform (to) informare; far sapere.
information informazione, f.; notizia.
ingenious ingegnoso, semplice.
ingenuity ingegno, ingegnosità.
ingratitude ingratitudine, f.
inhabit (to) abitare.
inhabitant abitante, m.
inherit (to) creditare.
inheritance eredità.
inhuman inumano.
initial (n. & adj.) iniziale, f.

initiate (to) iniziare.
initiative iniziativa.
injection puntura.
injurious offensivo, dannoso, nocivo.
injury danno, ingiuria.
injustice ingiustizia.
ink inchiostro.
inkwell calamaio.
inland interno.
inn albergo, osteria.
innate innato.
inner interno.
innkeeper albergatore, m.
innocence innocenza.
innocent innocente.
input (to) immettere.
inquire (to) domandare, ricercare.
inquiry inchiesta, indagine, f.
insane pazzo; malato di mente.
inscription iscrizione, f.
insect insetto.
insensible insensibile.
inseparable inseparabile.
inside di dentro; all'interno.
insight percezione, f.
insignificant insignificante.
insincere non sincero; falso.
insinuate (to) insinuare.
insist (to) insistere.
insistence insistenza.
insoluble insolubile.
insomnia insonnia.
inspect (to) esaminare, ispezionare.
inspection ispezione, f.; esame, m.
inspiration ispirazione, f.; estro.
inspire (to) ispirare.
install (to) installare.
installment installazione, f.; rata *(payment)*.
instance esempio.
instant istante, m.; attimo.
instantaneous istantaneo.
instantly all'istante; istantaneamente.
instead of invece di.
instigate (to) istigare.
instinct istinto.
instinctive istintivo.
institute istituto.
institute (to) istituire.
institution istituzione, f.
instruct (to) istruire, informare, ordinare.

instruction istruzione, f.
instructor istruttore, m.
instrument strumento.
insufficiency insufficienza.
insufficient insufficiente.
insular insulare.
insult insulto, offesa.
insult (to) insultare, offendere.
insuperable insuperabile.
insurance assicurazione, f.
insure (to) assicurare.
integral integrale.
intellect intelletto.
intellectual (n. & adj.) intellettuale, m.
intelligence intelligenza.
intelligent intelligente.
intend (to) intendere.
intense intenso.
intensity intensità.
intention intenzione, f.
interest interesse, m.
    interest rate tasso d'interesse.
interesting interessante.
interface interfaccia.
interfere (to) interferire, intromettersi.
interference interferenza.
interfering invadente.
interior (n. & adj.) interiore, m.;
    interno.
interjection interiezione.
intermediate (n. & adj.)
    intermediario.
interminable interminabile.
international internazionale.
interpose (to) interporre.
interpret (to) interpretare.
interpretation interpretazione, f.
interpreter interprete, m.
interrupt (to) interrompere.
interruption interruzione, f.
interval intervallo; intermezzo.
interview intervista, colloquio.
intimacy intimità.
intimate intimo.
intimidate (to) intimidire.
into entro, dentro, in.
intolerable intollerabile.
intolerance intolleranza.
intolerant intollerante.
intonation intonazione, f.
intransigent intransigente.
introduce (to) presentare.
introduction presentazione, f.

    letter of introduction lettera di
      presentazione.
introverted introverso.
intuition intuito, intuizione, f.
invade (to) invadere.
invariable invariabile.
invasion invasione, f.
invent (to) inventare.
invention invenzione, f.
inventor inventore, m.
invert (to) invertire.
invest (to) investire.
investment investimento.
invisible invisibile.
invitation invito.
invite (to) invitare.
invoice fattura.
invoke (to) invocare.
involuntary involontario.
involve (to) implicate.
iodine iodio.
iron ferro; ferro da stiro *(for
    pressing)*.
iron (to) stirare.
irony ironìa.
irregular irregolare.
irreparable irreparabile.
irresistible irresistibile.
irritate (to) irritare.
irritation irritazione, f.
island isola.
isolate (to) isolare.
issue emissione, f.
it lo, la, esso, essa.
    it is è.
    It's here. È qui.
    It's late. È tardi.
Italian (n. & adj.) Italiano.
italicize scrivere in corsivo;
    sottolineare; mettere in rilievo.
item dettaglio *(detail);* articolo.
its il suo; la sua; i suoi, le sue.
itself se stesso; se stessa; da se.
ivy edera.

J

jacket giacca *(for a suit)*.
jail prigione, f.
jail (to) incarcerare.
jam marmellata.

Japanese giapponese.

jar vaso.

jaw mascella.

jealous geloso.

jealousy gelosia.

jelly marmellata.

jest scherzo.

Jew (n. & adj.) ebreo.

jewel gioiello.

job impiego *(occupation);* lavoro *(work).*

join (to) unire, entrare a far parte.

joint giuntura.

joke burla, scherzo.

joke (to) burlare, scherzare.

jolly allegro.

journal giornale, m.; diario.

journalism giornalismo.

journalist giornalista, m.

journey viaggio.

joy gioia.

joyous gioioso.

judge giudice, m.

judge (to) giudicare.

judgment giudizio, discernimento.

judicial giudiziario.

juice succo.

July luglio.

jump salto.

jump (to) saltare.

jumper scamiciato.

June giugno.

junior più giovane; minore.

jurisdictional giurisdizionale.

jurisprudence giurisprudenza.

just (adj.) giusto; (adv.) appena.

　　just now proprio ora.

justice giustizia.

justify (to) giustificare.

K

keen acuto.

keep (to) tenere.

　　to keep back tenere indietro.

　　to keep from impedire *(prevent);* astenersi *(refrain).*

　　to keep quiet tacere.

　　to keep in mind tener conto di; ricordare.

　　to keep still star fermo.

kernel gheriglio; nocciolo *(of a discussion).*

kettle pentola.

key chiave, f.

keyboard tastiera.

keyhole buco della serratura.

khaki cachi, kaki.

kick calcio.

kick (to) dare un calcio.

kid capretto *(leather);* bambino.

kidney rene, m.

kill (to) uccidere.

kilogram chilogrammo (kg.).

kin parente, m. & f.

kind (n.) sorta, qualità; (adj.) benigno, gentile, amabile.

kindly benignamente.

　　Will you kindly . . . Volete avere la bontà di . . .; Per favore . . .

kindness bontà.

king re, m.

kingdom regno.

kiss bacio.

kiss (to) baciare.

kitchen cucina.

kite aquilone, m.

knee ginocchio.

　　on one's knees in ginocchio.

kneel (to) inginocchiarsi.

knife coltello.

　　penknife temperino.

knight cavaliere, m.

knit (to) lavorare a maglia.

knitting lavorazione a maglia.

knock colpo, battito.

knock (to) bussare.

knot nodo.

know (to) sapere, conoscere.

knowledge conoscenza, sapere, m.; sapienza.

known conosciuto.

L

label etichetta.

labor lavoro, fatica.

laboratory laboratorio.

labyrinth labirinto.

lace merletto, pizzo.

lace (to) allacciare.

lack mancanza.

lack (to) mancare.
ladder scala a pioli.
lady signora.
   the lady of the house la padrona di
     casa.
   Ladies Signore.
   Ladies and gentlemen. Signore e
     signori.
lagoon laguna.
lake lago.
lamb agnello; abbachio.
lame zoppo.
lamp lampada.
lance lancia.
land terra, terreno.
land (to) sbarcare *(ship);* atterrare
   (airplane).
landing atterraggio.
landscape paesaggio.
lane vicolo.
language linguaggio.
   foreign language lingua straniera.
languish (to) languire.
languor languore, m.
lantern lanterna.
lapel risvolto.
laptop portatile *(computer).*
large grande, spazioso.
last ultimo.
   at last finalmente.
   last month il mese scorso.
   last night ieri sera.
last (to) durare.
lasting duraturo.
latch saliscendi, m.
late tardi.
lately ultimamente, poco fa.
Latin latino.
latter ultimo.
laugh (to) ridere.
   to laugh at ridere di.
laughter risata, riso.
laundry lavanderia.
lavish prodigo, generoso, profuso.
lavish (to) prodigare.
law legge, f.
lawful legale.
lawn prato.
lay (to) deporre, collocare.
layer strato.
laziness pigrizia.
lazy pigro.

lead piombo.
lead (to) condurre, guidare.
leader capo; duce, m.
leadership direzione, f.
leaf foglia *(of a tree);* foglio, m.
league lega.
leak (to) gocciolare.
lean (to) appoggiarsi.
leap salto.
leap (to) saltare.
learn (to) apprendere, imparare.
learned erudito, colto.
learning cultura, erudizione, f.
lease (to) affittare.
least minore.
   at least almeno.
leather cuoio.
leave congedo, permesso.
leave (to) abbandonare *(desert);* partire;
   lasciare *(quit).*
   to leave again ripartire.
lecture conferenza, lezione
   universitaria.
left (n. & adj.) sinistra.
   left-handed mancino.
   to the left a sinistra.
leftover rimanente.
leftovers avanzi.
leg gamba.
legal legale.
legend leggenda.
legislation legislazione, f.
legitimacy legittimità.
legitimate legittimo.
leisure agio, ozio.
lemon limone, m.
   lemon juice succo di limone.
lemonade limonata.
lend (to) prestare.
length lunghezza; durata *(of time).*
lengthen (to) allungare.
lesbian lesbica.
less meno.
lesson lezione, f.
let (to) lasciare, permettere.
   to let alone lasciare in pace.
letter lettera.
level livello.
liable responsabile.
liar mentitore, m.; bugiardo.
liberal liberale.
liberty libertà.

librarian bibliotecaria.
library biblioteca.
license licenza, permesso, licenziosità.
lick (to) leccare.
lie menzogna.
lie (to) mentire *(tell a falsehood)*; sdraiarsi *(lie down)*; coricarsi *(go to bed)*.
lieutenant tenente *(first lieutenant)*; sottotenente *(second lieutenant)*.
life vita.
lift (to) sollevare, alzare.
light (n.) luce, f.; lume, m.; (adj.) chiaro; leggero *(in weight)*; lieve.
light (to) accendere.
    to light up illuminare.
lighten (to) alleggerire.
lighthouse faro.
lighting illuminazione, f.
lightning fulmine, m.
like (adj.) simile; (adv.) come.
like (to) voler bene a; piacere.
    Would you like to go? Le piacerebbe andare?
likely probabile.
likeness somiglianza.
likewise altrettanto.
liking piacere, m.; gusto.
limb membro, estremità, arto.
limit limite, m.
limit (to) limitare.
limp fiacco.
limp (to) zoppicare.
line linea, corda, riga, verso, discendenza.
    A-line svasato.
    straight line retta.
    to line up allineare.
lined foderato.
linen lino *(textile)*; biancheria.
linger (to) indugiarsi, indugiare.
lining fodera.
link anello *(in a chain)*.
link (to) concatenare, legare.
lion leone.
lip labbro.
lipstick rossetto.
liquid (n. & adj.) liquido; limpido; instabile.
liquor liquore, m.
list lista, elenco; tabella.
listen (to) ascoltare.

literary letterario.
literature letteratura; lettere.
little piccolo.
    little by little poco a poco.
    a little un po' di; poco.
live vivo.
live (to) vivere.
lively vivace.
liver fegato.
load carico.
load (to) caricare.
loan prestito.
loan (to) prestare.
lobster aragosta.
local locale.
locate (to) situare.
location sito, posizione, posto; locazione; ubicazione.
lock serratura.
lock (to) chiudere a chiave.
locomotive locomotiva.
log tronco.
logic logica.
logical logico.
loneliness solitudine, f.
lonely solitario.
long lungo.
    a long time lungo tempo.
    before long quanto prima.
    long ago tempo fa; molto tempo fa.
longing desiderio.
look sguardo; aspetto *(appearance)*.
look (to) guardare; sembrare *(seem)*.
    Look out! Attenzione!
    This dress looks good on me. Questo vestito mi sta bene.
    to look for ricercare.
loose sciolto, slegato.
loosen (to) sciogliere, slegare.
lord signore, m.; padrone, m.; Iddio *(God)*.
lose (to) perdere.
loss perdita.
lost perduto.
lot (a) molto, tanto.
    a lot of money molto denaro.
    a lot of people molta gente.
loud forte.
    Speak louder. Parlate più forte.
love amore, m.
love (to) amare.
lovely amabile, bello.

low basso.
lower (to) abbassare.
loyal leale, fedele.
loyalty lealtà, fedeltà.
luck fortuna.
    Good luck! In bocca al lupo!
lucky fortunato.
luggage bagaglio.
luminous luminoso.
lump massa.
lunch colazione, f.
lung polmone, m.
luxe lusso.
    de luxe di lusso.
luxurious lussuoso.
luxury lusso.
lyrics lirica, lyrics, parole di una canzone.

M

macaroni maccheroni, m. pl.
macaroons amaretti.
machine macchina.
mad irato *(angry)*.
madam signora.
madness follia.
magazine periodico, rivista.
magistrate magistrato.
magnificent magnifico.
maid cameriera, serva.
mail posta.
    e-mail e-mail, posta elettronica.
    voice mail audio-messaggeria.
    mail (to) impostare.
    main principale.
    main road via principale.
    main street strada principale.
maintain (to) mantenere, affermare, sostenere.
maintenance mantenimento, manutenzione.
majesty maestà.
major (n. & adj.) maggiore, m.; importante.
majority maggioranza, maggiore età.
make (to) fare.
male maschio.
malice malizia, dolo.
man uomo.
manage (to) gestire, amministrare.

management gestione, f.; amministrazione, f.; gerenza, f.
manager amministratore, m.
maneuver manovra.
mania mania, follia.
mankind unmanità.
manner maniera, modo.
manners buone maniere, educazione.
    good manners buone maniere.
manual manuale.
manufacture manifattura, lavorazione.
manufacture (to) fabbricare.
manufacturer fabbricante, m.
manuscript (n. & adj.) manoscritto.
many molti, molte.
map carta, mappa.
March marzo.
march (to) marciare.
margin margine, m.
marine marino.
marionette marionetta.
mark segno.
mark (to) segnare; prendere nota *(heed)*.
market mercato.
marriage matrimonio.
marry (to) sposare.
marvel meraviglia.
marvelous meraviglioso.
masculine maschile, virile.
mask maschera.
mask (to) mascherare.
mason muratore, m.
mass massa *(quantity);* messa *(religious rite)*.
massacre massacro.
massage massaggio.
mast albero.
master padrone, m.
master (to) dominare.
masterpiece capolavoro.
match fiammifero, cerino; incontro *(sports);* unione, f. *(marriage)*.
match (to) agguagliare.
material (n. & adj.) materiale, m.; importante; essenziale.
maternal materno.
mathematics matematica.
matter affare, m.; cosa, materia.
matter (to) importare.
mattress materasso.
mature maturo.
maturity maturità.

mausoleum mausoleo.
maximum massimo.
May maggio.
may potere *(to be able)*.
mayor sindaco.
me me, mi.
meadow praterìa; prato.
meal pasto.
mean cattivo.
mean (to) voler dire; significare.
meaning significato.
means mezzo; mezzi *(resources)*.
meanwhile frattanto.
   in the meanwhile nel frattempo.
measure misura.
measure (to) misurare.
meat carne, f.
mechanic (n. & adj.) meccanico.
mechanically meccanicamente.
medal medaglia.
meddle (to) intromettersi.
mediate (to) intervenire.
medical medico.
medicine medicina.
medieval medievale.
mediocre mediocre.
mediocrity mediocrità.
meditate (to) meditare.
meditation meditazione, f.
medium mezzo; intermedio; (adj.)
   medio.
meet (to) incontrare.
meeting incontro; riunione, f.
   (reunion); convegno.
melancholy malinconia.
melt (to) squagliare, liquefare,
   sciogliersi.
member membro.
memorize (to) imparare a memoria.
memory memoria.
mend (to) rappezzare, rattoppare.
mental mentale, pazzo.
mention menzione, f.
mention (to) menzionare.
merchandise merce, f.
merchant mercante, m.; commerciante,
   m., negoziante.
merciful clemente.
merciless inclemente.
mercury mercurio.
mercy clemenza, misericordia.
merit merito.
merry allegro.

merry-go-round giostra.
message messaggio, ambasciata.
messenger messaggero, fattorino.
metal metallo.
metallic metallico.
metaphor metafora, traslato.
meter metro.
method metodo.
metropolis metropoli, f.
microphone microfono.
microwave oven formo a microonde.
middle in mezzo; intermedio.
   in the middle of the night durante
    la notte.
   The Middle Ages Il Medio Evo.
midnight mezzanotte, f.
might forza, potere, m.
mild mite.
mildness mitezza.
military militare.
milk latte, m.
milkman lattaio.
mill mulino.
miller mugnaio.
million milione, m.
millionaire (n. & adj.) milionario.
mind mente, f.
mind (to) fare attenzione.
   Do you mind? Le dispiace?
mine (pron.) il mio; la mia; i miei; le
   mie; (n.) miniera *(coal or steel)*.
miner minatore, m.
mineral (n. & adj.) minerale, m.
minimum minimo.
minister ministro.
ministry ministero.
mink visone, m.
minor minore; poco importante; più
   giovane; minorenne.
minority minoranza.
minute minuto.
   Any minute now. Da un momento
    all'altro.
   Just a minute! Un minuto!
   Wait a minute. Attenda un minuto.
miracle miracolo.
mirror specchio.
miscarriage aborto spontaneo.
miscarry (to) abortire.
miscellaneous vario, miscellaneo.
mischief cattiveria, malizia.
mischievous cattivo, malizioso.
miser avaro.

miserable miserabile, infelice, sventurato.
miserably miseramente, con infelicità.
misery miseria.
misfortune sfortuna, disgrazia.
mishap infortunio, accidente, m.
misprint errore (di stampa), m.
Miss Signorina.
miss (to) mancare; sentire la mancanza di.
mission missione, f.
missionary missionario.
mist bruma, foschia.
mistake errore, m.
mistake (to) sbagliare, essare abbaglio.
mister Signore.
   Mr. Rossi Signor Rossi.
mistrust diffidenza.
mistrust (to) diffidare.
mistrustful diffidente.
misunderstand (to) capire male.
misunderstanding malinteso.
misuse abuso.
misuse (to) abusare.
mix (to) mischiare.
mixture miscuglio; mistura *(liquids and drugs)*.
mob folla.
mobile mobile.
mobility mobilità.
mobilization mobilitazione, f.
mobilize (to) mobilitare.
mock (to) deridere.
mockery derisione, f.
mode moda.
model (n. & adj.) modello.
model (to) modellare.
moderate moderato, conveniente.
moderate (to) moderare.
moderation moderazione, f.
modern moderno.
modernize (to) rimodemare.
modest modesto, pudore.
modesty modestia, pudore.
modification modifica.
modify (to) modificare.
moist umido.
moisten (to) inumidire.
moment momento.
   any minute now da un momento all'altro.
   Just a moment! Un momento!

monarchy monarchia.
monastery monastero.
Monday lunedì.
money denaro.
monk monaco.
monkey scimmia.
monologue monologo.
monopoly monopolio.
monotonous monotono.
monotony monotonìa.
monster mostro.
monstrosity mostruosità.
month mese, m.
   last month il mese passato.
   next month il mese prossimo.
monthly mensile.
monument monumento.
monumental monumentale.
mood umore, m.
moody di cattivo umore.
moon luna.
moonlight chiaro di luna.
moral morale, f. *(both fable and morality).*
morale morale, m.
moralist moralista, m.
morality moralità.
more di più.
morning mattina.
   this morning stamane.
mortal (n. & adj.) mortale, m.
mortgage ipoteca; finanziamento.
mortgage (to) ipotecare; finanziare.
mosquito zanzara.
most il più; la più; i più; le più.
mostly in gran parte; la maggior parte.
moth tignola.
mother madre.
mother-in-law suocera.
mother-of-pearl madreperla.
motion movimento, mozione, f.
motionless immobile.
motivate (to) motivare.
motive motivo.
motor motore, m.
motor (to) andare in auto.
motorcycle motocicletta.
motorist automobilista, m.
mount monte, m.
mount (to) montare.
mountain montagna.

mountainous montagnoso.
mourn (to) lamentare.
mournful triste, lugubre.
mourning lutto.
mouse topo.
mouth bocca; bocchetta.
movable movibile, mobile.
move movimento.
move (to) muovere, muoversi;
     proporre; sloggiare *(household);*
     traslocare.
movement movimento.
movies cinema, m.
moving commovente *(touching).*
Mr. Signore.
Mrs. Signora.
much molto.
mud fango.
muddy fangoso.
mule mulo.
multicolored variopinto, multicolore.
multiple molteplice *(numerous).*
multiply (to) moltiplicare.
multitude moltitudine, f.
mumble (to) borbottare.
municipal municipale.
municipality municipalità.
munitions munizioni, f.
murder omicidio.
murder (to) assassinare.
murmur mormorio.
murmur (to) mormorare.
muscle muscolo.
muscular muscolare.
museum musèo.
mushroom fungo.
music musica.
musical musicale.
musician musicista, m.
must dovere *(have to).*
mustard mostarda *(grain);* senape
     (prepared).
mute muto.
mutter mormorio, borbottamento.
mutter (to) mormorare, borbottare.
mutton montone, m.; carne di
     castrato. f.
my il mio; la mia; i miei; le mie.
myself io stesso; me stesso.
mysterious misterioso.
mystery mistero.
     mystery story racconto di mistero.

N

nail unghia *(finger);* chiodo
     (carpentry).
nail (to) inchiodare.
naive ingenuo.
naked nudo.
name nome, m.
     first name nome.
     last name cognome.
     What is your name? Come si
     chiama?
     My name is . . . Mi chiamo . . .
name (to) nominare, chiamare.
nameless senza nome; anonimo.
namely specialmente, cioè.
nap sonnellino.
nape (of the neck) nuca.
napkin salvietta, tovagliolo.
     sanitary napkin assorbente
     igienico.
narrow stretto.
narrow (to) restringere.
nasty offensivo, spiacevole.
nation nazione, f.
national nazionale.
nationality nazionalità.
nationalization nazionalizzazione, f.
nationalize (to) nazionalizzare.
native nativo, indigeno.
natural naturale.
naturalness naturalezza.
nature natural; indole.
     human nature natura umana.
naughty birichino.
naval navale.
navy marina.
Neapolitan napoletano.
near vicino.
nearly quasi.
neat nitido; ben tenuto.
neatness nitidezza.
necessarily necessariamente.
necessary necessario.
necessity necessità.
neck collo.
necklace collana.
necktie cravatta.
need bisogno, esigenza.
need (to) aver bisogno.
needle ago.

needless inutile.

needy bisognoso.

negative (n.) negativa *(denial or film)*; (adj.) negativo.

neglect negligenza.

neglect (to) trascurare.

negotiate (to) trattare, passare, superare.

negotiation trattativa; pratiche, pl.

neighbor vicino.

neighborhood rione, m.; vicinato.

neither nessuno.

   neither one nè l'uno, nè l'altro.

   neither ... nor ... nè ... nè ...

nephew nipote.

nerve nervo, coraggio, sangue freddo, spacciataggine.

   What a nerve! Che sfacciato!

nervous nervoso.

nest nido.

net (n.). rete, f.; (adj.) netto.

neurotic nevrotico.

neuter neutro.

neutral (n. & adj.) neutrale, m.

never mai.

nevertheless ció nonostante.

new nuovo.

news notizia.

news-dealer giornalaio.

newspaper giornale, m.

next prossimo.

nice piacevole.

nickname nomignolo, soprannome, m.

niece nipote.

night notte, f.

nightmare incubo.

nine nove.

nineteen diciannove.

nineteenth diciannovesimo.

ninetieth novantesimo.

ninety novanta.

ninth nono.

no no.

   no longer non più.

   No Smoking! Vietato Fumare!

nobility nobiltà.

noble nobile.

nobody nessuno.

nocturnal notturno.

nod cenno, saluto.

noise rumore, m.

noisy rumoroso.

nominate (to) nominare; propurre la candidatura.

nomination nomina.

none nessuno.

   She has none. Non ne ha.

nonsense assurdità, sciocchezza.

noon mezzogiorno.

nor nè ... non ...

   neither ... nor ... nè ... nè ...

normal normale.

north nord.

northern a nord; settentrionale.

northwest nord-ovest.

nose naso.

nostalgia nostalgia.

nostril narice, f.

not non.

   not at all niente affatto.

note nota, commenta; fama, biglietto.

note (to) notare.

noted conosciuto.

nothing niente.

notice avviso.

   notice to the public avviso al pubblico.

notice (to) notare.

notify (to) notificare.

notion nozione, f.; opinione, idea.

noun nome, m.

nourish (to) nutrire.

nourishment nutrimento.

novel (n.) romanzo *(literary)*; (adj.) nuovo.

novelty novità.

November novembre.

now ora.

   now and then di tanto in tanto.

   nowadays di questi tempi.

nowhere in nessun posto.

nuclear nucleare.

   nuclear energy energia nucleare.

   nuclear reactor reattore nucleare.

nude nudo.

nuisance seccatura.

null nullo, invalido.

numb insensibile, addormentato.

number numero.

number (to) numerare.

nun monaca.

nurse infermiera.

nursery giardino d'infanzia; asilo infantile.

nut noce, f.

O

oak quercia.

oar remo.

oat avena.

oath giuramento.

obedience obbedienza.

obedient obbediente.

obey (to) obbedire.

object oggetto; scopo *(aim)*.

object (to) opporsi, obbiettare.

objection obbiezione, f.
  I see no objection to it. Non ho
    nulla da obbiettare.

objective (n.) obbiettivo; (adj.) oggettivo.

objectively oggettivamente.

objectivity oggettivismo.

obligation obbligo.

obligatory obbligatorio.

oblige (to) obbligare, fare unfarore.

obliging gentile, cortese.

oblique obliquo.

obscene osceno.

obscure oscuro.

obscure (to) offuscare; oscurare.

obscurity oscurità.

observation osservazione, f.

observatory osservatorio.

observe (to) osservare.

observer osservatore, m.

obsolete obsoleto.

obstacle ostacolo.

obstinacy ostinazione, f.

obstinate ostinato.

obstruct (to) ostruire.

obvious ovvio.

obviously ovviamente.

occasion occasione, f.

occasion (to) cagionare, causare.

occasionally occasionalmente,
  irregolarmente.

occupation impiego.

occupy (to) occupare.

occur (to) avvenire, accadere.

occurrence avvenimento.

ocean oceano.

October ottobre.

odd dispari *(numbers)*; disuguale *(not
  matched)*; bizzarro *(strange)*.

odor odore, m.

of di.
  of course certo.

offend (to) offendere, insultare,
  trasgredire; scandalizzare.

offense offesa.

offensive (n.) offensiva *(military);* (adj.)
  offensivo, pericoloso, sgradevole,
  disgustoso.

offer offerta.

offer (to) offrire.

offering offerta.

office ufficio.

officer ufficiale, m.; agente,
  funzionario.

official (n. & adj.) funzionario;
  ufficiale, m.

often sovente, spesso.
  How often? Quante volte?

oil olio; petrolio *(mineral)*.

old vecchio.
  He is two years old. Ha due anni.
  old age vecchiaia.
  old man vecchio.

olive oliva.
  olive oil olio d'oliva.

on su, sopra.

once una volta.
  all at once d'un tratto.
  at once immediatamente.
  once a year una volta l'anno.
  once in a while di tanto in tanto.

oncology oncologia.

one (pron.) uno, qualcuno, si; (adj.)
  uno, un, una.

oneself se stesso; si.

onion cipolla.

only soltanto, solamente.

opaque opaco.

open (adj.) aperto.
  in the open all'aperto.

open (to) aprire.

opening apertura.

opera opera, melodrama.

operate (to) operare.

operation operazione, f.

opinion opinione, f.

opponent opponente, m.

opportune opportuno.

opportunist opportunista.

opportunity opportunità.

oppose (to) opporre.

opposite opposto.

opposition opposizione, f.

oppress (to) opprimere.

oppression oppressione, f.

oppressive oppressivo.
oppressor oppressore.
optician ottico.
optimism ottimismo.
optimist ottimista, f.
optimistic ottimista.
option opzione.
optional facoltativo.
or o.
    either ... or ... or ... o ...
oral verbale, orale.
orange arancia, arancio, arancione
    (color).
orator oratore, m.
oratory oratoria.
orchard orto, frutteto.
orchestra orchestra.
ordeal prova.
order ordine, m.; ordinazione.
    in order to per.
    to put in order mettere in ordine.
order (to) ordinare.
ordinary ordinario.
organ organo.
organism organismo.
organization organizzazione, f.
organize (to) organizzare.
Orient Oriente, m.
oriental orientale.
origin origine, f.
originality originalità.
originate (to) creare.
ornament ornamento.
orphan orfano, orfana.
orthodox ortodosso.
orthopedics ortopedia.
ostentation ostentazione, f.
other altro, altra, altri, altre.
ought dovere.
ounce oncia.
our(s) il nostro; la nostra; i nostri; le
    nostre.
ourselves noi stessi, noi stesse.
out fuori.
    out of danger fuori pericolo.
outcome conseguenza, risultato.
outdo (to) sorpassare.
outer esteriore.
outfit corredo *(clothes, trousseau)*;
    equipaggiamento.
outlast (to) sopravvivere.
outlaw proscritto, bandito.

outlaw (to) proscrivere, bandire.
outlay spesa.
outlet sbocco.
outline delineazione, f.; schizzo.
outline (to) delineare; tracciare a grandi
    linee.
outlook prospettiva.
output rendimento, produzione, f.
outrage oltraggio.
outrageous oltraggioso, eccessivo,
    violento.
outside fuori.
oval (n. & adj.) ovale, m.
oven forno.
overcoat cappotto.
overcome (to) sormontare.
overflow (to) inondare, traboccare.
overhang (to) sovrastare; minacciare.
overhead in alto.
overlook (to) trascurare.
overpower (to) sopraffare.
overrule (to) dominare, respingere.
overrun (to) invadere.
overseas oltre mare.
oversight inavvertenza.
overtake (to) raggiungere, sorpassare.
overthrow (to) rovesciare.
overwhelm (to) sopraffare.
owe (to) dovere.
own proprio.
own (to) possedere.
owner proprietario, possessore.
ox bue.
oxygen ossigeno.
oyster ostrica.

P

pace passo.
pacific pacifico.
pacifist pacifista.
pack pacco, pacchetto.
pack (to) imballare, impaccare.
package pacco.
packet pacchetto.
pact patto.
page pagina.
pain dolore, m.
pain (to) far male; addolorare.
painful doloroso.

painless indolore.
paint pittura, colore, m.
 Wet paint Pittura fresca.
paint (to) dipingere.
painter pittore, m.
painting pittura, quadro.
pair paio.
pale pallido.
paleness pallore.
palm palmo.
pamphlet opuscolo.
pan padella.
pancake frittella.
pane vetro.
panel pannello, gruppo di esperti,
 commissionare.
panic panico.
panorama panorama, m.
panties mutandine, f. pl.
pants pantaloni, m. pl.
paper carta; giornale; saggio;
 essamescritto.
parachute paracadute, m.
parade parata.
paradise paradiso.
paragraph paragrafo; comma.
parallel parallelo.
paralysis paralisi, f.
paralyze (to) paralizzare.
parcel pacco.
pardon perdono.
pardon (to) perdonare.
parent genitore, m.; genitrice, f.
parenthesis parentesi, f.
park parco; giardino pubblico.
park (to) parcheggiare.
 No parking! Divieto di sosta!
parkway autostrada.
parliament parlamento.
Parmesan parmigiano.
part parte, f.
part (to) separarsi, dividere.
partial parziale.
partially parzialmente; in parte.
particular (n. & adj.) particolare, m.;
 difficile, esigente.
particularity particolarità.
particularly particolarmente.
partner socio, socia, (business);
 compagno di giuoco (in games).
party partito (political); ricevimento
 (social); partita (sports).

pass permesso (permission).
pass (to) passare.
 to pass a law varare una legge.
passage passaggio; brano; traversatta.
passenger passeggero.
passion passione, f. sofferenza;
 emozione.
passive passivo.
past (n. & adj.) passato; (prep.) oltre
 (beyond).
 half-past seven le sette e mezzo.
 past ten o'clock le dieci passate.
 the past year l'anno passato.
paste colla (glue); conserva
 (preserve).
paste (to) incollare.
pastry paste, f. pl.; dolci, m. pl.
 (sweets).
pastry shop pasticcerìa.
patch pezza; rappezzo; benda
 (bandage); toppa.
patch (to) rattoppare.
patent brevetto, patente, f.
paternal paterno.
paternity paternità.
path sentiero.
pathetic patetico.
patience pazienza.
patient (n. & adj.) paziente, m. or f.
patriot patriota, m.
patriotism patriottismo.
patron cliente abituale.
patronize (to) patrocinare, proteggere,
 incoraggiare.
pattern modello; campione, m.;
 disegno.
pause pausa.
pause (to) fare una pausa; arrestarsi;
 esitare.
pave (to) pavimentare.
pavement selciato, lastricato.
paw zampa.
pay stipendio.
pay (to) pagare, fruttare.
 to pay in cash pagare in contanti.
payment pagamento, ricompensa.
pea pisello.
peace pace, f.
peaceful pacifico, tranquillo.
peach pesca.
peak cima.
peanut arachide.

pear pera.
pearl perla.
peasant contadino, contadina.
pebble sassolino, sasso.
peculiar peculiare, strano, bizzarro.
pecuniary pecuniario.
pedal pedale, m.
pedantic pedante.
pedestrian pedone, m.
peel buccia, corteccia.
peel (to) spellare, sbucciare.
pen penna.
    fountain pen penna stilografica.
penalty pena, multa.
pencil matita.
penetrate (to) penetrare.
peninsula penisola.
penitence penitenza.
pension pensione, m.
penthouse attico.
people gente, f.; popolo.
pepper pepe, m.; peperone.
peppermint menta.
perceive (to) scorgere, capire.
percent per cento.
percentage percentuale, f.
perennial perenne.
perfect perfetto.
perfect (to) perfezionare.
perfection perfezione, f.
perfectly perfettamente.
perform (to) compiere; eseguire;
    rappresentare *(in a play)*.
performance compimento; esecuzione;
    rappresentazione *(of a play)*.
perfume profumo.
perfume (to) profumare.
perhaps forse.
peril pericolo.
period punto fermo *(punctuation)*;
    epoca *(era)*.
periodical (n. & adj.) periodico.
perish (to) perire.
permanent (n. & adj.) permanente, f.
permission permesso.
permit permesso, licenza.
permit (to) permettere, concedere.
peroxide acqua ossigenata; perossido.
perplex (to) confondere; rendere
    perplesso.
persecute (to) perseguitare.
persecution persecuzione, f.
perseverance perseveranza.

persist (to) persistere, perseverare.
person persona.
personal personale.
personality personalità.
personnel personale, m.
perspective prospettiva *(art)*.
persuade (to) persuadere.
pertaining appartenente, riferendosi a.
pertinent pertinente.
perversion perversione.
petal petalo.
petty meschino.
pharmacist farmacista.
pharmacy farmacìa.
phenomenon fenomeno.
philosopher filosofo.
philosophy filosofia.
phoenix fenice.
photograph fotografia, foto.
    to take a photograph fare una
        fotografia.
phrase frase, f.
physic medicina.
physical fisico.
physician medico.
physiology fisiologia.
piano pianoforte, m.
pick (to) scegliere *(choose)*; rompere
    col piccone *(to break up with a*
    pick); mangiucchiare *(nibble on*
    food); sottrarre da *(a pocket)*.
pick up (to) raccogliere.
picnic merenda all'aperto; campagnata.
picture ritratto, disegno, dipinto,
    quadro, fotografia.
    to take a picture fare una
        fotografia.
picturesque pittoresco.
pie torta di frutta.
piece pezzo, brano.
pig maiale, m.; porco.
pigeon piccione, m.
pile ammasso, mucchio.
pile (to) ammassare.
pill pillola.
pillar colonna.
pillow guanciale, m.
pilot pilota, m.
pin spilla.
pinch (to) pizzicare.
pinewood pineta.
pink (adj.) rosa.
pin-striped gessato.

pious pio.

pipe pipa *(for smoking);* tubo *(plumbing);* zampogna *(musical).*

pitiful pietoso.

pity pietà.

   What a pity! Che peccato!

place luogo, località, posto.

   in my place al mio posto.

   to lose one's place perdere il segno.

   to take place aver luogo.

place (to) mettere.

plain (adj.) chiaro *(clear);* semplice *(simple);* bruttino.

plan progetto, piano.

plan (to) progettare.

plane aeroplano, aereo *(airplane);* pialla *(carpenter's tool).*

planet pianeta.

plant pianta.

plant (to) piantare.

plaster intonaco; gesso *(walls).*

plate piatto.

platform piattaforma, programa.

platter largo piatto.

play gioco; lavoro teatrale *(theatrical).*

play (to) giocare; recitare *(to act);* suonare *(musical instruments).*

player giocatore, m.

plea causa, processo, supplica.

plead (to) perorare *(court case);* dichiararsi *(plead guilty or innocent).*

   to plead with supplicare.

pleasant piacevole.

please (to) piacere, accontentare.

   if you please per piacere.

pleased contento, soddisfatto.

pleasure piacere, m.

pledge pegno, garanzia.

pledge (to) garantire.

plenty (n.) abbondanza; (adj.) abbondante.

plot complotto *(conspiracy);* pezzo di terra *(of ground);* intreccio *(of a play);* appezzamento.

plow aratro.

plow (to) arare.

plum prugna.

plunder (to) saccheggiare.

plural (n. & adj.) plurale, m.

plus più.

pneumonia polmonite, f.

pocket tasca.

poem poesia, poema, m.

poet poeta, m.

poetic poetico.

poetry poesia.

point punto.

point (to) indicare.

pointed appuntito *(sharp);* acuto *(incisive).*

poise equilibrio.

poison veleno.

poison (to) avvelenare, intossicare.

poisoning avvelenamento, intossicazione.

polar polare.

police polizia.

policeman vigile urbano; poliziotto.

policy politica; linea di condotta.

polish lucido, vernice, f.

polish (to) lucidare, lustrare.

polished raffinato, distinto.

polite cortese.

politeness cortesia.

political politico.

politics politica.

pollution inquinamento.

polychrome policromo.

pond stagno, laghetto.

poor povero.

popular popolare.

population popolazione, f.

porcelain porcellana.

pork carne di maiale, f.

port porto.

portable portatile.

porter portabagagli.

portion porzione.

portrait ritratto.

position posizione, f.; situazione, f.

positive positivo.

possess (to) possedere.

possession possesso.

possibility possibilità.

possible possibile, eventuale.

post palo *(pole).*

postage affrancatura.

postage stamp francobollo.

poster manifesto, affisso, cartellone, m.

posterity posterità.

post office posta; ufficio postale.

postpone (to) posticipare.

pot pentola, vaso, recipiente, m.

potato patata.

pound libbra.
pour (to) versare.
   It's pouring! Piove a dirotto!
poverty povertà.
powder polvere, f.
   face powder cipria.
power potere, m.; forza.
powerful potente; poderoso.
practical pratico.
practice pratica, abitudine, f.; esercizio.
practice (to) esercitarsi, esercitare, praticare.
praise elogio, lode, f.
praise (to) elogiare.
prank scherzo.
pray (to) pregare.
prayer preghiera.
preach (to) predicare.
precaution precauzione, f.
precede (to) precedere.
preceding precedente.
precept precetto.
precious prezioso.
precise preciso.
precision precisione, f.
predecessor predecessore, m.
preface prefazione, f.
prefer (to) preferire.
preference preferenza.
prehistoric preistorico.
prehistory preistoria.
prejudice pregiudizio.
preliminary preliminare.
preparation preparazione.
prepare (to) prepare, prepararsi.
preposition preposizione.
prescribe (to) prescrivere.
prescription ricetta medica.
presence presenza.
present (n.) dono *(gift);* presente *(present time);* (adj.) presente, attuale.
present (to) presentare.
preserve (to) preservare, conservare.
preside (to) presiedere.
presidency presidenza.
president presidente, m.
press stampa.
press (to) stirare *(iron clothes);* premere; comprimere.
pressing urgente.
pressure pressione, f.

prestige prestigio.
presume (to) presumere.
pretend (to) pretendere di; vantarsi di; fingere di.
pretext pretesto.
pretty (adj.) bello, grazioso; (adv.) quanto.
   pretty nearly quasi.
   pretty soon quanto prima.
prevail (to) prevalere.
prevent (to) impedire.
prevention prevenzione, f.
previous precedente.
   the previous year l'anno precedente.
prey preda.
price prezzo, costo.
pride orgoglio; fierezza.
priest prete.
prime primo, principale.
prince principe.
princess principessa.
principal principale.
principle principio.
print (to) stampare.
printer stampante.
priority precedenza.
prison prigione, f.
prisoner prigioniero, prigioniera.
private privato.
privilege privilegio.
prize premio.
prize (to) stimare molto.
probable probabile.
probably probabilmente.
problem problema, m.
procedure procedura.
   usual procedure prassi.
proceed (to) procedere.
process processo.
procession processione, f.
proclaim (to) proclamare.
produce (to) produrre.
product prodotto.
production produzione, f.
productive produttivo.
profession professione, f.
professional professionale.
professor professora, m.
profile profilo.
profit profitto, utile, m.
profit (to) trarre profitto.

profits profitti, utili.
program programma, m.
progress progresso.
progress (to) progredire.
prohibit (to) vietare.
prohibition divieto, probizione, f.
project progetto.
project (to) progettare.
prolong (to) prolungare.
promise promessa.
promise (to) promettere.
promoter promotore.
promotion promozione, f.
prompt pronto.
promptness prontezza.
pronoun pronome, m.
pronounce (to) pronunciare,
   pronunziare.
pronunciation pronuncia.
proof prova.
proper proprio, corretto.
property proprietà *(country home)*;
   beni, m. pl. *(estate, in legal sense)*;
   beni immobili *(real estate)*.
proportion proporzione, f.
proportional proporzionale.
proposal proposta.
propose (to) proporre.
prosaic prosaico.
prose prosa.
prospect prospetto, *(business)*;
   prospettiva, *(panorama)*.
prosper (to) prosperare.
prosperity prosperità.
prosperous prospero.
protagonist protagonista.
protect (to) proteggere.
protection protezione, f.
protective protettivo.
protector protettore, m.
protest protesta.
protest (to) protestare.
Protestant (n. & adj.) protestante, m.
proud orgoglioso, fiero.
prove (to) provare.
provenance provenienza.
proverb proverbio.
provide (to) provvedere.
   provided that purchè.
providential provvidenziale.
province provincia.
provincial provinciale.

provoke (to) provocare.
proximity prossimità.
prudence prudenza.
prune prugna secca.
psychological psicologico.
psychology psicologia.
public pubblico *(also adj.)*.
publication pubblicazione, f.
publish (to) pubblicare.
publisher editore, m.; casa editrice
   (publishing house).
pudding budino.
puddle pozzanghera.
pull (to) tirare.
pulpit pulpito.
pulse polso.
pump pompa.
punish (to) punire.
punishment punizione, f.
pupil allievo, allieva; pupilla *(eye)*.
purchase acquisto.
purchase (to) acquistare.
pure puro.
purify (to) depurare, purificare.
purity purezza.
purple porpora.
purpose scopo.
purse borsa.
pursue (to) inseguire.
pursuit inseguimento.
push (to) spingere.
put (to) mettere.
   to put away mettere via.
   to put off rimandare; rinviare.
   to put off balance sbilanciare.
   to put on indossare *(clothes)*.
   to put out spegnere *(light)*.
puzzle perplessità, indovinello,
   cruciverba, m.
puzzle (to) render perplesso;
   indovinare.

quaint pittoresco.
qualified qualificato.
qualify (to) essere adatto; qualificare.
quality qualità.
quantity quantità.
quarrel litigio.

quarrel (to) litigare.
quarter quarto; quartiere *(district)*.
queen regina.
quench (to) dissetare *(thirst);* estinguere *(flame)*.
question questione, f.; domanda.
question (to) domandare; interrogare; mettere in dubbio.
quick rapido.
quickly rapidamente.
    Come quickly! Venga subito!
quiet (adj.) quieto, tranquillo.
    Keep quiet. Stai zitto.
quiet (to) calmare, tranquillizzare.
quit (to) abbandonare, lasciare.
quite completamente; del tutto; proprio; affatto.
    quite good proprio buono.
quote (to) citare.

R

rabbi rabbino
rabbit coniglio; lepre, m. & f.
race corsa *(horse race, etc.);* razza *(of people)*.
racial razziale.
racism razzismo.
racist razzista.
radio radio, f.
rag cencio, straccio.
rage furia, collera, ira, indignazione.
ragged cencioso.
rail rotaia *(train);* sbarra *(wood or iron);* cancellata *(fence)*.
railroad ferrovia.
    railroad station stazione ferroviaria.
rain pioggia.
rain (to) piovere.
rainbow arcobaleno.
rainy piovoso.
raise aumento *(in pay)*.
raise (to) sollevare *(lift);* innalzare, produrre *(produce);* rincarare *(prices)*.
raisin uva secca.
rake rastrello.
rally (to) riunire insieme.
range estensione, f.; catena *(mountains)*.

range (to) percorrere, disporre.
rank grado, fila.
ransom riscatto.
rapid rapido.
rapidity rapidità.
rapidly rapidamente.
rapture estasi, f.
rare raro, eccezionale.
raspberry lampone.
rat topo.
rate velocità *(of speed);* tariffa *(fare)*.
    first rate di prim'ordine; tasso.
rate (to) valutare.
rather piuttosto.
    rather good piuttosto buono.
    rather than piuttosto che.
    I'd rather go. Preferirei andare.
ratify ratificare.
ration razione, f.
rational razionale, ragionevole.
rave (to) delirare.
raw crudo.
ray raggio.
razor rasoio.
    razor blade lametta.
reach portata, estensione, f.
reach (to) stendere; arrivare; pervenire; raggiungere; allungare *(with the arm)*.
react (to) reagire.
reaction reazione, f.
reactionary reazionario.
read (to) leggere.
    to re-read rileggere.
reading lettura.
ready pronto.
    to get ready prepararsi.
    ready-to-wear confezione.
real reale, vero.
realization realizzazione, f; comprensione, f.
realize (to) rendersi conto di.
really in verità; veramente.
rear di dietro.
rear (to) crescere *(children)*.
reason ragione, f.
reasonable ragionevole, abbastanza buono.
reasoning ragionamento.
reassure (to) rassicurare.
rebel (n. & adj.) ribelle, m.
rebel (to) ribellarsi.

rebellion ribellione, f.
rebirth rinascita.
rebuild (to) ricostruire.
recall richiamo.
recall (to) richiamare, ricordare.
receipt ricevuta.
receive (to) ricevere.
receiver ricevitore, m. *(telephone)*.
recent recente.
reception accoglienza; ricevimento
    (social).
recess recesso; sospensione del lavoro
    (rest period).
reciprocal reciproco, inverso, invertito.
recite (to) recitare.
recognize (to) riconoscere.
recollect (to) richiamare alla mente;
    ricordare.
recollection ricordo.
recommend (to) raccomandare.
recommendation raccomandazione, f.
reconcile (to) riconciliare.
reconstitute (to) ricostituire.
record disco *(phonograph)*; registro,
    documento *(file)*; primato *(sports)*.
recover (to) ritrovare *(find)*; guarire,
    ricuperare *(from illness)*.
recovery guarigione, f.
recruit coscritto, recluta.
rectangle rettangolo.
recycle (to) riciclare.
recycling riciclaggio.
red rosso.
    Red Cross Croce Rossa.
redeem (to) redimere, riscattare.
    to redeem a promise mantenere una
        promessa.
redouble (to) raddoppiare.
reduce (to) ridurre, dimagrire.
reduction riduzione, f.
reed canna.
refer (to) riferire, alludere.
reference riferimento, referenza,
    allusione, f.
referring to con riferimento.
refine (to) raffinare.
refinement raffinatezza.
reflect (to) riflettere.
reflection riflesso.
reform riforma, miglioramento.
reform (to) formare di nuovo;
    riformare.

refrain ritornello.
refrain (to) trattenersi.
refresh (to) rinfrescare, rianimare,
    rinvigorire.
refreshment rinfresco, ristoro.
refrigerator frigorifero.
refuge rifugio.
    to take refuge rifugiarsi.
refugee profugo.
refund (to) rimborsare.
refusal rifiuto, opzione.
refuse (to) rifiutare.
refute (to) confutare.
regard riguardo, stima, respetto.
    in regard to a proposito di;
        riguardo a.
regards ossequi, rispettosi saluti.
regatta regata.
regime regime, m.
regiment reggimento.
region regione, f.
regional regionale.
register registro.
register (to) registrare, iscriversi.
regret rimpianto, rammarico.
regret (to) rimpiangere, rammaricarsi di.
regular regolare.
regulate (to) regolare.
regulation regola; ordinamento.
rehearsal prova.
rehearse (to) provare.
reign regno.
reign (to) regnare.
reinforce (to) rinforzare.
reject scarto.
reject (to) respingere, rifiutare.
rejoice (to) gioire, rallegrarsi.
relapse ricaduta.
relate (to) raccontare.
    relating to attinente a, che riguarda.
relation relazione, f.; rapporto.
    in relation to in riferimento a.
relationship rapporto, parentela.
relative (n.) parente, m. & f. (adj.)
    relativo, affine.
relax (to) rilassarsi; rallentare; riposare
    (rest); calmarsi *(calm)*.
relaxation diminuzione, f.;
    rallentamento; ricreazione, f.
release liberazione, f.; scarico.
relent (to) cedere; divenire meno
    severo.

relentless inflessibile.

relevant pertinente, relativo, in questione.

reliable degno di fiducia; fidato.

reliance fiducia.

relic reliquia.

relief sollievo, soccorso.

relieve (to) sollevare.

religion religione, f.

religious religioso.

relinquish (to) abbandonare, cedere.

relish gusto, sapore, m.

relish (to) trovar piacevole.

reluctance riluttanza.

reluctant riluttante.

rely upon (to) fare assegnamento su (di).

remain (to) rimanere.

remainder resto, residuo.

remark osservazione, f.; commento.

remark (to) osservare, notare.

remarkable notevole, straordinario.

remedy rimedio.

remember (to) ricordare.

remembrance ricordo.

remind (to) richiamare alla mente.

remorse rimorso.

remote remoto.

removal rimozione, f.

remove (to) rimuovere.

renew (to) rinnovare.

rent affitto.

rent (to) dare in affitto; prendere in affitto.

  For Rent Si Affitta.

repair riparazione, f.; condizione.

repair (to) riparare.

repeat (to) ripetere.

repent (to) pentirsi.

repentance pentimento.

repetition ripetizione, f.

reply risposta.

reply (to) rispondere.

report notizia, resoconto, rapporto, relazione.

represent (to) rappresentare.

representation rappresentazione, f.; dichiarazione.

representative rappresentante, deputato.

repress (to) reprimere.

reprimand rimprovero.

reprimand (to) rimproverare.

reprisal rappresaglia.

reproach rimprovero.

reproach (to) rimproverare.

reproduce (to) riprodurre.

reproduction riproduzione.

republic repubblica.

reputation riputazione, f.

request domanda, richiesta.

request (to) richiedere.

require (to) esigere; aver bisogna di; chiedere.

rescue salvezza, soccorso.

rescue (to) salvare, soccorrere.

research ricerca.

resemblance somiglianza; rassomiglianza.

resemble (to) rassomigliare.

resent (to) offendersi di.

resentment risentimento.

reservation riserva; prenotazione *(for tickets, etc.).*

reserve riserva.

reserve (to) riservare; prenotare *(tickets, tables, etc.).*

resign (to) dimettersi; dare le dimissioni.

resignation dimissione, f. *(from a position);* rassegnazione, f. *(acquiescence).*

resist (to) resistere.

resistance resistenza.

resolute risoluto.

resolution soluzione, f. *(solution or explanation);* risoluzione, f. *(determination).*

resolve (to) risolvere.

resort stazione climatica.

resort (to) ricorrere.

resource risorsa.

respect rispetto.

respect (to) rispettare.

respectful rispettoso.

respective rispettivo.

respite tregua.

responsibility responsabilità.

responsible responsabile, competente.

rest riposo.

rest (to) riposare.

restaurant ristorante, m.

restless inquieto, irrequieto.

restoration restauro.

restore (to) restaurare.

restrain (to) reprimere, trattenere.

restraint restrizione; controllo.

restrict (to) restringere, limitare.

restriction restrizione, f.

result risultato, esito.

result (to) risultare, resolversi.

résumé curriculum vitae.

resume (to) riprendere, riassumere.

retail vendita al minuto.

retail (to) vendere al minuto.

retain (to) trattenere, ritenere.

retaliate (to) vendicarsi di; ritorcere.

retaliation rappresaglia.

retire (to) ritirarsi, andare in pensione.

retired pensionato.

retirement ritiro, isolamento.

retract (to) ritrarre.

retreat ritirata.

return ritorno.

return (to) ritornare; restituire *(give back)*.

reveal (to) rivelare.

revelation rivelazione, f.

revenge vendetta.

revenue entrata, reddito, ricavo.

reverence riverenza.

reverend reverendo.

reverse (n. & adj.) inverso, contrario.

reverse (to) rovesciare, invertire, rivoltare.

revert (to) tornare indietro; spettare *(go to, as in a will)*.

review rivista *(periodical)*; recensione.

review (to) recensire *(a book, play, etc.)*.

    to pass in review *(as troops)* passare in rivista.

revise (to) rivedere, emendare; revisionare.

revision revisione, f.

revive (to) fare rivivere; rianimare; risvegliare *(memories)*.

revoke (to) revocare.

revolt (to) ribellarsi *(rebel)*; disgustare *(disgust or offend)*.

revolution rivoluzione, f.

revolutionize rivoluzionare.

revolve (to) roteare *(rotate)*; meditare *(think, consider)*.

reward ricompensa.

reward (to) ricompensare.

rhyme rima.

rib costola.

ribbon nastro.

rice riso.

rich ricco.

richness ricchezza.

rid (to get) sbarazzarsi.

    to get rid of something sbarazzarsi di quaiche cosa.

riddle enigma, indovinello.

ride corsa *(in a car)*; galoppata *(on horseback)*; passeggiata.

ride (to) andare.

    to ride a horse andare a cavallo.

    to ride a bicycle andare in bicicletta.

    to ride in a car andare in auto.

    to go for a boatride andare in barca.

    to go for a plane ride andare in aeroplano.

ridiculous ridicolo.

rifle fucile, m.

right (n.) destra, bene, m.; (adj.) corretto, diritto, esatto, giusto.

    to have a right to aver il diritto di.

    to be right aver ragione.

    to the right a destra.

    Right! Bene!

righteous giusto, retto.

righteousness giustizia, rettitudine, f.

rightful giusto, legittimo.

rigid rigido.

rigor rigore, m.

rigorous rigoroso.

ring anello *(finger)*; cerchio *(circle)*; recinto *(enclosure)*; suono *(of a bell)*.

ring (to) suonare.

rinse (to) sciacquare.

riot tumulto, rivolta.

ripe maturo.

ripen (to) maturare.

rise ascesa, salita.

rise (to) alzarsi, levarsi, sollevarsi.

risk rischio.

risk (to) rischiare; mettere in pericolo.

rite rito.

ritual (n. & adj.) rituale, m.

rival (n. & adj.) rivale, m. & f.

rivalry rivalità.

river fiume, m.

road strada, via.

roar ruggito *(of an animal);* rombo *(of cannon, motor).*
roar (to) ruggire.
roast arrosto.
roast (to) arrostire.
rob (to) derubare.
robber ladro.
robbery furto.
robe mantello.
robust robusto.
rock roccia, scoglio.
rock (to) dondolare, cullare.
rocky roccioso.
rod bacchetta, asta.
role ruolo.
roll rotolo; rullìo *(drums);* panino *(bread).*
roll (to) rotolare.
    to roll up arrotolare, avvolgere.
Roman (n. & adj.) romano, romana.
Romanesque romanico.
romantic romantico.
romanticism romanticismo.
roof tetto.
room camera *(of a house);* spazio *(space or area).*
    make room for fare largo.
    There's no room. Non c'è spazio.
root radice, f.
rope corda.
rose rosa.
rosy roseo.
rot (to) marcire.
rough ruvido, rozzo.
round (adj.) rotondo; (adv.) attorno; in giro; (n.) ripresa *(in boxing);* giro *(inspection);* ronda *(patrol).*
    to round off arrotondire.
route via, percorso.
row fila.
row (to) remare.
royal reale.
rub (to) strofinare.
rubber gomma (also *tire);* caucciù (also *overshoes).*
rubbish scarti, m. pl; rifiuti, m. pl.
rude rude; grossolano; scortese *(impolite).*
ruffle increspatura.
ruffle (to) increspare.
ruin rovina.
ruin (to) rovinare.

rule regola, dominio; norma.
rule (to) regolare, governare.
ruler governante *(boss);* sovrano *(of a country);* riga *(for drawing lines).*
rumor diceria; voce generale, f.
run (to) correre.
    to run away fuggire.
rural rurale.
rush assalto, impeto.
rush (to) precipitarsi.
    rush hour ora di punta.
Russian (n. & adj.) russo, russa.
rust ruggine, f.
rustic rustico.
rusty arrugginito.
rye segala.

S

sacred sacro.
sacrifice sacrificio.
sacrifice (to) sacrificare.
sacrificial espiatorio.
sacrilege sacrilegio.
sad triste.
sadden (to) rattristare.
saddle sella.
sadness tristezza.
safe salvo, sicuro.
safe (to be) essere al sicuro.
safely sicuramente.
safety sicurezza.
sail vela.
sail (to) salpare, navigare.
sailor marinaio.
saint (n. & adj.) santo, m.; santa, f.
sake amore, motivo, scopo.
    for my sake per amor mio.
    for the sake of per amor di.
salad insalata.
salami salame.
salary stipendio.
sale vendita.
salt sale, m.
salt (to) salare.
salute saluto.
salute (to) salutare.
salvation salvezza.
same medesimo, stesso.
    all the same lo stesso.

sample campione, m.
sanctuary santuario.
sand sabbia.
sandal sandalo.
sandwich panino ripieno.
sandy sabbioso.
sane sano.
sanitary sanitario.
sap linfa.
sarcasm sarcasmo.
sarcastic sarcastico.
sardine sardina.
satiate (to) saziare.
satin raso.
satisfaction soddisfazione, f.
satisfactory soddisfacente.
satisfy (to) soddisfare.
saturate (to) saturare.
Saturday sabato.
sauce salsa.
saucer piattino.
sausage salsiccia.
savage (n. & adj.) selvaggio; violento,
     incivile, feroce.
save (prep.) tranne, eccetto.
save (to) salvare *(person);* fare delle
     economic *(money).*
   to save time guadagnar tempo.
   to save as salvare con nome
       (computer).
savings risparmi, m. pl.
saviour salvatore, m.
say (to) dire.
scales bilancia.
scalp cuoio capelluto.
scan (to) scandire, scrutare.
scandal scandalo.
scanty scarso, ristretto.
scar cicatrice, f., diffamazione.
scarce scarso, raro.
scarcely appena, scarsamente.
scare (to) spaventare.
scarf sciarpa.
scatter (to) spargere.
scene scena.
scenery paesaggio *(landscape);*
     scenario *(theater).*
schedule tabella, lista, inventario,
     orario.
scheme disegno, piano, schema.
scholar dotto, erudito.
school scuola.

science scienza.
scientific scientifico.
scientist scienziato.
scissors forbici, f. pl.
scold (to) rimproverare.
scope scopo, campo, prospettiva.
score punteggio.
scorn sdegno.
scorn (to) sdegnare.
scornful sdegnoso.
scrape grattare.
scratch (to) graffiare.
scream urlo, grido.
scream (to) gridare, urlare.
screen paravento; schermo *(movie,*
     computer).
screw vite, f.
screwdriver cacciavite, m.
scribble (to) scribacchiare.
scruple scrupolo.
scrupulous scrupoloso.
scrutinize (to) scrutare.
sculpture scultura.
sea mare, m.
seagull gabbiano.
seal sigillo.
seal (to) sigillare.
seam cucitura.
search ricerca.
search (to) ricercare.
seashore spiaggia.
seasickness mal di mare, m.
season stagione, f.
season (to) condire.
seasonal stagionale.
seat sedile, m.; posto.
seat (to) sedere.
seaweed alga, alghe.
second (n.) secondo *(unit of time);*
     (adj.) secondo *(numeral).*
secondary secondario.
secret (n. & adj.) segreto.
secretariat segreteria.
secretary segretario, segretaria.
sect setta.
section sezione, f.
secular laico.
secure (adj.) sicuro.
secure (to) procurarsi, ottenere *(get or*
     obtain); assicurare *(make secure).*
security sicurezza, cauzine.
seductive seducente.

see (to) vedere.
   to see again rivedere.
seed seme, m.
seek (to) cercare; sforzarsi di.
seem (to) sembrare.
seize (to) afferrare, catturare,
   impadronirsi.
seldom raramente.
select (to) scegliere, selezionare.
selection scelta, assortimento,
   selezione.
self stesso, stessa.
   self-confidence fiducia in se
     stesso.
selfish egoista, egoistico.
selfishness egoismo.
sell (to) vendere.
semi- mezzo, metà.
semicolon punto e virgola.
semolina semolino.
senate senato.
senator senatore, m.
send (to) inviare; mandare.
senior (n. & adj.) maggiore, m. or f.;
   anziano.
sensation sensazione, f.
sense senso.
senseless insensibile.
sensibility sensibilità.
sensible sensibile, ragionevole.
sensitive sensibile, sensitivo, delicato,
   suscettibile.
sensitivity sensibilità.
sentence proposizione, f.; sentenza.
sentiment sentimento.
sentimental sentimentale.
separate separato.
separate (to) separare.
separately separatamente.
separation separazione, f.
September settembre.
sergeant sergente, m.
series serie, f.
serious serio.
seriously seriamente.
sermon sermone, m.; predica.
servant servo, m.; serva, f.
serve (to) servire, rompiere.
service servizio, assistenza.
session sessione, f.
set (n.) serie, f.; assortimento; (adj.)
   fisso, stabilito.

set (to) mettere a posto.
settle (to) fissare, stabilire.
settlement sistemazione, f.;
   accomodamento; colonizzazione, f.
   (colonization).
seven sette.
seventeen diciassette.
seventeenth diciassettesimo.
seventh settimo.
seventieth settantesimo.
seventy settanta.
several diversi, parecchi.
   several times diverse volte.
severe severo.
severity severità.
sew (to) cucire.
sewer fogna.
sex sesso.
shabby meschino, logoro.
shade ombra.
shade (to) ombreggiare.
shadow ombra.
shady ombreggiato.
shake (to) scuotere; agitare; tremare
   (tremble).
shallow poco profondo.
shame vergogna.
shame (to) gettar vergogna su.
shameful vergognoso.
shameless impudente.
shape forma.
shape (to) formare.
shapeless informe; senza forma.
share parte, f.; porzione, f.; azione, f.
   (of stock); quota.
share (to) dividere; ripartire.
shareholder azionista, m.
shark squalo.
sharp (n.) diesis, m. *(in music);* (adj.)
   tagliente.
sharpen (to) affilare.
shave (to) radersi.
she essa, ella, lei.
shed capannone, m.
shed (to) versare; spandere; perdere
   (leaves).
sheep pecora.
sheer puro; sottile *(thin)*.
sheet lenzuolo.
shelf scaffale, m.
shell guscio.
shellfish crostaceo.

shelter ricovero.
shelter (to) ricoverare.
shepherd pastore, m.
shield scudo.
shield (to) proteggere.
shift cambiamento.
shift (to) cambiare, trasferire, spostarsi.
shine splendore, m. *(of the sun);*
  lucidatura.
shine (to) brillare.
ship nave, f.
  steamship vaporetto.
ship (to) spedire.
shipment imbarco, spedizione, f.
shirt camicia.
shiver brivido.
shiver (to) rabbrividire, tremare.
shock scossa.
shock (to) sparare.
shoe scarpa.
shoemaker calzolaio.
shoot (to) sparare.
shooting sparata, sparatoria.
shop bottega.
shop (to) fare delle spese; fare delle
  compere.
shore riva.
  sandy shore arenile.
short corto, breve.
shortly fra poco.
shorten (to) abbreviare.
shorthand stenografia.
shorts mutande, f. pl.
shot colpo.
shoulder spalla.
shout grido.
shout (to) gridare.
shove (to) spingere.
shovel pala, paletta.
show spettacolo.
show (to) mostrare.
shower doccia.
shrill stridente.
shrimp gambero, gamberetto.
shrink (to) ritirarsi.
  unshrinkable irrestringibile.
shrub cespuglio; arbusto.
shun (to) evitare, schivare.
shut (adj.) chiuso.
shut (to) chiudere.
shy timido.
Sicilian (n. & adj.) siciliano, siciliana.

sick infermo, malato.
sickness infermità, malattia.
side lato, parte.
  side dish contorno.
sidewalk marciapiede, m.
siege assedio.
sigh sospiro.
sigh (to) sospirare.
sight vista.
sign segno, simbolo, targa, cartello.
sign (to) firmare; sottoscrivere.
signal segnale, m.
signature firma.
significance significato.
signify (to) significare.
silence silenzio.
silence (to) far tacere.
silent silenzioso.
silk seta.
silken di seta; delicato *(soft).*
silly sciocco.
silver argento.
silverware posate.
silvery argentato.
similar simile.
similarity somiglianza.
simple semplice.
simplicity semplicità.
simply semplicemente.
simulate (to) simulare.
simultaneous simultaneo.
sin peccato.
sin (to) peccare.
since da quando.
sincere sincero.
sincerely sinceramente.
  Yours sincerely Vostro sincero
    amico.
sincerity sincerità.
sing (to) cantare.
singer cantante, m. & f.
single solo; celibe *(unmarried man);*
  nubile *(unmarried woman);* singolo.
singular singolare.
sinister sinistro.
sink lavandino *(kitchen).*
sink (to) affondare.
sinner peccatore, m.; peccatrice, f.
sip (to) centellinare, sorbire.
sir signore.
  Thank you, sir! Grazie, signore!
siren sirena.

sister sorella.
sister-in-law cognata.
sit (to) sedere, accomodarsi.
site sito, luogo.
situation situazione, f.
six sei.
sixteen sedici.
sixteenth sedicesimo.
sixth sesto.
sixtieth sessantesimo.
sixty sessanta.
size misura.
skate (to) pattinare.
skates pattini, m. pl.
skeleton scheletro.
skeptic(al) (n. & adj.) scettico.
sketch schizzo, abbozzo.
ski sci.
ski (to) sciare.
skill destrezza.
skillful destro, abile.
skin pelle, f.
skirt sottana, gonna.
skull teschio, cranio.
sky cielo.
slam (to) sbattere.
slander calunnia.
slang gergo.
slap schiaffo.
slate lavagna.
slaughter macello.
slave schiavo, schiava.
slavery schiavitù.
sleep sonno.
sleep (to) dormire.
sleeve manica.
sleigh slitta.
slender snello.
slice fetta.
slide (to) scivolare.
slight lieve, esile.
slight (to) disprezzare.
slip (to) scivolare.
slipper pantofola.
slippery sdrucciolevole.
slope pendio.
slot fessura.
slovenly disordinato.
slow lento.
slowness lentezza.
slumber sonno.
slumber (to) sonnecchiare, dormire.

sly furbo.
small piccolo.
smart elegante; abile (skillful); piccante.
smash (to) fare a pezzi.
smear macchia.
smear (to) lordare, macchiare.
smell odore, m.
smell (to) odorare, fiutare.
smile sorriso.
smile (to) sorridere.
smoke fumo.
smoke (to) fumare.
smoker fumatore, m.
smooth liscio.
smother (to) soffocare.
smuggle (to) far entrare di
     contrabbando.
snake serpente, m.; rettile, m.
snapshot istantanca.
snatch frammento (fragment).
sneer (to) sogghignare.
sneeze (to) stamutire.
sniff (to) annusare.
snore (to) russare.
snow neve, f.
snow (to) nevicare.
so (thus) cosi.
     and so on e via di seguito.
soak (to) mettere a bagno.
soap sapone, m.
sob singhiozzo.
sober sobrio.
soccer calcio.
sociable socievole.
social sociale.
socialism socialismo.
society società.
sock calzino.
socket orbita.
soft morbido, cedevole.
soften (to) ammorbidire.
soil (to) sporcare.
solar solare.
soldier soldato.
sole unico, solo; suola (shoes); sogliola
     (fish).
solemn solenne.
solemnity solennità.
solicit (to) sollecitare.
solid solido; massiccio, tinta unita.
solidarity solidarietà.
solitary solitario.

solitude solitudine, f.
solution soluzione, f.
solve (to) risolvere.
some del; qualche; alcuni, m. pl;
     alcune, f. pl.
somebody qualcuno.
somehow in un modo o in un'altro.
someone qualcuno, m.; qualcuna, f.
something qualche cosa.
sometime un tempo; qualche volta.
sometimes talvolta; delle volte.
somewhat piuttosto.
somewhere in qualche luogo.
son figlio.
song canzone, f.
son-in-law genero.
soon presto.
soot fuliggine, f.
soothe (to) calmare.
sophisticated sofisticato.
sore piaga, ferita.
sorrow dolore, m.
sorry spiacente.
     to be sorry about essere
          spiacente di.
     I am sorry. Mi dispiace.
sort sorta; generale; m.
sort (to) scegliere; selezionare.
soul anima.
sound suono.
sound (to) suonare.
soup minestra, brodo.
sour acido *(milk, etc.);* acerbo *(fruit);*
     amaro *(bitter).*
source fonte, f.
south sud, m. pl., meridione, m.
southern meridionale (also noun, m.);
     al sud.
southwest sudovest, m.
sovereign (n. & adj.) sovrano, sovrana.
sow (to) seminare.
space spazio.
space (to) spaziare.
spacecraft astronave.
spacious spazioso.
spade vanga; badile; m.; picche, f.
     (playing cards).
spaghetti spaghetti.
Spanish (n. & adj.) spagnolo.
spare disponibile; di ricambio *(said of
     a tire).*
spare (to) risparmiare, disporre.

spark scintilla.
sparkle (to) scintillare.
sparkling frizzante.
sparrow passero.
speak (to) parlare.
speaker oratore, m.; parlatore, m.
special speciale, particolare.
specialty specialità.
specific specifico.
specify (to) specificare.
spectacle spettacolo.
spectacular spettacolare.
spectator spettatore, m.
speculate (to) speculare.
speech discorso.
speed velocità.
speedy rapido, veloce.
spell incanto.
spell (to) compitare, scrivere.
     How do you spell this word? Come
          si scrive questa parola?
spelling ortografia.
spend (to) spendere.
sphere sfera; ambito.
spice spezie, f. pl.
spider ragno.
spill (to) versare; far cadere.
spin (to) filare.
spirit spirito.
spiritual spirituale.
spit sputo; spiedo.
spit (to) sputare.
spite dispetto.
spite (to) contrariare.
spiteful dispettoso.
splash (to) schizzare.
splendid splendido.
splendor splendore, m.
split (to) fendere, spaccare.
spoil (to) guastare, sciupare.
spokesperson portavoce.
sponge spugna.
spontaneous spontaneo.
spoon cucchiaio.
spoonful cucchiaiata.
sport sport, m.; giuoco.
spot luogo determinato *(location);*
     punto; *macchia* (stain).
spread (to) stendere, spandere.
spring primavera *(season);* balzo
     (leap); molla *(machine);* sorgente, f.
     (of water).

spring (to) saltare; balzare; nascere; derivare; provenire da; far scattare *(a trap)*.

sprinkle (to) spruzzare, aspergere, cospargere.

sprout (to) germogliare.

spry vivace, attivo.

spur (to) spronare.

spurn (to) respingere, disprezzare.

spy spia.

spy (to) spiare.

squadron squadrone, m.

squalid squallido.

squander (to) sprecare.

square quadrato; piazza *(city).*

squeeze (to) spremere.

squirrel scoiattolo.

stability stabilità.

stabilize (to) stabilizzare.

stable stalla.

stable (adj.) stabile.

stack catasta, mucchio.

stack (to) ammucchiare.

stadium stadio.

staff bastone, m.; stato maggiore *(military).*

stage palcoscenico.

stain macchia.

stain (to) macchiare.

stairs scale, f. pl.

stammer balbuzie, f.

stammer (to) balbettare.

stamp francobollo *(postage);* marchio *(seal).*

stand edicola *(newsstand);* leggio *(music);* posizione.

stand (to) stare in piedi; subire *(endure).*

star stella.

stare (to) fissare.

start (to) sobbalzare, trasalire, cominciare.

    (to) start again ricominciare.

starve (to) morire di fame.

state stato; (adj.) statale; rango.

state (to) affermare, dichiarare.

stateless apolide.

stately imponente.

statement dichiarazione, f.

stateroom cabina.

station stazione, f.

    first aid station pronto soccorso.

stationery articoli di cancelleria.

statistics statistiche, f. pl.

statue statua.

statute statuto.

stay permanenza, soggiorno.

stay (to) stare, restare, soggiornare.

steady fermo, saldo.

steak bistecca.

steal (to) rubare.

steam vapore, m.

steamer piroscafo; vapore, m.

steel acciaio.

steep ripido.

steeple campanile, m.

steer (to) dirigere, guidare.

stem ramo, stelo, fusto.

stenographer stenografa, f.; stenografo, m.

stenography stenografia.

step gradino.

step (to) camminare.

sterile sterile.

sterilized sterilizzato.

stern severo.

stew stufato.

stew (to) cuocere in umido; stufare.

steward dispensiere m.; cameriere, m. *(on a ship).*

stick bacchetta.

stick (to) conficcare, appiccicare.

stiff rigido.

stiffen (to) irrigidire.

stiffness rigidezza.

still (adj.) fermo, calmo; (adv.) ancora, sempre.

    Keep still! Stá fermo!

stimulate (to) stimolare.

stimulating stimolante.

stimulus stimolo.

sting puntura.

sting (to) pungere.

stinginess tirchieria.

stingy tirchio.

stir (to) agitare, incitare, muoversi.

stitch punto; puntura *(of pain).*

stock bestiame, m. *(cattle);* merce, f. *(wares).*

stock exchange borsa valori.

stocking calza.

stomach stomaco, pancia.

stone pietra.

stool sgabello.

stop fermata.
stop (to) fermare, arrestare, smettere.
store negozio.
stork cicogna.
storm tempesta.
story storia.
    short story novella, racconto.
stove stufa.
straight diritto.
straighten (to) raddrizzare.
strain sforzo, tensione, f.
strange strano.
stranger straniero.
strap cinghia.
straw paglia.
strawberry fragola.
stream corrente, f.; ruscello.
street strada.
streetcar tranvia, m.
strength forza.
strengthen (to) rafforzare.
strenuous strenuo.
stress pressione, f.; forza, enfasi, f.
stretch stiramento; sforzo *(effort)*; tratto
    (of road).
stretch (to) stendere, allargare;
    sgranchire.
strict stretto, rigido, severo.
stride passo lungo; andatura.
stride (to) camminare a gran passi.
strife contesa, conflitto.
strike sciopero.
strike (to) colpire, battere.
string spago.
strip (to) spogliare.
stripe striscia.
strive (to) sforzarsi, lottare.
stroke colpo, tocco.
stroll breve passeggiata.
stroll (to) andare a passeggio.
strong forte.
structure struttura, edificio.
struggle lotta, sforzo.
struggle (to) lottare.
stubborn ostinato.
student studente, m.; studentessa, f.
studious studioso.
study studio.
study (to) studiare.
stuff stoffa.
stuff (to) imbottire.
stuffing ripieno.

stumble (to) inciampare.
stump ceppo.
stun (to) stordire.
stunt ostentazione di forza, f.
stupendous stupendo.
stupid stupido.
stupidity stupidità.
stupor stupore, m.
sturdy forte, tenace, stordimento,
    torpore.
stutter (to) balbettare.
style moda *(fashion);* stile, m.
subdue (to) soggiogare.
subject soggetto.
subject (to) sottoporre, assoggettare.
subjective soggettivo.
subjugate (to) soggiogare.
subjunctive congiuntivo.
sublime sublime.
submission sottomissione, f.
submissive sottomesso.
submit (to) sottomettere, sottoporre.
subordinate subordinato,
    subalterno.
subscribe (to) sottoscrivere.
subscription sottoscrizione, f.
subside (to) abbassarsi.
subsidy sovvenzione, f.
subsist (to) sussistere.
substance sostanza.
substantial sostanziale, sostanzioso,
    importante.
substantive sostantivo.
substitute sostituto, surrogato.
substitute (to) sostituire.
substitution sostituzione, f.
subtitles didascalie; sottotitoli.
subtle sottile, fine.
subtlety sottigliezza.
subtract (to) sottrarre.
subtraction sottrazione, f.
suburb sobborgo.
suburban extraurbano.
subway ferrovia sotterranea;
    metropolitana.
succeed (to) succedere, seguire,
    riuscire.
success successo.
successful fortunato.
succession successione, f.
successor successore, m.
such tale.

sudden improvviso.
suddenly improvvisamente.
sue (to) chiamare in giudizio.
suede scamosciato.
suffer (to) soffrire, sopportare, permotare.
suffering sofferenza.
sufficient sufficiente.
suffocation soffocamento.
sugar zucchero.
suggest (to) suggerire.
suggestion suggerimento.
suicide suicidio.
suit vestito *(clothes)*; petizione, f. *(lawsuit)*.
suit (to) adattare.
suitable adatto.
sulk (to) essere di cattivo umore.
sullen imbronciato.
sum somma.
   to sum up fare la somma; fare un riassunto.
summary riassunto.
summer estate, f.
summit sommità, vertice.
summon (to) citare, convocare.
sumptuous sontuoso.
sun sole, m.
sunbeam raggio di sole.
Sunday domenica.
sunny solatìo.
sunrise sorgere del sole, m.
sunset tramonto.
sunshine luce di sole, f.; sole, m.
superb superbo.
superficial superficiale.
superfluous superfluo.
superimpose (to) sovrapporre.
superintendent sovrintendente, m.
superior (n. & adj.) superiore, m.
superiority superiorità.
supermarket supermercato.
superstition superstizione, f.
supervise (to) sorvegliare.
supper cena.
supplement supplemento.
supplementary supplementare.
supply provvista.
supply (to) fornire.
support sostegno.
support (to) sostenere, reggere, mantenere.

suppose (to) supporre.
suppress (to) sopprimere.
supreme supremo.
sure sicuro.
surety sicurezza.
surface superficie, f.
surgeon chirurgo.
surgery chirurgia, sala operatoria *(operation room)*.
surmount (to) sormontare.
surname cognome, m.
surpass (to) sorpassare.
surplus eccedenza; sopprappiù, m.
surprise sorpresa.
surprise (to) sorprendere.
surrender resa.
surrender (to) arrendersi.
surround (to) circondare.
surroundings dintorni, m. pl.
survey esame, m.; ispezione, f.
survey (to) esaminare.
survive (to) sopravvivere.
susceptibility suscettibilità.
susceptible suscettibile.
suspect sospetto.
suspect (to) sospettare.
suspenders bretelle.
suspense sospensione d'animo, f.
suspension sospensione, f.
suspicion sospetto.
suspicious sospettoso.
sustain (to) sostenere.
swallow (to) inghiottire.
swamp palude, f.
swan cigno.
sway (to) oscillare.
swear bestemmiare *(curse)*; giurare *(take an oath)*.
sweat sudore, m.
sweat (to) sudare.
Swedish svedese.
sweep (to) scopare, spazzare.
sweet dolce.
sweetness dolcezza.
swell (to) gonfiare.
swift veloce, rapido.
swim (to) nuotare.
swindler truffatore, m.
swing (to) dondolare.
switch interruttore, m. *(electric)*.
sword spada.
syllable sillaba.

symbol simbolo.
symbolic simbolico.
symbolize (to) simboleggiare.
symmetrical simmetrico.
symmetry simmetrìa.
sympathetic tenero, sensibile, comprensivo.
sympathy compassione, f.
symposium simposio; riunione; raccolta discretti.
symptom sintomo.
synagogue sinagoga.
syntax sintassi.
synthesis sintesi.
syringe siringa.
syrup sciroppo.
system sistema, m.
systematic sistematico.

T

table tavola, tavolo.
tablecloth tovaglia.
tablet tavoletta.
tacit tacito.
tacitly tacitamente.
taciturn taciturno.
tact tatto.
tactfully con tatto.
tail coda.
tailor sarto.
take (to) prendere.
takeoff decollo.
talcum powder borotalco.
tale storia, racconto.
talent talento.
talk (to) parlare, chiacchierare, discorrere.
talkative ciarliero.
tall alto.
tame mansueto, addomesticato, domato.
tan (to) abbronzare.
    (to) get tanned abbronzarsi.
tangle (to) ingarbugliare.
tank serbatoio; cisterna *(cistern);* carro armato *(army).*
tape nastro.
tape recorder magnetòfono, m.; registratore magnètico, m.

tapestry tappezzerìa, arazzo.
tar catrame, m.
tardy lento, tardino.
target bersaglio.
tarnish (to) appannare; rendere opaco.
task compito, incarico.
taste gusto.
taste (to) assaggiare.
tavern osteria.
tax tassa, imposta.
taxi tassì.
tea tè.
teach (to) insegnare.
teacher insegnante, m. & f.; docente.
team squadra.
tear strappo.
tear (to) strappare.
tease (to) molestare, tormentare.
teaspoon cucchiaino.
technical tecnico.
technique tecnica.
technology tecnologia.
tedious tedioso.
teetotaler astemio, m.
telecommunications telecomunicazioni.
telegram telegramma, m.
telegraph telegrafo.
telegraphic telegrafico.
telephone telefono.
    cellular phone telefonino.
    cordless phone telefono portatile.
    telephone call telefonata.
    telephone operator telefonista, m. & f.
telephone (to) telefonare.
teletype telescrivente, f.
tell (to) dire.
temper umore, m. *(mood);* temperamento *(disposition).*
temperance temperanza.
temperate temperato, moderato.
temperature temperatura.
tempest tempesta.
temple tempio.
temporary temporaneo.
tempt (to) tentare.
temptation tentazione, f.
ten dicci.
tenacious tenace.
tenant inquilino, locatorio.
tend (to) tendere.

tendency tendenza.
tender tenero.
tennis tennis, m.
tense (n.) tempo *(grammar);* (adj.) teso.
tension tensione, f.
tent tenda.
tenth decimo.
tepid tiepido.
term termine, m.
terrace terrazzo.
terrible terribile.
terrify (to) atterrire.
territory territorio.
terror terrore, m.
terrorism terrorismo.
test prova, esame, m.
test (to) provare; esaminare *(school).*
testament testamento.
testify (to) attestare, deporre.
testimony testimonianza.
text testo.
textbook libro di testo.
textiles tessile.
than di; che; di quello che; di quanto che.
thank (to) ringraziare.
thanks grazie, f. pl.*;* ringraziamenti, m. pl.
that (pron.) quello, quella, ciò, quelle, quelli; (adj.) quel, quello, quella, quelle, quei, quelli, quegli.
    that is vale a dire.
    That's it. È così.
thaw disgelo.
thaw (to) disgelare.
the il, lo, la, i, gli, le.
theater teatro.
their il loro; la loro; i loro; le loro.
theirs il loro; la loro; i loro; le loro; di loro.
them essi, esse, loro, li, le, quelli, quelle, coloro.
theme tema, m.
themselves essi stessi; esse stesse; se stessi; se stesse; sè; si.
then allora, perciò, dunque.
theoretical teorico.
theory teoria.
there là, lì.
    there is c'è.
    there are ci sono.
thereafter d'allora in poi.

thereupon in conseguenza di ciò.
thermometer termometro.
these queste, questi.
thesis tesi, f.
they essi, esse, loro.
thick spesso.
thicken (to) ingrossare *(make larger);* far restringere *(a gravy or sauce).*
thickness spessore, m.
thief ladro.
thigh coscia.
thimble ditale, m.
thin sottile, magro *(referring to people).*
thing cosa.
think (to) pensare, credere, ritenere.
thinness sottigliezza.
third terzo.
thirst sete, f.
thirteen tredici.
thirteenth tredicesimo.
thirtieth trentesimo.
thirty trenta.
this questo, questa.
thorn spina.
thorough intero, completo.
though sebbene, quantunque, però.
thought pensiero.
thoughtful pensieroso, pensoso; riflessivo.
thoughtless spensierato.
thousand mille.
thread filo.
thread (to) infilare.
threat minaccia.
threaten (to) minacciare.
three tre.
threshold soglia.
thrift economìa.
thrifty economico.
thrill palpito, tremito.
thrill (to) elettrizzare.
thrilling emozionante.
throat gola.
throb (to) pulsare.
throne trono.
throng folla, ressa.
through attraverso; tramite.
throughout per tutta la durata di.
throw lancio, tiro.
throw (to) lanciare, gettare.
thumb pollice, m.
thunder tuono.

thunder (to) tuonare.
thunderbolt fulmine, m.
Thursday giovedì.
thus così; in tal modo.
ticket biglietto.
    ticket window biglietterìa; sportello del biglietti.
tickle solletico.
ticklish sensitivo, delicato.
tide marèa.
tidiness pulizia, accuratezza, ordine, m.
tidy ordinato.
tie cravatta.
tie (to) legare.
tiger tigre, f.
tight stretto, attillato.
tights calzamaglia.
tile piastrella.
till fino a; finchè.
till (to) coltivare.
tilt (to) inclinare.
timber legname da costruzione, m.
time tempo.
    behind time in ritardo.
    from time to time di volta in volta.
    in time a tempo.
    to have a good time divertirsi.
    What time is it? Che ora è?
timid timido.
timidity timidezza.
tin stagno.
tinkle tintinnìo.
tiny piccolo, minuscolo.
tip punta; mancia *(money)*.
tip (to) dare la mancia.
    tip over far ribaltare.
tire gomma, pneumatico.
tire (to) stancare, stancarsi, affaticarsi.
tired stanco.
tireless instancabile.
tiresome stanchevole, noioso.
title titolo.
to a, ad, verso.
toad rospo.
toast pane tostato; pane abbrustolito.
toast (to) brindare *(drink to)*; tostare *(bread)*.
tobacco tabacco.
    tobacco store tabaccherìa.
today oggi.
toe dito del piede.
together insieme.

toil fatica.
toil (to) faticare.
toilet toilette, gabinetto.
token segno; simbolo; pegno *(of affection)*.
tolerable tollerabile.
tolerance tolleranza.
tolerant tollerante.
tolerate (to) tollerare.
tomato pomodoro.
tomb tomba.
tomorrow domani, m.
ton tonnellata.
tonality tonalità.
tone tono.
tongs mollette, f. pl. *(tool)*; pinze, f. pl. *(tweezers, pincers)*.
tongue lingua.
tonight stasera.
too anche *(also)*; pure.
    too much troppo.
tool strumento; arnese, m.; utensile, m.
tooth dente, m.
toothache mal di denti.
toothbrush spazzolino da denti.
toothpaste dentifricio.
toothpick stuzzicadenti, m.
top sommità, cima, vertice.
topic soggetto.
torch torcia, fiaccola.
torment tormento.
torrid torrido.
torture tortura.
toss (to) lanciare; agitarsi *(in sleep)*.
total (n. & adj.) totale, m.
totally totalmente.
touch tocco.
touch (to) toccare.
touching commovente.
touchy suscettibile.
tough duro, rude.
tour viaggio *(journey)*; giro.
tour (to) fare un viaggio.
tourist turista, m. or f.
    tourist agency agenzia di viaggi.
tournament tornèo, gara.
toward verso.
towel asciugamano.
tower torre, f.
town città.
    town hall palazzo municipale.
toy giocattolo.

trace traccia.

trace (to) tracciare.

track orma; binario *(railroad);* traccia; pista.

trade commercio; mestiere, m. *(occupation).*

    trade union camera del lavoro.

trade (to) commerciare.

tradition tradizione, f.

traditional tradizionale.

traffic traffico.

trafficker trafficante.

traffic light semaforo.

tragedy tragedia.

tragic tragico.

trail sentiero, traccia.

trail (to) seguire le tracce di; strisciare.

train treno.

    freight train treno merci.

train (to) ammaestrare, allenarsi, addestrare.

training esercitazione, f.; allenamento.

traitor traditore, m.; traditrice, f.

trample (to) calpestare.

tranquil tranquillo.

tranquillity tranquillità.

transaction affare, m.; trattamento.

transfer trasferimento.

transfer (to) trasferire.

transition transizione, f.

transitory transitorio.

translate (to) tradurre.

translation traduzione, f.

translator traduttore, m.

transmission trasmissione, f.

transmit (to) trasmettere.

transparency trasparenza.

transparent trasparente.

transplant (to) trapiantare.

transplantation trapianto.

transport trasporto.

transport (to) trasportare.

transportation trasportazione, f.; trasporto.

transverse trasverso.

trap trappola.

trap (to) prendere in trappola.

trash rifiuto, spazzatura.

trash can pattumiera.

travel viaggio.

    travel agency agenzia di viaggi.

travel (to) viaggiare.

traveler viaggiatore, m.; viaggiatrice, f.

tray vassoio.

treacherous perfido, sleale, traditore.

treachery tradimento.

treason tradimento.

treasure tesoro.

treasurer tesoriere, m.

treasury tesoro.

treat cosa offerta; gioia; festa.

treat (to) trattare.

treatment trattamento; cura *(medical).*

treaty trattato.

tree albero.

tremble (to) tremare.

trembling (n.) tremito; (adj.) tremulo.

tremendous tremendo.

trench trincèa.

trend tendenza.

trial prova; esperimento; processo *(court).*

triangle triangolo.

tribe tribù, f.

tribulation tribolazione, f.

tribunal tribunale, m.

tribute tributo.

trick stratagemma, m.; trucco.

trick (to) ingannare.

trifle inezia.

trifling insignificante.

trim (to) guarmire.

trimming guarnizione, f.

trip viaggio; gita; incespicamento *(fall).*

trip (to) inciampare.

triple triplice.

triptych trittico.

triumph trionfo.

triumph (to) trionfare.

triumphant trionfante.

trivial insignificante.

trolley car tranvia, m.

troop truppa.

trophy trofèo.

trot trotto.

trot (to) trottare; mettere al trotto.

trouble disturbo, incomodo.

trouble (to) importunare, disturbare.

    Don't trouble yourself. Non si disturbi.

trousers calzoni, m. pl.

truck carro, autocarro.

true vero.

truly veramente, sinceramente.
  yours truly suo devotissimo, m.; sua
    devotissima, f.
trump briscola.
trump (to) giocare una briscola.
trumpet tromba.
trunk tronco *(tree);* baule, m.
  (luggage); proboscide, f.
  (elephant's).
trust fiducia.
trust (to) aver fiducia in.
trusting fidente.
trustworthy fidato.
truth verità.
truthful sincero, veritiero.
truthfully sinceramente.
truthfulness sincerità.
try tentativo.
try (to) tentare.
  Try to come. Cerchi di venire.
  Try to be on time. Cerchi di arrivare
    in tempo.
tube tubo, tubetto.
tumble (to) cadere, precipitare.
tumult tumulto.
tune aria, tono, melodìa.
tune (to) accordare.
tunnel gallerìa.
turf terreno erboso.
turkey tacchino.
turmoil tumulto.
turn giro, turno.
turn (to) voltare, rivoltare.
  Left turn. Voltare a sinistra.
turnip rapa.
twelfth dodicesimo.
twelve dodici.
twentieth ventesimo.
twenty venti.
twenty-five venticinque.
twenty-four ventiquattro.
twenty-six ventisei.
twice due volte.
twilight crepuscolo.
twin gemello, m.; gemella, f.
twist torcere, contorcere, torcersi.
two due.
type tipo.
type (to) dattilografare.
typewriter macchina da scrivere.
tyranny tirannìa.
tyrant tiranno.

ugliness bruttezza.
ugly brutto.
ulterior ulteriore.
ultimate ultimo, finale, definitivo.
ultimately finalmente; in definitiva.
umbrella ombrello.
umpire arbitro.
unable to (to be) essere incapace di.
unanimity unanimità.
unanimous unanime.
unanimously unanimemente.
unaware (to be) essere inconsapevole.
unbearable insopportabile.
unbelievable incredibile.
unbutton (to) sbottonare.
uncertain incerto.
uncertainty incertezza.
unchangeable immutabile.
unchanged inalterato.
uncle zio.
uncomfortable scomodo.
uncommon raro; non comune.
unconscious inconscio; privo di sensi;
  subcosciente.
unconsciously inconsciamente.
uncouth goffo, agraziato, grossolano.
uncover (to) scoprire.
undecided indeciso.
undefinable indefinibile.
undefined indefinito.
undeniable innegabile.
under sotto.
undergo (to) subire; sottomettersi a.
underground sottoterra; sotterraneo.
underhand (adj.) clandestino, subdolo.
underline (to) sottolineare.
underneath sotto; al disotto.
understand (to) comprendere;
  sottintendere.
understanding comprensione, f.;
  intesa; accordo.
undertake (to) intraprendere.
undertaker direttore di pompe
  funebri, m.
undertaking impresa.
underwater subacqueo.
undesirable non desiderabile.
undignified poco dignitoso.
undo (to) disfare.

undress (to) svestirsi.
uneasiness inquietudine, f.; ansia.
uneasy inquieto; non comodo.
unemployed non impiegato;
   disoccupato.
unemployment disoccupazione.
unequal ineguale.
uneven ineguale; dispari *(numbers)*.
uneventful tranquillo; senza importanti
   avvenimenti.
unexpected inaspettato, imprevisto.
unexpectedly inaspettatamente,
   improvvisamente.
unfailing immancabile.
unfair ingiusto.
unfaithful infedele.
unfamiliar non familiare; poco noto.
unfasten (to) slacciare.
unfavorable sfavorevole.
unfit inadatto.
unfold (to) spiegare, stendere, svelare.
unforeseen impreveduto, imprevisto.
unforgettable indimenticabile.
unfortunate sfortunato.
unfortunately sfortunatamente.
ungrateful ingrato.
unhappily infelicemente.
unhappiness infelicità.
unhappy infelice.
unharmed incolume.
unhealthy non sano.
unheard (of) inaudito.
unhesitatingly senza esitazione.
unhook (to) sganciare.
unhoped for insperato.
unhurt illeso, incolume.
uniform (n. & adj.) uniforme, f.
uniformity uniformità.
uniformly uniformemente.
unify (to) unificare.
unimportant insignificante.
unintentional involontario.
unintentionally involontariamente.
uninviting non invitante.
union unione, f.; sindicato *(labor)*.
unique unico.
unit unità; unitario.
unite (to) unire.
united unito, congiunto.
unity unità.
universal universale.
universe universo.
university università.

unjust ingiusto.
unjustifiable ingiustificabile.
unkind poco gentile; scortese.
unknown sconosciuto.
unlawful illegale, illecito.
unleavened azzimo, non lievitato.
unless a meno che.
unlikely improbabile; inverosimile.
unlimited illimitato.
unload (to) scaricare.
unluckily sfortunatamente,
   disgraziatamente.
unmistakably chiaramente.
unnecessary non necessario.
unoccupied non occupato; disponibile;
   libero.
unofficial non ufficiale.
unpack (to) disfare le valigie.
unpleasant spiacevole, doloroso,
   sgradevole.
unprepared impreparato.
unpublished inedito.
unquestionably indubitatamente,
   indubbiamente.
unravel (to) dipanare, sbrogliare;
   chiarire.
unreadable illeggibile.
unreal irreale.
unreasonable irragionevole.
unrecognizable irriconoscibile.
unreliable immeritevole di fiducia.
unrest inquietudine, f.
unrestrained sfrenato.
unrestricted libero; sfrenato; senza
   restrizioni.
unroll (to) svolgere, distendere.
unsafe pericoloso.
unsatisfactory non soddisfacente.
unsatisfied insoddisfatto.
unscrupulous senza scrupoli.
unseemly sconveniente.
unseen (adj.) inosservato.
unselfish disinteressato.
unspeakable indicibile.
unsteady instabile, incostante.
unsuccessful senza successo.
unsuitable inadatto.
unthinkable impensabile.
untidy disordinato.
untie (to) sciogliere, slegare.
until fino a; finchè.
   until now fino ad ora.
untrimmed senza guarnizione.

untrue falso, infedele.
untrustworthy indegno di fiducia.
untruth menzogna.
unusable inutilizzabile.
unusual insolito, raro.
unwell indisposto, sofferente.
unwholesome malsano, nocivo.
unwilling non disposto; mal disposto.
unwillingly a malincuore.
unwise non saggio; insensato.
unworthy indegno, immeritevole.
up su; sopra; in alto; in piedi.
update (to) aggiornare.
upheaval sollevamento.
uphold (to) sostenere, mantenere.
upkeep mantenimento, sostentamento.
upon sopra.
upper superiore.
upright diritto; in piedi; retto.
uprising rivolta, insurrezione, f.
uproar tumulto, clamore, m.
upset capovolgimento, rovesciamento.
upset (to) capovolgere, sconvolgere.
upside down sottosopra.
upstairs al piano superiore; sopra.
upward in su; in alto.
urge (to) esortare.
urgency urgenza.
urgent urgente, impellente.
us noi, ci.
use uso, usanza.
use (to) usare; servirsi di.
used to abituato.
    to get used to abituarsi.
useful utile.
useless inutile.
user utente.
usual solito, usuale.
usually usualmente.
utensil utensile, m.
utility utilità, profitto, vantaggio.
utilize (to) utilizzare.
utter estremo, assoluto.
utter (to) emettere.
utterly estremamente, totalmente.

V

vacancy vacanza, posto vacante, vuoto.
vacant vuoto; non occupato.
vacation vacanze, f.

vagabond vagabondo.
vague vago.
vain vano, vanitoso.
    in vain in vano.
    vain ambition velleità.
valiant valoroso, intrepido.
valid valido.
validity validità.
valley valle, f.
valuable costoso, prezioso.
value valore, m.
value (to) valutare, stimare.
valued stimato, apprezzato.
valve valvola.
vandalism vandalismo.
vanilla vaniglia.
vanish (to) svanire.
vanity vanità.
vanquish (to) vincere, conquistare.
vapor vapore, m.
variable variabile.
variant variante.
variation variazione, f.
varied vario, variato.
variety varietà; varietà, m. *(show)*.
various diverso, vario.
varnish vernice, f.
varnish (to) verniciare.
vary (to) variare, mutare.
vase vaso.
vast vasto.
vault volta.
VCR video registratore.
veal vitello.
vegetable verdura, ortaggio; legume, m.
vehemence veemenza.
vehicle veicolo.
veil velo.
veil (to) velare.
vein vena.
velocity velocità.
velvet velluto.
venerable venerabile.
venerate (to) venerare.
veneration venerazione, f.
Venetian (n. & adj.) veneziano.
vengeance vendetta.
venom veleno.
ventilation ventilazione, f.
ventilator ventilatore, m.
venture (to) azzardare, osare.
verb verbo.
verdict verdetto.

verge limite; punto estremo.
verification verifica, conferma prova, dimostrare.
verify (to) verificare.
versatile versatile.
versatility versatilità.
verse verso.
version versione, f.
vertical verticale.
very molto.
vessel recipiente, m. *(container);* vascello; nave, f.
vest panciotto.
veterinarian veterinario.
vex (to) irritare.
via via.
vibrate (to) oscillare; far vibrare.
vice vizio, difetto.
   vice president vice presidente, m.
vice versa viceversa.
vicinity vicinanza; prossimità.
victim vittima.
victor vincitore, m.
victorious vittorioso.
victory vittoria.
victuals vettovaglie, f. pl.
video camera telecamera.
videodisc videodisco, m.
video games video giocchi.
videotape nastro televisivo, m.
view vista, veduta, visuale.
view (to) guardare, considerare.
vigor vigore, m.
vigorous vigoroso.
vile abbietto.
village villaggio.
villain furfante, m.
vindicate (to) rivendicare.
vindictive vendicativo.
vine vigna.
vinegar aceto.
vineyard vigneto.
violence violenza.
violent violento.
violet viola, mammola.
violin violino.
virile virile.
virtual virtuale.
virtue virtù, f.
virtuous virtuoso.
visibility visibilità.
visible visibile.

visibly visibilmente.
vision visione, f.; vista *(eyesight);* intuizione.
visit visita.
visitor visitatore, m.; ospite, m.; turista.
visual visivo.
visualize (to) immaginare, raffigurarsi.
vital vitale.
vitality vitalità.
vivacious vivace.
vivid vivido.
vocabulary vocabolario.
vocal vocale.
vocation vocazione, f.
vogue voga.
voice voce, f.
void non valido; privo; nullo.
volubility fluidità, abbondanza.
voluble volubile.
volume volume, m.
voluminous voluminoso.
voluntary volontario.
vote voto.
vote (to) votare.
vow voto.
vow (to) far voto di.
vowel vocale, f.
vulgar volgare.
vulnerable vulnerabile.

W

wager scommessa.
wager (to) scommettere.
wages salario.
waist vita, cintura.
wait (to) attendere.
waiter cameriere.
wake (to) svegliarsi.
walk cammino, passeggiata, passeggio.
walk (to) camminare.
   to go for a walk fare una passeggiata.
wall muro.
wallet portafogli, m.
walnut noce, f.
wander (to) vagabondare, divagare.
want bisogno.

want (to) volere; desiderare; aver bisogno.
war guerra.
    prewar period anteguerra.
ward pupillo *(person);* corsìa *(hospital).*
wardrobe guardaroba, corredo.
ware, wares merce, f.; merci, f. pl.
warehouse magazzino.
warfare guerra.
warm caldo.
    to be warm (hot) aver caldo *(a person);* essere caldo *(an object);* far caldo *(the weather).*
warm (to) riscaldare.
warmth calore, m.
warn (to) mettere in guardia; avvertire.
warning avvertimento, ammonimento.
warrant autorizzazione, f.; mandato.
warrant (to) assicurare, giustificare.
warrior guerriero.
wary cauto, guardingo.
wash bucato.
wash (to) lavare.
washing lavaggio.
washing machine lavatrice.
washroom lavandino.
waste sperpero, spreco.
waste (to) consumare; sperperare; deperire *(waste away).*
watch guardia *(guard);* orologio *(clock);* veglia *(vigil).*
watch (to) stare in guardia; guardare.
watchful guardingo.
water acqua.
    fresh water acqua dolce.
waterfall cascata d'acqua; cataratta.
waterproof impermeabile.
wave onda.
wave (to) ondeggiare *(speaking of sea);* far segno *(to signal);* fare la piega *(set hair).*
waver (to) vacillare.
wax cera.
way via, modo, maniera.
we noi.
weak debole.
weaken (to) indebolire.
weakly debolmente.
weakness debolezza.
wealth ricchezza.
wealthy ricco.

weapon arma.
wear (to) portare; indossare; consumare *(consume).*
weariness stanchezza.
weary stanco.
weather tempo.
weave (to) tessere.
wedding sposalizio.
Wednesday mercoledì.
weed erbaccia.
week settimana.
weekend fine settimana.
weekly settimanalmente.
weep (to) piangere.
weigh (to) pesare.
weight peso.
weird strano, bizzarro.
welcome benvenuto.
    Welcome! Benvenuto!
    You're welcome. Non e'è di che. Prego.
welfare assistenza sociale.
well pozzo.
    Well! Bene!
well-being benessere, m.
west ovest; ponente.
western occidentale.
wet bagnato.
whale balena.
what quale; quali; che; ciò che; quello che, *etc.; (interrog.)* come?; che cosa?
    What? Come?
    What is it? Che cos'è?
whatever qualunque cosa; tutto ciò che; tutto quello che.
wheat grano.
wheel ruota.
when quando.
whenever ogni qual volta.
where dove.
wherever dovunque.
whether se; sia che.
which quale, sing.; quali, pl.
while mentre.
    Wait a while. Attenda un po'.
whim capriccio; estro.
whine (to) piagnucolare.
whip frusta.
whip (to) frustare.
whirlwind turbine, m.
whisper bisbiglio, mormorio.

whisper (to) bisbigliare.
whistle fischio.
whistle (to) fischiare.
white bianco.
who, whom chi; che; il quale; la quale; i quali; le quali; colui che; colei che.
whoever chiunque.
whole (n.) il tutto, totalità; (adj.) tutto, intero.
wholesale all'ingrosso.
wholesome sano, salubre.
whose di chi; di cui.
Why perchè.
    Why not? Perchè no?
wicked cattivo.
wide largo.
widen (to) allargare.
widow vedova.
widower vedovo.
width larghezza.
wife moglie.
wig parrucca.
wild selvaggio.
wilderness deserto.
wildness selvatichezza.
wile astuzia, inganno.
will volontà; testamento.
will (to) volere; lasciare per testamento (*bequeath*).
willful volontario, premeditato.
willing disposto, pronto.
willingly volentieri.
win (to) vincere.
wind vento.
wind (to) attorcigliare; caricare (*a watch*).
windmill mulino a vento.
window finestra.
    mullioned window bifora.
    rose window rosone.
    stained glass window vetrata.
windshield parabrezza.
windy ventoso.
wine vino.
    sparkling wine spumante.
wing ala; quinte, pl. (*theater*).
wink strizzatina d'occhio.
winner vincitore, m.; vincitrice, f.
winter inverno, invernale.
wipe (to) asciugare, pulire.
wire filo metallico (*metal*); telegramma, m. (*telegram*).

wire (to) telegrafare.
wisdom saggezza.
wise saggio.
wish desiderio.
wit senso, spirito.
witch strega.
with con.
withdraw (to) ritirarsi, prelevare.
withdrawal ritirata; prelievo.
wither (to) disseccare, inaridirsi, appassire.
within di dentro.
without senza.
witness testimone, m.
witty spiritoso.
woe dolore, m.
wolf lupo.
woman donna.
wonder meraviglia.
wonder (to) meravigliarsi, domandarsi.
wonderful meraviglioso.
    Wonderful! Meraviglioso!
wood legno.
woods bosco.
work lavoro.
    work of art lavoro d'arte.
work (to) lavorare.
worker lavoratore, m.; lavoratrice, f.
workman lavoratore, m.; operaio.
workshop laboratorio; officina.
world mondo.
worldliness mondanità.
worldly mondano.
worldwide mondiale.
worm verme, m.
worry preoccupazione, f.; inquietudine, f.
worry (to) essere inquieto; preoccuparsi.
    Don't worry. Non si preoccupi.
worse peggiore, peggio.
worship adorazione, f.; culto.
worship (to) adorare, venerare.
worst il peggiore; il peggio.
worth valore, m.; merito.
worthless senza valore; immeritevole.
worthy degno, meritevole.
wound ferita.
wound (to) ferire.
wounded ferito.

wrap (to) avvolgere, coprirsi.
wrapping involucro.
wrath ira.
wrathful irato.
wreath ghirlanda, corona.
wreck rovina; naufragio *(ship)*.
wreck (to) rovinare; demolire *(a building)*; naufragare *(ship)*.
wrestle (to) lottare.
wrestler lottatore, m.
wrestling lotta.
wretched miserabile, misero.
wring (to) torcere, spremere, estorcere.
wrinkle ruga, grinza.
wrinkle (to) produrre rughe o grinze; corrugare.
wrist polso.
write (to) scrivere.
writer scrittore, m.; scrittrice, f.
writing scrittura.
  in writing per iscritto.
written scritto.
wrong (n.) torto, ingiustizia; (adj.) erroneo, sbagliato.
wrong (to) fare torto; offendere; giudicare erroneamente.

X ray radiografia.

yacht panfilo.
yard cortile, m.; recinto; cantiere, m. *(shipyard)*.
yarn filato.
yawn sbadiglio.
yawn (to) sbadigliare.
year anno.

yearly (adv.) annualmente; (adj.) annuale.
yearn for (to) aver desiderio di; bramare.
yearning desiderio.
yeast lievito.
yell (to) urlare.
yellow giallo.
yes sì.
yesterday ieri, m.
yet ancora, tuttora.
yield precedenza.
yield (to) produrre *(produce)*; cedere *(give in)*; arrendersi *(surrender)*.
yielding cedevole.
yoke giogo, vincolo.
yolk torlo *(egg)*.
you (subj. pron.) tu, sing. fam.; lei, sing. pol.; voi, pl. fam. & sing. pol.; loro, pl. pol.; (obj. pron.) ti, la, vi, li; (ind. obj. pron.) ti, le, vi, loro.
young (n. & adj.) giovane, m. & f.
  young lady signorina.
  young man giovanetto.
your(s) il vostro; la vostra; i vostri; le vostre; il tuo; la tua; i tuoi; le tue; il suo; la sua; i suoi; le sue.
yourself voi stesso; tu stesso; te stesso; Lei stesso.
youth giovinezza.
youthful giovanile.
youthfulness giovinezza.

Z

zeal zelo.
zealous zelante.
zebra zebra.
zero zero.
zipper cerniera.
zone zona.
zoo giardino zoologico.
zoology zoologia.

GLOSSARY OF
PROPER NAMES

Adrian Adriana.
Albert Alberto.
Alexander Alessandro.
Alfred Alfredo.
Alice Alice.
Andrew Andrèa.
Anita Anita.
Anthony Antonio.
Arnold Arnoldo.
Arthur Arturo.

Beatrice Beatrice.
Blanche Bianca.

Carol Carolina.
Charles Carlo.
Charlotte Carlotta.

Daniel Daniele.
David Davide.

Edith Editta.
Edmond Edmondo.
Edward Edoardo.
Eleanor Eleonora.
Evelyn Evelina.

Ferdinand Ferdinando.
Frances Francesca.
Francis Francesco.
Frederick Federico.

Gabriel Gabriele.
George Giorgio.
Gertrude Gertrude.
Gregory Gregorio.
Guy Guido.

Harriet Enrichetta.
Harry Enrico.
Henry Enrico.
Hugh Ugo.

Irene Irene.

Jane Gianna.
Jerome Geronimo.
Joan Giovanna.
Judith Giuditta.
Julian Giuliano.

Lawrence Lorenzo.
Lewis Luigi.
Lucy Lucìa.

Mark Marco.
Mary Marìa.
Maurice Maurizio.
Michael Michele.

Paul Paolo.
Peter Pietro.

Raphael Raffaele.
Richard Riccardo.
Robert Roberto.

Sylvia Silvia.

Theresa Teresa.
Thomas Tommaso.

Vincent Vincenzo.
Vivian Viviana.

William Guglielmo.

GLOSSARY OF GEOGRAPHICAL NAMES

Africa Africa.
Alps Alpi.
America America.
   North America America del Nord.
   Central America America
      Centrale.
   South America America del Sud.
Argentina Argentina.
Asia Asia.
Atlantic Atlantico.
Australia Australia.
Austria Austria.

Belgium Belgio.
Bermuda Bermude.
Bolivia Bolivia.
Brazil Brasile.
Brussels Brusselle.

Canada Canadà.
Chile Cile.
China Cina.
Colombia Colombia.
Commonwealth of Independent
   States Confederazione Stati
   Independenti.
Costa Rica Costa Rica.
Cuba Cuba.
Czech Republic Repubblica Ceca.

Denmark Danimarca.
Dominican Republic Repubblica
   Dominicana.
Dover Dover.

Ecuador Ecuador.
Egypt Egitto.
El Salvador Il Salvador.
England Inghilterra.
Europe Europa.

Finland Finlanda.
Florence Firenze.
France Francia.

Geneva Ginevra.
Genoa Genova.
Germany Germania.

Great Britain Gran Brettagna.
Greece Grecia.
Guatemala Guatemala.

Hamburg Amburgo.
Holland Olanda.
Honduras Onduras.
Hungary Ungherìa.

Iceland Islanda.
India India.
Iraq Iraq.
Ireland Irlanda.
Ischia Ischia.
Israel Israele.
Italy Italia.

Japan Giappone.

Kenya Kenya.
Korea Corea.

Lisbon Lisbona.
London Londra.

Mexico Messico.
Milan Milano.
Moscow Mosca.

Naples Napoli.
New Zealand Nuova Zelanda.
Nicaragua Nicaragua.
Norway Norvegia.

Pacific Pacifico.
Palermo Palermo.
Paraguay Paraguay.
Poland Polonia.
Portugal Portogallo.
Puerto Rico Porto Rico.

Rhine Reno.
Rome Roma.
Romania Romanìa.
Russia Russia.

Sardinia Sardegna.
Scotland Scozia.
Siberia Siberia.
Sicily Sicilia.
Slovakia Slovachia.
Spain Spagna.

Sweden Svezia.
Switzerland Svizzera.

Turkey Turchìa.
Tuscany Toscana.

United States Stati Uniti.
Uruguay Uriguay.

Vatican Vaticano.
Venezuela Venezuela.
Venice Venezia.
Vienna Vienna.

Wales Galles.